party foods

party foods

Mouthwatering recipes for every occasion, from light bites, brunches and buffets to dinner parties, shown in 1000 photographs

BRIDGET JONES

LORENZ BOOKS

This edition is published by Lorenz Books, an imprint of Anness Publishing Ltd,
Blaby Road, Wigston, Leicestershire LE18 4SE; info@anness.com

www.lorenzbooks.com; www.annesspublishing.com

If you like the images in this book and would like to investigate using them for publishing,
promotions or advertising, please visit our website www.practicalpictures.com for more information.

Publisher: Joanna Lorenz
Project Editor: Lucy Doncaster
Production Manager: Steve Lang
Editorial Readers: Jane Bamforth and Richard McGinlay
Designers: Nigel Partridge and Jonathan Harley
Illustrator: Anna Koska
Recipes: Catherine Atkinson, Alex Barker, Angela Boggiano, Carla Capalbo, Kit Chan, Jacqueline Clarke,
Maxine Clarke, Andi Cleverly, Roz Denny, Matthew Drennan, Joanna Farrow, Rafi Fernandez, Christine
France, Silvano Franco, Sarah Gates, Shirley Gill, Brian Glover, Nicola Graimes, Rosamund Grant, Carole
Handslip, Deh-Ta Hsing, Peter Jordan, Lucy Knox, Elisabeth Lambert Ortiz, Ruby Le Bois, Clare Lewis,
Sara Lewis, Christine McFadden, Leslie Mackley, Norma MacMillan, Sue Maggs, Sally Mansfield,
Sallie Morris, Jane Milton, Keith Richmond, Rena Salaman, Marlena Spieler, Jenny Stacey, Liz Trigg,
Linda Tubby, Oona van den Berg, Hilaire Walden, Laura Washburn, Steven Wheeler, Kate Whiteman,
Elizabeth Wolf-Cohen, Jeni Wright
Photographers: Karl Adamson, Edward Allwright, Caroline Arber, Steve Baxter, Martin Brigdale, Nicki
Dowey, James Duncan, Gus Filgate, John Freeman, Ian Garlick, Michelle Garrett, Peter Henley, John
Heseltine, Amanda Heywood, Janine Hosegood, David Jordan, Maris Kelly, Dave King, Don Last,
William Lingwood, Patrick McLeavy, Michael Michaels, Roisin Neild, Thomas Odulate, Spike Powell,
Craig Robertson, Simon Smith, Sam Stowell, Polly Wreford
Food for photography (chapter openers): Becky Johnson

Previously published as part of a larger volume, 400 *Party Foods* and *Appetizers*

COOKING NOTE
• Bracketed terms are intended for American readers.
• For all recipes, quantities are given in both metric and imperial measures and, where appropriate, in standard
cups and spoons. Follow one set of measures, but not a mixture, because they are not interchangeable.
• Standard spoon and cup measures are level. 1 tsp = 5ml, 1 tbsp = 15ml, 1 cup = 250ml/8fl oz.
Australian standard tablespoons are 20ml. Australian readers should use 3 tsp in place of 1 tbsp for
measuring small quantities of gelatine, flour, salt, etc.
• American pints are 16fl oz/2 cups. American readers should use 20fl oz/2.5 cups in place of 1 pint
when measuring liquids.
• Electric oven temperatures in this book are for conventional ovens. When using a fan oven, the temperature will probably need to be reduced by about 10–20°C/20–40°F. Since ovens vary, you should
check with your manufacturer's instruction book for guidance.
• The nutritional analysis given for each recipe is calculated per portion (i.e. serving or item), unless
otherwise stated. If t[...]
the smaller portion si[...]
• Medium (US large) [...]

PUBLISHER'S NOTE
Although the advice [...]
going to press, neith[...]
errors or omissions th[...]
that comes about fro[...]

contents

Introduction

Party-giving should be enjoyable, and timely planning ensures that any event is as relaxed for the organizer as for the guests. The following pages provide guidelines and reminders to ensure that the organizing is easy and the occasion successful. Included are more than 320 easy-to-follow step-by-step recipes that will provide inspiration as well as detailed instructions for creating stunning dishes for every occasion.

Getting started
The process of deciding on dates, times, venues and style often starts the roller-coaster task of putting together

Below Approach entertaining with a clear sense of occasion and a few concise lists. Involve others and share the planning with friends and family.

Above Simple snacks, drinks and bright decorations are key basics for a party.

once-in-a-lifetime gatherings. It can be a stressful time when you are making decisions such as whether traditional ceremonies take precedence over a relaxed celebration or how to assemble different groups of family and friends. Side-stepping a frantic start helps to

avoid dips in enthusiasm later on. Often the initial problems are not as complicated as they appear.

Enthusiasm and energy are the first requirements for overcoming any uncertainties, backed up by making useful lists such as important dates, numbers of guests, types of food and drink. It is vital to do this before any celebration, large or small, in advance of getting down to the practicalities of invitation writing, room clearing, cooking and greeting.

Making to-do lists
Lists are essential when planning for a special occasion. Suggesting that there should be a system for making them may sound like overkill, but even the most super-efficient notes can become so mottled with additions that they

become uninterpretable. The answer is to have separate lists with different information. Using a computer or a spiral-bound notepad is brilliant for keeping them on separate pages but together in one place. Jot the date on each page and include notes of discussions with suppliers, orders placed and ideas, as well as the guest list, special requirements, shopping and so on. Using this system, it is easy to flip through to check detail, and you can flag significant pages you refer to frequently. Start with a list of the usual requirements for different occasions and then personalize it to your style.

Enlisting support

There is no point in playing the party hero and trying to juggle every last item alongside a normal busy life – it is far more sensible and fun to share the load and satisfaction with at least one helper, if not a team of supporters. Hand-pick a reliable and hard-working friend who shares your aims, ethos and humour to join in the process – most people are flattered to be asked for their support, especially on important occasions. Then be thoughtful about who to add to the team. For children's parties, unless the occasion is a surprise, involve the child whose party it is and allow one special friend to be included in the pre-party organization.

Below *One-pot feasts, such as moussaka, are good for supper parties.*

Mix and match

If the occasion is so formal, such as a wedding or christening, or the approach so traditional that there is little room for changing the style and form, it is best to follow the rules of etiquette. For all parties adopt a sensible attitude to all numbers, catering and entertainment and use tried and tested approaches to ensure success.

When the occasion allows for flexibility, aim for enjoyment rather than perfection. Mixing and matching can be an inspiring approach to party planning, especially for informal events. Those who are not keen on cooking for crowds often do best by selecting just one or two practical one-pot dishes and complementing them with well-chosen bought foods.

The same goes for party drinks: while all the experts may dictate offering chilled champagne or certain wines and liqueurs to go with individual courses during a meal, if you – or your budget – dictate otherwise, then do so with conviction and without

Above *Make lists for organizing all aspects of party planning.*

apology. And if you expect guests to make a contribution by bringing a bottle, spell it out on the invitations.

Enjoy!

Great atmosphere is the most important feature of any party or celebration – and that does not mean ambience alone. Whether you are entertaining in a palace or on a building site, remember to do so with a genuine and warm welcome. Make your guests aware of the type, context and style of the party so that they all come suitably dressed and in the right frame of mind to enjoy themselves. Greet everyone and be sure to encourage them to mingle, making them feel relaxed, at home and with a certain responsibility to participate. At the end of the day, no matter how brilliant the tables, food and decorations, it is the people who make the party.

Party Planning

A clear picture of the party style and size is the secret of success every time. Before planning venues, invitations, settings, entertainment and food and drink, decide on exactly the right type of party. Energy and enthusiasm are essential for getting things moving, but it is best to sort out guidelines within which to plan before ideas snowball and practicalities are forgotten in an initial wave of excitement.

There are established routines and etiquette for many occasions and utilizing these is often sensible. They range from formal dinner parties, society drinks gatherings or balls to weddings, anniversaries and seasonal gatherings. There are also just as many small or substantially large gatherings that are organized for no particular reason other than meeting up and socializing, for example overcoming winter blues, making the most of the summer sun or catching up with a group of friends.

Below *Informal supper parties are a good choice for midweek entertaining.*

Who's who?

Start with an outline guest plan: is this a gathering for six or sixty, under-fives or over-fifties, family or friends, best buddies or business associates? If you are inviting a complete mix of family, friends, colleagues and neighbours, a proper plan would be a sensible starting point. Identify the different types and ages; by fitting individuals into groups you will be sure to include something for everyone.

Which day?

Work functions are best from midweek onwards. Friday can be a good day for lunch or an evening party if partners are invited; Wednesday or Thursday are more convenient for "colleague only" events (especially if there will be a comparatively early finish).

Weekday dinner parties can be inconvenient, but midweek evenings are a good choice for drinks gatherings or supper parties designed to end early. Relaxed dinner and drinks parties are good Friday affairs, as are after-theatre or post-exhibition suppers.

Above *Summer barbecues can be day or early evening social events.*

Weekends are popular for group events for families and for activity club get-togethers or excursions. While weekend brunches are generally great for those without young children, Saturday brunch can also start family activities on a high note and the afternoon is a good choice for children's parties. If Saturday lunch is difficult for working hosts and guests who have to juggle family commitments, the evening is good for large and/or formal dinner parties. Saturday is popular for weddings, allowing time for guests to travel; Friday is ideal when the marriage is witnessed by a small number of relations and followed by a party for friends and associates.

Sunday lunch is extremely versatile: it allows plenty of time for preparation and is suitable for informal or smart arrangements for families, couples, singles or a mixture.

Parties and celebrations for clubs and classes are usually planned for the day and time when the meetings are normally held.

Time of day

The party may be to celebrate a marriage, baby naming or christening, or it may be a social event. It may not be a particularly jolly occasion, for example a post-funeral wake. Double-check arrangements that cannot be changed later, for example timings for ceremonies, photography or performances and estimated travelling time between event and party venue.

Consider the different ages of, or relationship between, guests before fixing times. A two-phase celebration is popular for very different groups; it would typically comprise a formal meal, low-key lunch or early evening drinks party followed by a lively gathering later for younger guests or close friends. Plan the transition between day and evening, and decide whether those invited to the first part of the party will also stay late.

Party price

As each name is added to the guest list and every idea mulled and jotted bear in mind the cost. Decide on the type of party to suit the funds available, then work out a realistic budget in more detail before progressing from idea to plan.

Sorting an outline budget at this stage is essential: make a list of every aspect of the party, adding a realistic (generous rather than mean) cost and contacting suppliers to check special prices. For extravagant occasions involving hotels, venues, caterers, entertainers and so on, make specific enquiries at this first stage. Divide the costs into fixed amounts for the occasion and variable prices that increase with the number of guests – refreshments in particular – remember that the venue size may change if the guest list grows too long. Spreading the cost by paying for some items in advance is one way of easing an overstretched budget.

Above *Send out invitations to major events, such as weddings, in good time.*

Invitation information

Once you have established the venue, time and theme, you can send out invitations, making sure you allow plenty of time for guests to respond and for you to finalize numbers well in advance of the big day. It may seem like a statement of the obvious but it is surprisingly easy to miss details or to include incorrect information. Invitations need to include the following:
• Guest names, with correct titles.
• Host and/or hostess names.
• Occasion or reason for party.
• Venue.
• Day and date.
• Time: this may be approximate or precise. Before a formal meal, it is usual to indicate a period of about 30 minutes during which guests are expected (within the first 15 minutes). The time may include a time when an evening will end – expressed as "carriages at …" on formal dinner invitations.
• RSVP (*répondez s'il vous plaît* – reply please), sometimes with a date, is a polite way of reminding guests that a reply is required.

• Address, telephone and other contact details for replying.
• Dress code and other information: white tie indicating wing collars, white ties and tails for men, ball gowns for women; black tie and dinner jacket (tuxedo) is standard evening wear for men, when women may wear long or short dresses. Notes on a theme should be included. Indicate any special requirements, such as swimming things and towels for poolside parties, sun hats and picnic blankets to sit on, and warm clothes for evenings outdoors.

Before and after

Guests may need accommodation for the night before and/or after the party. After a long journey, house guests will usually want to arrive early enough to freshen up. Include the preparation of guests' rooms in your plans, remembering the little things that make people feel welcome, such as towels, soap, shampoo and tissues.

For large gatherings, check the local hotels and provide guests with details of price, location and availability when sending out invitations. Remember breakfast on the morning after the party and make flexible arrangements.

Planning Your Party Food

The easiest way to make sure a party is successful is by tailoring your requirements to a list of key points. Consider the following planning points:
• The occasion and type of meal are good starting points. Is the celebration formal or informal? Is it for adults or children, or both? Are you serving nibbles and finger food, a fork supper or a sit-down meal? A mixture of dishes can come together successfully as refreshment without fitting into accepted menu courses.
• Numbers and special requirements are important. Thinking up a menu that is over-ambitious to cook for a large number of guests can lead to disaster. An extravagant spread of many courses that is suitable for a dozen guests to sample in small quantities may be difficult to prepare. You should plan to accommodate special diets right from the beginning, for example, include vegetarian, vegan, or low-fat dishes on the menu. If guests have specific needs, such as gluten-free food, it is easier to plan suitable dishes as part of the main menu rather than preparing a set of alternatives at the last minute.

Above *Lobster Thermidor and fillets of turbot with oysters are stylish dishes for special occasions.*

• Facilities should come high on the list of considerations. When finishing or serving food away from home, at a hired venue or a picnic for example, make sure that every dish can be transported, reheated or cooked at the venue as appropriate. Check the facilities available at the venue, if necessary. At home, the danger is overstretching facilities, so avoid planning too many dishes requiring last-minute cooking or heating to fit in the oven or for the top of the stove. Some recipes cooked at different temperatures cannot be adapted for cooking in the same oven. Also make sure you have enough crockery and cutlery for the menu.
• Food options are endless, so cost and capabilities are vital. When buying ready-made or commissioning caterers, be aware of prices before dreaming up a menu to blow the budget. When planning to cook, work within your capabilities; being adventurous is fun

within reasonable limitations but beyond this it can become a problem. Enlist the help of others or combine bought and home-made to be practical when there is a lot to be done.

Money can evaporate when using expensive ingredients and it is easy to isolate a pricey shopping list and get carried away, forgetting that it all adds up with drinks and other party costs.

Selecting recipes

Confident cooks who entertain often and enjoy providing culinary theatre for guests may opt for lots of last-minute cooking, especially when they have kitchen space to accommodate spectators. Otherwise it is sensible to plan the menu around cook-ahead dishes, with complicated cooking limited according to ability and the occasion. Being with your guests at a dinner party is important, while doing whirling dervish impressions between stove and buffet table can be stressful for both partygoers and you. Consider the following points:
• Balance hot and cold dishes to minimize the amount of work. One or two hot dishes are usually sufficient for a formal, main-meal buffet.
• Go for recipes that are based on familiar techniques.
• Select dishes that are practical to serve as well as prepare.
• For stand-up buffets, avoid dishes that are difficult to eat with only a fork.
• When arranging a finger buffet, select foods that are bitesize or easy to handle and bite without being messy.
• Leafy salads fill plates and can be difficult to eat when standing up, so guests tend to take less from buffets. Serve dressings separately from salads that are likely to wilt so that they can be added to taste when served; this prevents the salad from become soggy.
• Creamy salads and dishes that can be piled neatly on plates are popular.

Above *Tarts and quiches are popular choices for a buffet or brunch.*

Increasing quantities

Recipes that can be increased in quantity successfully include soups, casseroles, sauces for pasta and recipes for individual portions.

• When increasing the volume of stews and casseroles by more than three times, re-assess the volume of liquid as the proportion can be reduced slightly.

• Pies with pre-cooked fillings and a lid can be made in larger portions and cooked in larger dishes without vastly increasing the cooking time.

• Baked pasta dishes (such as lasagne or cannelloni) are excellent candidates for cooking in quantity.

• It is easier to boil large quantities of pasta in separate batches than to try to overfill a pan. Undercook it very slightly, drain and rinse, then toss with a little olive oil and reheat briefly in a suitable covered dish in the microwave.

• When increasing quantities by more than double, do not multiply up the herbs, spices and garlic several times as they may become overpowering.

• Accompanying sauces for hot dishes and dressings for salads do not have to be increased by as much as the main ingredients when increasing the recipe by more than two or three times.

Cooking plan

Make a list of all the cooking. It is a good idea to copy the recipes and keep them together in a plastic folder in the kitchen when preparing them.

Divide the list into those recipes to cook well in advance and freeze, adding notes on when to remove them from the freezer, with likely thawing time and any finishing touches or reheating times. Note down any seasonings or enriching ingredients that have to be added at the last minute and include this on the checklist of things to do.

List the dishes that have to be cooked just before the party, that is the day before or on the same day. Note any advance preparation next to each dish. For example, salad dressings can be made a day or two ahead and chilled; some salad ingredients can be trimmed or peeled and washed the day before, then chilled ready for use – spring onions (scallions), celery sticks and tomatoes are good examples.

When all the dishes are listed, with the days on which they have to be made, it is then easier to draw up a cooking plan. Order the recipes according to the day on which they have to be made, then go through this list to make sure it is all possible. If you have far too much work for any one day, check whether any can be made in advance. If you have chosen too many last-minute dishes, adjust the menu before embarking on a shopping spree.

On your cooking plan, list different items to be prepared separately – this way you are less likely to underestimate the time involved. As well as volume of work, make sure that you have enough containers, work surfaces and note the cooking appliance needed for each dish.

Shopping lists

Working from numbers and the menu, check the recipes and increase the quantities if necessary. Then work out your shopping list, checking store-cupboard (pantry) ingredients. Rather than having one mammoth list, divide it according to types of food, such as items that can be bought in advance and perishable last-minute purchases. Be sure to include any notes, reminders or alternatives on the lists to make shopping as efficient as possible.

Below *Stocks, sauces and casserole dishes can usually be cooked ahead.*

welcome nibbles

Stylish snacks and little bites set every gathering off to the right start. Choose a variety of different tastes and textures to complement the drinks you serve.

Tortilla Chips

A useful and quick-to-prepare appetizer, tortilla chips or *totopos* as they are also known are excellent for scooping up a salsa or dip. They can also be sprinkled with a little grated cheese and grilled until golden, then served with a selection of other nibbles. Use corn tortillas that are a few days old; fresh tortillas will not crisp up so well.

Makes 48

8 corn tortillas
oil, for frying
salt

COOK'S TIP
The oil needs to be very hot for cooking the tortillas chips – test it first by carefully adding one of the wedges to the frying pan. It should float and begin to bubble in the oil immediately.

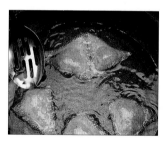

1 Cut each corn tortilla into six triangular wedges. Pour oil into a large, heavy frying pan to a depth of about 1cm/½ in, place the frying pan over a medium heat and heat until very hot (see Cook's Tip).

VARIATION
To give a spicy flavour to the chips, prepare a mixture of garlic salt, paprika and a pinch of mace. Sprinkle over the freshly drained tortilla chips while they are still hot.

2 Fry the tortilla wedges in the hot oil in small batches until they turn golden and are crisp. This will only take a few moments. Remove with a slotted spoon and drain on kitchen paper. Sprinkle with salt.

3 The tortillas should be served warm. They can be cooled completely and stored in an airtight container for a few days, but will need to be reheated in a microwave or a warm oven before being served.

Pepitas

These crunchy, spicy and slightly sweet pumpkin seeds are absolutely irresistible, especially if you use hot and tasty chipotle chillies to spice them up. Their smoky flavour is the perfect foil for the nutty taste of the pumpkin seeds and the hint of sweetness provided by the sugar. Serve bowls of pepitas with pre-dinner drinks and cocktails as an alternative to nuts.

Makes 2 bowls

250g/9oz/2 cups pumpkin seeds
8 garlic cloves, crushed
2.5ml/½ tsp salt
20ml/4 tsp crushed dried chillies
10ml/2 tsp caster (superfine) sugar
2 wedges of lime

1 Heat a small, heavy frying pan, add the pumpkin seeds and dry-fry for a few minutes, stirring constantly as they swell.

COOK'S TIPS
• It is important to keep the pumpkin seeds moving as they cook. Watch them carefully and do not let them burn, or they will taste bitter.
• Chipotle chillies are smoke-dried jalapeño chillies.

2 When all the seeds have swollen, add the garlic and cook for a few minutes more, stirring constantly. Add the salt and the crushed chillies and stir to mix. Turn off the heat, but keep the pan on the stove. Sprinkle the sugar over the seeds and shake the pan to make sure that they are all coated.

3 Tip the pepitas into a bowl and serve with the wedge of lime for squeezing over the seeds. If the lime is omitted, the seeds can be cooled and stored in an airtight container for serving cold or reheating later, but they are best served fresh and warm.

VARIATION
If you are using the pepitas cold, they can be mixed with cashew nuts and dried cranberries to make a spicy and fruity bowl of nibbles.

Chips: Energy 230kcal/964kJ; Protein 3.8g; Carbohydrate 30.1g, of which sugars 0.6g; Fat 11.3g, of which saturates 2g; Cholesterol 0mg; Calcium 75mg; Fibre 3g; Sodium 430mg.
Pepitas: Energy 299kcal/1242kJ; Protein 10.3g; Carbohydrate 11.2g, of which sugars 2g; Fat 23.8g, of which saturates 2.3g; Cholesterol 0mg; Calcium 57mg; Fibre 3.2g; Sodium 2mg.

Marinated Feta Cheese with Capers

Marinating cubes of feta cheese with herbs and spices gives it a really marvellous flavour.

Serves 6

350g/12oz feta cheese
2 garlic cloves
2.5ml/½ tsp mixed peppercorns
8 coriander seeds
1 bay leaf
15–30ml/1–2 tbsp drained capers
fresh oregano or thyme sprigs
olive oil, to cover
hot toast and chopped tomatoes,
*   to serve*

1 Cut the feta cheese into cubes. Thickly slice the garlic. Put the mixed peppercorns and coriander seeds in a mortar and crush lightly with a pestle.

2 Pack the feta cubes into a large preserving jar with the bay leaf, interspersing layers of cheese with garlic, crushed peppercorns and coriander, capers and the fresh oregano or thyme sprigs.

3 Pour in enough olive oil to cover the cubes of cheese. Close tightly and leave to marinate for 2 weeks in the refrigerator.

4 Lift out the feta cubes and serve on hot toast, with some chopped tomatoes and a little of the flavoured oil from the jar drizzled over.

COOK'S TIP
Add 50–75g/2–3oz/½–¾ cup pitted black or green olives to the feta cheese in the marinade if you like.

Energy 165kcal/683kJ; Protein 9.3g; Carbohydrate 1.3g, of which sugars 0.9g; Fat 13.6g, of which saturates 8.3g; Cholesterol 41mg; Calcium 211mg; Fibre 0.1g; Sodium 840mg.

Tapas of **Almonds, Olives** and **Cheese**

These three simple ingredients are lightly flavoured to create a Spanish tapas medley that is perfect to serve with pre-dinner drinks.

Serves 6–8

For the marinated olives
2.5ml/½ tsp coriander seeds
2.5ml/½ tsp fennel seeds
5ml/1 tsp chopped fresh rosemary
10ml/2 tsp chopped fresh parsley
2 garlic cloves, crushed
15ml/1 tbsp sherry vinegar
30ml/2 tbsp olive oil
225g/8oz/1⅓ cup black and green pitted or stuffed olives

For the marinated cheese
150g/5oz goat's cheese
90ml/6 tbsp olive oil
15ml/1 tbsp white wine vinegar
5ml/1 tsp black peppercorns
1 garlic clove, sliced
3 fresh tarragon or thyme sprigs
fresh tarragon sprigs, to garnish

For the salted almonds
1.5ml/¼ tsp cayenne pepper
30ml/2 tbsp sea salt
25g/1oz/2 tbsp butter
60ml/4 tbsp olive oil
200g/7oz/1¾ cups blanched almonds

1 To marinate the olives, crush the coriander and fennel seeds. Mix with the rosemary, parsley, garlic, vinegar and oil and pour over the olives in a bowl. Cover and chill for up to 1 week.

2 To make the marinated cheese, cut the cheese into bitesize pieces, leaving the rind on. Mix together the oil, vinegar, peppercorns, garlic and herb sprigs and pour over the cheese in a bowl. Cover and chill for up to 3 days. Use a spoon and fork to turn the cheese cubes in the marinade.

3 To make the salted almonds, mix together the cayenne pepper and salt in a bowl. Melt the butter with the olive oil in a frying pan. Add the almonds and cook, stirring constantly, for 5 minutes, or until the almonds are golden.

4 Tip the almonds out of the frying pan, into the salt mixture and toss together until the almonds are coated. Leave to cool, then store them in a jar or airtight container for up to 1 week.

5 To serve the tapas, arrange in small, shallow serving dishes. Use fresh sprigs of tarragon to garnish the cheese and sprinkle the almonds with a little more salt, if you like.

Energy 432kcal/1784kJ; Protein 10.3g; Carbohydrate 1.8g, of which sugars 1.1g; Fat 42.3g, of which saturates 9.7g; Cholesterol 25mg; Calcium 217mg; Fibre 2.7g; Sodium 805mg.

Dates Stuffed with Chorizo

This is a delicious combination from Spain, using fresh dates and spicy chorizo sausage. Serve as a hot snack at a drinks party or before a robust meal.

Makes 12

50g/2oz chorizo sausage
12 fresh dates, stoned (pitted)
6 streaky (fatty) bacon
　rashers (strips)
oil, for frying
plain (all-purpose) flour,
　for dusting
1 egg, beaten
50g/2oz/1 cup fresh breadcrumbs

1 Using a sharp knife, trim the ends of the chorizo sausage and then peel off the skin with your fingers and discard. Cut the sausage into three 2cm/¾in slices. Cut the slices in half lengthways, then cut them into quarters, giving 12 pieces in total.

2 Stuff the cavity of each date with a piece of chorizo, closing the date around it. Stretch the bacon, by running the back of a knife along the rasher. Cut each rasher in half, widthways. Wrap a piece of bacon around each date and secure with a wooden cocktail stick (toothpick).

3 In a deep pan, heat 1cm/½in of oil. Dust the dates with flour, dip them in the beaten egg, then coat in breadcrumbs. Cook the dates in the hot oil, turning them, frequently until golden. Remove the dates with a slotted spoon, and drain on kitchen paper. Serve immediately.

Energy 204kcal/851kJ; Protein 5.9g; Carbohydrate 17.9g, of which sugars 10.8g; Fat 12.6g, of which saturates 3.1g; Cholesterol 46mg; Calcium 29mg; Fibre 0.8g; Sodium 355mg.

Spicy Peanut Balls

Tasty rice balls, rolled in chopped peanuts and deep-fried, make a delicious party snack. Serve them as they are, or with a sweet chilli sauce for dipping.

Makes 16

1 garlic clove, crushed
1cm/½ in piece fresh root ginger, peeled and finely chopped
1.5ml/¼ tsp ground turmeric
5ml/1 tsp granulated sugar
2.5ml/½ tsp salt
5ml/1 tsp chilli sauce
10ml/2 tsp Thai fish sauce or soy sauce
30ml/2 tbsp chopped fresh coriander (cilantro)
juice of ½ lime
225g/8oz/2 cups cooked white long grain rice
115g/4oz/1 cup peanuts, chopped
vegetable oil, for deep-frying
lime wedges and chilli dipping sauce, to serve (optional)

1 Put the garlic, ginger and turmeric in a food processor or blender and process until the mixture forms a paste. Add the sugar, salt, chilli sauce and fish sauce or soy sauce, with the chopped coriander and lime juice. Process briefly to mix the ingredients.

COOK'S TIP
Be sure to include a variety of nibbles so that guests with a nut allergy will have plenty to eat too.

2 Add three-quarters of the cooked rice to the paste in the food processor and process until smooth and sticky. Scrape into a mixing bowl and stir in the remainder of the rice. Wet your hands and shape the mixture into thumb-size balls.

3 Place the chopped peanut in a dish and roll the balls in them, making sure they are evenly coated.

4 Heat the oil in a deep-fryer or wok. Add the peanut balls and cook until crisp. Drain well on kitchen paper and then pile on to a warmed platter. Serve hot with lime wedges and chilli dipping sauce, if you like.

Energy 123kcal/512kJ; Protein 2.9g; Carbohydrate 12.4g, of which sugars 0.8g; Fat 6.8g, of which saturates 1g; Cholesterol 0mg; Calcium 7mg; Fibre 0.4g; Sodium 45mg.

Potato and Onion Tortilla with Broad Beans

This Spanish omelette, which includes herbs and broad beans, is ideal for a summer party when cut into pieces and served as a tapa.

Serves 8–10

45ml/3 tbsp olive oil
2 Spanish onions, thinly sliced
300g/11oz waxy potatoes, cut into
 1cm/½in dice
250g/9oz/1½ cups shelled broad
 (fava) beans
5ml/1 tsp chopped fresh thyme or
 summer savory
6 large (US extra large) eggs
45ml/3 tbsp mixed chopped chives
 and chopped flat leaf parsley
salt and ground black pepper

1 Heat 30ml/2 tbsp of the oil in a 23cm/9in deep non-stick frying pan. Add the onions and potatoes and stir to coat. Cover and cook gently, stirring frequently, for 20–25 minutes, until the potatoes are cooked and the onions collapsed. Do not let the vegetables turn brown.

2 Meanwhile, cook the beans in salted, boiling water for 5 minutes. Drain well and set aside to cool.

3 When the beans are cool enough to handle, peel off the grey outer skins. Add the beans to the frying pan, together with the thyme or savory and season with salt and pepper to taste. Stir well and cook for 2–3 minutes.

4 Beat the eggs with salt and pepper to taste, add the mixed herbs, then pour over the potatoes and onions and increase the heat slightly. Cook gently until the egg on the bottom sets and browns, gently pulling the omelette away from the sides of the pan and tilting it to allow the uncooked egg to run underneath.

5 Invert the tortilla on to a plate. Add the remaining oil to the pan and heat until hot. Slip the tortilla back into the pan, uncooked side down, and cook for another 3–5 minutes to allow the underneath to brown.

6 Slide the tortilla out on to a clean plate. Use a sharp knife to cut the tortilla into eight to ten pieces or small squares and serve warm.

COOK'S TIP
Cook the tortilla very gently once the eggs have been added to the pan – trying to speed up the cooking process by raising the temperature browns the underneath much too soon, before the egg has had time to set.

Energy 673kcal/2812kJ; Protein 34.9g; Carbohydrate 59.2g, of which sugars 18.1g; Fat 35.2g, of which saturates 7.3g; Cholesterol 571mg; Calcium 272mg; Fibre 14.3g; Sodium 252mg.

Little Onions Cooked with **Wine, Coriander** and **Olive Oil**

If you can find the small, flat Italian cipolla or borettane onions, they are excellent in this recipe – otherwise use pickling onions, small red onions or shallots.

Serves 6

105ml/7 tbsp olive oil
675g/1½lb small onions, peeled
150ml/¼ pint/⅔ cup dry white wine
2 bay leaves
2 garlic cloves, bruised
1–2 small dried red chillies
15ml/1 tbsp coriander seeds, toasted
   and lightly crushed
2.5ml/½ tsp sugar
a few fresh thyme sprigs
30ml/2 tbsp currants
10ml/2 tsp chopped fresh oregano
5ml/1 tsp grated lemon rind
15ml/1 tbsp chopped fresh flat
   leaf parsley
30–45ml/2–3 tbsp pine nuts, toasted
salt and ground black pepper

1 Place 30ml/2 tbsp olive oil in a wide pan. Add the onions and cook gently over a medium heat for about 5 minutes, or until they begin to colour. Remove from the pan and set aside.

2 Add the remaining oil, the wine, bay leaves, garlic, chillies, coriander seeds, sugar and thyme to the pan. Bring to the boil and cook briskly for 5 minutes. Return the onions to the pan.

3 Add the currants, reduce the heat and cook gently for 15–20 minutes, or until the onions are tender but not falling apart. Use a slotted spoon to transfer the onions to a serving dish.

4 Boil the liquid over a high heat until it reduces considerably. Taste and adjust the seasoning, if necessary, then pour the reduced liquid over the onions. Sprinkle the oregano over the onions, set aside to cool and then chill.

5 Just before serving stir in the grated lemon rind, chopped flat leaf parsley and toasted pine nuts.

COOK'S TIP
Serve this dish with other small dishes such as an antipasto, or with some thinly sliced prosciutto or other air-dried ham.

Energy 265kcal/1094kJ; Protein 3g; Carbohydrate 13g, of which sugars 11g; Fat 23g, of which saturates 3g; Cholesterol 0mg; Calcium 50mg; Fibre 2g; Sodium 6mg.

Party Eggs

Hard-boiled eggs make perfect party food. Use a variety of fillings for a stunning centrepiece. Double the quantities if you are making larger batches.

Each variation fills 6 eggs

EGGS WITH CAVIAR

6 eggs, hard-boiled
4 spring onions (scallions), trimmed
   and very thinly sliced
30ml/2 tbsp sour cream
5ml/1 tsp lemon juice
25g/1oz/2 tbsp caviar
salt and ground black pepper
lemon rind and caviar, to garnish

Mix all the ingredients with the egg yolks, spoon back into the egg whites and garnish with lemon rind and caviar.

PRAWN AND CUCUMBER EGGS

6 eggs, hard-boiled
75g/3oz/scant 1 cup cooked peeled
   prawns (shrimp), reserving 12 for
   garnish and the rest chopped
25g/1oz cucumber, peeled and diced
5ml/1 tsp tomato ketchup
15ml/1 tbsp lemon mayonnaise
salt and ground black pepper
fennel sprigs, to garnish

Mix all the ingredients with the egg yolks, spoon back into the egg whites and garnish with the reserved prawns and fennel sprigs.

NUTTY DEVILLED EGGS

6 eggs, hard-boiled
40g/1½oz cooked ham, chopped
4 walnut halves, very finely chopped
15ml/1 tbsp Dijon mustard
15ml/1 tbsp mayonnaise
5ml/1 tsp white wine vinegar
few large pinches of cayenne pepper
salt and ground black pepper
paprika and gherkins, to garnish

Mix together all the ingredients with the egg yolks, spoon into the whites and garnish with paprika and gherkin slices.

GARLIC AND GREEN PEPPERCORN EGGS

5ml/1 tsp garlic purée or 1 large garlic
   clove, crushed
45ml/3 tbsp crème fraîche
6 eggs, hard-boiled
salt and ground black pepper
2.5ml/½ tsp green peppercorns,
   crushed, to garnish

Mix the garlic, crème fraîche, egg yolks and seasoning. Place in a piping (pastry) bag and pipe into the egg whites. Sprinkle with the peppercorns.

Energy 118kcal/492kJ; Protein 9g; Carbohydrate 0g, of which sugars 0g; Fat 9g, of which sugars 3g; Cholesterol 249mg; Calcium 45mg; Fibre 0g; Sodium 217mg.

Pickled Quail's Eggs

3 Gently tap the eggs all over to crack the shells, but do not peel them. Place in a large, airtight, sterilized jar and fill up with the liquid, totally covering the eggs. Seal the jar and leave the eggs to stand in a cool, dark place for about 7–8 days.

4 To serve, remove the eggs from the liquid and peel off the shells carefully. Serve whole with a dipping sauce and a bowl of toasted sesame seeds.

COOK'S TIPS

• Although you can buy Chinese dipping sauces in the supermarket, it is very easy to make your own at home. To make a quick dipping sauce, mix equal quantities of soy sauce and hoisin sauce.

• Be sure to use only boiled water or distilled water for the eggs, as the water must be completely free of bacteria or it will enter the porous shells.

• You can also pickle hard-boiled hen's eggs in the same way. Shell, then cut in half or quarters to serve. You will need to increase the quantity of liquid.

These Chinese eggs are pickled in alcohol and can be stored in a preserving jar in a cool, dark place for several months. They will make delicious bitesize snacks at a drinks party and are sure to delight guests.

Makes 12

12 quail's eggs
15ml/1 tbsp salt
750ml/1¼ pints/3 cups distilled or
   previously boiled water
15ml/1 tsp Sichuan peppercorns
150ml/¼ pint/⅔ cup spirit such as
   Mou-tal (Chinese brandy), brandy,
   whisky, rum or vodka
dipping sauce (see Cook's Tip) and
   toasted sesame seeds, to serve

1 Boil the eggs for about 4 minutes until the yolks are soft but not runny.

2 Place the salt and the distilled or previously boiled water in a large pan and heat gently until the salt has dissolved. Add the peppercorns, then remove the pan from the heat, leave the water to cool, then add the spirit.

Energy 20kcal/82kJ; Protein 1.7g; Carbohydrate 0g, of which sugars 0g; Fat 1.5g, of which saturates 0.4g; Cholesterol 51mg; Calcium 8mg; Fibre 0g; Sodium 19mg.

Eggs Mimosa

The use of the word mimosa describes the fine yellow and white grated egg which looks not unlike the flower of the same name. It can be used to finish any dish.

Makes 20

12 eggs, hard-boiled
2 ripe avocados, halved and
*   stoned (pitted)*
1 garlic clove, crushed
Tabasco sauce, to taste
15ml/1 tbsp virgin olive oil
salt and ground black pepper
20 chicory (Belgian endive) leaves or
*   small crisp lettuce leaves, to serve*
basil leaves, to garnish

1 Reserve 2 eggs, halve the remaining eggs and put the yolks in a mixing bowl. Blend or beat the yolks with the avocados, garlic, Tabasco sauce, oil and salt and pepper. Check the seasoning and adjust as necessary. Pipe or spoon this mixture back into the halved egg whites.

2 Sieve the two remaining egg whites and sprinkle this fine white over the filled eggs. Sieve the yolks on top. Arrange each half egg on a chicory or lettuce leaf and place them on a serving platter. Sprinkle the shredded basil leaves over the filled egg halves before serving.

Energy 79kcal/327kJ; Protein 4.1g; Carbohydrate 0.5g, of which sugars 0.2g; Fat 6.8g, of which saturates 1.6g; Cholesterol 114mg; Calcium 22mg; Fibre 0.6g; Sodium 43mg.

Mozzarella and Tomato Skewers

There's stacks of flavour in these layers of oven-baked mozzarella, tomatoes, basil and bread. These colourful kebabs will be popular with children and adults alike, so make plenty for everyone to enjoy.

Makes 32

24 slices white country bread, each
  about 1cm/½in thick
90ml/6 tbsp olive oil
250g/9oz mozzarella cheese, cut into
  5mm/¼in slices
6 ripe plum tomatoes, cut into
  5mm/¼in slices
25g/1oz/1 cup fresh basil leaves,
  plus extra to garnish
salt and ground black pepper
60ml/4 tbsp chopped fresh flat leaf
  parsley, to garnish

1 Preheat the oven to 220°C/425°F/ Gas 7. Trim the crusts from the bread and cut each slice into four equal squares. Arrange on baking sheets and brush with half the olive oil. Bake for 3–5 minutes, until the squares are a pale golden colour.

2 Remove the bread squares from the oven and place them on a chopping board with the other ingredients.

3 Make 32 stacks, each starting with a square of bread, then a slice of the mozzarella topped with a slice of tomato and a basil leaf. Sprinkle with salt and pepper, then repeat, ending with a piece of bread. Push a skewer through each stack and place on the baking sheets. Drizzle with the remaining oil and bake for 10–15 minutes, until the cheese begins to melt. Garnish with basil and parsley.

Energy 336kcal/1416kJ; Protein 12g; Carbohydrate 45g, of which sugars 4g; Fat 14g, of which saturates 4g; Cholesterol 12mg; Calcium 180mg; Fibre 4g; Sodium 544mg.

Cherry Tomatoes with Pesto

These make a colourful and tasty appetizer to go with drinks before you move to the table. Make the pesto when fresh basil is plentiful, and freeze it in batches.

Serves 8–10

450g/1lb small cherry tomatoes

For the pesto
90g/3¹/₂ oz/3¹/₂ cups fresh basil leaves
3–4 garlic cloves
60ml/4 tbsp pine nuts
5ml/1 tsp salt, plus extra to taste
120ml/4fl oz/¹/₂ cup olive oil
*45ml/3 tbsp freshly grated
  Parmesan cheese*
*90ml/6 tbsp freshly grated
  Pecorino cheese*
ground black pepper

1 Wash the tomatoes. Slice off the top of each tomato and carefully scoop out the seeds with a melon baller or small spoon.

2 To make the pesto, place the basil, garlic, pine nuts, salt and olive oil in a blender or food processor and process until smooth. Remove the contents to a bowl with a rubber spatula. If you like, the pesto may be frozen at this point, before the cheeses are added.

3 If you have frozen the pesto, allow it to thaw completely before use.

4 Fold in the grated Parmesan and Pecorino cheeses. Season with pepper, and more salt if necessary.

5 Use a small spoon to fill each tomato with a little pesto. This dish is at its best if chilled in the refrigerator for about an hour before serving.

Energy 185kcal/765kJ; Protein 6.7g; Carbohydrate 1.9g, of which sugars 1.8g; Fat 16.8g, of which saturates 4.2g; Cholesterol 14mg; Calcium 184mg; Fibre 1g; Sodium 154mg.

Stilton Croquettes

These are perfect little party bites, which you can make in advance and reheat at the last minute. For a really crisp result, double coat the croquettes in breadcrumbs.

Makes about 20

350g/12oz floury (mealy)
  potatoes, cooked
75g/3oz/¾ cup creamy Stilton
  cheese, crumbled
3 eggs, hard-boiled, peeled
  and chopped
few drops of Worcestershire sauce
plain (all-purpose) flour, for coating
1 egg, beaten
45–60ml/3–4 tbsp fine,
  dry breadcrumbs
vegetable oil, for deep-frying
salt and ground black pepper
dipping sauce or salsa, to serve

1 Mash the potatoes with a potato masher or fork until they are quite smooth. Work in the crumbled Stilton, chopped egg and Worcestershire sauce. Season with salt and ground black pepper to taste.

2 Divide the potato and cheese mixture into about 20 equal portions. Dust your hands lightly with flour and shape the pieces into small sausage shapes, no longer than about 2.5cm/1in in length.

3 Coat in flour, shaking off the excess, then dip into the beaten egg and, finally, coat evenly in breadcrumbs. Reshape, if necessary. Chill for about 30 minutes then deep-fry, seven to eight at a time, in hot oil turning frequently until they are golden brown all over. Drain well on kitchen paper, transfer to a serving dish and keep warm for up to 30 minutes. Serve with a dipping sauce, such as soy sauce or a tomato salsa.

Energy 79kcal/328kJ; Protein 2.2g; Carbohydrate 3.8g, of which sugars 0.2g; Fat 6.2g, of which saturates 1.4g; Cholesterol 35mg; Calcium 18mg; Fibre 0.2g; Sodium 57mg.

Cheese Aigrettes

Choux pastry is often associated with sweet pastries, such as profiteroles, but these little savoury buns, flavoured with Gruyère and dusted with grated Parmesan, are just delicious. They are best made ahead and deep-fried to serve.

Makes 30

90g/3¹/₂ oz/scant 1 cup strong plain (all-purpose) flour
2.5ml/¹/₂ tsp paprika
2.5ml/¹/₂ tsp salt
75g/3oz/6 tbsp cold butter, diced
200ml/7fl oz/scant 1 cup water
3 eggs, beaten
75g/3oz/³/₄ cup mature (sharp) coarsely grated Gruyère cheese
corn or vegetable oil, for deep-frying
50g/2oz/²/₃ cup freshly grated Parmesan cheese
ground black pepper

1 Mix the flour, paprika and salt together by sifting them on to a large sheet of baking parchment. Add a generous amount of ground black pepper.

2 Put the diced butter and water into a medium pan and heat gently. As soon as the butter has melted and the liquid starts to boil, quickly tip in all the seasoned flour at once and beat very hard with a wooden spoon. Continue beating vigorously over a low heat until the paste comes away cleanly from the sides of the pan.

3 Remove the pan from the heat and leave the paste to cool for 5 minutes. Gradually beat in enough of the beaten egg to give a stiff dropping consistency that still holds a shape on the spoon. Mix in the Gruyère.

4 Heat the oil for deep-frying to 180°C/350°F or until a cube of bread, added to it, browns in 45 seconds. Take a teaspoonful of the choux paste and use a second spoon to slide it into the oil. Make more aigrettes in the same way. Deep-fry for 3–4 minutes, then drain on kitchen paper and keep warm while you are cooking successive batches. To serve, pile the aigrettes on a warmed serving dish and sprinkle with Parmesan.

COOK'S TIP
Filling these aigrettes gives a delightful surprise as you bite through their crisp shell. Make slightly larger aigrettes by dropping a slightly larger spoonful of paste into the hot oil. Slit them open and scoop out any soft paste. Fill the centres with taramasalata, hummus or crumbled Roquefort mixed with a little fromage frais (farmer's cheese).

Energy 84kcal/348kJ; Protein 2.2g; Carbohydrate 2.4g, of which sugars 0.1g; Fat 7.3g, of which saturates 2.7g; Cholesterol 28mg; Calcium 46mg; Fibre 0.1g; Sodium 58mg.

Aromatic Tiger Prawns

There is no elegant way to eat these delicious aromatic prawns – just hold them by the tails, pull them off the sticks with your fingers and pop them into your mouth.

Makes 8

16 raw tiger prawns (jumbo shrimp)
2.5ml/½ tsp chilli powder
5ml/1 tsp fennel seeds
5 Sichuan or black peppercorns
1 star anise, broken into segments
1 cinnamon stick, broken into pieces
30ml/2 tbsp groundnut (peanut) oil
2 garlic cloves, chopped
2cm/¾in piece fresh root ginger,
  peeled and finely chopped
1 shallot, chopped
30ml/2 tbsp water
30ml/2 tbsp rice vinegar
30ml/2 tbsp soft brown or palm sugar
salt and ground black pepper
lime slices and chopped spring onion
  (scallion), to garnish

1 Peel the prawns, but leave the tails intact. Cut along the back of each prawn and remove the dark vein. Thread the prawns in pairs on to 8 wooden cocktail sticks (toothpicks) or small skewers. Set aside.

2 Heat a heavy frying pan, add the chilli powder, fennel seeds, Sichuan or black peppercorns, star anise and cinnamon stick and dry-fry for 1–2 minutes to release the flavours. Leave to cool, then grind coarsely in a grinder or tip into a mortar and crush with a pestle.

3 Heat the groundnut oil in a shallow pan, add the garlic, ginger and chopped shallot and cook over a low heat, stirring occasionally, until very lightly coloured.

4 Add the crushed spices, season with salt and pepper and cook the mixture gently for 2 minutes. Pour in the water and simmer gently, stirring constantly, for about 5 minutes.

5 Add the rice vinegar and soft brown or palm sugar, stir until dissolved, then add the prawns. Cook for about 3–5 minutes, until the prawns have turned pink, but are still very juicy. Serve hot, garnished with lime slices and spring onion.

COOK'S TIP
You can use whole prawns (shrimp), but remove the heads before cooking them.

Energy 142kcal/593kJ; Protein 13.4g; Carbohydrate 9g, of which sugars 8.7g; Fat 6g, of which saturates 0.7g; Cholesterol 146mg; Calcium 67mg; Fibre 0.2g; Sodium 144mg.

Deep-fried Whitebait

A spicy coating on these fish gives
this favourite dish a crunchy bite.

Serves 6

115g/4oz/1 cup plain (all-purpose) flour
2.5ml/¹/₂ tsp curry powder
2.5ml/¹/₂ tsp ground ginger
2.5ml/¹/₂ tsp cayenne pepper
1.2kg/2¹/₂ lb whitebait, thawed if frozen
vegetable oil, for deep-frying
salt
lemon wedges, to garnish

1 Mix together the flour, curry powder,
ginger, cayenne pepper and a little salt
in a large bowl or shallow dish.

2 Coat the fish in the seasoned flour,
covering them evenly. Shake off
any excess.

COOK'S TIP
To coat the fish evenly, place the seasoned
flour in a clean plastic bag, add a few fish
at a time and shake well.

3 Heat the oil in a large, heavy pan to
190°C/375°F or until a cube of bread,
added to the oil, browns in about
30 seconds. Fry the whitebait, in
batches, for 2–3 minutes, until the fish
is golden and crispy.

4 Drain the whitebait well on kitchen
paper. Transfer to a dish and keep
warm in a low oven until you have
cooked all the fish. Serve immediately
garnished with lemon wedges for
squeezing over.

Energy 1050kcal/4348kJ; Protein 39g; Carbohydrate 10.6g, of which sugars 0.2g; Fat 95g, of which saturates 0g; Cholesterol 0mg; Calcium 1720mg; Fibre 0.4g; Sodium 460mg.

Mini Sausage Rolls

These miniature versions of old-fashioned sausage rolls are always popular – the Parmesan cheese gives them an extra special flavour.

Makes about 48

15g/¹/₂oz/1 tbsp butter
1 onion, finely chopped
350g/12oz good quality sausage meat
    (bulk sausage)
15ml/1 tbsp dried mixed herbs, such as
    oregano, thyme, sage, tarragon or dill
25g/1oz finely chopped pistachio
    nuts (optional)
350g/12oz puff pastry, thawed if frozen
60–90ml/4–6 tbsp freshly grated
    Parmesan cheese
salt and ground black pepper
1 egg, lightly beaten, for glazing
poppy seeds, sesame seeds, fennel
    seeds and aniseeds, for sprinkling

1 Melt the butter in a small frying pan over a medium heat. Add the onion and cook, stirring occasionally, for about 5 minutes, until softened. Remove the pan from the heat and leave to cool. Put the softened onion, sausage meat, herbs and nuts (if using) in a mixing bowl. Season with a little salt and pepper and stir together until completely blended.

2 Divide the sausage mixture into four equal portions and roll into thin sausages measuring about 25cm/10in long. Set aside.

3 On a lightly floured surface, roll out the pastry to about 3mm/¹/₈in thick. Cut the pastry into four strips measuring 25 × 7.5cm/10 × 3in. Place a long sausage on each pastry strip and sprinkle each with a little grated Parmesan cheese.

VARIATION

Filo pastry can be used instead of puff pastry for a very light effect. Depending on the size of the filo sheets, cut into eight pieces 25 × 7.5cm/10 × 3in. Brush four of the sheets with a little melted butter or vegetable oil and place a second pastry sheet on top. Place one sausage log on each of the four layered sheets and roll up and bake as above.

4 Brush one long edge of each of the pastry strips with a little of the egg glaze and roll up to enclose each sausage. Set them seam side down and press gently to seal. Brush each one with the egg glaze and sprinkle with one type of seeds. Repeat with remaining pastry strips, sprinkling each with different seeds.

5 Preheat the oven to 220°C/425°F/Gas 7. Lightly grease a large baking sheet. Cut each of the pastry logs into 2.5cm/1in lengths and arrange them on the baking sheet. Bake for about 15 minutes, until the pastry is crisp and brown. Serve warm or leave to cool before serving.

COOK'S TIP

For best results, handle pastry dough as little as possible and keep it cool. Although frozen pastry needs to be thawed before use, keep it chilled until required. Rinse your hands in cold water and use a marble or glass rolling pin. Alternatively, use a rolling pin that can be filled with cold water. This helps to make sure that the pastry is crisp when cooked.

Energy 59kcal/245kJ; Protein 1.8g; Carbohydrate 3.7g, of which sugars 0.3g; Fat 4.3g, of which saturates 1.2g; Cholesterol 9mg; Calcium 24mg; Fibre 0.1g; Sodium 99mg.

Tuna in Rolled Red Peppers

This lovely savoury combination originated in southern Italy. Grilled peppers have a sweet, smoky taste that combines particularly well with a robust fish like tuna. You could try canned mackerel instead.

Makes 12

3 large red (bell) peppers
200g/7oz can tuna, drained
30ml/2 tbsp lemon juice
45ml/3 tbsp olive oil
6 green or black olives, pitted
*   and chopped*
30ml/2 tbsp chopped fresh parsley
1 garlic clove, finely chopped
1 celery stick, very finely chopped
salt and ground black pepper

1 Arrange the peppers on a baking sheet and place under a hot grill (broiler). Cook, turning them occasionally, until they are charred and blistered on all sides. Remove from the heat with tongs and place them in a plastic bag. Tie the top.

2 Leave for 5 minutes until cool enough to handle. then remove from the bag and peel. Cut the peppers into quarters and remove and discard the stems, seeds and membranes.

3 Meanwhile, flake the tuna and combine with the lemon juice and oil. Stir in the olives, parsley, garlic and celery. Season with salt and plenty of ground black pepper.

4 Lay the pepper segments out flat, skinned side down. Divide the tuna mixture equally among them. Spread it out, pressing it into an even layer. Roll the peppers up. Place the pepper rolls in the refrigerator for at least 1 hour. Just before serving, cut each roll in half with a sharp knife, then arrange on a large serving platter.

Energy 90kcal/374kJ; Protein 6.1g; Carbohydrate 3.8g, of which sugars 3.6g; Fat 5.7g, of which saturates 0.9g; Cholesterol 10mg; Calcium 16mg; Fibre 1.2g; Sodium 119mg.

Smoked Trout Mousse in **Cucumber Cups**

This delicious creamy mousse can be made in advance and chilled for 2–3 days in the refrigerator. Serve it in crunchy cucumber cups or simply with crudités if you like.

Makes about 24

115g/4oz/¹/₂ cup cream cheese, softened
2 spring onions (scallions), chopped
15–30ml/1–2 tbsp, chopped fresh dill
   or parsley
5ml/1 tsp horseradish sauce
225g/8oz smoked trout fillets, flaked
   and any fine bones removed
30–60ml/2–4 tbsp double
   (heavy) cream
salt and cayenne pepper
2 cucumbers
fresh dill sprigs, to garnish

1 Start by making the trout mouse. Put the cream cheese, spring onions, dill or parsley and horseradish sauce into a blender or the bowl of a food processor and process until well blended. Add the trout and process until smooth, scraping down the sides of the bowl once. With the machine running, pour in the cream through the feeder tube until a soft mousse-like mixture forms. Season with salt and cayenne pepper to taste, turn into a bowl and chill for 15 minutes.

2 To make the cucumber cups, using a cannelle knife (zester) or vegetable peeler, score the length of each cucumber to create a striped effect. Cut each cucumber into 2cm/¾in thick rounds. Using a small spoon or melon baller, scoop out the seeds from the centre of each round.

3 Spoon the smoked trout mousse into a piping (pastry) bag fitted with a medium-sized star nozzle and pipe swirls of the mousse mixture into the prepared cucumber rounds. Arrange the cucumber cups on a serving platter and chill until ready to serve. Garnish the cucumber cups with small sprigs of dill.

COOK'S TIP
The easiest way to remove any fine bones remaining in the fish fillets is to pull them out with a small pair of tweezers.

Energy 44kcal/182kJ; Protein 2.8g; Carbohydrate 0.4g, of which sugars 0.4g; Fat 3.5g, of which saturates 1.9g; Cholesterol 10mg; Calcium 20mg; Fibre 0.4g; Sodium 193mg.

Cheese and Potato Bread Twists

These individual "ploughman's lunch" twists have the cheese cooked in the bread. They can be filled with smoked salmon seasoned with lemon juice after cooking to make them extra special.

Makes 12

225g/8oz potatoes, diced
225g/8oz/2 cups strong white bread
*   flour, plus extra for dusting*
5ml/1 tsp easy-blend (rapid-rise)
*   dried yeast*
150ml/¼ pint/⅔ cup lukewarm water
175g/6oz/1½ cups finely grated red
*   Leicester cheese*
10ml/2 tsp olive oil, for greasing
salt

1 Cook the potatoes in a large pan in plenty of lightly salted boiling water for 20 minutes, or until tender. Drain through a colander and return to the pan. Mash with a potato masher or fork until smooth and set aside to cool.

2 Meanwhile, sift the flour into a large bowl and add the yeast and a good pinch of salt. Stir in the mashed potatoes and rub with your fingers to form a crumb consistency.

VARIATION
Any hard, well-flavoured cheese can be used. Mature (sharp) Cheddar is the traditional choice for a ploughman's lunch, or you could try a smoked cheese or a variety with added herbs.

3 Make a well in the centre of the mixture and pour in the lukewarm water. Start by bringing the mixture together with a round-bladed knife, then use your hands. Turn out on to a well-floured surface and knead for 5 minutes. Return the dough to the bowl. Cover with a damp dishtowel and leave to rise in a warm place for 1 hour, or until doubled in size.

4 Turn the dough out and knock back (punch down) the air bubbles. Knead again for a few seconds.

5 Divide the dough into 12 even pieces and shape into rounds.

6 Sprinkle the cheese over a baking sheet. Take each ball of dough and roll it in the cheese.

7 Roll each cheese-covered roll on a dry surface to form a long sausage shape. Fold the two ends together and twist the bread. Lay the bread twists on an oiled baking sheet.

8 Cover with a damp cloth and leave the bread to rise in a warm place for 30 minutes. Preheat the oven to 220°C/425°F/Gas 7. Bake the bread for 10–15 minutes. These bread twists stay moist and fresh for up to 3 days if stored in airtight food bags.

Energy 231kcal/971kJ; Protein 8.7g; Carbohydrate 26.4g, of which sugars 0.8g; Fat 10.4g, of which saturates 5.2g; Cholesterol 21mg; Calcium 203mg; Fibre 1.2g; Sodium 162mg.

Bitesize Cheese Brioches

These mouthfuls of golden, buttery dough have a surprise in the middle: a nugget of melting cheese, so be sure to serve them warm to enjoy them at their best.

Makes about 40

450g/1lb/4 cups plain (all-purpose) or strong white bread flour, plus extra for dusting
5ml/1 tsp salt
5ml/1 tsp ground turmeric
1 sachet (envelope) easy-blend (rapid-rise) dried yeast
150ml/¼ pint/⅔ cup warm milk
2 eggs, plus 2 egg yolks
75g/3oz/6 tbsp butter, melted and slightly cooled
50g/2oz/½ cup grated Cheddar cheese
oil, for greasing
50g/2oz/½ cup cubed cheese, such as Cheshire, Gouda or Port Salut

1 Sift the dry ingredients into a large bowl with the yeast and make a hollow in the middle. Mix the milk, eggs and one yolk with the butter and Cheddar.

2 Pour the liquid into the well in the dry ingredients and blend with a fork to bring the mixture together. Continue mixing in the bowl or in a food processor with a dough blade, until it is evenly mixed. Turn out the mixture on to a lightly floured surface and knead, working in as little flour as possible, until the surface of the mixture becomes smooth and dry.

3 Place the dough in a lightly oiled bowl. Lightly oil the top of the dough, cover with a clean dishtowel and leave in a warm place for at least 1 hour, until the dough has doubled in bulk.

4 Turn out on to a floured surface and knead the dough until it becomes firm and elastic again.

5 Divide the dough into four batches, then divide each batch into eight to ten pieces. Knead each piece until smooth.

COOK'S TIP

For a special party, use gold petits fours cases; they are firmer and give more support, and they look smart and elegant.

6 Press a cube of cheese into the middle of each piece of dough, then shape into a round and place in paper sweet (candy) cases. Place the paper cases in mini muffin trays to support the soft dough during baking or, alternatively, put the dough in doubled paper cases. Set the brioches aside in a warm place until they are well risen and have almost doubled in size.

7 Preheat the oven to 200°C/400°F/ Gas 6. Mix the remaining yolk with 15ml/1 tbsp water and glaze the brioches with the mixture, using a pastry brush. Bake for 15 minutes, or until golden brown, well-risen and firm underneath if tapped.

Energy 64kcal/270kJ; Protein 2.1g; Carbohydrate 9g, of which sugars 0.4g; Fat 2.5g, of which saturates 1.3g; Cholesterol 25mg; Calcium 27mg; Fibre 0.3g; Sodium 75mg.

Pretzels

Pretzels or brezeln, as they are known in Germany, are said to be derived from the Latin *bracellae* or arms, referring to the crossed "arms" of dough inside the oval. In Alsace the pretzel shape is part of the emblem of quality that bakers display outside their shops.

Makes 12

For the yeast sponge
10g/¼ oz fresh yeast
75ml/5 tbsp water
*15ml/1 tbsp unbleached plain
   (all-purpose) flour*

For the dough
10g/¼ oz fresh yeast
150ml/¼ pint/⅔ cup lukewarm water
75ml/5 tbsp lukewarm milk
*400g/14oz/3½ cups unbleached strong
   white bread flour*
7.5ml/1½ tsp salt
25g/1oz/2 tbsp butter, melted

For the topping
1 egg yolk
15ml/1 tbsp milk
sea salt or caraway seeds, for sprinkling

1 Flour a baking sheet and grease two baking sheets. Cream the yeast for the yeast sponge with the water. Mix in the flour, cover and leave to stand at room temperature for 2 hours.

2 Mix the yeast for the dough with the water, then stir in the milk. Sift 350g/ 12oz/3 cups of the flour and the salt into a bowl. Add the yeast sponge and the butter and mix for 3–4 minutes. Turn out on to a lightly floured surface and knead in the remaining flour. Place in a lightly oiled bowl, cover with lightly oiled clear film (plastic wrap) and leave to rise in a warm place for 30 minutes.

3 Turn out on to a floured surface and knock back (punch down) the dough. Knead into a ball, return to the bowl, cover and leave to rise for 30 minutes.

4 Turn out the dough on to a floured surface, divide into 12 pieces and form into balls. Take one ball of dough and cover the remainder with a dishtowel.

5 Roll the dough into a stick 46cm/18in long and about 1cm/½in thick in the middle and thinner at the ends. Bend each end of the dough stick into a horseshoe. Cross over and place the ends on top of the thick part of the pretzel. Repeat with the remaining dough balls.

6 Place on the floured baking sheet to rest for 10 minutes. Preheat the oven to 190°C/375°F/Gas 5. Bring a large pan of water to the boil, then reduce to a simmer. Add the pretzels, in batches of 2–3 at a time, and poach for about 1 minute. Drain on a dishtowel and place on the greased baking sheets, spaced well apart.

7 Mix the egg yolk and milk and brush over the pretzels. Sprinkle with sea salt or caraway seeds and bake the pretzels for 25 minutes.

Energy 142kcal/601kJ; Protein 3.8g; Carbohydrate 27.3g, of which sugars 0.9g; Fat 2.8g, of which saturates 1.4g; Cholesterol 22mg; Calcium 60mg; Fibre 1.1g; Sodium 264mg.

Parmesan Thins

These thin, crisp, savoury biscuits will melt in the mouth, so make plenty for guests. They are a great snack at any time of the day, so don't just keep them for parties.

Makes 16–20

50g/2oz/¹/₂ cup plain
  (all-purpose) flour
40g/1¹/₂ oz/3 tbsp butter, softened
1 egg yolk
40g/1¹/₂oz/²/₃ cup freshly grated
  Parmesan cheese
pinch of salt
pinch of mustard powder

1 Rub together the flour and the butter in a bowl using your fingertips, then work in the egg yolk, Parmesan cheese, salt and mustard powder. Mix to bring the dough together into a ball. Shape the mixture into a log, wrap in foil or clear film (plastic wrap) and chill for 10 minutes.

2 Preheat the oven to 200°C/400°F/ Gas 6. Cut the Parmesan log into very thin slices, 3–5mm/¹/₈–¹/₄in maximum, and arrange on a baking sheet. Flatten with a fork to give a pretty ridged pattern. Bake for 10 minutes, or until the Parmesan thins are crisp but not changing colour.

Energy 36kcal/148kJ; Protein 1.2g; Carbohydrate 2g, of which sugars 0.1g; Fat 2.6g, of which saturates 1.5g; Cholesterol 16mg; Calcium 29mg; Fibre 0.1g; Sodium 34mg.

dips and dippers

Smooth or slightly chunky, luscious or
refreshing, dips and dippers are ideal for large
gatherings or instead of a formal appetizer
for supper with friends.

Walnut and Garlic Dip, Salsa Verde and Yogurt with Garlic, Cucumber and Mint

Full-flavoured classic sauces and salsas make terrific dips.

WALNUT AND GARLIC DIP

Makes 1 bowl

2 × 1cm/½ in slices white bread
60ml/4 tbsp milk
150g/5oz/1¼ cups shelled walnuts
4 garlic cloves, chopped
120ml/4fl oz/½ cup mild olive oil
15–30ml/1–2 tbsp walnut
  oil (optional)
juice of 1 lemon
salt and ground black pepper
walnut or olive oil, for drizzling
paprika, for dusting (optional)

1 Remove the crusts from the bread, and soak the slices in the milk for 5 minutes, then process with the walnuts and chopped garlic in a food processor or blender to a coarse paste.

2 Gradually add the olive oil to the paste with the motor still running, until the mixture forms a smooth thick sauce. Blend in the walnut oil, if using.

3 Scoop the sauce into a bowl and add lemon juice to taste, season with salt and pepper and beat well.

4 Transfer the dip to a serving bowl, drizzle over a little more walnut or olive oil, then dust lightly with paprika, if using.

SALSA VERDE

Makes 1 bowl

1–2 garlic cloves, finely chopped
25g/1oz/1 cup flat leaf parsley leaves
15g/½oz/½ cup fresh basil, mint
  or coriander (cilantro) or a mixture
  of fresh herbs
15ml/1 tbsp chopped fresh chives
15ml/1 tbsp salted capers, rinsed
5 anchovy fillets in olive oil, drained
  and rinsed
10ml/2 tsp French mustard (tarragon or
  fines herbes mustard are both good)
120ml/4fl oz/½ cup extra virgin olive oil
grated lemon rind and juice (optional)
ground black pepper

1 Process the garlic, parsley, basil, mint or coriander, chives, capers, anchovies, mustard and 15ml/1 tbsp of the oil in a blender or food processor.

2 Gradually add the remaining oil in a thin stream with the motor running.

3 Transfer to a bowl and adjust the seasoning to taste – there should be enough salt from the capers and anchovies. Add a little lemon juice and rind if you like. Serve immediately.

VARIATIONS

If dipping prawns (shrimp), substitute fresh chervil, tarragon, dill or fennel, for the basil, mint or coriander (cilantro).

YOGURT WITH GARLIC, CUCUMBER AND MINT

Makes 1 bowl

15cm/6in piece cucumber
5ml/1 tsp sea salt
300ml/½ pint/1¼ cups Greek
  (US strained plain) yogurt
3–4 garlic cloves, crushed
45ml/3 tbsp chopped fresh mint
ground black pepper
chopped fresh mint and/or ground
  toasted cumin seeds, to garnish

1 Slice the cucumber, place in a sieve and sprinkle with half the salt. Leave over a bowl for 30 minutes to drip.

2 Rinse the cucumber in cold water, pat dry and mix with the yogurt, garlic and mint. Season to taste. Leave for 30 minutes, stir and sprinkle with fresh mint and/or toasted cumin seeds.

COOK'S TIP

To make a yogurt and garlic dressing, spoon 150ml/¼ pint/⅔ cup Greek (US strained plain) yogurt into a bowl. Beat in 1 chopped garlic clove, 5ml/1 tsp French mustard and a pinch of sugar. Season. Beat in 15–30ml/1–2 tbsp olive oil and 15–30ml/1–2 tbsp chopped herbs.

Right, from top to bottom:
Walnut and Garlic Dip, Yogurt with Garlic, Cucumber and Mint, and Salsa Verde.

Dip: Energy 2361kcal/9755kJ; Protein 32g; Carbohydrate 52g, of which sugars 10g; Fat 227g, of which saturates 27g; Cholesterol 8mg; Calcium 313mg; Fibre 12g; Sodium 495mg.
Salsa: Energy 1147kcal/4722kJ; Protein 7g; Carbohydrate 4g, of which sugars 2g; Fat 123g, of which saturates 17g; Cholesterol 9mg; Calcium 156mg; Fibre 2g; Sodium 999mg.
Yogurt: Energy 306kcal/1276kJ; Protein 17g; Carbohydrate 20g, of which sugars 17g; Fat 18g, of which saturates 13g; Cholesterol 42mg; Calcium 498mg; Fibre 1g; Sodium 2421mg.

Avocado Salsa

A popular chunky dip that is
excellent with tortilla chips.

Makes 1 bowl

2 large ripe avocados
1 small red onion, very finely chopped
1 fresh red or green chilli, seeded and
   very finely chopped
½–1 garlic clove, crushed (optional)
finely shredded rind of ½ lime and
   juice of 1–1½ limes
pinch of caster (superfine) sugar
225g/8oz tomatoes, seeded
   and chopped
30ml/2 tbsp coarsely chopped fresh
   coriander (cilantro)
2.5–5ml/½–1 tsp ground cumin seeds
15ml/1 tbsp olive oil
15–30ml/1–2 tbsp sour cream (optional)
salt and ground black pepper
lime wedges dipped in sea salt, and
   coriander (cilantro) sprigs, to garnish

1 Halve, stone (pit) and peel the
avocados. Set half the flesh aside and
coarsely mash the remainder in a bowl
using a fork.

COOK'S TIPS
• Leaving some of the avocado in chunks
adds a slightly different texture, but if you
like a smoother salsa, mash all the
avocado together.
• Hard avocados will soften in a few
seconds in a microwave. Check frequently
until you get the softness that you like.

2 Add the onion, chilli, garlic, if using,
lime rind, juice of 1 lime, sugar,
tomatoes and coriander. Add the
ground cumin, seasoning and more
lime juice to taste. Stir in the olive oil.

3 Dice the remaining avocado and stir
into the avocado salsa, then cover and
leave to stand for 15 minutes so that
the flavour develops. Stir in the sour
cream, if using. Serve immediately with
lime wedges dipped in sea salt and
fresh coriander sprigs.

Energy 891kcal/3686kJ; Protein 12g; Carbohydrate 26g, of which sugars 18g; Fat 83g, of which saturates 20g; Cholesterol 18mg; Calcium 146mg; Fibre 4g; Sodium 65mg.

Guacamole

Avocados discolour quickly so make this dip just before serving. If you do need to keep it for any length of time, cover the surface of the sauce with clear film and chill in the refrigerator.

Makes 1 bowl

2 large ripe avocados
2 fresh red chillies, seeded
1 garlic clove
1 shallot
20ml/2 tbsp olive oil,
    plus extra to serve
juice of 1 lemon
salt and ground black pepper
fresh flat leaf parsley leaves, to garnish

1 Halve the avocados, remove the stones (pits) and scoop out the flesh into a large bowl.

2 Using a fork or potato masher, mash the avocado flesh until smooth.

3 Finely chop the chillies, garlic and shallot, then stir into the mashed avocado with the olive oil and lemon juice. Season to taste with salt and pepper and stir again.

4 Spoon the mixture into a small serving bowl. Drizzle over a little olive oil and sprinkle with a few flat leaf parsley leaves. Serve immediately.

VARIATION
Substitute lime juice for the lemon juice and fresh coriander (cilantro) leaves for the flat leaf parsley.

Energy 108kcal/445kJ; Protein 1.6g; Carbohydrate 3.1g, of which sugars 2.3g; Fat 9.9g, of which saturates 2.1g; Cholesterol 0mg; Calcium 13mg; Fibre 2.3g; Sodium 8mg.

Basil and Lemon Dip

This lovely dip is based on fresh mayonnaise flavoured with lemon juice and two types of basil. Serve with crispy potato wedges for a delicious appetizer.

Makes 1 bowl

2 large (US extra large) egg yolks
15ml/1 tbsp lemon juice
150ml/¼ pint/⅔ cup olive oil
150ml/¼ pint/⅔ cup sunflower oil
4 garlic cloves
handful of fresh green basil
handful of fresh opal basil
salt and ground black pepper

1 Place the egg yolks and lemon juice in a blender or food processor and process them briefly until they are just lightly blended.

2 Pour the olive oil and sunflower oil into a jug (pitcher) and stir them together. With the motor running, very gradually pour the oil into the blender or food processor, a little at a time.

3 Once half of the oil has been added, the remaining oil can be incorporated more quickly in a steady stream. Continue processing to form a thick, creamy mayonnaise.

4 Peel and crush the garlic cloves. Alternatively, place them on a chopping board and sprinkle with salt, then flatten them with the heel of a heavy-bladed knife and chop the flesh. Flatten the garlic again to make a coarse purée.

COOK'S TIPS
• Make sure all the ingredients are at room temperature before you start to help prevent the mixture from curdling.
• To make a really quick and easy version of this dip, use good quality bottled mayonnaise and simply stir in the garlic and chopped herbs.

5 Tear both types of basil into small pieces and then stir them into the mayonnaise along with the crushed garlic purée.

6 Add salt and pepper to taste, then transfer the dip to a serving dish. Cover with clear film (plastic wrap) and chill until ready to serve.

Energy 484kcal/1992kJ; Protein 1.8g; Carbohydrate 0.4g, of which sugars 0.3g; Fat 52.9g, of which saturates 7.4g; Cholesterol 101mg; Calcium 37mg; Fibre 0.6g; Sodium 9mg.

Hummus Bi Tahina

Blending chickpeas with garlic and oil creates a surprisingly creamy purée that is delicious as part of a Turkish-style mezze, or as a dip with vegetables. Leftovers make a good sandwich filler.

Makes 1 bowl

150g/5oz/¾ cup dried chickpeas
juice of 2 lemons
2 garlic cloves, sliced
30ml/2 tbsp olive oil
pinch of cayenne pepper
150ml/¼ pint/⅔ cup tahini paste
salt and ground black pepper
extra olive oil and cayenne pepper,
 for sprinkling
fresh flat leaf parsley sprigs, to garnish

1 Put the chickpeas in a bowl and add cold water to cover. Leave to soak for 8 hours or overnight.

2 Drain the chickpeas, place in a pan and add fresh water to cover. Bring to the boil over a high heat and boil rapidly for 10 minutes. Reduce the heat and simmer gently for about 2 hours, until soft. (The cooking time depends on how long the chickpeas have been stored.) Drain in a colander.

3 Process the chickpeas in a food processor to a smooth purée. Add the lemon juice, garlic, olive oil, cayenne pepper and tahini paste and blend until creamy, scraping the mixture down from the sides of the bowl.

4 Season the purée with plenty of salt and ground black pepper and transfer to a serving dish. Sprinkle with a little olive oil and cayenne pepper, and serve garnished with a few parsley sprigs.

COOK'S TIPS

• For convenience, canned chickpeas can be used instead. Allow two 400g/14oz cans and drain them thoroughly.
• Tahini paste can now be purchased from most good supermarkets or health-food stores.
• The cooking time for chickpeas will vary, depending on how long they've been allowed to soak.

Energy 265kcal/1101kJ; Protein 10g; Carbohydrate 12.6g, of which sugars 0.8g; Fat 19.7g, of which saturates 2.8g; Cholesterol 0mg; Calcium 210mg; Fibre 4.7g; Sodium 15mg.

Baba Ganoush with Lebanese Flatbread

Baba Ganoush is a delectable aubergine dip from the Middle East. Tahini, a sesame seed paste with cumin, is the main flavouring, giving a subtle hint of spice.

Makes 1 bowl

2 small aubergines (eggplants)
1 garlic clove, crushed
60ml/4 tbsp tahini
25g/1oz/¼ cup ground almonds
juice of ½ lemon
2.5ml/½ tsp ground cumin
30ml/2 tbsp fresh mint leaves
30ml/2 tbsp olive oil
salt and ground black pepper

For the flatbread
4 pitta breads
45ml/3 tbsp sesame seeds
45ml/3 tbsp fresh thyme leaves
45ml/3 tbsp poppy seeds
150ml/¼ pint/⅔ cup olive oil

1 Start by making the Lebanese flatbread. Split the pitta breads through the middle and carefully open them out. Mix the sesame seeds, chopped thyme and poppy seeds in a mortar. Grind them lightly with a pestle to release the flavour.

2 Stir in the olive oil. Spread the mixture over the cut sides of the pitta bread. Grill (broil) until golden brown and crisp. Leave to cool, then break into pieces and set aside in an airtight container until required.

3 Grill the aubergines, turning them frequently, until the skin is blackened and blistered. Peel off the skins, chop the flesh coarsely and leave to drain in a colander.

4 Squeeze out as much liquid from the aubergines as possible. Place the flesh in a blender or food processor, then add the garlic, tahini, ground almonds, lemon juice and cumin, with salt to taste. Process to a smooth paste, then coarsely chop half the mint and stir it into the dip.

5 Spoon the aubergine paste into a serving bowl, sprinkle the remaining mint leaves on top of the dip and drizzle with the olive oil. Serve with the Lebanese flatbread.

Energy 451kcal/1878kJ; Protein 9.3g; Carbohydrate 29.5g, of which sugars 3.1g; Fat 33.8g, of which saturates 4.7g; Cholesterol 0mg; Calcium 204mg; Fibre 4.2g; Sodium 225mg.

Taramasalata

This smoked roe speciality is one of the most famous Greek dips. It is ideal for a buffet or for handing round with drinks. Fingers of warm pitta bread, breadsticks or crispy crackers all make good dippers.

Makes 1 bowl

*115g/4oz smoked grey mullet roe
 (see Cook's Tip)*
2 garlic cloves, crushed
30ml/2 tbsp grated onion
60ml/4 tbsp olive oil
4 slices white bread, crusts removed
juice of 2 lemons
30ml/2 tbsp milk or water
ground black pepper
*warm pitta bread, breadsticks or
 crackers, to serve*

1 Place the smoked roe, garlic, onion, oil, bread and lemon juice in a blender or food processor and process briefly until just smooth.

COOK'S TIP
Since the roe of grey mullet is expensive, smoked cod's roe is often used instead for this dish. It is paler than the burnt-orange colour of mullet roe but is still very good.

2 Add the milk or water and process again for a few seconds. (This will give the taramasalata a creamier texture.)

3 Pour the taramasalata into a serving bowl, cover with clear film (plastic wrap) and chill for 1–2 hours in the refrigerator before serving. Sprinkle the dip with freshly ground black pepper just before serving.

Energy 807kcal/3374kJ; Protein 36.2g; Carbohydrate 60.6g, of which sugars 5.4g; Fat 48.4g, of which saturates 7.1g; Cholesterol 380mg; Calcium 147mg; Fibre 3g; Sodium 700mg.

Tzatziki

Serve this classic Greek dip with toasted small pitta breads.

Makes 1 bowl

1 mini cucumber
4 spring onions (scallions)
1 garlic clove
200ml/7fl oz/scant 1 cup Greek
*   (US strained plain) yogurt*
45ml/3 tbsp chopped fresh mint
fresh mint sprigs, to garnish (optional)
salt and ground black pepper

3 Spoon the yogurt into a bowl and beat until it is completely smooth, if necessary, then gently stir in the diced cucumber, spring onions, garlic and chopped mint.

4 Add salt and plenty of freshly ground black pepper to taste. Transfer the mixture to a serving bowl. Cover and chill until ready to serve; garnish with mint if you like.

1 Trim the ends from the mini cucumber, then cut it into 5mm/¼in dice, using a sharp knife.

2 Trim the spring onions and garlic, then chop both very finely.

COOK'S TIP
Choose Greek (US strained plain) yogurt for this dip – it has a higher fat content than most yogurts, which gives it a deliciously rich, creamy texture.

Energy 67kcal/279kJ; Protein 4g; Carbohydrate 2.3g, of which sugars 1.6g; Fat 5.3g, of which saturates 2.6g; Cholesterol 0mg; Calcium 107mg; Fibre 0.3g; Sodium 39mg.

Lemon and Coconut Dhal Dip

A warm spicy dish, this can be served either as a dip or as an accompaniment to cold meats.

Makes 2 bowls

5cm/2in piece fresh root ginger
1 onion
2 garlic cloves
2 small fresh red chillies, seeded
30ml/2 tbsp sunflower oil
5ml/1 tsp cumin seeds
150g/5oz/²/3 cup red lentils
250ml/8fl oz/1 cup water
15ml/1 tbsp hot curry paste
200ml/7fl oz/scant 1 cup coconut cream
juice of 1 lemon
handful of fresh coriander
  (cilantro) leaves
25g/1oz/¹/4 cup flaked (sliced) almonds
salt and ground black pepper

1 Use a vegetable peeler to peel the ginger, then chop it finely with the onion, garlic and chillies.

VARIATION
Try making this dhal with yellow split peas: they take longer to cook and a little extra water has to be added but the result is equally tasty.

2 Heat the sunflower oil in a large, shallow pan. Add the ginger, onion, garlic, chillies and cumin. Cook over a medium heat, stirring occasionally, for about 5 minutes, until the onion is softened but not coloured.

3 Stir the lentils, measured water and curry paste into the pan. Bring to the boil, then reduce the heat to low, cover and simmer gently, stirring occasionally, for 15–20 minutes, until the lentils are just tender but have not yet broken up.

4 Stir in all but 30ml/2 tbsp of the coconut cream. Bring to the boil and cook, uncovered, for 15–20 minutes, until the mixture is thick and pulpy. Remove the pan from the heat, stir in the lemon juice and coriander leaves. Season to taste.

5 Heat a large, heavy frying pan and dry-fry the flaked almonds for about 1–2 minutes on each side, until golden brown. Stir about three-quarters of the toasted almonds into the dhal. Reserve the remainder for the garnish.

6 Transfer the dhal to a serving bowl; swirl in the remaining coconut cream. Sprinkle the reserved almonds on top and serve warm.

Energy 1177kcal/4888kJ; Protein 29g; Carbohydrate 59g, of which sugars 15g; Fat 94g, of which saturates 62g; Cholesterol 0mg; Calcium 150mg; Fibre 11g; Sodium 183mg.

Chilli Bean Dip

This deliciously spicy and creamy bean dip is best served warm with triangles of grilled pitta bread or a bowl of crunchy tortilla chips.

Makes 1 bowl

2 garlic cloves
1 onion
2 fresh green chillies
30ml/2 tbsp vegetable oil
5–10ml/1–2 tsp hot chilli powder
400g/14oz can kidney beans
75g/3oz/³/4 cup grated Cheddar cheese
1 fresh red chilli
salt and ground black pepper

1 Finely chop the garlic and onion. Slit the green chillies and remove and discard the seeds, then chop finely.

2 Heat the vegetable oil in a large sauté pan or deep frying pan and add the garlic, onion, green chillies and chilli powder. Cook over a low heat, stirring frequently, for about 5–8 minutes, until the onion has softened and become translucent, but is not browned.

3 Drain the kidney beans, reserving the can juice. Process all but 30ml/2 tbsp of the beans to a purée in a food processor.

4 Add the puréed beans to the pan with 30–45ml/2–3 tbsp of the reserved can juice and stir well. Cook over a low heat, stirring occasionally.

5 Stir in the reserved whole beans and the grated Cheddar cheese. Cook gently for a further 2–3 minutes, stirring until the cheese has melted. Season with salt and pepper to taste.

6 Slit the red chilli and remove and discard the seeds, then cut the flesh into tiny strips.

7 Spoon the dip into a serving bowl or into several small bowls and sprinkle the chilli strips over the top to garnish. Serve warm.

COOK'S TIP

To make a dip with a coarser texture, do not purée the beans; instead mash them roughly with a potato masher.

Energy 240kcal/1002kj; Protein 12.3g; Carbohydrate 20.3g; of which sugars 5.4g; Fat 12.3g; of which saturates 4.8g; Cholesterol 18mg; Calcium 219mg; Fibre 6.6g; Sodium 527mg.

Potato Skins with Cajun Dip

Divinely crisp, these potato skins are great on their own or served with this piquant dip as a garnish or on the side.

Serves 4

2 large baking potatoes
vegetable or groundnut (peanut) oil, for deep-frying

For the dip
120ml/4fl oz/¹/₂ cup natural (plain) yogurt
1 garlic clove, crushed
5ml/1 tsp tomato purée (paste) or 2.5ml/¹/₂ tsp green chilli purée (paste) or ¹/₂ small fresh green chilli, seeded and chopped
1.5ml/¹/₄ tsp celery salt
salt and ground black pepper

1 Preheat the oven to 180°C/350°F/ Gas 4. Prick the potatoes with a fork and bake, for 45–50 minutes until tender. Cut them in half and scoop out the flesh, leaving a thin layer on the skins. Keep the flesh for another recipe. Cut the potato skins in half once more.

2 To make the dip, mix together all the ingredients and chill.

3 Heat a 1cm/¹/₂in layer of oil in a large pan or deep-fat fryer. Deep-fry the potato skins until crisp and golden on both sides. Drain well on kitchen paper, then sprinkle with salt and black pepper. Serve the potato skins immediately with a bowl of dip or a spoonful of dip in each skin.

Energy 211kcal/873kJ; Protein 2.7g; Carbohydrate 12.5g, of which sugars 3.3g; Fat 17g, of which saturates 2.2g; Cholesterol 0mg; Calcium 62mg; Fibre 0.7g; Sodium 35mg.

Spicy Potato Wedges with Chilli Dip

These dry-roasted potato wedges with crisp spicy crusts are delicious with the chilli dip. They make a tasty appetizer or can be served with other dishes as part of a barbecue or informal buffet supper.

Serves 6

4 baking potatoes, about 225g/
  8oz each
60ml/4 tbsp olive oil
4 garlic cloves, crushed
10ml/2 tsp ground allspice
10ml/2 tsp ground coriander
30ml/2 tbsp paprika
salt and ground black pepper

For the dip
30ml/2 tbsp olive oil
2 small onions, finely chopped
2 garlic clove, crushed
400g/14oz can chopped tomatoes
2 fresh red chillies, seeded and
  finely chopped
30ml/2 tbsp balsamic vinegar
30ml/2 tbsp chopped fresh coriander
  (cilantro), plus extra to garnish

1 Preheat the oven to 200°C/400°F/ Gas 6. Cut the potatoes in half, then into eight wedges.

2 Add the wedges to a large pan of cold water. Bring to the boil, reduce the heat and simmer for 10 minutes, or until the wedges have softened but the flesh has not started to disintegrate. Drain well and pat dry on kitchen paper.

3 Mix the olive oil, garlic, allspice, coriander and paprika in a roasting pan. Add salt and pepper to taste. Add the potatoes to the pan and shake to coat them thoroughly. Roast for 20–25 minutes, until the wedges are browned, crisp and fully cooked. Turn the potato wedges occasionally during the roasting time.

4 Meanwhile, make the chilli dip. Heat the oil in a small pan, add the onion and garlic, and cook for 5–10 minutes, until softened.

5 Tip in the chopped tomatoes, with any juice. Stir in the chilli and vinegar. Cook gently for 10 minutes, until the mixture has reduced and thickened, then taste and check the seasoning. Stir in the chopped fresh coriander.

6 Pile the spicy potato wedges on a plate, garnish with the extra coriander and serve with the chilli dip.

VARIATION
Instead of balsamic vinegar, try brown rice vinegar, which has a mellow flavour.

Energy 239kcal/1001kJ; Protein 4g; Carbohydrate 30.8g, of which sugars 4.9g; Fat 11.9g, of which saturates 1.9g; Cholesterol 0mg; Calcium 23mg; Fibre 2.6g; Sodium 28mg.

Stilton-stuffed Mushrooms Baked with Garlic Breadcrumbs

Serve these succulent stuffed mushrooms with warm bread.

Serves 8

900g/2lb chestnut mushrooms
6 garlic cloves, finely chopped
200g/7oz/scant 1 cup butter, melted
juice of 1 lemon
225g/8oz Stilton cheese, crumbled
115g/4oz/1 cup walnuts, chopped
200g/7oz/3 cups white breadcrumbs
50g/2oz/²⁄₃ cup freshly grated
   Parmesan cheese
60ml/4 tbsp chopped fresh parsley
salt and ground black pepper

For the sauce

225g/8oz/1 cup fromage frais or
   Greek (US strained plain) yogurt
1 bunch chopped fresh herbs
15ml/1 tbsp Dijon mustard

1 Preheat the oven to 200°C/400°F/ Gas 6. Place the mushrooms in an ovenproof dish and sprinkle half the garlic over them. Drizzle with 50g/ 2oz/¼ cup of the butter and the lemon juice. Season with salt and pepper, and bake for 15–20 minutes. Remove from the oven and leave to cool.

2 Cream the crumbled Stilton with the chopped walnuts and mix in 30ml/2 tbsp of the breadcrumbs.

3 Divide the Stilton mixture among the chestnut mushrooms.

4 To make the sauce, mix the fromage frais or Greek yogurt with the chopped fresh herbs and the Dijon mustard until thoroughly combined.

5 Preheat the grill (broiler). Mix the remaining garlic, breadcrumbs and melted butter together. Stir in the grated Parmesan and chopped, fresh parsley and season with plenty of ground black pepper. Cover the mushrooms with the breadcrumb mixture and grill (broil) for about 5 minutes, or until crisp and browned. Serve immediately with the sauce.

VARIATION
Use other types of mushrooms such as large flat mushrooms or ceps.

Vegetable Tempura

Tempura is a Japanese type of savoury fritter. Originally prawns were used, but vegetables can be cooked in the egg batter successfully too. The secret of making the incredibly light batter is to use really cold water, and to have the oil at the right temperature before you start cooking the fritters.

Serves 4

2 courgettes (zucchini)
$^{1}/_{2}$ aubergine (eggplant)
1 large carrot
$^{1}/_{2}$ small Spanish (Bermuda) onion
1 egg
120ml/4fl oz/$^{1}/_{2}$ cup iced water
115g/4oz/1 cup plain
    (all-purpose) flour
salt and ground black pepper
vegetable oil, for deep-frying
sea salt flakes, lemon slices and
    Japanese soy sauce (shoyu), to serve

1 Pare strips of peel from the courgettes and aubergine.

2 Using a chef's knife, cut the courgettes, aubergine and carrot into strips measuring about 7.5–10cm/ 3–4in long and 3mm/$^{1}/_{8}$in wide. Place in a colander and sprinkle with salt. Put a small plate over and weigh it down. Leave for 30 minutes, then rinse under cold running water to remove all traces of salt. Drain well, then dry with kitchen paper.

3 Thinly slice the onion from top to base, discarding the plump pieces in the middle. Separate the layers so that there are lots of fine, long strips. Mix all the vegetables together and season with salt and pepper.

4 Make the batter immediately before frying, as it should not be left to stand. Mix the egg and iced water in a bowl, then sift in the flour. Mix briefly with a fork or chopsticks. Do not overmix: the batter should remain fairly lumpy. Add the vegetables to the batter and mix to combine and coat.

COOK'S TIP

Other suitable vegetables for tempura include mushrooms, cauliflower florets and slices of red, green, yellow or orange (bell) peppers.

5 Half-fill a wok with oil and heat to 180°C/350°F or until a cube of bread, added to it, browns in about 45 seconds. Scoop up a generous tablespoonful of the mixture at a time and carefully lower it into the oil. Deep-fry in batches for about 3 minutes, until golden brown and crisp. Remove with a slotted spoon and drain well on kitchen paper. Keep warm while you cook the remaining batches.

6 Serve each portion with sea salt, slices of lemon and a tiny bowl of Japanese soy sauce for dipping.

Energy 313kcal/1305kJ; Protein 7.1g; Carbohydrate 30.6g, of which sugars 7.3g; Fat 18.9g, of which saturates 2.5g; Cholesterol 48mg; Calcium 94mg; Fibre 3.6g; Sodium 28mg.

Quail's Eggs with Herbs and Dips

For *al fresco* eating or informal entertaining this platter of contrasting tastes and textures is delicious and certainly encourages a relaxed atmosphere. Choose the best seasonal vegetables and substitute for what is available.

Serves 6

1 large Italian focaccia or 2–3 Indian parathas or other flatbread
extra virgin olive oil, plus extra to serve
1 large garlic clove, finely chopped
small handful chopped fresh mixed herbs, such as coriander (cilantro), mint, parsley and oregano
18–24 quail's eggs
30ml/2 tbsp home-made mayonnaise
30ml/2 tbsp thick sour cream
5ml/1 tsp chopped capers
5ml/1 tsp finely chopped shallot
225g/8oz fresh beetroot (beet), cooked, peeled and sliced
1/2 bunch spring onions (scallions), trimmed and coarsely chopped
60ml/4 tbsp red onion or tamarind and date chutney
salt and ground black pepper
coarse sea salt and mixed ground peppercorns, to serve

1 Preheat the oven to 190°C/375°F/ Gas 5. Brush the focaccia or flatbread liberally with olive oil, sprinkle with garlic and your choice of herbs and season with salt and pepper. Bake for 10–15 minutes, or until golden. Keep warm until ready to serve.

2 Put the quail's eggs into a pan of cold water, bring to the boil over a medium heat and boil for 5 minutes. Arrange in a serving dish. Peel the eggs, if you like, or leave guests to do their own.

3 To make the dip, combine the mayonnaise, sour cream, capers, shallot and seasoning.

4 To serve, cut the bread into wedges and serve with dishes of the quail's eggs, mayonnaise dip, beetroot, spring onion and chutney. Serve with tiny bowls of the coarse salt, ground peppercorns and olive oil for dipping.

VARIATION
For a truly impressive dish for a special occasion, use guinea fowl eggs, which are slightly larger than quail's eggs and have attractive brown shells. They have a rich flavour and are delicious hard-boiled. However, they are difficult to obtain.

COOK'S TIP
If you don't have time to make your own mayonnaise use the best commercial variety available. You will probably find that you need to add less seasoning to it.

Energy 297kcal/1241kJ; Protein 12g; Carbohydrate 18g, of which sugars 7g; Fat 21g, of which saturates 4g; Cholesterol 262mg; Calcium 83mg; Fibre 2g; Sodium 248mg.

Sesame Seed-coated Falafel with **Tahini dip**

Sesame seeds are used to give a delightfully crunchy coating to these spicy chickpea patties.

Serves 6

250g/9oz/1¹/₃ cups dried chickpeas
2 garlic cloves, crushed
1 fresh red chilli, seeded and sliced
5ml/1 tsp ground coriander
5ml/1 tsp ground cumin
15ml/1 tbsp chopped fresh mint
15ml/1 tbsp chopped fresh parsley
2 spring onions (scallions),
   finely chopped
1 large (US extra large) egg, beaten
sesame seeds, for coating
sunflower oil, for frying
salt and ground black pepper

For the tahini yogurt dip
30ml/2 tbsp light tahini
200g/7oz/scant 1 cup natural (plain)
   live yogurt
5ml/1 tsp cayenne pepper, plus extra
   for sprinkling
15ml/1 tbsp chopped fresh mint
1 spring onion (scallion), thinly sliced
fresh herbs, to garnish

1 Place the chickpeas in a bowl, cover with cold water and leave to soak overnight. Drain and rinse the chickpeas, then place in a pan and cover with fresh cold water. Bring to the boil over a medium heat and boil rapidly for 10 minutes. Reduce the heat to low and simmer gently for 1½–2 hours, until tender.

2 Meanwhile, make the tahini yogurt dip. Mix together the tahini, yogurt, cayenne pepper and mint in a small bowl. Sprinkle the spring onion and extra cayenne pepper on top, cover with clear film (plastic wrap) and chill in the refrigerator until required.

3 Drain the chickpeas and combine with the garlic, chilli, coriander, cumin, mint, parsley, spring onions and seasoning, then mix in the egg. Place in a food processor and process until the mixture forms a coarse paste. If the paste seems too soft, chill it for about 30 minutes.

4 Spread out the sesame seeds on a plate. Form the chilled chickpea paste into 12 patties with your hands, then roll each one in the sesame seeds to coat thoroughly.

5 Heat enough oil to cover the base of a large frying pan. Add the falafel, in batches if necessary, and cook for 6 minutes, turning once. Serve with the tahini yogurt dip garnished with fresh herbs.

Energy 315kcal/1314kJ; Protein 14.3g; Carbohydrate 23.8g, of which sugars 3.8g; Fat 18.8g, of which saturates 2.6g; Cholesterol 32mg; Calcium 237mg; Fibre 5.8g; Sodium 63mg.

Cheese-crusted Party Eggs

Similar to the popular Scotch egg, these whole small eggs are wrapped in a tasty herb-flavoured coating, then deep-fried. Tiny bantam or quail's eggs will look dainty and are ideal for dipping into mayonnaise.

Makes 12–20

225g/8oz/4 cups stale
white breadcrumbs
1 small leek, very finely chopped
225g/8oz mild but tasty cheese, grated
10ml/2 tsp garlic and herb seasoning
60ml/4 tbsp chopped fresh parsley
10ml/2 tsp mild mustard
4 eggs, separated
60–90ml/4–6 tbsp milk
12–20 small spinach or sorrel leaves,
stalks removed
12 very small eggs, such as bantam,
guinea fowl, or 16–20 quail's eggs,
hard-boiled and peeled
50–75g/2–3oz/½–⅔ cup plain
(all-purpose) flour, for coating,
plus extra for dusting
50g/2oz/4 tbsp sesame seeds
vegetable oil, for deep-frying
salt and ground black pepper
mayonnaise, for dipping

1 Mix the breadcrumbs, leek, cheese, seasoning, parsley and mustard. Beat the egg yolks with the milk and blend into the mixture. Whisk two egg whites until stiff and gradually work sufficient stiff egg white into the breadcrumb mixture to give a firm, dropping (pourable) consistency. Chill for 1 hour.

2 Divide the mixture into 12 portions (or 16–20 if using the smaller eggs). Mould one portion in the palm of your hand, place a spinach leaf inside and then an egg and carefully shape the mixture around the egg to enclose it completely within a thin crust. Seal well and dust lightly with flour. Repeat with the remaining portions.

3 Beat the remaining egg white with 30ml/2 tbsp water, then pour into a shallow dish. Mix the flour with salt and pepper and the sesame seeds and place in another shallow dish. Dip the eggs first in the beaten egg white, then in the sesame flour. Cover and chill for at least 20 minutes.

4 Heat the oil in a pan until a crust of bread turns golden in about 1¼ minutes. Deep-fry the eggs in the hot oil, turning frequently, until they are golden brown all over. Remove the eggs with a slotted spoon, drain on kitchen paper and leave to cool completely. Serve the cooked eggs whole or sliced in half, with a bowl of good mayonnaise for dipping.

Energy 188kcal/784kJ; Protein 10g; Carbohydrate 11g, of which sugars 1g; Fat 12g, of which saturates 4g; Cholesterol 149mg; Calcium 148mg; Fibre 1g; Sodium 236mg.

Crisp-fried Crab Claws

Crab claws are readily available in the freezer cabinet in many Asian stores and supermarkets. Thaw out thoroughly and dry on kitchen paper before dipping in the batter. They are just the right size to munch on for a burst of flavour.

Makes 12

50g/2oz/½ cup rice flour
15ml/1 tbsp cornflour (cornstarch)
2.5ml/½ tsp sugar
1 egg
60ml/4 tbsp cold water
1 lemon grass stalk, root trimmed
2 garlic cloves, finely chopped
15ml/1 tbsp chopped fresh
    coriander (cilantro)
1–2 fresh red chillies, seeded and
    finely chopped
5ml/1 tsp Thai fish sauce
vegetable oil, for frying
12 half-shelled crab claws
ground black pepper

For the chilli vinegar dip
45ml/3 tbsp sugar
120ml/4fl oz/½ cup water
120ml/4fl oz/½ cup red wine vinegar
15ml/1 tbsp Thai fish sauce
2–4 fresh red chillies, seeded
    and chopped

1 Combine the rice flour, cornflour and sugar in a bowl. Beat the egg with the cold water, then stir the egg and water mixture into the flour mixture and mix well until it forms a light batter.

2 Cut off the lower 5cm/2in of the lemon grass stalk and chop it finely. Add the lemon grass to the batter, with the garlic, coriander, red chillies and fish sauce. Stir in pepper to taste.

3 Make the chilli dip. Mix the sugar and water in a pan, stirring until the sugar has dissolved, then bring to the boil. Lower the heat and simmer for 5–7 minutes. Stir in the rest of the dip ingredients and set aside.

4 Heat the vegetable oil in a wok or deep-fryer. Pat the crab claws dry and dip into the batter. Drop the battered claws into the hot oil, a few at a time. Deep-fry until golden brown. Drain on kitchen paper and keep hot. Pour the chilli vinegar dip into a serving bowl and serve with the hot crab claws.

VARIATION

This Asian-style batter can also be used to coat king prawns (jumbo shrimp).

Energy 222kcal/926kJ; Protein 10.1g; Carbohydrate 16.9g, of which sugars 0g; Fat 12.8g, of which saturates 1.7g; Cholesterol 78mg; Calcium 62mg; Fibre 0.3g; Sodium 256mg.

Parmesan Fish Goujons

The batter used here is light and crisp, making it the perfect choice for these moreish strips of fish. Serve as an appetizer or as part of a fork buffet.

Serves 4

*375g/13oz plaice, flounder or sole
    fillets, or thicker fish such as cod,
    haddock or hoki
plain (all-purpose) flour, for dusting
vegetable oil, for deep-frying
salt and ground black pepper
fresh dill sprigs, to garnish*

For the cream sauce
*60ml/4 tbsp sour cream
60ml/4 tbsp mayonnaise
2.5ml/^{1}/$_2$ tsp grated lemon rind
30ml/2 tbsp chopped gherkins
    or capers
15ml/1 tbsp chopped mixed fresh
    herbs, or 5ml/1 tsp dried*

For the batter
*75g/3oz/^{3}/$_4$ cup plain (all-
    purpose) flour
25g/1oz/^{1}/$_4$ cup freshly grated
    Parmesan cheese
5ml/1 tsp bicarbonate of soda
    (baking soda)
1 egg, separated
150ml/^{1}/$_4$ pint/^{2}/$_3$ cup milk*

1 To make the cream sauce, mix the sour cream, mayonnaise, lemon rind, gherkins or capers, fresh or dried herbs and seasoning together, then place in the refrigerator to chill.

2 To make the batter, sift the flour into a bowl. Mix in the cheese, soda and a pinch of salt, then whisk in the egg yolk and milk to give a thick yet smooth batter. Then gradually whisk in 90ml/6 tbsp water. Season, cover with clear film (plastic wrap) and place in the refrigerator to chill.

3 Skin the fish and cut into thin strips of similar length. Season the flour and then dip the fish strips lightly in the flour, shaking off any excess.

4 Heat at least 5cm/2in oil in a large pan with a lid. Whisk the egg white until stiff and gently fold it into the batter until just blended.

5 Dip the floured fish into the batter, drain off any excess and then drop gently into the hot oil.

6 Cook the fish for only 3–4 minutes, turning once. You may need to cook the goujons in batches to prevent them from sticking to each other. When the batter is golden and crisp, remove the fish with a slotted spoon. Place on kitchen paper on a plate and keep warm in a low oven while you are cooking the remaining goujons.

7 Serve the goujons hot garnished with sprigs of dill and accompanied by the cream sauce.

Energy 358kcal/1497kJ; Protein 24.2g; Carbohydrate 21.4g, of which sugars 3.2g; Fat 20.2g, of which saturates 5.9g; Cholesterol 116mg; Calcium 243mg; Fibre 1.4g; Sodium 293mg.

Thai Tempeh Cakes with Dipping Sauce

Made from soya beans, tempeh is similar to tofu but has a nuttier taste. Here, it is combined with a fragrant blend of lemon grass, coriander and ginger, and formed into small patties, then served with a spicy dipping sauce.

Makes 8

1 lemon grass stalk, outer leaves
   removed, finely chopped
2 garlic cloves, finely chopped
2 spring onions (scallions),
   finely chopped
2 shallots, finely chopped
2 fresh red or green chillies, seeded
   and finely chopped
2.5cm/1in piece fresh root ginger,
   peeled and finely chopped
60ml/4 tbsp chopped fresh coriander
   (cilantro), plus extra to garnish
250g/9oz/2¼ cups tempeh, thawed if
   frozen, sliced
15ml/1 tbsp lime juice
5ml/1 tsp caster (superfine) sugar
45ml/3 tbsp plain (all-
   purpose) flour
1 large (US extra large) egg,
   lightly beaten
vegetable oil, for frying
salt and ground black pepper

For the dipping sauce
45ml/3 tbsp mirin
45ml/3 tbsp white wine vinegar
2 spring onions (scallions),
   thinly sliced
15ml/1 tbsp sugar
2 fresh red or green chillies,
   finely chopped
30ml/2 tbsp chopped fresh
   coriander (cilantro)
large pinch of salt

1 To make the dipping sauce, mix together the mirin, vinegar, spring onions, sugar, chillies, coriander and salt in a small bowl and set aside.

2 To make the tempeh cakes, place the lemon grass, garlic, spring onions, shallots, chillies, ginger and coriander in a food processor or blender, then process to a coarse paste. Add the tempeh, lime juice and sugar, then process until combined.

3 Add the flour and beaten egg to the food processor or blender and season well with salt and pepper. Process again until the mixture forms a coarse, sticky paste.

4 Take a generous tablespoonful of the tempeh paste mixture at a time and form into rounds with your hands. The mixture will be quite sticky.

5 Heat enough oil to cover the base of a large, heavy frying pan. Add the tempeh cakes, in batches if necessary, and cook over a medium heat, turning once, for 5–6 minutes, until golden. Drain well on kitchen paper and serve warm with the dipping sauce, and garnished with chopped coriander.

Energy 79kcal/332kJ; Protein 4.5g; Carbohydrate 9.1g, of which sugars 4.3g; Fat 2.3g, of which saturates 0.4g; Cholesterol 26mg; Calcium 192mg; Fibre 0.8g; Sodium 15mg.

Butterfly Prawn Spiedini with Chilli and Raspberry Dip

The success of this dish depends upon the quality of the prawns, so it is worthwhile getting really good ones, which have a fine flavour and firm texture. A fruity, slightly spicy dip is an astonishingly easy, but fabulous accompaniment.

Makes 30

30 raw king prawns (jumbo shrimp), peeled
15ml/1 tbsp sunflower oil
sea salt

For the chilli and raspberry dip
30ml/2 tbsp raspberry vinegar
15ml/1 tbsp sugar
115g/4oz/²/₃ cup raspberries
1 large fresh red chilli, seeded and finely chopped

1 Soak 30 wooden skewers in cold water for about 30 minutes. Make the dip by mixing the vinegar and sugar in a small pan. Heat gently until the sugar has dissolved, stirring constantly, then add the raspberries.

2 When the raspberry juices start to flow, tip the mixture into a sieve set over a bowl. Push the raspberries through the sieve using the back of a ladle. Discard the seeds. Stir the chilli into the purée. When the dip is cold, cover and place in a cool place until it is needed.

COOK'S TIP
These mini kebabs also taste really delicious with a vibrant chilli and mango dip. Use 1 large, ripe mango in place of the raspberries.

3 Preheat the grill (broiler) or barbecue. Remove the dark spinal vein from the prawns using a small, sharp knife.

4 Make an incision down the curved back and butterfly each prawn.

5 Mix the sunflower oil with a little sea salt in a bowl. Add the prawns and toss to coat them completely.

6 Thread the prawns on to the drained skewers, spearing them head first.

7 Grill (broil) the prawns for about 5 minutes, depending on their size, turning them over once. Serve hot, with the chilli and raspberry dip.

VARIATIONS
• Thin strips of chicken or turkey escalope (scallop) can be seasoned and threaded on to the skewers and grilled (broiled) instead of the prawns. They are delicious with the fruity dip.
• For a vegetarian version, use chunks of halloumi cheese or firm tofu.

Energy 21kcal/88kJ; Protein 3g; Carbohydrate 1g, of which sugars 1g; Fat 1g, of which saturates 0g; Cholesterol 37mg; Calcium 16mg; Fibre 0g; Sodium 210mg.

Seafood Spring Onion Skewers
with **Tartare Sauce**

Make these skewers quite small to serve as a canapé at a drinks party or before dinner, with the tartare sauce offered as a dip.

Makes 9

675g/1½lb monkfish, filleted, skinned
    and membrane removed
1 bunch thick spring onions (scallions)
75ml/5 tbsp olive oil
1 garlic clove, finely chopped
15ml/1 tbsp lemon juice
5ml/1 tsp dried oregano
30ml/2 tbsp chopped fresh flat
    leaf parsley
12–18 small scallops or raw king
    prawns (jumbo shrimp)
75g/3oz/1½ cups fine
    fresh breadcrumbs
salt and ground black pepper

For the tartare sauce
2 egg yolks
300ml/½ pint/1¼ cups olive oil, or
    vegetable oil and olive oil mixed
15–30ml/1–2 tbsp lemon juice
5ml/1 tsp French mustard, preferably
    tarragon mustard
15ml/1 tbsp chopped gherkin or
    pickled cucumber
15ml/1 tbsp chopped capers
30ml/2 tbsp chopped fresh flat
    leaf parsley
30ml/2 tbsp chopped fresh chives
5ml/1 tsp chopped fresh tarragon

1 Soak nine wooden skewers in water for 30 minutes to prevent them from scorching under the grill (broiler).

2 To make the tartare sauce, whisk the egg yolks and a pinch of salt. Whisk in the oil, a drop at a time at first. When about half the oil is incorporated, add it in a thin stream, whisking constantly. Stop when the mayonnaise is thick.

3 Whisk in 15ml/1 tbsp of the lemon juice, then a little more oil. Stir in the mustard, gherkin or cucumber, capers, parsley, chives and tarragon. Add more lemon juice and seasoning to taste.

4 Cut the monkfish into 18 even-size pieces. Cut the spring onions into 18 pieces about 5cm/2in long. In a bowl, mix the oil, garlic, lemon juice, oregano and half the parsley with seasoning. Add the seafood and the spring onions, then marinate for 15 minutes.

5 Mix the breadcrumbs and remaining parsley together. Toss the seafood and spring onions in the mixture to coat.

6 Preheat the grill. Drain the wooden skewers and thread the monkfish, scallops or prawns and spring onions on to them. Drizzle with a little of the marinade, then grill (broil), turning once and drizzling with the marinade, for 5–6 minutes, until the seafood is just cooked. Serve immediately with the tartare sauce.

Energy 408kcal/1692kJ; Protein 15g; Carbohydrate 8g, of which sugars 2g; Fat 35g, of which saturates 5g; Cholesterol 59mg; Calcium 46mg; Fibre 1g; Sodium 88mg.

Chicken Satay with Peanut Sauce

A great choice for parties, these skewers of marinated chicken can be prepared in advance and served at room temperature. Beef, pork or even lamb fillet can be used instead of chicken if you prefer.

Makes about 24

450g/1lb boneless, skinless chicken
    breast portions
groundnut (peanut) oil,
    for brushing
sesame seeds, for sprinkling
red (bell) pepper strips,
    to garnish

For the marinade
90ml/6 tbsp vegetable oil
60ml/4 tbsp tamari or light soy sauce
60ml/4 tbsp fresh lime juice
2.5cm/1in piece fresh root ginger,
    peeled and chopped
3–4 garlic cloves
30ml/2 tbsp light brown sugar
5ml/1 tsp Chinese-style chilli sauce or
    1 small fresh red chilli, seeded
    and chopped
30ml/2 tbsp chopped fresh
    coriander (cilantro)

For the peanut sauce
30ml/2 tbsp smooth peanut butter
30ml/2 tbsp soy sauce
15ml/1 tbsp sesame or vegetable oil
2 spring onions (scallions),
    finely chopped
2 garlic cloves
15–30ml/1–2 tbsp fresh lime or
    lemon juice
15ml/1 tbsp brown sugar

COOK'S TIP
When using metal skewers, look for flat ones which prevent the food from spinning around. If using wooden skewers, be sure to soak them in cold water for at least 30 minutes to prevent them from burning.

1 Prepare the marinade. Place all the marinade ingredients in a food processor or blender and process until smooth and well blended, scraping down the sides of the bowl once or twice. Pour the marinade into a shallow, non-metallic dish and set aside.

2 Put all the peanut sauce ingredients into the same food processor bowl or blender goblet and process until well blended. If the sauce is too thick, add a little water and process again. Pour into a small bowl, cover and set aside until ready to serve.

3 Slice the chicken breast portions into thin strips, then cut the strips into 2cm/¾in pieces.

4 Add the chicken pieces to the marinade. Toss well to coat, cover with clear film (plastic wrap) and marinate for about 3–4 hours in a cool place, or overnight in the refrigerator.

5 Preheat the grill (broiler). Line a baking sheet with foil and brush lightly with oil. Thread 2–3 pieces of the marinated chicken on to skewers and sprinkle with the sesame seeds. Grill (broil) for 4–5 minutes until golden, turning once. Serve hot or cold with the peanut sauce and a garnish of red pepper strips.

Energy 375kcal/1564kJ; Protein 42.9g; Carbohydrate 3.9g, of which sugars 2.4g; Fat 20.9g, of which saturates 5.6g; Cholesterol 149mg; Calcium 27mg; Fibre 1.3g; Sodium 249mg.

Yakitori Chicken

These Japanese-style kebabs are easy to eat and ideal for barbecues or parties.

Makes 12

6 boneless, skinless chicken thighs
1 bunch of spring onions (scallions)
shichimi (seven-flavour spice),
*   to serve (optional)*

For the yakitori sauce
150ml/¼ pint/⅔ cup Japanese
*   soy sauce*
90g/3½ oz/½ cup sugar
25ml/1½ tbsp sake or dry white wine
15ml/1 tbsp plain (all-purpose) flour

1 Soak 12 wooden skewers in water for at least 30 minutes. Make the sauce. Stir the soy sauce, sugar and sake or wine into the flour in a small pan and bring to the boil, stirring. Lower the heat and simmer the mixture for 10 minutes, or until the sauce is reduced by one-third. Set aside.

2 Cut each chicken thigh into bitesize pieces and set aside.

3 Cut the spring onions into 3cm/1¼ in pieces. Preheat the grill (broiler) or prepare the barbecue.

COOK'S TIP
If shichimi is difficult to obtain, paprika can be used instead.

4 Thread the chicken and spring onions alternately on to the drained skewers. Grill (broil) under a medium heat or cook on the barbecue, brushing generously several times with the sauce. Allow 5–10 minutes, or until the chicken is cooked but still moist.

5 Serve with yakitori sauce, offering shichimi with the kebabs if available.

VARIATION
Bitesize chunks of turkey breast fillet, lean boneless pork or lamb fillet can be used instead of chicken. Small, whole button (white) mushrooms are also delicious for a vegetarian alternative.

Energy 56kcal/238kJ; Protein 7g; Carbohydrate 2g, of which sugars 1g; Fat 2g, of which saturates 1g; Cholesterol 33mg; Calcium 19mg; Fibre 0g; Sodium 729mg.

Tandoori Chicken Sticks

This aromatic chicken dish is a sure-fire success at any party.

Makes about 25

450g/1lb boneless, skinless chicken breast portions

For the coriander yogurt
250ml/8fl oz/1 cup natural (plain) yogurt
30ml/2 tbsp whipping cream
1/2 cucumber, peeled, seeded and finely chopped
15–30ml/1–2 tbsp fresh chopped mint or coriander (cilantro)
salt and ground black pepper

For the marinade
175ml/6fl oz/3/4 cup natural yogurt
5ml/1 tsp garam masala or curry powder
1.5ml/1/4 tsp ground cumin
1.5ml/1/4 tsp ground coriander
1.5ml/1/4 tsp cayenne pepper (or to taste)
5ml/1 tsp tomato purée (paste)
1–2 garlic cloves, finely chopped
2.5cm/1in piece fresh root ginger, peeled and finely chopped
grated rind and juice of 1/2 lemon
15–30ml/1–2 tbsp chopped fresh mint or coriander

1 Prepare the coriander yogurt. Combine all the ingredients in a bowl and season with salt and ground black pepper to taste. Cover with clear film (plastic wrap) and chill until you are ready to serve.

2 Prepare the marinade. Place all the ingredients in the bowl of a food processor and process until the mixture is smooth. Pour the marinade into a shallow, non-metallic dish.

3 Place the chicken breast portions in the freezer for 5 minutes to firm, then slice in half horizontally. Cut the slices into 2cm/3/4in strips and add them to the marinade. Toss to coat all over. Cover and chill in the refrigerator for 6–8 hours or overnight.

4 Preheat the grill (broiler) and line a baking sheet with foil. Using a slotted spoon, remove the chicken from the marinade and arrange the pieces in a single layer on the baking sheet. Scrunch up the chicken strips slightly so that they make wavy shapes. Grill (broil) for 4–5 minutes, until golden brown and just cooked, turning once. When cool enough to handle, thread 1–2 pieces on to cocktail sticks (toothpicks) or short skewers and serve with the coriander yogurt dip.

Energy 32kcal/134kJ; Protein 5g; Carbohydrate 1.1g, of which sugars 0.8g; Fat 0.9g, of which saturates 0.4g; Cholesterol 14mg; Calcium 29mg; Fibre 0.2g; Sodium 23mg.

Duck Wontons with Spicy Mango Sauce

These Chinese-style wontons are easy to make using ready-cooked smoked duck or chicken, or even leftovers from the Sunday roast.

Makes about 40

15ml/1 tbsp light soy sauce
5ml/1 tsp sesame oil
2 spring onions (scallions), chopped
grated rind of ½ orange
5ml/1 tsp brown sugar
275g/10oz/1½ cups chopped
    smoked duck
about 40 small wonton wrappers
15ml/1 tbsp vegetable oil
whole fresh chives, to garnish (optional)

For the mango sauce

30ml/2 tbsp vegetable oil
5ml/1 tsp ground cumin
2.5ml/½ tsp ground cardamom
1.5ml/¼ tsp ground cinnamon
250ml/8fl oz/1 cup mango purée
    (about 1 large mango)
15ml/1 tbsp clear honey
2.5ml/½ tsp Chinese chilli sauce (or
    to taste)
15ml/1 tbsp cider vinegar
chopped fresh chives, to garnish

1 First, prepare the sauce. Heat the oil in a medium-sized pan over a medium-low heat. Add the ground cumin, cardamom and cinnamon and cook for about 3 minutes, stirring constantly.

2 Stir in the mango purée, honey, chilli sauce and vinegar. Remove the pan from the heat and leave to cool. Pour the sauce into a bowl and cover until ready to serve.

3 Prepare the wonton filling. Mix together the soy sauce, sesame oil, spring onions, orange rind and brown sugar in a large bowl until thoroughly blended. Add the chopped duck and toss to coat well.

4 Place a teaspoonful of the duck mixture in the centre of each wonton wrapper. Brush the edges of the wrappers with water and then draw them up to the centre, twisting to seal and forming a pouch shape.

5 Preheat the oven to 190°F/375°C/Gas 5. Line a large baking sheet with foil and brush lightly with oil. Arrange the wontons on the baking sheet and bake for 10–12 minutes, until crisp and golden.

6 Transfer the wontons to a warm platter and serve with the mango sauce garnished with chopped fresh chives. If you like, tie each wonton with a fresh chive.

COOK'S TIP

Wonton wrappers, available in some large supermarkets and Asian food shops, are usually sold in 450g/1lb packets and can be stored in the freezer almost indefinitely. Remove as many as you need, keeping the rest frozen.

Energy 16kcal/165kJ; Protein 1g; Carbohydrate 0g, of which sugars 0g; Fat 1g, of which saturates 0g; Cholesterol 8mg; Calcium 2mg; Fibre 0g; Sodium 35mg.

Pork and **Peanut Wontons** with **Plum Sauce**

These crispy filled wontons are delicious served with a sweet plum sauce. They can be filled for up to 8 hours before they are cooked.

Makes 40–50

175g/6oz/1¹/₂ cups minced
   (ground) pork
2 spring onions (scallions), chopped
30ml/2 tbsp peanut butter
10ml/2 tsp oyster sauce (optional)
40–50 wonton wrappers
30ml/2 tbsp flour paste (see Cook's Tip)
vegetable oil, for deep-frying
salt and ground black pepper
lettuces and radishes, to garnish

For the plum sauce
225g/8oz/generous ³/₄ cup dark
   plum jam
15ml/1 tbsp rice or white wine vinegar
15ml/1 tbsp dark soy sauce
2.5ml/¹/₂ tsp chilli sauce

1 Combine the minced pork, spring onions, peanut butter, oyster sauce, if using, in a bowl and season with salt and pepper, then set aside.

2 For the plum sauce, combine the plum jam, vinegar, soy and chilli sauces in a serving bowl and set aside.

COOK'S TIP
To make the flour paste, mix 4 parts cornflour (cornstarch) with 5 parts cold water in a small bowl, stirring well to make a smooth paste.

3 To fill the wonton wrappers, place eight wrappers at a time on a work surface, moisten the edges with the flour paste and place 2.5ml/¹/₂ tsp of the filling on each one. Fold them in half, corner to corner, and twist.

4 Fill a large wok or deep frying pan one-third full with vegetable oil and heat to 190°C/375°F or until a cube of bread, added to the oil, browns in 30 seconds. Have ready a wire strainer or frying basket and a tray lined with kitchen paper. Drop the wontons, eight at a time, into the hot oil and deep-fry for 1–2 minutes, until golden all over. Lift the wontons out on to the paper-lined tray and sprinkle with fine salt. Serve hot with the plum sauce, and garnished with lettuce and radishes.

Energy 56kcal/236kJ; Protein 1.5g; Carbohydrate 7.9g, of which sugars 4.1g; Fat 2.3g, of which saturates 0.4g; Cholesterol 3mg; Calcium 8mg; Fibre 0.2g; Sodium 35mg.

Pork Balls with a Minted Peanut Sauce

This recipe is equally delicious when made with chicken.

Serves 4–6

275g/10oz leg of pork, trimmed and diced
1cm/½in piece fresh root ginger,
   peeled and grated
1 garlic clove, crushed
10ml/2 tsp sesame oil
15ml/1 tbsp medium-dry sherry
15ml/1 tbsp soy sauce
5ml/1 tsp sugar
1 egg white
2.5ml/½ tsp salt
pinch of white pepper
350g/12oz/scant 1¾ cups long grain rice,
   washed and cooked for 15 minutes
50g/2oz ham, diced
1 iceberg or Bibb lettuce, to serve

For the peanut sauce
90ml/6 tbsp coconut cream
30ml/2 tbsp smooth peanut butter
juice of 1 lime
1 fresh red chilli, seeded and chopped
1 garlic clove, crushed
15ml/1 tbsp chopped fresh mint
15ml/1 tbsp chopped fresh
   coriander (cilantro)
15ml/1 tbsp Thai fish sauce (optional)

1 Place the diced pork, ginger and garlic in a food processor and process for 2–3 minutes, until smooth. Add the sesame oil, sherry, soy sauce and sugar and blend with the pork mixture. Finally, add the egg white, salt and white pepper.

2 Spread the cooked rice and ham in a shallow dish. Using wet hands, shape the pork mixture into thumb-size balls. Roll in the rice to coat and pierce each ball with a bamboo skewer.

3 To make the peanut sauce, heat the coconut cream in a small pan over a medium heat. Meanwhile, place the peanut butter, lime juice, chilli, garlic, mint and coriander in a bowl. Stir until thoroughly combined, then add the creamed coconut and season with the fish sauce if using. Stir well to mix, cover with clear film (plastic wrap) and set aside until ready to serve.

4 Place the pork balls in a bamboo steamer, then steam over a pan of boiling water for about 8–10 minutes. Arrange the pork balls on a bed of lettuce leaves on a plate with the sauce to one side and serve.

Energy 337kcal/1409kJ; Protein 17.5g; Carbohydrate 47.9g, of which sugars 1g; Fat 7.8g, of which saturates 3g; Cholesterol 33mg; Calcium 35mg; Fibre 0.7g; Sodium 322mg.

Nonya Pork Satay

These skewers of tender pork with a spicy nut coating make tasty snacks for a drinks party.

Makes 8–12

450g/1lb pork fillet (tenderloin)
15ml/1 tbsp light muscovado
   (brown) sugar
1cm/½in cube shrimp paste
1–2 lemon grass stalks
30ml/2 tbsp coriander seeds, dry-fried
6 macadamia nuts or blanched almonds
2 onions, coarsely chopped
3–6 fresh red chillies, seeded and
   coarsely chopped
2.5ml/½ tsp ground turmeric
300ml/½ pint/1¼ cups canned
   coconut milk
30ml/2 tbsp groundnut (peanut) oil
   or sunflower oil
salt

1 Soak 8–12 bamboo skewers in water for at least 30 minutes to prevent them from scorching when they are placed under the grill (broiler).

2 Cut the pork into small, bitesize chunks, then spread it out in a single layer in a shallow dish. Sprinkle with the sugar, to help release the juices, and set aside.

3 Fry the shrimp paste briefly in a foil parcel in a dry frying pan. Alternatively, warm the foil parcel on a skewer held over the gas flame.

COOK'S TIP

Nonya Pork Satay can be served either as part of a buffet or as a light party snack – in which case serve it with cubes of cooling cucumber, which contrast well with the spicy meat.

4 Cut off the lower 5cm/2in of the lemon grass stalks and chop finely. Process the dry-fried coriander seeds to a powder in a food processor. Add the nuts and chopped lemon grass, process briefly, then add the onions, chillies, shrimp paste, turmeric and a little salt and process to a fine paste.

5 Pour in the coconut milk and oil. Switch the machine on very briefly to mix. Pour the mixture over the pork and leave to marinate for 1–2 hours.

6 Preheat the grill or prepare the barbecue. Thread three or four pieces of marinated pork on to each bamboo skewer and grill (broil) or cook on the barbecue for 8–10 minutes, or until tender, basting frequently with the remaining marinade. Serve the skewers immediately while hot.

Energy 105kcal/439kJ; Protein 9g; Carbohydrate 5g, of which sugars 4g; Fat 6g, of which saturates 1g; Cholesterol 26mg; Calcium 26mg; Fibre 0g; Sodium 69mg.

Beef Satay with a Hot Mango Dip

Strips of tender beef are flavoured with a delicious spicy marinade before being grilled then served with a fruit dip.

Makes 12

450g/1lb sirloin steak, trimmed

For the marinade
15ml/1 tbsp coriander seeds
5ml/1 tsp cumin seeds
50g/2oz/^{1}/$_3$ cup cashew nuts
15ml/1 tbsp vegetable oil
2 shallots, or 1 small onion, finely chopped
1cm/^{1}/$_2$in piece fresh root ginger, peeled and finely chopped
1 garlic clove, crushed
30ml/2 tbsp tamarind sauce
30ml/2 tbsp dark soy sauce
10ml/2 tsp sugar
5ml/1 tsp rice or white wine vinegar

For the mango dip
1 ripe mango
1–2 small fresh red chillies, seeded and finely chopped
15ml/1 tbsp Thai fish sauce
juice of 1 lime
10ml/2 tsp sugar
1.5ml/^{1}/$_4$ tsp salt
30ml/2 tbsp chopped fresh coriander (cilantro)

1 Soak 12 bamboo skewers in cold water for 30 minutes. Slice the beef into long narrow strips and thread, zigzag-style, on to the skewers. Place on a flat plate and set aside.

2 For the marinade, dry-fry the coriander and cumin seeds and cashews in a large wok over a low heat until evenly brown. Transfer to a mortar with a rough surface and crush finely with the pestle. Add the oil, shallots or onion, ginger, garlic, tamarind and soy sauces, sugar and rice or white wine vinegar.

3 Spread this marinade over the beef, cover and leave to marinate for up to 8 hours. Cook the beef skewers under a moderate grill (broiler) or over a barbecue for 6–8 minutes, turning to make sure that they are evenly cooked. Meanwhile, make the mango dip.

4 Cut away the skin and remove the stone (pit) from the mango. Put the mango flesh, chillies, fish sauce, lime juice, sugar and salt into a food processor or blender and process until smooth, then add the coriander. Serve the skewers with the dip.

Energy 62kcal/263kJ; Protein 9g; Carbohydrate 2.9g, of which sugars 2.8g; Fat 1.7g, of which saturates 0.8g; Cholesterol 19mg; Calcium 5mg; Fibre 0.3g; Sodium 205mg.

finger food and light bites

Standing-and-eating food has to be easy to eat

and sufficiently satisfying to keep everyone

munching through hours of chatting.

Grilled Polenta with Gorgonzola

This delicious, hot Italian-style snack can be served with any creamy cheese, but a richly flavoured blue cheese looks attractive and tastes fabulous. Here the polenta is cut into triangles but you could make different shapes if you like.

Serves 6–8

1.5 litres/2¹/₂ pints/6¹/₄ cups water
15ml/1 tbsp salt
350g/12oz/2¹/₂ cups polenta
  (corn) flour
225g/8oz Gorgonzola or other creamy
  blue cheese, at room temperature

1 Bring the water to the boil in a large heavy pan over a medium heat. Add the salt. Reduce the heat so that the water is simmering and begin to add the polenta flour in a steady stream. Stir constantly with a whisk until the polenta has all been incorporated.

2 Switch to a long-handled wooden spoon and continue to stir the polenta over a low to medium heat until it is a thick mass and pulls away from the sides of the pan. This may take from 25–50 minutes, depending on the type of flour used. For best results, never stop stirring the polenta until you remove it from the heat. However, note that if you are using quick-cook polenta, it will take far less time to thicken – about 5 minutes.

3 When the polenta is cooked, sprinkle a work surface or large board with a little water. Spread the polenta out on the surface in a layer 2cm/³/₄in thick. Leave to cool completely. Preheat the grill (broiler).

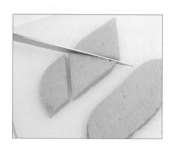

4 Cut the polenta into triangles. Grill (broil) until hot and speckled with brown on both sides. Spread the triangles with the Gorgonzola or other cheese. Serve immediately.

Energy 257kcal/1073kJ; Protein 9.9g; Carbohydrate 32g, of which sugars 0g; Fat 9.6g, of which saturates 5.4g; Cholesterol 21mg; Calcium 139mg; Fibre 1g; Sodium 343mg.

Buckwheat Blinis with Mushroom Caviar

These little Russian pancakes are traditionally served with fish roe, caviar and sour cream. Here is a vegetarian alternative that uses a selection of delicious wild mushrooms in place of the fish roe. The blinis can be made ahead of time and warmed in the oven just before topping.

Serves 4

115g/4oz/1 cup strong white
   bread flour
50g/2oz/^{1}/$_2$ cup buckwheat flour
2.5ml/^{1}/$_2$ tsp salt
300ml/^{1}/$_2$ pint/1^1/$_4$ cups milk
5ml/1 tsp easy-blend (rapid-rise)
   dried yeast
2 eggs, separated
200ml/7fl oz/scant 1 cup sour cream or
   crème fraîche

For the caviar
350g/12oz mixed wild mushrooms
   such as field (portabello)
   mushrooms, orange birch bolete,
   bay boletus and oyster
5ml/1 tsp celery salt
30ml/2 tbsp walnut oil
15ml/1 tbsp lemon juice
45ml/3 tbsp chopped fresh parsley
ground black pepper

1 To make the caviar, trim and chop the mushrooms, then place them in a glass bowl, toss with the celery salt and cover with a weighted plate.

2 Leave the mushrooms for about 2 hours, until the juices have run out into the base of the bowl. Rinse the mushrooms thoroughly to remove the salt, drain and press out as much liquid as you can with the back of a spoon. Return them to the bowl and toss with walnut oil, lemon juice, parsley and a twist of pepper. Chill in the refrigerator until ready to serve.

3 Sift the white bread flour and buckwheat flour together with the salt into a large mixing bowl. Gently warm the milk to approximately blood temperature. Add the yeast, stirring until dissolved, then pour into the flour, add the egg yolks and stir to make a smooth batter. Cover with a clean damp dishtowel and leave in a warm place for 1 hour.

4 Whisk the egg whites in a clean grease-free bowl until stiff, then fold them into the risen batter.

COOK'S TIP
It is important that there are no traces of grease in the bowl or yolk in the egg whites when they are whisked. Otherwise, they will not foam up and become stiff.

5 Heat an iron pan or griddle to a moderate temperature. Moisten with oil, then drop spoonfuls of the batter on to the surface. When bubbles rise to the top, turn them over and cook briefly on the other side.

6 Transfer to a serving plate. Spoon on the mushroom caviar top with the sour cream or crème fraîche, and serve.

Energy 380kcal/1586kJ; Protein 12.5g; Carbohydrate 38.8g, of which sugars 6.2g; Fat 20.6g, of which saturates 8.5g; Cholesterol 130mg; Calcium 205mg; Fibre 2.3g; Sodium 94mg.

Potato Pancakes

These light pancakes originate from Russia, where they are served with caviar. Here they are topped with an equally luxurious mixture of sour cream and smoked salmon.

Serves 6

115g/4oz floury (mealy) potatoes, boiled and mashed
15ml/1 tbsp easy-blend (rapid-rise) dried yeast
175g/6oz/1½ cups plain (all-purpose) flour
oil, for frying
90ml/6 tbsp sour cream
6 slices smoked salmon
salt and ground black pepper
lemon slices, to garnish

COOK'S TIP

These small pancakes can easily be prepared in advance and stored in the refrigerator until ready for use. Simply warm them through in a low oven.

1 Place the mashed potatoes, dried yeast and flour in a large bowl and pour in 300ml/½ pint/1¼ cups lukewarm water. Mix together well.

2 Leave to rise in a warm place for about 30 minutes, until the mixture has doubled in size.

VARIATIONS

• Substitute salmon roe for the smoked salmon and garnish with fresh dill.
• For a vegetarian version, top the pancakes with sour cream or tapenade and halved, hard-boiled quail's eggs or cherry tomatoes.

3 Heat a non-stick frying pan and add a little oil. Drop spoonfuls of the mixture on to the preheated pan. Cook the potato pancakes over a medium heat for about 2 minutes, until lightly golden on the underside, turn with a spatula and cook on the second side for about 1 minute.

4 Season the pancakes with some salt and pepper and transfer them to a warm platter. Top with a little sour cream and a small slice of smoked salmon folded on top. Garnish with a final grind of black pepper and slices of lemon and serve immediately.

Energy 291kcal/1221kJ; Protein 6g; Carbohydrate 35.4g, of which sugars 2.9g; Fat 15g, of which saturates 2.2g; Cholesterol 63mg; Calcium 36mg; Fibre 2.1g; Sodium 42mg.

Cannellini Bean and Rosemary Bruschetta

This sophisticated, Italian variation
on the theme of beans on toast
makes an unusual party snack.

Makes 12

150g/5oz/²/₃ cup dried cannellini beans
5 tomatoes
45ml/3 tbsp olive oil, plus extra
    for drizzling
2 sun-dried tomatoes in oil, drained
    and finely chopped
1 garlic clove, crushed
30ml/2 tbsp chopped fresh rosemary
12 slices Italian-style bread, such
    as ciabatta
1 large garlic clove
salt and ground black pepper
handful of fresh basil leaves, to garnish

4 Add the tomato mixture to the
cannellini beans and season to taste
with salt and pepper. Mix together
well. Keep the bean mixture warm.

5 Rub the cut sides of the bread slices
with the garlic clove, then toast them
lightly on both sides. Spoon the
cannellini bean mixture evenly on top
of the toast. Sprinkle with basil leaves
and drizzle with a little extra olive oil
before serving.

1 Put the beans in a bowl, add
sufficient cold water to cover and leave
to soak overnight.

2 Drain and rinse the beans, then
place in a pan and cover with fresh
water. Bring to the boil and boil rapidly
for 10 minutes. Then simmer for
50–60 minutes, or until tender. Drain,
return to the pan and keep warm.

3 Meanwhile, place the tomatoes in a
bowl, cover with boiling water; leave
for 30 seconds, then peel, seed and
chop the flesh. Heat the oil in a frying
pan, add the fresh and sun-dried
tomatoes, garlic and rosemary. Cook
for 2 minutes until the tomatoes
begin to break down and soften.

Energy 499kcal/2111kJ; Protein 20.2g; Carbohydrate 84.3g, of which sugars 8.5g; Fat 11.3g, of which saturates 1.7g; Cholesterol 0mg; Calcium 195mg; Fibre 8.1g; Sodium 749mg.

Deep-fried New Potatoes with Saffron Aioli

Serve these crispy golden potatoes dipped into a garlicky mayonnaise – and watch them disappear.

Makes 20

20 baby, new or salad potatoes
vegetable oil, for deep-frying
salt and ground black pepper

For the aioli
1 egg yolk
2.5ml/¹/₂ tsp Dijon mustard
300ml/¹/₂ pint/1¹/₄ cups extra virgin
   olive oil
15–30ml/1–2 tbsp lemon juice
1 garlic clove, crushed
2.5ml/¹/₂ tsp saffron threads

1 To make the aioli put the egg yolk in a bowl with the Dijon mustard and a pinch of salt. Stir to mix together well. Using a balloon whisk or an electric mixer, beat in the olive oil very gradually, drop by drop at first and then in a very thin stream. Stir in the lemon juice.

2 Season the mayonnaise with salt and pepper to taste, then add the crushed garlic and beat the mixture thoroughly to combine.

3 Place the saffron in a small bowl and add 10ml/2 tsp hot water. Press the saffron with the back of a teaspoon to extract the colour and flavour, then leave to infuse (steep) for 5 minutes. Beat the saffron and the soaking liquid into the aioli.

4 Cook the potatoes in their skins in a large pan of lightly salted, boiling water for 5 minutes, then turn off the heat. Cover the pan and leave to stand for 15 minutes. Drain the potatoes well, then dry them thoroughly in a clean dishtowel.

5 Heat a 1cm/¹/₂in layer of vegetable oil in a deep pan. When the oil is very hot, add the potatoes and cook quickly, turning them constantly, until crisp and golden all over. Drain well on kitchen paper, transfer to a warm platter and serve immediately with the saffron aioli.

Energy 795kcal/3282kJ; Protein 2.9g; Carbohydrate 20.1g, of which sugars 1.6g; Fat 78.7g, of which saturates 10.5g; Cholesterol 50mg; Calcium 13mg; Fibre 1.3g; Sodium 16mg.

Fried Rice Balls Stuffed with Mozzarella

These deep-fried balls of risotto go by the name of *Suppli al Telefono* in their native Italy because the strings of melted mozzarella resemble telephone wires. Stuffed with mozzarella cheese, they are very popular snacks, which is hardly surprising as they are quite delicious. They make wonderful party bites or a great start to any dinner party meal.

Makes 6–8

1 quantity Risotto alla Milanese
3 eggs
breadcrumbs and plain (all-purpose)
*   flour, for dusting*
115g/4oz mozzarella cheese, cut into
*   small cubes*
vegetable oil, for deep-frying
dressed frisée lettuce leaves and cherry
*   tomatoes, to serve (optional)*

1 Put the risotto in a bowl and leave it to cool completely. Beat two of the eggs and stir them into the cooled risotto until well mixed.

2 Use your hands to form the rice mixture into balls the size of a large egg. If the mixture is too moist to hold its shape well, stir in a few spoonfuls of breadcrumbs.

3 Poke a hole in the centre of each ball with your finger, then fill it with small cubes of mozzarella and close the hole over again with the rice mixture.

4 Heat the oil for deep-frying until a small piece of bread sizzles as soon as it is dropped in.

5 Spread out some flour on a plate. Beat the remaining egg in a shallow bowl. Sprinkle another plate with breadcrumbs. Roll the risotto balls in the flour, then in the egg and, finally, in the breadcrumbs.

6 Deep-fry the rice balls, a few at a time, in the hot oil until golden and crisp. Drain on kitchen paper while the remaining balls are being fried, and keep warm. Transfer to warm plates and serve immediately, with dressed frisée leaves and cherry tomatoes if serving as an appetizer. For finger food, transfer to a warm platter and serve plain.

COOK'S TIP
These provide the perfect solution for the problem of to what to do with leftover risotto, as they are best made with a cold mixture, cooked the day before. This also makes them a perfect choice for parties as much of the preparation is done ahead.

Energy 505kcal/2111kJ; Protein 15g; Carbohydrate 44.8g, of which sugars 1.1g; Fat 30.9g, of which saturates 8.5g; Cholesterol 160mg; Calcium 168mg; Fibre 0.7g; Sodium 1095mg.

Mini Baked Potatoes with Blue Cheese

These miniature potatoes can be eaten with the fingers. They provide a great way of starting off an informal supper party.

Makes 20

20 small new or salad potatoes
60ml/4 tbsp vegetable oil
coarse salt
120ml/4fl oz/¹/₂ cup sour cream
25g/1oz/¹/₄ cup crumbled blue cheese, such as Dolcelatte
30ml/2 tbsp chopped fresh chives, to garnish

VARIATION
Use a strong-flavoured cheddar in place of the blue cheese.

1 Preheat the oven to 180°C/350°F/Gas 4. Wash and dry the potatoes. Toss with the oil in a bowl to coat.

2 Dip the potatoes in the coarse salt to coat lightly, then spread them out on a baking sheet. Bake for 45–50 minutes, until the potatoes are tender.

3 In a small bowl, combine the sour cream and blue cheese, mixing them together well.

COOK'S TIP
This dish works just as well as a light snack; if you don't want to be bothered with lots of fiddly small potatoes, simply bake an ordinary baking potato.

4 Cut a cross in the top of each potato. Press gently with your fingers to open the potatoes.

5 Top each potato with a generous spoonful of the blue cheese mixture. Place on a serving dish and garnish with the chives. Serve hot or leave to cool to room temperature.

Energy 63kcal/262kJ; Protein 1.1g; Carbohydrate 6.3g, of which sugars 0.7g; Fat 3.9g, of which saturates 1.3g; Cholesterol 5mg; Calcium 14mg; Fibre 0.4g; Sodium 22mg.

Glamorgan Sausages

These tasty, traditional "sausages" are ideal for vegetarians.

Makes 8

150g/5oz/2¹/₂ cups fresh breadcrumbs
150g/5oz/1¹/₄ cups grated
   Caerphilly cheese
1 small leek, very finely chopped
15ml/1 tbsp chopped fresh parsley
leaves from 1 thyme sprig, chopped
2 eggs
7.5ml/1¹/₂ tsp English (hot)
   mustard powder
about 45ml/3 tbsp milk
plain (all-purpose) flour, for coating
15ml/1 tbsp oil
15g/¹/₂oz/1 tbsp butter, melted
salt and ground black pepper
salad leaves and tomato halves, to serve

1 Mix the breadcrumbs, cheese, leek, herbs and seasoning. Whisk the eggs with the mustard and reserve 30ml/ 2 tbsp. Stir the rest into the cheese mixture with enough milk to bind.

2 Divide the cheese mixture into eight portions and form into sausage shapes with your hands.

3 Dip the sausages into the reserved egg and mustard mixture to coat. Spread out the flour on a plate and season with a little salt and pepper, then roll the sausages in it to give a light, even coating. Transfer to a plate, cover with clear film (plastic wrap) and chill in the refrigerator for about 30 minutes, until firm.

4 Preheat the grill (broiler) and oil the grill rack. Mix the oil and melted butter together and brush the mixture all over the sausages. Grill (broil) the sausages for 5–10 minutes, turning them carefully every now and then, until they are golden brown all over. Serve hot or cold, with salad leaves and tomato halves.

COOK'S TIPS
• You can make these sausages well in advance of the party and open freeze them, then transfer to a bag and seal. To serve, thaw for about 1 hour and reheat in a moderately hot oven for 10–15 minutes.
• Make 16 smaller sausages to serve as finger food. Grill (broil) for 5–6 minutes and serve on cocktail sticks (toothpicks).

Energy 193kcal/809kJ; Protein 8.8g; Carbohydrate 15.1g, of which sugars 0.9g; Fat 10.9g, of which saturates 5.7g; Cholesterol 70mg; Calcium 179mg; Fibre 0.8g; Sodium 309mg.

Son-in-law Eggs

This fascinating name comes from a delightful story about a prospective bridegroom who was anxious to impress his future mother-in-law and devised a recipe from the only other dish he knew how to make – boiled eggs. The hard-boiled eggs are deep-fried and then drenched with a sweet piquant tamarind sauce before serving.

Makes 6

75g/3oz/generous ¹/₃ cup palm sugar
60ml/4 tbsp light soy sauce
105ml/7 tbsp tamarind juice
vegetable oil, for frying
6 shallots, thinly sliced
6 garlic cloves, thinly sliced
6 fresh red chillies, sliced
6 hard-boiled eggs, shelled
coriander (cilantro) sprigs, to garnish
lettuce, to serve

1 Combine the palm sugar, soy sauce and tamarind juice in a small pan. Bring to the boil over a low heat, stirring until the sugar dissolves, then simmer the sauce, without stirring, for about 5 minutes.

2 Taste the sauce and add more palm sugar, soy sauce or tamarind juice, if necessary. It should be a balanced combination of sweet, salty and slightly sour. Transfer the sauce to a bowl and set aside until needed.

3 Heat a couple of spoonfuls of the oil in a frying pan. Add the shallots, garlic and chillies and cook over a low heat, until golden brown. Transfer the mixture to a bowl and set aside.

4 Deep-fry the eggs in hot oil for 3–5 minutes, until golden brown. Drain on kitchen paper, cut into quarters and arrange on a bed of lettuce. Sprinkle the shallot mixture over them, drizzle with the sauce and garnish with coriander.

Energy 138kcal/578kJ; Protein 6.9g; Carbohydrate 16.3g, of which sugars 15.4g; Fat 5.6g, of which saturates 1.6g; Cholesterol 190mg; Calcium 45mg; Fibre 0.5g; Sodium 547mg.

Thai Fish and Egg Cakes

These tangy little mouthfuls, with a kick of Eastern spice, make great party food or appetizers.

Makes about 20

225g/8oz smoked cod or haddock
fillet (undyed)
225g/8oz fresh cod or haddock fillet
1 small fresh red chilli, seeded and
finely chopped
2 garlic cloves, grated
1 lemon grass stalk, very finely chopped
2 large spring onions (scallions), very
finely chopped
30ml/2 tbsp Thai fish sauce or
30ml/2 tbsp soy sauce and a few
drops anchovy essence (extract)
60ml/4 tbsp thick coconut milk
2 large (US extra large) eggs, beaten
15ml/1 tbsp chopped fresh
coriander (cilantro)
15ml/1 tbsp cornflour (cornstarch),
plus extra for moulding
vegetable oil, for frying
soy sauce, rice vinegar or Thai fish
sauce, for dipping

1 Place the smoked fish in a bowl of cold water and leave to soak for 10 minutes. Dry well on kitchen paper. Remove and discard the skin and any stray bones from the smoked and fresh fish, chop the flesh coarsely and place in a food processor.

2 Add the chilli, garlic, lemon grass, spring onions, fish or soy sauce and the coconut milk and process until the fish is well blended with the spices. Add the eggs and coriander and process for a further few seconds. Cover with clear film (plastic wrap) and chill in the refrigerator for 1 hour.

3 To make the fish cakes, flour your hands with cornflour and shape large teaspoonfuls of the fish mixture into neat balls, coating them with the flour.

4 Heat 5–7.5cm/2–3in oil in a medium pan until a crust of bread turns golden in about 1 minute. Add the fish balls, 5–6 at a time, turning them carefully with a slotted spoon for 2–3 minutes, until they turn golden all over.

5 Remove with a slotted spoon and drain on kitchen paper. Keep the fish cakes warm in the oven until they are all cooked. Serve with a dish of soy sauce, rice vinegar or Thai fish sauce or a combination of sauces for dipping.

Energy 38kcal/161kJ; Protein 1.1g; Carbohydrate 6.6g, of which sugars 0.6g; Fat 1g, of which saturates 0.1g; Cholesterol 0mg; Calcium 15mg; Fibre 0.5g; Sodium 88mg.

Crispy Spring Rolls

These small and dainty spring rolls
are ideal served as appetizers or as
cocktail snacks.

Makes 40 rolls

115g/4oz small leeks or spring
    onions (scallions)
115g/4oz carrots
115g/4oz bamboo shoots
115g/4oz mushrooms
225g/8oz fresh beansprouts
45–60ml/3–4 tbsp vegetable oil
5ml/1 tsp salt
5ml/1 tsp light brown sugar
15ml/1 tbsp light soy sauce
15ml/1 tbsp Chinese rice wine or
    dry sherry
20 frozen spring roll wrappers, thawed
15ml/1 tbsp cornflour (cornstarch)
    paste (see Cook's Tip)
plain (all-purpose) flour,
    for dusting
vegetable oil, for deep-frying

1 With a sharp knife, cut the leeks or
spring onions, carrots, bamboo shoots
and mushrooms into thin shreds,
about the same size and shape as
the beansprouts.

2 Heat the oil in a wok. Add the
vegetables and stir-fry for about
1 minute. Add the salt, sugar, soy
sauce and rice wine or sherry, and
continue stirring and tossing the
vegetables for 1½–2 minutes. Remove
from the heat and drain away the
excess liquid, then leave to cool.

3 To make the spring rolls, cut each
spring roll wrapper in half diagonally,
then place about a tablespoonful of
the cooled vegetable mixture one-third
of the way down on the wrapper, with
the triangle pointing away from you.

4 Lift the lower edge of the spring roll
wrapper over the filling and roll once.
Fold in both ends and roll once more,
then brush the upper pointed edge
with a little cornflour paste and roll
into a neat package, pressing lightly to
seal. Lightly dust a tray with flour and
place the spring rolls on the tray with
the flapside underneath.

5 To cook, heat the oil in a wok or
deep-fryer to 180°C/350°F or until a
cube of bread added to it browns in
about 30 seconds. Reduce the heat
to low. Deep-fry the spring rolls in
batches – about 8–10 at a time – for
2–3 minutes, or until golden and
crispy, then remove and drain on
kitchen paper. Serve the spring rolls
hot with a dipping sauce, such as soy
sauce, or mixed salt and pepper.

COOK'S TIPS

• To make cornflour (cornstarch) paste,
put 4 parts cornflour and 5 parts cold
water into a small bowl and stir well
until smooth.

• Classic Chinese salt and pepper sauce
is made with Sichuan peppercorns and
sea salt. Dry-fry 30ml/2 tbsp Sichuan
peppercorns and 60ml/4 tbsp sea salt in a
heavy frying pan, stirring frequently, until
the mixture begins to brown. Remove the
pan from the heat and leave to cool, then
grind in a mortar with a pestle or in a
spice grinder.

Energy 57kcal/236kJ; Protein 5g; Carbohydrate 1g, of which sugars 0g; Fat 3g, of which saturates 1g; Cholesterol 35mg; Calcium 11mg; Fibre 0g; Sodium 275mg.

Samosas

Crisp and spicy, these tasty party snacks are enjoyed the world over. Throughout the East, they are sold by street vendors, and eaten at any time of day. Filo pastry can be used if you like a lighter, flakier texture.

Makes about 20

1 packet 25cm/10in square spring roll wrappers, thawed if frozen
30ml/2 tbsp plain (all-purpose) flour, mixed to a paste with water
vegetable oil, for deep-frying
fresh coriander (cilantro) leaves, to garnish

For the filling

25g/1oz/2 tbsp ghee or unsalted (sweet) butter
1 small onion, finely chopped
1cm/½in piece fresh root ginger, peeled and chopped
1 garlic clove, crushed
2.5ml/½ tsp chilli powder
1 large potato, about 225g/8oz cooked until just tender and finely diced
50g/2oz/½ cup cauliflower florets, lightly cooked, chopped into small pieces
50g/2oz/½ cup frozen peas, thawed
5–10ml/1–2 tsp garam masala
15ml/1 tbsp chopped fresh coriander (cilantro) leaves and stems
squeeze of lemon juice
salt

1 Heat the ghee or butter in a large frying pan. Add the onion, ginger and garlic and cook over a low heat, stirring occasionally, for 5 minutes, until the onion has softened but not browned. Add the chilli powder and cook for 1 minute, then stir in the potato, cauliflower and peas. Sprinkle with garam masala and set aside to cool. Stir in the chopped coriander, lemon juice and salt.

2 Cut the spring roll wrappers into three strips (or two for larger samosas). Brush the edges with a little of the flour paste. Place a small spoonful of filling about 2cm/¾in in from the edge of one strip. Fold one corner over the filling to make a triangle and continue this folding until the entire strip has been used and a triangular pastry has been formed. Seal any open edges with more flour and water paste, if necessary adding more water if the paste is very thick.

3 Heat the vegetable oil in a large pan or a deep-fryer to 190°C/375°F or until a cube of bread added to it browns in about 45 seconds. Add the samosas, a few at a time, and deep-fry until golden and crisp. Drain well on kitchen paper and serve hot garnished with chopped coriander leaves.

COOK'S TIP

You can prepare samosas in advance of the party by deep-frying them until they are just cooked through, then drain well. Cook in hot oil for a few minutes to brown and heat through, then drain again before serving.

Energy 56kcal/235kJ; Protein 1.3g; Carbohydrate 10g, of which sugars 0.8g; Fat 1.4g, of which saturates 0.2g; Cholesterol 0mg; Calcium 16mg; Fibre 0.7g; Sodium 8mg.

Futo-Maki

Thick-rolled sushi, such as futo-maki, is a fashionable and attractive food to serve as canapés with drinks.

Makes 16

2 nori seaweed sheets

For the su-meshi (vinegared rice)
200g/7oz/1 cup short grain rice
275ml/9fl oz/scant 1¼ cups water
45ml/3 tbsp rice vinegar
37.5ml/7½ tsp sugar
10ml/2 tsp salt

For the omelette
2 eggs, beaten
25ml/1½ tbsp dashi stock
10ml/2 tsp sake
2.5ml/½ tsp salt
vegetable oil, for frying

For the fillings
4 dried shiitake mushrooms,
 soaked in water overnight
120ml/4fl oz/½ cup dashi stock
15ml/1 tbsp shoyu
7.5ml/1½ tsp sugar
5ml/1 tsp mirin
6 raw king prawns (jumbo shrimp),
 heads and shells removed
4 asparagus spears, boiled and cooled
10 fresh chives, about 23cm/9in long
salt
wasabi, gari and soy sauce, to serve

1 To make the su-meshi, wash the rice in cold water, drain and set aside for one hour. Put the rice into a pan and add the water. Cover and boil for 5 minutes, then simmer until the water has been absorbed. Remove from the heat and set aside for 10 minutes.

2 Mix the rice vinegar with the sugar and salt. Tip the rice into a bowl and sprinkle with the vinegar mixture. Fold into the rice with a spatula, but do not stir. Cool the su-meshi before shaping.

3 To make the omelette, mix the beaten eggs, dashi stock, sake and salt in a bowl. Heat a little oil in a frying pan on a medium-low heat. Pour in just enough egg mixture to cover the base of the pan. As soon as the mixture sets, fold the omelette in half towards you and wipe the space left with a little oil. With the first omelette still in the pan, repeat until all the mixture is used.

4 Each new omelette is laid on to the first to form a multi-layered omelette. Slide the layered omelette on to a chopping board. When cool, cut lengthways into 1cm/½in wide strips.

5 Put the shiitake mushrooms and the water, stock, shoyu, sugar and mirin in a small pan. Bring to the boil, then reduce the heat to low. Cook for 20 minutes, or until half of the liquid has evaporated. Drain the shiitake mushrooms, remove and discard the stalks, and slice the caps thinly. Squeeze out any excess liquid, then dry on kitchen paper. Discard the liquid.

6 Make three cuts in the belly of each of the prawns to stop them curling up, and boil in salted water for 1 minute, or until they turn bright pink. Drain and cool, then remove the vein using a cocktail stick (toothpick).

COOK'S TIP
If you make the rolled sushi ahead, wrap each roll in clear film (plastic wrap) until ready to slice and serve the rolls.

7 Place a nori sheet, rough side up, at the front edge of a sushi rolling mat. Scoop up half of the su-meshi and spread it on the nori. Leave a 1cm/½in margin at the side nearest you, and 2cm/¾in at the side furthest from you. Make a shallow depression lengthways across the centre of the rice. Fill this with half the omelette strips and half the asparagus. Place half the prawns along the egg and asparagus. Top with five chives and half the shiitake slices.

8 Lift the mat with your thumbs while pressing the filling with your fingers. Roll the mat up gently. When completed, gently roll the mat to firm it up. Unwrap and set the futo-maki aside. Repeat to make another roll.

9 Cut each futo-maki into eight pieces, using a very sharp knife. Wipe the knife with a clean dishtowel dampened with rice vinegar after each cut.

10 Line up all the pieces on a large tray or serving platter. Serve with small dishes of wasabi, gari and soy sauce for dipping.

Energy 107kcal/447kJ; Protein 3.8g; Carbohydrate 16.3g, of which sugars 1.3g; Fat 2.9g, of which saturates 0.6g; Cholesterol 52mg; Calcium 17mg; Fibre 0.2g; Sodium 112mg.

Sushi-style Tuna Cubes

These tasty tuna cubes are easier to prepare than classic Japanese sushi but retain the same fresh taste.

Makes about 24

675g/1 1/2 lb fresh tuna steak, about
    2cm/3/4in thick
1 large red (bell) pepper, seeded and
    cut into 2cm/3/4in pieces
sesame seeds, for sprinkling

For the marinade
15–30ml/1–2 tbsp lemon juice
2.5ml/1/2 tsp salt
2.5ml/1/2 tsp sugar
2.5ml/1/2 tsp wasabi paste
120ml/4 fl oz/1/2 cup vegetable oil
30ml/2 tbsp chopped fresh
    coriander (cilantro)

For the soy dipping sauce
105ml/7 tbsp soy sauce
15ml/1 tbsp rice wine vinegar
5ml/1 tsp lemon juice
1–2 spring onions (scallions), chopped
5ml/1 tsp sugar
2–3 dashes Asian hot chilli oil

1 Cut the tuna into 2.5cm/1in pieces and then arrange them in a single layer in a large non-metallic ovenproof dish.

2 Prepare the marinade. In a small bowl, stir the lemon juice with the salt, sugar and wasabi paste. Slowly whisk in the oil until thoroughly blended and slightly creamy. Stir in the coriander. Pour the marinade over the tuna cubes and toss to coat. Cover with clear film (plastic wrap) and marinate for about 40 minutes in a cool place.

3 Meanwhile, prepare the soy dipping sauce. Put the soy sauce, vinegar, lemon juice, spring onions, sugar and chilli oil to taste in a small bowl and stir until thoroughly blended. Cover with clear film and set aside until ready to serve.

4 Preheat the grill (broiler) and line a baking sheet with foil. Thread a cube of tuna, then a piece of pepper on to each skewer and arrange on the baking sheet.

5 Sprinkle with sesame seeds and grill (broil) for 3–5 minutes, turning once or twice, until just beginning to colour but still pink inside. Serve immediately with the soy dipping sauce.

COOK'S TIP
Wasabi is a hot, pungent Japanese horseradish available in powder form and as paste in a tube from gourmet and Japanese food stores. The powdered form needs to be reconstituted with water in the same way as mustard powder.

VARIATIONS
• Substitute spring onions (scallions) for the (bell) pepper. Cut them into short lengths, about 2.5cm/1in long and thread them on to the skewers in the same way.
• Use another firm-fleshed fish, such as swordfish instead of the tuna.

Energy 42kcal/179kJ; Protein 6.9g; Carbohydrate 0.8g, of which sugars 0.8g; Fat 1.3g, of which saturates 0.3g; Cholesterol 8mg; Calcium 6mg; Fibre 0.1g; Sodium 325mg.

Rice Triangles

These rice shapes – *Onigiri* – are very popular in Japan. You can put anything you like in the rice, so you could invent your own *Onigiri*.

Makes 8

1 salmon steak
15ml/1 tbsp salt
450g/1lb/4 cups freshly cooked
*   sushi rice*
¼ cucumber, seeded and cut
*   into thin batons*
½ sheet yaki-nori seaweed, cut into
*   four equal strips*
white and black sesame seeds,
*   for sprinkling*

1 Grill (broil) the salmon steak on each side until the flesh flakes easily when tested with a sharp knife. Set aside to cool while you make the cucumber *onigiri*. When the salmon is cold, flake it, discarding any skin and bones.

2 Put the salt in a bowl. Spoon an eighth of the warm, cooked rice into a small rice bowl. Make a hole in the middle of the rice and put in a few cucumber batons. Smooth the rice over to cover.

3 Wet the palms of both hands with cold water, then rub the salt evenly on to your palms.

4 Empty the rice and cucumbers from the bowl on to one hand. Use both hands to shape the rice into a triangular shape, using firm but not heavy pressure, and making sure that the cucumber is encased by the rice. Make three more rice triangles the same way, dampening your palms and sprinkling with salt as before.

5 Mix the flaked salmon into the remaining rice, then shape it into triangles as before.

6 Wrap a strip of yaki-nori around each of the cucumber triangles. Sprinkle sesame seeds on the salmon triangles. Set aside to cool completely before serving.

COOK'S TIP
Always use warm rice to make the triangles. Leave them to cool completely, then wrap each in foil or clear film (plastic wrap) and store in a cool place.

Energy 341kcal/1426kJ; Protein 10.5g; Carbohydrate 29.8g, of which sugars 1.8g; Fat 20.7g, of which saturates 7.7g; Cholesterol 37mg; Calcium 140mg; Fibre 1.1g; Sodium 38mg.

Paella Croquettes

Paella is probably Spain's most famous dish, and here it is used for a tasty fried tapas.

Makes 16

pinch of saffron threads
150ml/¼ pint/⅔ cup white wine
30ml/2 tbsp olive oil
1 small onion, finely chopped
1 garlic clove, finely chopped
150g/5oz/⅔ cup risotto rice
300ml/½ pint/1¼ cups hot
  chicken stock
50g/2oz /½ cup cooked prawns
  (shrimp), peeled, deveined and
  coarsely chopped
50g/2oz cooked chicken,
  coarsely chopped
75g/3oz/⅔ cup petits pois (baby peas),
  thawed if frozen
30ml/2 tbsp freshly grated
  Parmesan cheese
1 egg, beaten
30ml/2 tbsp milk
75g/3oz/1½ cups fresh white
  breadcrumbs
vegetable or olive oil, for shallow-frying
salt and ground black pepper
fresh flat leaf parsley, to garnish

1 Stir the saffron into the wine in a small bowl; set aside.

2 Heat the measured olive oil in a pan and gently cook the onion and garlic for 5 minutes, until softened. Stir in the risotto rice and cook, stirring, for 1 minute.

3 Keeping the heat fairly high, add the wine and saffron mixture to the pan, stirring until it is completely absorbed. Gradually add the stock, a little at a time, stirring until all the liquid has been absorbed and the rice is cooked – this should take about 20 minutes.

COOK'S TIP
If you can find Valencia rice, use that instead as it is more authentic.

4 Stir in the prawns, chicken, petits pois and freshly grated Parmesan. Season to taste with salt and pepper. Remove the pan from the heat and leave to cool slightly, then use two tablespoons to shape the mixture into 16 small lozenges.

5 Mix the egg and milk in a shallow bowl. Spread out the breadcrumbs on a sheet of foil. Dip the croquettes in the egg mixture, then coat them evenly in the breadcrumbs.

6 Heat the oil for shallow-frying in a large, heavy frying pan. Then add the croquettes and cook for 4–5 minutes, until crisp and golden brown. Work in batches. Drain on kitchen paper and keep hot. Serve garnished with a sprig of flat leaf parsley.

Energy 524kcal/2183kJ; Protein 16.2g; Carbohydrate 48.4g, of which sugars 2.3g; Fat 27.3g, of which saturates 4.9g; Cholesterol 85mg; Calcium 160mg; Fibre 1.5g; Sodium 280mg.

Spinach Empanadillas

These are little Spanish pastry turnovers, filled with ingredients that have a strong Moorish influence – pine nuts and raisins. Serve with pre-dinner drinks at an informal supper party, allowing two to three per person.

Makes 20

25g/1oz/2 tbsp raisins
25ml/1¹/₂ tbsp olive oil
450g/1lb fresh spinach, washed
    and chopped
6 drained canned anchovies, chopped
2 garlic cloves, finely chopped
25g/1oz/¹/₃ cup pine nuts, chopped
1 egg, beaten
350g/12oz puff pastry
salt and ground black pepper

1 To make the filling, soak the raisins in a little warm water for 10 minutes. Drain, then chop coarsely.

2 Heat the oil in a large sauté pan or wok, add the spinach, stir, then cover and cook over a low heat for about 2 minutes. Uncover, increase the heat to medium and cook until any liquid has evaporated. Add the anchovies, garlic and seasoning, then cook, stirring, for a further minute. Remove from the heat, add the raisins and pine nuts and leave to cool.

3 Preheat the oven to 180°C/350°F/ Gas 4. Roll out the pastry to a 3mm/ ¹/₈in thickness.

4 Using a 7.5cm/3in pastry (cookie) cutter, stamp out 20 rounds, re-rolling the dough if necessary. Place about two teaspoonfuls of the filling in the middle of each round, then brush the edges with a little water. Bring up the sides of the pastry and press together gently to seal.

5 Press the edges of the pastry together with the back of a fork. Brush the turnovers, with a little beaten egg, then place them on a lightly greased baking sheet and bake for about 15 minutes, until well risen and golden brown. Serve the empanadillas warm.

COOK'S TIP

If using frozen pastry, make sure that it is completely thawed before you try to roll it out. Once the pastry has thawed, store in the refrigerator until required. It is essential to keep it chilled so that it puffs up when cooked.

Energy 98kcal/409kJ; Protein 2.5g; Carbohydrate 8.6g, of which sugars 1.9g; Fat 6g, of which saturates 0.6g; Cholesterol 14mg; Calcium 29mg; Fibre 0.2g; Sodium 92mg.

Thai-style Seafood Turnovers

These elegant appetizer-size
turnovers are filled with fish,
prawns and fragrant Thai rice.

Makes 18

plain (all-purpose) flour, for dusting
500g/1¼lb puff pastry, thawed
    if frozen
1 egg, beaten with 30ml/2 tbsp water
lime twists, to garnish

For the filling
275g/10oz skinned white fish fillets
seasoned plain (all-purpose) flour
8–10 large raw prawns (shrimp)
15ml/1 tbsp sunflower oil
about 75g/3oz/6 tbsp butter
6 spring onions (scallions),
    finely sliced
1 garlic clove, crushed
225g/8oz/2 cups cooked jasmine rice
4cm/1½in piece fresh root
    ginger, grated
10ml/2 tsp finely chopped fresh
    coriander (cilantro)
5ml/1 tsp finely grated lime rind

1 Preheat the oven to 190°C/375°F/
Gas 5. Make the filling. Cut the fish
into 2cm/¾in cubes and dust with
seasoned flour, shaking off any excess.
Peel and devein the prawns and cut
each one into four pieces.

2 Heat half of the oil and 15g/½oz/
1 tbsp of the butter in a large frying
pan. Add the spring onions and cook
gently for 2 minutes.

3 Add the garlic and cook for a further
5 minutes, until the spring onions are
very soft. Transfer to a large bowl.

4 Heat the remaining oil and a further
25g/1oz/2 tbsp of the butter in a clean
pan. Add the fish pieces and cook
briefly. As soon as they begin to turn
opaque, use a slotted spoon to
transfer them to the bowl with the
spring onions.

5 Cook the prawns in the oil mixture
remaining in the pan. When they
begin to change colour, lift them out
with a slotted spoon and add them
to the bowl.

6 Add the cooked rice to the bowl,
with the fresh root ginger, coriander
and grated lime rind. Mix gently,
taking care not to break up the fish.

7 Dust the work surface with a little
flour. Roll out the pastry and cut into
10cm/4in rounds. Place spoonfuls of
filling just off centre on the pastry
rounds. Dot with a little of the
remaining butter. Dampen the edges
of the pastry with a little of the beaten
egg mixture, fold one side of the
pastry over the filling and press
the edges together firmly.

8 Place the turnovers on two lightly
greased baking sheets. Decorate them
with the pastry trimmings, if you like,
and brush them with remaining beaten
egg to glaze. Bake the turnovers for
12–15 minutes, or until golden brown
all over.

9 Transfer the turnovers to a warm
platter and garnish with lime twists,
then serve immediately.

Energy 175kcal/732kJ; Protein 8g; Carbohydrate 14g, of which sugars 1g; Fat 10g, of which saturates 3g; Cholesterol 57mg; Calcium 42mg; Fibre 1g; Sodium 139mg.

Herbed Fish Fritters

Serve these mini fritters with a tartare sauce if you like. Simply chop some capers and gherkins, and stir into home-made or good quality ready-made mayonnaise.

Makes 20

450g/1lb plaice or flounder fillets
300ml/½ pint/1¼ cups milk
450g/1lb cooked potatoes
1 fennel bulb, finely chopped
45ml/ 3 tbsp chopped fresh parsley
2 eggs
15g/½oz/1 tbsp unsalted
   (sweet) butter
250g/9oz/2 cups white breadcrumbs
25g/1oz/2 tbsp sesame seeds
vegetable oil, for deep-frying
salt and ground black pepper

1 Gently poach the fish fillets in the milk for about 15 minutes, until the flesh flakes easily. Drain and reserve the milk.

2 Peel the skin off the fish and remove any stray bones. In a food processor fitted with a metal blade, process the fish, potatoes, fennel, parsley, eggs and butter.

3 Transfer the mixture to a bowl, add 30ml/2 tbsp of the reserved cooking milk and season with salt and plenty of ground black pepper. Mix well. Cover with clear film (plastic wrap) and chill for 30 minutes, then shape into twenty even-size fritters with your hands.

4 Mix together the breadcrumbs and sesame seeds in a shallow dish, then roll the croquettes in this mixture to form a good coating.

5 Heat the oil in a large, heavy pan until it is hot enough to brown a cube of stale bread in 30 seconds. Deep-fry the croquettes, in small batches, for about 4 minutes, until they are golden brown all over. Drain well on kitchen paper and serve the fritters hot.

Energy 149kcal/626kJ; Protein 7.4g; Carbohydrate 14.3g, of which sugars 1.6g; Fat 7.4g, of which saturates 1.4g; Cholesterol 31mg; Calcium 65mg; Fibre 0.9g; Sodium 147mg.

Mussels in **Black Bean Sauce**

The large green-shelled mussels from New Zealand are perfect for this delicious dish. Buy the cooked mussels on the half-shell – it is an elegant way to serve them.

Makes 20

15ml/1 tbsp vegetable oil
2.5cm/1in piece fresh root ginger,
   finely chopped
2 garlic cloves, finely chopped
1 fresh red chilli, seeded
   and chopped
15ml/1 tbsp black bean sauce
15ml/1 tbsp dry sherry
5ml/1 tsp granulated sugar
5ml/1 tsp sesame oil
10ml/2 tsp dark soy sauce
20 cooked New Zealand
   green-shelled mussels
2 spring onions (scallions), 1 shredded
   and 1 cut into fine rings

1 Heat the vegetable oil in a frying pan or wok. Cook the ginger, garlic and chilli with the black bean sauce for a few seconds, then add the sherry and sugar and cook for 30 seconds more, stirring with chopsticks or a wooden spoon until the sugar is dissolved.

2 Remove from the heat, stir in the oil and soy sauce. Mix thoroughly.

COOK'S TIP
Provide cocktail sticks (toothpicks) for spearing the mussels and removing them from their half-shells.

3 Have ready a bamboo steamer or a medium pan holding 5cm/2in of simmering water and fitted with a metal trivet. Place the mussels in layers on a heatproof plate that will fit inside the steamer or pan. Spoon the prepared sauce evenly over the half-shell mussels.

4 Sprinkle all the spring onions over the mussels. Place in the steamer or cover the plate tightly with foil and place it on the trivet in the pan. It should be just above the level of the water. Cover and steam over a high heat for about 10 minutes, or until the mussels have heated through. Serve immediately.

Energy 19kcal/56kJ; Protein 1g; Carbohydrate 0g, of which sugars 0g; Fat 1g, of which saturates 0g; Cholesterol 1mg; Calcium 4mg; Fibre 0g; Sodium 63mg.

Marinated Mussels

This is an ideal recipe to prepare and arrange well in advance. Remove from the refrigerator 15 minutes before serving to allow the flavours to develop fully.

Makes about 48

1kg/2¼lb mussels, large if possible
    (about 48)
175ml/6fl oz/¾ cup dry white wine
1 garlic clove, finely crushed
120ml/4fl oz/½ cup olive oil
50ml/2fl oz/¼ cup lemon juice
5ml/1 tsp hot chilli flakes
2.5ml/½ tsp mixed (apple pie) spice
15ml/1 tbsp Dijon mustard
10ml/2 tsp sugar
5ml/1 tsp salt
15–30ml/1–2 tbsp chopped fresh dill
    or coriander (cilantro)
15ml/1 tbsp capers, drained and
    chopped if large
ground black pepper

1 With a stiff kitchen brush, under cold running water, scrub the mussels to remove any sand and barnacles; pull out and remove the beards. Discard any open shells that will not shut when they are tapped.

2 In a large, flameproof casserole or pan set over a high heat, bring the white wine to the boil with the garlic and ground black pepper. Add the mussels and cover tightly. Reduce the heat to medium and simmer for 2–4 minutes, until the shells open, shaking the pan occasionally.

3 In a large bowl combine the olive oil, lemon juice, chilli flakes, mixed spice, Dijon mustard, sugar, salt, chopped dill or coriander and capers. Stir well, then set aside.

4 Discard any mussels with closed shells. With a small sharp knife, carefully remove the remaining mussels from their shells, reserving the half shells for serving. Add the mussels to the marinade. Toss the mussels to coat thoroughly, then cover with clear film (plastic wrap) and chill in the refrigerator for 6–8 hours or overnight, stirring gently from time to time.

5 With a teaspoon, place one mussel with a little marinade in each shell. Arrange on a platter and cover until ready to serve.

VARIATION
You can prepare other shellfish in the same way. Venus, Amandes and other medium-size clams would work well and, if you can find them, razor clams would look very impressive. This would also be an unusual way to serve scallops.

COOK'S TIP
Mussels can be prepared ahead of time and marinated for up to 24 hours. To serve, arrange the mussel shells on a bed of crushed ice, well-washed seaweed or even coarse salt to prevent them from wobbling on the plate.

Energy 26kcal/109kJ; Protein 0g; Carbohydrate 0g, of which sugars 0g; Fat 3g, of which saturates 0g; Cholesterol 1mg; Calcium 2mg; Fibre 0g; Sodium 61mg.

Crab Egg Rolls

These wonderful crab rolls are similar to authentic Chinese spring rolls. They are made with wafer-thin pancakes, which provide the very crisp case for the filling. If you prefer a softer version the rolls can be steamed – they are equally delicious and quite light. These are ideal for buffets, children's parties and summer picnics.

Makes about 12

3 eggs
450ml/¾ pint/scant 2 cups water
175g/6oz/1½ cups plain
    (all-purpose) flour
2.5ml/½ tsp salt
vegetable oil, for deep-frying
45ml/3 tbsp light soy sauce mixed with
    5ml/1 tsp sesame oil, for dipping
lime wedges, to serve

For the filling
225g/8oz/1⅓ cups white crab meat
    or small prawns (shrimp)
3 large spring onions
    (scallions), shredded
2.5cm/1in piece fresh root
    ginger, grated
2 large garlic cloves, chopped
115g/4oz bamboo shoots, chopped,
    or beansprouts
15ml/1 tbsp soy sauce
10–15ml/2–3 tsp cornflour (cornstarch)
    blended with 15ml/1 tbsp water
1 egg, separated
salt and ground black pepper

1 Lightly beat the eggs and gradually stir in the water. Sift the flour and salt into another bowl and work in the egg mixture. Blend to a smooth batter, then remove any lumps if necessary. Leave to rest for 20 minutes.

2 When ready to use, lightly whisk the batter and stir in 15ml/1 tbsp cold water to thin it slightly if necessary.

3 Lightly grease a 25cm/10in non-stick frying pan and heat gently. To make smooth, pale wrappers for the egg rolls, the frying pan must be hot enough to set the batter, but should not be hot enough for the batter to brown, bubble or develop holes. Pour in about 45ml/3 tbsp batter and swirl around the pan to spread evenly and very thinly. Cook for 2 minutes, or until loose underneath. There is no need to cook the pancake on the other side.

4 Make a further 11 pancakes. Stack the pancakes, cooked side upwards, between sheets of baking parchment. Set aside until ready to use.

5 To make the filling, combine the crab or prawns, spring onions, ginger, garlic, bamboo shoots or beansprouts, soy sauce, cornflour and water, egg yolk and seasoning.

6 Lightly beat the egg white. Place a spoonful of filling in the middle of each pancake, brush the edges with egg white and fold into neat parcels, tucking in the ends well.

7 Heat the oil in a deep-frying pan and when a cube of bread turns light golden in 1 minute, carefully add four of the parcels, fold side downwards. Cook for 1–2 minutes, or until golden and crisp. Remove with a slotted spoon and place on kitchen paper. Keep warm in the oven while you cook the remaining egg rolls. Alternatively, using a stacking bamboo steamer, arrange four parcels in each layer, cover with a lid and steam for 30 minutes.

8 Serve with the soy sauce and sesame oil dipping sauce and wedges of lime.

Energy 313kcal/1309kJ; Protein 15.1g; Carbohydrate 26.1g, of which sugars 1g; Fat 17.3g, of which saturates 2.5g; Cholesterol 154mg; Calcium 67mg; Fibre 1.3g; Sodium 351mg.

Crab and **Ricotta Tartlets**

Use the meat from a freshly cooked crab, weighing about 450g/1lb, if you can. Otherwise, look out for frozen brown and white crab meat.

Makes 4

225g/8oz/2 cups plain
  (all-purpose) flour
pinch of salt
115g/4oz/¹/₂ cup butter, diced
225g/8oz/1 cup ricotta cheese
15ml/1 tbsp grated onion
30ml/2 tbsp freshly grated
  Parmesan cheese
2.5ml/¹/₂ tsp mustard powder
2 eggs, plus 1 egg yolk
225g/8oz crab meat
30ml/2 tbsp chopped fresh parsley
2.5–5ml/¹/₂–1 tsp anchovy
  essence (extract)
5–10ml/1–2 tsp lemon juice
salt and cayenne pepper
salad leaves, to garnish

1 Sift the flour and salt into a bowl, add the butter and rub it in until the mixture resembles fine breadcrumbs. Stir in about 60ml/4 tbsp cold water to make a firm dough.

2 Turn the dough on to a lightly-floured surface and knead lightly. Roll out the pastry and use to line four 10cm/4in tartlet tins (muffin pans). Prick the bases all over with a fork, then chill in the refrigerator for about 30 minutes. Preheat the oven to 200°C/400°F/Gas 6.

3 Line the pastry cases (pie shells) with baking parchment or foil and fill with baking beans. Bake them for 10 minutes, then remove the paper or foil and beans. Return to the oven and bake for a further 10 minutes.

4 Place the ricotta, grated onion, Parmesan and mustard powder in a bowl and beat until soft and well combined. Gradually beat in the eggs and egg yolk.

5 Gently stir in the crab meat and chopped parsley, then add the anchovy essence and lemon juice and season with salt and cayenne pepper, to taste.

6 Remove the tartlet cases from the oven and reduce the temperature to 180°C/350°F/Gas 4. Spoon the filling evenly into the cases and bake for 20 minutes, until set and golden brown. Serve hot with a garnish of salad leaves.

Energy 644kcal/2685kJ; Protein 28.1g; Carbohydrate 46.3g, of which sugars 3.3g; Fat 39.8g, of which saturates 23g; Cholesterol 278mg; Calcium 288mg; Fibre 2.4g; Sodium 609mg.

Foie Gras Pâté in Filo Cups

This is an extravagantly rich hors d'oeuvre – so save it for a special anniversary or celebration.

Makes 24

3–6 sheets fresh or thawed filo pastry
40g/1¹/₂oz/3 tbsp butter, melted
225g/8oz canned foie gras pâté
  or other fine liver pâté, at
   room temperature
50g/2oz/4 tbsp butter, softened
30–45ml/2–3 tbsp Cognac (optional)
chopped pistachio nuts, to garnish

1 Preheat the oven to 200°C/400°F/ Gas 6. Grease a bun tray (muffin pan) with 24 × 4cm/1½in cups. Stack the filo sheets on a work surface and cut into 6cm/2½in squares. Cover with a damp dishtowel to prevent them from drying out.

COOK'S TIPS

• The pâté and pastry are best eaten soon after preparation. If preparing ahead of time and then chilling in the refrigerator, be sure to bring the cups back to room temperature before serving.

• Pâté de foie gras is made from the liver of specially fattened geese or ducks. Duck liver – foie gras de canard – is more delicate in texture, but stronger in flavour than goose liver – foie gras d'oie. Both are regarded as a great delicacy and are very expensive. However, some people object to the method used to produce the enlarged livers of these birds and so prefer to buy more conventional pâté.

2 Keeping the rest of the filo squares covered until required, place one square on a work surface and brush lightly with melted butter, then turn and brush the other side.

3 Butter a second square and place it over the first at an angle. Butter a third filo square and place it at an angle over the first two sheets to form an uneven edge.

4 Press the stacked layers into one cup of the bun tray. Continue with the remaining filo pastry and melted butter until all the cups in the bun tray have been filled.

5 Bake the filo cups for about 4–6 minutes, until they are crisp and golden, then remove and cool in the tray for 5 minutes. Carefully transfer each filo cup to a wire rack and leave to cool completely.

6 In a small bowl, beat the pâté with the softened butter until smooth and well blended. Add the Cognac to taste, if using.

7 Spoon the filling into a piping (pastry) bag fitted with a medium star nozzle and pipe a swirl into each filo cup. Sprinkle with pistachio nuts and chill until you are ready to serve.

Energy 71kcal/295kJ; Protein 1.5g; Carbohydrate 2.5g, of which sugars 0.1g; Fat 6.2g, of which saturates 2.9g; Cholesterol 24mg; Calcium 7mg; Fibre 0.1g; Sodium 93mg.

Chicken Bitki

This is a popular Polish dish and makes an attractive appetizer when offset by deep red beetroot.

Makes 12

15g/¹/₂oz/1 tbsp butter, melted
115g/4oz flat mushrooms,
   finely chopped
50g/2oz/1 cup fresh white breadcrumbs
350g/12oz skinless chicken breast
   portions or guinea fowl, minced
   (ground) or finely chopped
2 eggs, separated
1.5ml/¹/₄ tsp grated nutmeg
30ml/2 tbsp plain (all-purpose) flour
45ml/3 tbsp vegetable oil
salt and ground black pepper
salad leaves and grated pickled
   beetroot (beet), to serve

1 Melt the butter in a pan and cook the mushrooms for about 5 minutes, until softened and the juices have evaporated. Leave to cool.

2 Mix together the mushrooms, breadcrumbs, minced or chopped chicken or guinea fowl, egg yolks and nutmeg in a bowl and season to taste with salt and pepper.

3 Whisk the egg whites until stiff in a clean, grease-free bowl. Gently stir half the whites into the chicken or guinea fowl mixture to slacken it, then fold in the remainder with a rubber spatula or metal spoon.

4 Shape the mixture into 12 even-size meatballs, about 7.5cm/3in long and 2.5cm/1in wide. Spread out the flour on a shallow plate. Roll the meatballs in the flour to coat.

5 Heat the oil in a large, heavy frying pan, add the bitki and cook over a medium heat for about 10 minutes, turning occasionally until evenly golden brown and cooked through. Serve hot with salad leaves and grated pickled beetroot.

Energy 112kcal/470kJ; Protein 9g; Carbohydrate 5g, of which sugars 0g; Fat 6g, of which saturates 1g; Cholesterol 62mg; Calcium 17mg; Fibre 0g; Sodium 71mg.

Chicken Parcels

These home-made chicken parcels look splendid piled high and golden brown.

Makes 35

225g/8oz/2 cups strong white bread
  flour, plus extra for dusting
2.5ml/¹/₂ tsp salt
2.5ml/¹/₂ tsp caster (superfine) sugar
5ml/1 tsp easy-blend (rapid-rise)
  dried yeast
25g/1oz/2 tbsp butter, softened
1 egg, beaten, plus a little extra
90ml/6 tbsp warm milk
lemon wedges, to serve

For the filling
15ml/1 tbsp sunflower oil
1 small onion, finely chopped
175g/6oz/1¹/₂ cups minced
  (ground) chicken
75ml/5 tbsp chicken stock
30ml/2 tbsp chopped fresh parsley
pinch of grated nutmeg
salt and ground black pepper

1 Sift the flour, salt and sugar into a large bowl. Stir in the dried yeast, then make a well in the centre of the flour.

2 Add the butter, egg and milk and mix to a soft dough. Turn on to a lightly-floured surface and knead for 10 minutes, until smooth and elastic.

3 Put the dough in a clean bowl, cover with clear film (plastic wrap) and leave in a warm place to rise for 1 hour, or until the dough has doubled in size.

4 Meanwhile, heat the oil in a frying pan. Add the onion and chicken and cook over a low heat, stirring occasionally, for about 10 minutes, until the onion has softened and the chicken is beginning to colour. Add the stock and simmer for 5 minutes. Stir in the parsley, grated nutmeg and salt and ground black pepper. Then leave to cool.

5 Preheat the oven to 220°C/425°F/Gas 7. Knead the dough, then roll it out on a lightly floured surface until it is 3mm/¹/₈in thick. Stamp out rounds with a 7.5cm/3in cutter.

6 Brush the edges with beaten egg. Put a little filling in the middle, then press the edges together. Place on oiled baking sheets, cover with oiled clear film, leave in a warm place to rise for 15 minutes.

7 Brush the parcels with a little more egg, then bake for 5 minutes. Lower the oven temperature to 190°C/375°F/Gas 5, and bake for about 10 minutes more, until well risen and golden. Serve with lemon wedges.

Energy 42kcal/175kJ; Protein 2g; Carbohydrate 5g, of which sugars 0g; Fat 1g, of which saturates 1g; Cholesterol 12mg; Calcium 14mg; Fibre 0g; Sodium 49mg.

Tunisian Brik

You can make these little parcels into any shape you like, but the most important thing is to encase the egg white quickly before it starts to escape.

Makes 6

45ml/3 tbsp butter, melted
1 small red onion, finely chopped
150g/5oz skinless chicken or turkey
    fillet, minced (ground)
1 large garlic clove, crushed
juice of ½ lemon
30ml/2 tbsp chopped fresh parsley
12 sheets of filo pastry, each about
    15 × 25cm/6 × 10in, thawed
    if frozen
6 small (US medium) eggs, such as
    bantam, pheasant or guinea fowl
vegetable oil, for deep-frying
salt and ground black pepper

1 Heat half the butter in a pan and cook the onion for 3 minutes. Add the chicken or turkey, garlic, lemon juice, parsley and seasoning, and cook, stirring, for 2–3 minutes, or until the meat is just cooked. Set aside to cool.

COOK'S TIP
If you prefer to cook these pastries in the oven, preheat it to 220°C/425°F/Gas 7. Brush the pastries with butter or beaten egg and cook for 8–10 minutes.

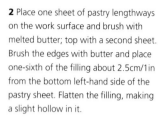

2 Place one sheet of pastry lengthways on the work surface and brush with melted butter; top with a second sheet. Brush the edges with butter and place one-sixth of the filling about 2.5cm/1in from the bottom left-hand side of the pastry sheet. Flatten the filling, making a slight hollow in it.

3 Carefully crack an egg into the hollow and fold up the pastry immediately so the egg white does not run out. Lift the right-hand edge and fold it over to the left edge to enclose the filling and seal quickly. Fold the bottom left-hand corner straight up and then fold the bottom left corner up to the right edge, forming a triangle.

4 Use the remaining pastry sheets and filling to make another five parcels, then heat the oil in a frying pan until a cube of bread turns golden in about 1½ minutes. Cook the pastries, two or three at a time, until golden. Lift them out of the pan with a slotted spoon and drain on kitchen paper. Serve hot or cold.

Energy 316kcal/1321kJ; Protein 15g; Carbohydrate 24g, of which sugars 2g; Fat 18g, of which saturates 6g; Cholesterol 210mg; Calcium 36mg; Fibre 1g; Sodium 225mg.

Golden Parmesan Chicken

Served cold with the garlicky mayonnaise, these morsels of chicken make great finger food.

Makes 16–20

4 skinless chicken breast fillets
75g/3oz/1¹/₂ cups fresh
   white breadcrumbs
40g/1¹/₂ oz/¹/₂ cup finely grated
   Parmesan cheese
30ml/2 tbsp chopped fresh parsley
2 eggs, beaten
120ml/4fl oz/¹/₂ cup mayonnaise
120ml/4fl oz/¹/₂ cup fromage frais or
   natural (plain) yogurt
1–2 garlic cloves, crushed
50g/2oz/4 tbsp butter, melted
salt and ground black pepper

1 Cut each fillet into four or five chunks. Mix together the breadcrumbs, Parmesan, parsley and salt and pepper in a shallow dish.

2 Dip the chicken pieces in the egg, then into the breadcrumb mixture. Place in a single layer on a baking sheet and chill for 30 minutes.

3 Meanwhile, to make the garlic mayonnaise, combine the mayonnaise, fromage frais or yogurt and garlic, and season to taste with ground black pepper. Spoon the mayonnaise into a small serving bowl, cover with clear film (plastic wrap) and chill in the refrigerator until required.

4 Preheat the oven to 180°C/350°F/Gas 4. Drizzle the melted butter over the chicken pieces and cook them for about 20 minutes, until crisp and golden. Transfer to a warm platter and serve the chicken immediately, accompanied by the garlic mayonnaise for dipping.

Energy 591kcal/2460kJ; Protein 35.7g; Carbohydrate 16.7g, of which sugars 2.4g; Fat 43g, of which saturates 14.7g; Cholesterol 227mg; Calcium 216mg; Fibre 0.8g; Sodium 571mg.

Chicken Croquettes

This recipe comes from Rebato's, a tapas bar in London. The chef there makes croquettes with a number of different flavourings.

Makes 8

25g/1oz/2 tbsp butter
25g/1oz/¼ cup plain
   (all-purpose) flour
150ml/¼ pint/⅔ cup milk
15ml/1 tbsp olive oil
1 boneless chicken breast portion with
   skin, about 75g/3oz, diced
1 garlic clove, finely chopped
1 small (US medium) egg, beaten
50g/2oz/1 cup fresh white breadcrumbs
vegetable oil, for deep-frying
salt and ground black pepper
fresh flat leaf parsley, to garnish
lemon wedges, to serve

1 Melt the butter in a small pan over a low heat. Add the flour and cook gently, stirring constantly, for 1 minute. Gradually add the milk, whisking constantly to make a smooth, very thick sauce. Cover with a lid and remove from the pan from the heat.

2 Heat the oil in a heavy frying pan. Add the chicken and garlic and cook over a low heat, stirring frequently, for 5 minutes, until the chicken is lightly browned and cooked through.

3 Turn the contents of the frying pan into a food processor or blender and process until finely chopped. Do not over-process to a paste. Stir the chicken into the sauce, mixing it well. Season with salt and pepper to taste. Leave to cool completely.

4 Shape the mixture into eight even-sized sausages, then dip each in egg and then breadcrumbs. Deep-fry in hot oil for 4 minutes, until crisp and golden. Drain on kitchen paper and serve garnished with parsley and lemon wedges for squeezing.

Energy 286kcal/1195kJ; Protein 13.9g; Carbohydrate 16.4g, of which sugars 2.2g; Fat 18.9g, of which saturates 5.8g; Cholesterol 89mg; Calcium 80mg; Fibre 0.5g; Sodium 189mg.

Chicken with Lemon and Garlic

Extremely easy to cook and delicious to eat, serve this succulent tapas dish with home-made aioli if you like.

Makes 12–16

225g/8oz skinless chicken breast fillets
30ml/2 tbsp olive oil
1 shallot, finely chopped
4 garlic cloves, finely chopped
5ml/1 tsp paprika
juice of 1 lemon
30ml/2 tbsp chopped fresh parsley
salt and ground black pepper
fresh flat leaf parsley, to garnish
lemon wedges, to serve

1 Sandwich the chicken breast fillets between two sheets of clear film (plastic wrap) or baking parchment. Bat out with a rolling pin or meat mallet until the fillets are about 5mm/¼in thick.

2 Using a sharp knife, cut the chicken into strips about 1cm/½ in wide.

3 Heat the oil in a large, heavy frying pan or wok until it is very hot but not smoking. Add the chicken strips, shallot, garlic and paprika and stir-fry over a high heat for about 3 minutes, until the chicken is lightly browned and cooked through.

4 Stir in the lemon juice and parsley and season with salt and pepper to taste. Transfer to a warm platter and serve immediately with lemon wedges, garnished with flat leaf parsley.

Energy 138kcal/579kJ; Protein 18.5g; Carbohydrate 1.5g, of which sugars 1.1g; Fat 6.5g, of which saturates 1g; Cholesterol 53mg; Calcium 30mg; Fibre 0.8g; Sodium 49mg.

Prosciutto and Mozzarella Parcels on Frisée Salad

Italian prosciutto crudo is a delicious raw smoked ham. Here it is baked with melting mozzarella in a light, crisp pastry case, making it an ideal finger food.

Makes 6

a little hot chilli sauce
6 prosciutto crudo slices
200g/7oz mozzarella cheese, cut into
*   6 slices*
6 sheets filo pastry, each measuring
*   45 × 28cm/18 × 11in, thawed*
*   if frozen*
50g/2oz/¼ cup butter, melted
150g/5oz frisée lettuce, to serve

1 Preheat the oven to 200°C/400°F/ Gas 6. Sprinkle a little of the chilli sauce over each slice of prosciutto crudo. Place a slice of mozzarella on each slice of prosciutto, then fold it around the cheese. The cheese should be enclosed by the ham.

2 Brush a sheet of filo pastry with melted butter and fold it in half to give a double-thick piece measuring 23 × 14cm/9 × 5½in. Place a ham and mozzarella parcel in the middle of the pastry and brush the remaining pastry with a little butter, then fold it over to enclose the prosciutto and mozzarella in a neat parcel. Place on a baking sheet with the edges of the pastry underneath and brush with a little butter. Repeat with the remaining parcels and sheets.

3 Bake the filo parcels for 15 minutes, or until the pastry is crisp and evenly golden. Arrange the salad on six plates and add the parcels. Serve immediately.

Smoked Chicken with Peach Mayonnaise in Filo Tartlets

These tartlets require the minimum of culinary effort because smoked chicken is widely available ready cooked. The filling can be prepared a day in advance and chilled overnight but do not fill the pastry cases until you are ready to serve.

Makes 12

25g/1oz/2 tbsp butter, melted
3 sheets filo pastry, each measuring
*   45 × 28cm/18 × 11in, thawed*
*   if frozen*
2 skinless cooked smoked chicken
*   breast fillets, thinly sliced*
150ml/¼ pint/⅔ cup mayonnaise
grated rind of 1 lime
30ml/2 tbsp lime juice
2 ripe peaches, peeled, stoned (pitted)
*   and chopped*
salt and ground black pepper
fresh tarragon sprigs, lime slices and
*   salad leaves, to garnish*

1 Preheat the oven to 200°C/400°F/ Gas 6. Brush 12 small individual tartlet tins (muffin pans) with a little of the melted butter. Cut each sheet of filo pastry into 12 equal rounds large enough to line the tins, allowing just enough to stand up above the tops of the tins.

2 Place a round of pastry in each tin and brush with a little butter, then add another round of pastry. Brush each with more butter and add a third round of pastry.

COOK'S TIP
To peel peaches, place them in a bowl and pour in freshly boiled water to cover. Leave to stand for 30–60 seconds (the riper the peaches, the quicker their skins loosen). Use a slotted spoon to remove a peach from the water. Working quickly, slit the skin with the point of a knife, then slip it off. Repeat with the remaining peaches.

3 Bake the tartlets for 5 minutes, or until the pastry is golden brown. Leave in the tins for a few moments before transferring to a wire rack to cool.

4 In a mixing bowl combine the chicken, mayonnaise, lime rind and juice, peaches and salt and pepper. Chill the mixture for at least 30 minutes, or up to 12 hours overnight. When you are ready to serve the tartlets, spoon the chicken mixture into the filo tartlets. Garnish with the fresh tarragon sprigs, lime slices and salad leaves.

Parcels: Energy 136kcal/566kJ; Protein 3g; Carbohydrate 10g, of which sugars 1g; Fat 9g, of which saturates 5g; Cholesterol 23mg; Calcium 9mg; Fibre 1g; Sodium 268mg.
Tartlets: Energy 164kcal/682kJ; Protein 10g; Carbohydrate 5g, of which sugars 2g; Fat 12g, of which saturates 3g; Cholesterol 40mg; Calcium 5mg; Fibre 1g; Sodium 92mg.

Savoury Pork Pies

These little pies come from Spain and are really delicious.

Makes 12

350g/12oz shortcrust pastry, thawed
   if frozen

For the filling
15ml/1 tbsp vegetable oil
1 onion, chopped
1 garlic clove, crushed
5ml/1 tsp fresh thyme
115g/4oz/1 cup minced (ground) pork
5ml/1 tsp paprika
1 hard-boiled egg, chopped
1 gherkin, chopped
30ml/2 tbsp chopped
   fresh parsley
vegetable oil, for deep-frying
salt and ground black pepper

1 To make the filling, heat the oil in a large, heavy frying pan or wok. Add the onion, garlic and thyme and cook over a medium heat, stirring occasionally, for about 3–4 minutes, until softened but not browned. Add the pork and paprika, then brown evenly for 6–8 minutes. Season well, turn out into a bowl and cool. When the mixture is cool, add the hard-boiled egg, gherkin and parsley.

2 Turn the pastry out on to a lightly floured work surface and roll out to a 38cm/15in square. Cut out 12 rounds 13cm/5in in diameter. Place 15ml/1 tbsp of the filling on each round, moisten the edges with a little water, fold over and seal.

3 Heat the vegetable oil in a deep-fryer fitted with a basket, to 196°C/385°F. Place three pies at a time in the basket and deep-fry until golden brown. Frying should take at least 1 minute or the inside filling will not be heated through. Serve warm in a basket covered with a napkin.

COOK'S TIP
For the best flavour and texture, buy lean pork and mince (grind) it yourself.

Energy 209kcal/868kJ; Protein 4.2g; Carbohydrate 14.2g, of which sugars 0.7g; Fat 15.4g, of which saturates 3.8g; Cholesterol 26mg; Calcium 38mg; Fibre 0.9g; Sodium 131mg.

Chorizo Pastry Puffs

These flaky pastry puffs, filled with spicy chorizo sausage and grated cheese, make a really superb accompaniment to a glass of cold sherry or beer. You can use any type of hard cheese for the puffs, but for best results, choose a mild variety, as the chorizo has plenty of flavour.

Makes 16

225g/8oz puff pastry, thawed if frozen
115g/4oz cured chorizo sausage,
*   finely chopped*
50g/2oz/¹/₂ cup grated cheese
1 small (US medium) egg, beaten
5ml/1 tsp paprika

1 Roll out the pastry thinly on a lightly floured work surface. Using a 7.5cm/3in cutter, stamp out as many rounds as possible, then re-roll the trimmings, if necessary, and stamp out more rounds to make 16 in all.

2 Preheat the oven to 230°C/450°F/Gas 8. Put the chorizo sausage and grated cheese in a bowl and toss together lightly.

3 Lay one of the pastry rounds in the palm of your hand and place a little of the chorizo mixture across the centre.

COOK'S TIP
There are many varieties of chorizo sausages, but they are all made from pork and are flavoured and coloured with paprika. Some are spicier than others.

4 Using your other hand, pinch the edges of the pastry together along the top to seal, as when making a miniature turnover. Repeat the process with the remaining rounds to make 16 puffs in all.

5 Place the pastries on a non-stick baking sheet and brush lightly with the beaten egg to glaze. Using a small sifter or strainer, dust the tops lightly with a little of the paprika.

6 Bake the pastries for 10–12 minutes, until they are puffed and golden brown. Transfer the pastries to a wire rack. Leave to cool slightly for about 5 minutes, then transfer to a warm platter and serve the chorizo pastry puffs warm, lightly dusted with the remaining paprika.

Energy 183kcal/763kJ; Protein 5.4g; Carbohydrate 12.1g, of which sugars 0.6g; Fat 13.1g, of which saturates 3g; Cholesterol 36mg; Calcium 73mg; Fibre 0.1g; Sodium 258mg.

Mini Ham, Roasted Pepper and Mozzarella Ciabatta Pizzas

These quick ciabatta pizzas are eye-catching with their bright pepper topping and great for children.

Makes 8

2 red (bell) peppers
2 yellow (bell) peppers
1 loaf ciabatta bread
8 slices prosciutto or other thinly-sliced ham, cut into thick strips
150g/5oz mozzarella cheese
ground black pepper
tiny basil leaves, to garnish

1 Preheat a grill (broiler). Grill (broil) the peppers, skin sides up, until they are black. Place them in a bowl, cover and leave for 10 minutes. Peel off the skins.

2 Cut the bread into eight thick slices and toast both sides until golden.

3 Cut the roasted peppers into thick strips and arrange them on the toasted bread with the strips of prosciutto or other ham.

4 Thinly slice the mozzarella cheese and arrange on top. Grind over plenty of black pepper. Place under a hot grill for 2–3 minutes, until the cheese is bubbling.

5 Arrange the fresh basil leaves on top and to serve, transfer to a serving dish or platter. Leave the cheese to cool for a few minutes, if serving the mini-pizzas to children.

Energy 161kcal/675kJ; Protein 9g; Carbohydrate 18g, of which sugars 5g; Fat 7g, of which saturates 3g; Cholesterol 16mg; Calcium 105mg; Fibre 2g; Sodium 366mg.

Monte Cristo Triangles

These opulent little sandwiches are stuffed with ham, cheese and turkey, dipped in egg, then fried in butter and oil. They are rich, very filling – and very popular too.

Makes 64

16 slices firm-textured thin-sliced white bread
120g/4oz/¹/₂ cup butter, softened
8 slices oak-smoked ham
45–60ml/3–4 tbsp wholegrain mustard
8 slices Gruyère or Emmenthal cheese
45–60ml/3–4 tbsp mayonnaise
8 slices turkey or chicken breast
5 eggs
50ml/2 fl oz/¹/₄ cup milk
5ml/1 tsp Dijon mustard
vegetable oil, for frying
butter, for frying
salt and ground white pepper
64 pimiento-stuffed green olives and fresh parsley leaves, to garnish

1 Arrange eight of the bread slices on a work surface and spread with half the softened butter. Lay a slice of ham on each slice of bread and spread with a little mustard. Cover with a slice of Gruyère or Emmenthal cheese and spread with a little of the mayonnaise, then cover with a slice of turkey or chicken breast.

2 Butter the rest of the bread slices and use to top the sandwiches. Cut off and discard the crusts, trimming to an even square.

3 Place the eggs, milk and Dijon mustard in a large, shallow dish and beat until thoroughly combined. Season with a little salt and pepper. Add the sandwiches in a single layer and leave them in the egg mixture to soak, turning them once, until all the egg has been absorbed.

4 Heat about 1cm/¹/₂in of the oil with a little butter in a large heavy frying pan until hot but not smoking. Add the sandwiches, in batches, and cook for about 4–5 minutes, until crisp and golden, turning once. Add more oil and butter as necessary. Drain well on kitchen paper.

5 Transfer the sandwiches to a bread board or chopping board and cut each into four triangles, then cut each triangle in half to make 64 triangles in total. Thread an olive and parsley leaf on to a cocktail stick (toothpick), then stick into each triangle. Arrange on a platter and serve immediately, while the triangles are still warm.

Energy 84kcal/351kJ; Protein 4.3g; Carbohydrate 5.1g, of which sugars 0.3g; Fat 5.3g, of which saturates 2.1g; Cholesterol 29mg; Calcium 38mg; Fibre 0.2g; Sodium 120mg.

Deep-fried Lamb Patties

These patties are a tasty North African speciality – called kibbeh – of minced meat and bulgur wheat. They are sometimes stuffed with additional meat and deep fried. Moderately spiced, they're good served with yogurt.

Makes 12

450g/1lb lean lamb or lean minced (ground) lamb or beef
salt and ground black pepper
vegetable oil, for deep-frying
avocado slices and fresh coriander (cilantro) sprigs, to serve

For the patties
225g/8oz/1⅓ cups bulgur wheat
1 red chilli, seeded and coarsely chopped
1 onion, coarsely chopped

For the stuffing
1 onion, finely chopped
50g/2oz/⅔ cup pine nuts
30ml/2 tbsp olive oil
7.5ml/1½ tsp ground allspice
60ml/4 tbsp chopped fresh coriander (cilantro)

1 If necessary, coarsely cut up the lamb and process the pieces in a blender or food processor until minced. Divide the minced meat into two equal portions.

2 For the patties, soak the bulgur wheat for 15 minutes in cold water. Drain then process in a blender or a food processor with the chilli, onion, half the meat and salt and pepper.

3 For the stuffing, cook the onion and pine nuts in the oil for 5 minutes. Add the allspice and remaining meat and cook gently, breaking up the meat with a wooden spoon, until browned. Stir in the coriander and seasoning.

4 Turn the patty mixture out on to a work surface and shape into a cake. Cut into 12 wedges.

5 Flatten one piece and spoon some of the stuffing into the centre. Bring the edges of the patty up over the stuffing, making sure that the filling is completely encased.

6 Pour the oil into a large pan to a depth of 5cm/2in and heat until a few patty crumbs sizzle on the surface.

7 Gently lower half of the filled patties into the oil and deep-fry for about 5 minutes, until golden. Drain well on kitchen paper and keep hot while you are cooking the remainder. Serve immediately, with avocado slices and coriander sprigs.

COOK'S TIPS
• When you are filling the kibbeh, it helps to dampen your hands with cold water to prevent the mixture from sticking to them.
• You can prepare the kibbeh a day in advance and store them, covered, in the refrigerator until ready to cook.

Energy 518kcal/2149kJ; Protein 20g; Carbohydrate 33g, of which sugars 3g; Fat 34g, of which saturates 7g; Cholesterol 56mg; Calcium 35mg; Fibre 1g; Sodium 50mg.

Spicy Koftas

These koftas will need to be cooked in batches. Keep them hot when they are cooked while you cook the rest.

Makes 20–25

450g/1lb minced (ground) lamb
30ml/2 tbsp ground ginger
30ml/2 tbsp finely chopped garlic
4 green chillies, finely chopped
1 small onion, finely chopped
1 egg
2.5ml/½ tsp ground turmeric
5ml/1 tsp garam masala
50g/2oz/2 cups coriander (cilantro)
  leaves, chopped
4–6 mint leaves, chopped
175g/6oz potato
salt, to taste
vegetable oil, for deep-frying

1 Place the meat in a large bowl with the ginger, garlic, chillies, onion, egg, turmeric, garam masala, coriander and mint. Grate the potato into the bowl, and season with salt. Knead together to blend well and form a soft dough.

VARIATION
Although lamb is traditionally used for making koftas, they are also delicious made with lean minced (ground) beef.

COOK'S TIP
Leftover koftas can be coarsely chopped and packed into pitta bread spread with chutney or relish for a quick, easy and delicious snack.

2 Using your fingers, shape the kofta mixture into portions about the size of golf balls. You should be able to make 20–25 koftas. Place the balls in a single layer on a baking sheet or large tray, cover with a clean dishtowel and leave to rest at room temperature for about 25 minutes.

3 Heat the oil in a large, heavy frying pan or wok to medium-hot. Add the koftas, in small batches, and deep-fry until they are golden brown in colour. Drain the koftas well on kitchen paper and keep hot in a low oven while you are cooking the remaining batches. Transfer to a platter and serve.

Energy 96kcal/404kJ; Protein 5.2g; Carbohydrate 11.8g, of which sugars 1.2g; Fat 3.4g, of which saturates 1.4g; Cholesterol 18mg; Calcium 16mg; Fibre 1g; Sodium 28mg.

brunches, lunches and fork suppers

Stylish dishes that are understated and easy to eat, go down well for these light meal occasions, bringing a sophisticated touch to informal entertaining.

Griddled Tomatoes on Soda Bread

Nothing could be simpler than this appetizing snack, yet a drizzle of olive oil and balsamic vinegar and shavings of Parmesan cheese transform it into something really rather special. It's the perfect choice for a brunch party that includes children.

Serves 4

extra virgin olive oil, for brushing
    and drizzling
6 tomatoes, thickly sliced
4 thick slices soda bread
balsamic vinegar, for drizzling
salt and ground black pepper
thin shavings of Parmesan cheese,
    to serve

1 Brush a griddle pan with olive oil and heat. Add the tomato slices and cook, turning them once, for about 4 minutes, until softened and slightly blackened. Alternatively, heat the grill (broiler) to high and line the rack with foil. Brush the tomato slices with oil and grill (broil), turning them once, for 4–6 minutes, until softened.

2 Meanwhile, lightly toast the soda bread. Place the tomatoes on top of the toast and drizzle each portion with a little olive oil and balsamic vinegar. Season to taste with salt and pepper and serve immediately with the shavings of Parmesan cheese.

COOK'S TIP

Using a griddle pan reduces the amount of oil required for cooking the tomatoes, which is useful for those guests who are watching their weight. It also gives the tomatoes a delicious flavour as if they have been cooked on a barbecue.

VARIATION

Substitute sherry vinegar for the balsamic if you like.

Energy 172kcal/724kJ; Protein 3.9g; Carbohydrate 25.1g, of which sugars 5.8g; Fat 6.9g, of which saturates 0.9g; Cholesterol 0mg; Calcium 63mg; Fibre 2.3g; Sodium 171mg.

Baked Mediterranean Vegetables

Crisp and golden crunchy batter surrounds these vegetables, turning them into a substantial vegetarian dish. Use other vegetables instead if you prefer.

Serves 10–12

1 small aubergine (eggplant), trimmed,
    halved and thickly sliced
1 egg
115g/4oz/1 cup plain
    (all-purpose) flour
300ml/½ pint/1¼ cups milk
30ml/2 tbsp fresh thyme leaves
1 red onion
2 large courgettes (zucchini)
1 red (bell) pepper
1 yellow (bell) pepper
60–75ml/4–5 tbsp sunflower oil
salt and ground black pepper
30ml/2 tbsp freshly grated
    Parmesan cheese and fresh herbs,
    to garnish

1 Place the aubergine in a colander or sieve, sprinkle generously with salt and leave for 10 minutes. Drain, rinse and pat dry on kitchen paper.

2 Meanwhile, to make the batter, beat the egg in a large bowl, then gradually beat in the flour and a little milk to make a smooth, thick paste. Blend in the rest of the milk, add the thyme leaves and season to taste with salt and pepper, blend until smooth. Cover with clear film (plastic wrap) and leave in a cool place until required.

3 Cut the onion into quarters and slice the courgettes. Seed and quarter the peppers. Put the oil in a roasting pan and place in the oven. Preheat the oven to 220°C/425°F/Gas 7. Add all the vegetables to the roasting pan, turn in the oil to coat them well and return to the oven for 20 minutes, until they start to cook.

4 Whisk the batter again, then pour it over the vegetables and return the roasting pan to the oven for a further 30 minutes, until the batter is well puffed up and golden.

5 Reduce the oven temperature to 190°C/375°F/Gas 5 and cook for a further 10–15 minutes, until the batter is crisp around the edges. Sprinkle with Parmesan and herbs and serve.

COOK'S TIP

It is essential to get the oil in the roasting pan really hot before adding the batter, or it will not rise well. Use a roasting pan or ovenproof dish that is not too deep.

Energy 113kcal/473kJ; Protein 4.3g; Carbohydrate 11.9g, of which sugars 4.3g; Fat 5.7g, of which saturates 1.4g; Cholesterol 17mg; Calcium 89mg; Fibre 1.5g; Sodium 45mg.

Scrambled Eggs with Smoked Salmon

For a luxury brunch, you cannot beat this special combination. Try it with a glass of champagne or sparkling wine mixed with freshly squeezed orange juice.

Serves 8

8 slices of pumpernickel or wholemeal (whole-wheat) bread, crusts trimmed
115g/4oz/½ cup butter
250g/9oz thinly sliced smoked salmon
12 eggs
90–120ml/6–8 tbsp double (heavy) cream
120ml/8 tbsp crème fraîche
salt and ground black pepper
generous 120ml/8 tbsp lumpfish roe or salmon caviar and fresh dill sprigs, to garnish

VARIATION

Another real treat is to grate a little fresh truffle into the scrambled eggs.

1 Spread the slices of bread with half of the butter and place them on eight individual plates. Arrange the smoked salmon on top and cut each slice in half. Set aside while you make the scrambled eggs.

2 Lightly beat the eggs together and season with salt and freshly ground black pepper. Melt the remaining butter in a pan until it is sizzling, then quickly pour in the beaten eggs, stirring vigorously with a wooden spoon. Do not let the eggs burn.

3 Stir constantly until the eggs begin to thicken. Just before they have finished cooking, stir in the cream.

4 Remove the pan from the heat and stir in the crème fraîche, add more salt and ground black pepper to taste.

5 Spoon the scrambled eggs on to the smoked salmon and bread on each plate. Top each serving with a spoonful of lumpfish roe or the salmon caviar and garnish with fresh sprigs of dill. Serve immediately.

Egg Crostini with Rouille

Crostini are extremely quick to make so are perfect for brunch parties. The spicy rouille gives them a hint of a Mediterranean flavour, providing the perfect complement to lightly fried eggs.

Serves 8

8 slices of ciabatta bread
extra virgin olive oil, for brushing
90ml/6 tbsp home-made mayonnaise
10ml/2 tsp harissa
8 eggs
8 small slices smoked ham
watercress or salad leaves, to serve

COOK'S TIP

Harissa is a fiery North African chilli paste made from dried red chillies, cumin, garlic, coriander, caraway and olive oil.

1 Preheat the oven to 200°C/400°F/ Gas 6. Use a pastry brush to brush each slice of ciabatta bread lightly with a little olive oil. Place the bread on a baking sheet and bake for 10 minutes, or until crisp and turning golden brown.

VARIATION

You can use four small portions of smoked haddock instead of ham and poach them for 5–7 minutes.

2 Meanwhile, make the rouille. Put the mayonnaise and harissa in a small bowl and mix well together.

3 Fry the eggs lightly in a little oil in a large non-stick frying pan.

4 Top the baked bread with the ham, eggs and a small spoonful of rouille. Serve immediately with watercress or salad leaves.

Scrambled: Energy 447kcal/1862kJ; Protein 37.3g; Carbohydrate 0.4g, of which sugars 0.4g; Fat 33.6g, of which saturates 13.1g; Cholesterol 734mg; Calcium 128mg; Fibre 0g; Sodium 1370mg.
Crostini: Energy 259kcal/1083kJ; Protein 15.8g; Carbohydrate 13.6g, of which sugars 1.3g; Fat 16.3g, of which saturates 3.4g; Cholesterol 220mg; Calcium 62mg; Fibre 0.6g; Sodium 705mg.

Eggs Benedict

There is still debate over who created this recipe but the most likely story credits a Mr and Mrs LeGrand Benedict, regulars at New York's Delmonico's restaurant, who complained there was nothing new on the lunch menu. This dish was created as a result.

Serves 4

5ml/1 tsp vinegar
4 eggs
2 English muffins or
    4 rounds of bread
butter, for spreading
4 thick slices cooked ham, trimmed to
    fit the muffins
fresh chives, to garnish

For the sauce
3 egg yolks
30ml/2 tbsp fresh lemon juice
1.5ml/¼ tsp salt
115g/4oz/½ cup butter
30ml/2 tbsp single (light) cream
ground black pepper

1 To make the sauce, place the egg yolks, lemon juice, and salt in a food processor or blender and process for 15 seconds.

2 Melt the butter in a small pan until it bubbles, but do not let it brown. With the motor running, pour the hot butter into the food processor through the feeder tube in a slow, steady stream. Turn off the machine as soon as all the butter has been added.

3 Scrape the sauce into the top of a double boiler or into a heatproof bowl set over barely simmering water. Stir for 2–3 minutes, until thickened. If it curdles, whisk in 15ml/1 tbsp boiling water. Stir in the cream and season to taste with pepper. Keep the sauce warm over the hot water.

4 Bring a shallow pan of water to the boil. Stir in the vinegar. Break each egg in turn, into a cup or jug (pitcher), then slide it carefully into the water. Carefully and gently turn the white around the yolk with a slotted spoon.

5 Cook for about 3–4 minutes, until the egg is set to your taste. Remove from the pan and place on kitchen paper to drain. Very gently cut any ragged edges off the eggs with a small knife or scissors.

6 While the eggs are poaching, split and toast the muffins or bread slices. Spread them with butter while they are still warm.

7 Place a piece of ham, which you may brown in butter if you like, on each muffin half or slice of toast. Place an egg on each ham-topped muffin. Spoon the warm sauce over the eggs, garnish with chives and serve.

COOK'S TIPS
• Use the freshest possible eggs for poaching, or the whites will coagulate immediately and the eggs will not spread out in the water.
• Cook each egg separately, so that they do not merge with each other.

VARIATION
For a special treat grate a little white or black truffle on top before serving.

Energy 553kcal/2304kJ; Protein 19.8g; Carbohydrate 31.6g, of which sugars 2.2g; Fat 39.7g, of which saturates 18.9g; Cholesterol 427mg; Calcium 148mg; Fibre 1.3g; Sodium 635mg.

Chive Scrambled Eggs in Brioches

This is an indulgent, truly delicious dish to serve for brunch.

Serves 4

*115g/4oz/¹/₂ cup unsalted
    (sweet) butter*
*75g/3oz/generous 1 cup brown cap
    (cremini) mushrooms, thinly sliced*
4 individual brioches
8 eggs
*15ml/1 tbsp chopped fresh chives, plus
    extra to garnish*
salt and ground black pepper

1 Preheat the oven to 180°C/350°F/
Gas 4. Place a quarter of the butter in
a frying pan and heat until melted.
Add the mushrooms and cook over a
low heat, stirring occasionally, for
about 3 minutes, or until soft, then set
aside and keep warm.

2 Slice the tops off the brioches, then
scoop out the centres and discard.
(Make them into breadcrumbs and
store in the refrigerator for another
recipe.) Put the brioches and lids on a
baking sheet and bake for 5 minutes,
until they are hot and slightly crisp.

3 Meanwhile, beat the eggs lightly
and season to taste with salt and
pepper. Heat the remaining butter in
a heavy pan over a low heat. When
the butter has melted and is foaming
slightly, add the eggs. Using a wooden
spoon, stir constantly to make sure
that the eggs do not stick.

4 Continue to stir fairly gently for
about 2–3 minutes, until about three-
quarters of the egg is semi-solid and
creamy. Remove the pan from the heat
or turn off the heat – the eggs will
continue to cook in the residual heat
from the pan. Stir in the chopped
fresh chives.

5 To serve, spoon a little of the
mushrooms into the base of each
brioche and top with the scrambled
eggs. Sprinkle with extra chopped
chives, balance the brioche lids on top
and serve immediately.

COOK'S TIP
Timing and temperature are crucial for
perfect scrambled eggs. When cooked for
too long over too high a heat, eggs
become dry and crumbly; if they are
undercooked, they will not set and be
sloppy and unappealing.

VARIATION
If fresh chervil is available, use it instead
of the chives.

Energy 533kcal/2218kJ; Protein 17.9g; Carbohydrate 31.9g, of which sugars 9.9g; Fat 38.2g, of which saturates 19.2g; Cholesterol 443mg; Calcium 137mg; Fibre 1.7g; Sodium 507mg.

Poached Eggs Florentine

The term "à la Florentine" means "in the style of Florence", referring to dishes cooked with spinach and topped with mornay sauce.

Serves 4

675g/1½lb spinach
25g/1oz/2 tbsp butter
60ml/4 tbsp double (heavy) cream
pinch of freshly grated nutmeg
salt and ground black pepper

For the topping
25g/1oz/2 tbsp butter
25g/1oz/¼ cup plain
   (all-purpose) flour
300ml/½ pint/1¼ cups hot milk
pinch of ground mace
115g/4oz/1 cup grated Gruyère cheese
4 eggs
15ml/1 tbsp grated Parmesan cheese,
   plus shavings to serve

1 Cut off any tough stalks, then wash the spinach in cold water and drain well. Place it in a large pan with very little water. Cook over a medium heat for 3–4 minutes, or until tender and wilted, then drain thoroughly and chop finely. Return the spinach to the pan, add the butter, cream and grated nutmeg and season to taste with salt and pepper, then heat through gently, stirring occasionally. Spoon the spinach mixture into the base of one large or four small gratin dishes.

2 To make the topping, heat the butter in a small pan, add the flour and cook, stirring constantly, for 1 minute to make a paste. Gradually blend in the hot milk, beating well as it thickens to break up any lumps.

3 Cook for 1–2 minutes, stirring constantly. Remove the pan from the heat and stir in the mace and three-quarters of the Gruyère.

4 Preheat the oven to 200°C/400°F/ Gas 6. Poach the eggs, one at a time, in lightly salted water for 3–4 minutes. Make hollows in the spinach with the back of a spoon, and place a poached egg in each one. Cover with the cheese sauce and sprinkle with the remaining Gruyère and the grated Parmesan. Bake for 10 minutes, or until golden. Serve immediately with Parmesan shavings.

Energy 459kcal/1901kJ; Protein 21.7g; Carbohydrate 11.5g, of which sugars 6.5g; Fat 36g, of which saturates 20.3g; Cholesterol 270mg; Calcium 636mg; Fibre 3.8g; Sodium 626mg.

Egg and Salmon Puff Parcels

These crisp elegant parcels hide a mouthwatering collection of flavours and textures, and make a delicious lunch dish.

Serves 6

75g/3oz/scant ¹/₂ cup long grain rice
300ml/¹/₂ pint/1¹/₄ cups fish stock
350g/12oz piece salmon tail
juice of ¹/₂ lemon
15ml/1 tbsp chopped fresh dill
15ml/1 tbsp chopped fresh parsley
10ml/2 tsp mild curry powder
6 small eggs, soft-boiled and cooled
425g/15oz flaky pastry, thawed
    if frozen
1 small (US medium) egg, beaten
salt and ground black pepper

1 Cook the rice in the fish stock according to the packet instructions, then drain and set aside to cool. Preheat the oven to 220°C/425°F/Gas 7.

2 Poach the salmon in a large pan with just enough water to cover, then remove and discard the bones and skin. Flake the fish into the rice. Add the lemon juice, dill, parsley and curry powder, then season to taste with salt and pepper and mix well. Shell the soft-boiled eggs.

COOK'S TIP
You can also add a spoonful of cooked spinach to each parcel.

3 Roll out the pastry on a floured surface and cut into six 14–15cm/5½–6in squares. Brush the edges with the beaten egg. Place a spoonful of the rice mixture in the middle of each square, push an egg into the middle and top with a little more rice.

4 Pull over the pastry corners to the middle to form a square parcel, squeezing the joins together well to seal. Brush with more beaten egg to glaze, place on a baking sheet and bake the puffs for 20 minutes.

5 Reduce the oven temperature to 190°C/375°F/Gas 5 and cook the puffs for a further 10 minutes, or until golden and crisp underneath.

6 Cool slightly before transferring the puffs to serving plates and serving, with a curry flavoured mayonnaise or hollandaise sauce, if you like. Alternatively, serve them on their own.

Energy 540kcal/2252kJ; Protein 36g; Carbohydrate 36g, of which sugars 1g; Fat 35g, of which saturates 10g; Cholesterol 255mg; Calcium 104mg; Fibre 1g; Sodium 433mg.

Courgette Fritters with Chilli Jam

Chilli jam is hot, sweet and sticky –
rather like a thick chutney. It adds a
delicious piquancy to these light
courgette fritters which are always
a popular dish.

Serves 6

*450g/1lb/3¹/₂ cups coarsely grated
   courgettes (zucchini)
50g/2oz/²/₃ cup freshly grated
   Parmesan cheese
2 eggs, beaten
60ml/4 tbsp plain (all-purpose) flour
vegetable oil, for frying
salt and ground black pepper*

For the chilli jam
*75ml/5 tbsp olive oil
4 large onions, diced
4 garlic cloves, chopped
1–2 green chillies, seeded and sliced
30ml/2 tbsp dark brown soft sugar*

1 First make the chilli jam. Heat the oil
in a large, heavy frying pan, then add
the onions and the garlic. Reduce the
heat to low, then cook for 20 minutes,
stirring frequently, until the onions are
very soft.

VARIATION
If you don't like chillies or you are short of
time, serve the fritters with an easy-to-
make dip. Chop a bunch of spring onions
(scallions) and stir them into a 150ml/
5fl oz/²/₃ cup sour cream or simply mix
finely chopped fresh herbs into a bowl of
good-quality mayonnaise.

2 Remove the pan from the heat and
leave the onion mixture to cool, then
transfer to a food processor or blender.
Add the chillies and sugar and process
until smooth, then return the mixture
to the pan. Cook over a low heat for a
further 10 minutes, stirring frequently,
until the liquid evaporates and the
mixture has the consistency of jam.
Cool slightly.

3 To make the fritters, squeeze the
courgettes in a dishtowel to remove
any excess liquid, then combine with
the grated Parmesan, eggs and flour
and season with salt and pepper.

COOK'S TIP
Stored in an airtight jar in the refrigerator,
the chilli jam will keep for up to 1 week.

4 Pour in enough oil to cover the base
of a large frying pan and heat. Add
30ml/2 tbsp of the courgette mixture
for each fritter and cook three fritters
at a time. Cook for 2–3 minutes on
each side until golden, then keep
warm while you cook the rest of the
fritters. Drain well on kitchen paper
and serve warm with a spoonful of
the chilli jam.

Energy 157kcal/652kJ; Protein 4.4g; Carbohydrate 11.1g, of which sugars 6.1g; Fat 10.8g, of which saturates 2.2g; Cholesterol 36mg; Calcium 85mg; Fibre 1.2g; Sodium 59mg.

Kansas City Fritters

These tasty fritters are always popular at brunch parties.

Serves 4

210g/7¹/₂oz/1¹/₄ cups canned corn
2 eggs, separated
40g/1¹/₂oz/¹/₃ cup plain
(all-purpose) flour
90ml/6 tbsp milk
1 small courgette (zucchini), grated
2 bacon rashers (strips), diced
2 spring onions (scallions), chopped
good pinch of cayenne pepper
45ml/3 tbsp sunflower oil
salt and ground black pepper
fresh coriander (cilantro) sprigs,
to garnish

For the salsa

3 tomatoes, peeled, seeded and diced
¹/₂ red (bell) pepper, seeded and diced
¹/₂ small onion, diced
15ml/1 tbsp lemon juice
15ml/1 tbsp chopped fresh
coriander (cilantro)
dash of Tabasco sauce

1 To make the salsa, place all the ingredients in a bowl, mix well and season to taste with salt and pepper. Cover with clear film (plastic wrap) and chill until required.

2 To make the fritters, drain the corn, place in a bowl and mix in the egg yolks. Add the flour and blend in with a wooden spoon. When the mixture begins to thicken, gradually blend in the milk.

3 Stir in the grated courgette, bacon, spring onions and cayenne pepper and season with salt and pepper, then set aside until required.

4 Place the egg whites in a clean, grease-free bowl and whisk until stiff. Gently fold the whites into the corn batter mixture with a metal spoon.

5 Heat 30ml/2 tbsp of the oil in a large, heavy frying pan and place four large spoonfuls of the mixture into the oil. Cook over a medium heat for 2–3 minutes on each side until golden, then drain on kitchen paper. Keep warm while you are cooking the remaining four fritters, adding the rest of the oil if necessary.

6 Serve two fritters each, garnished with coriander sprigs and a spoonful of the chilled tomato salsa.

COOK'S TIP

These fritters would also be delicious served with avocado salsa, guacamole or any strongly flavoured salsa spiced with fresh chillies.

Energy 126kcal/527kJ; Protein 4.5g; Carbohydrate 11.7g, of which sugars 3.4g; Fat 7.2g, of which saturates 1.5g; Cholesterol 52mg; Calcium 33mg; Fibre 0.7g; Sodium 190mg.

Potato and Red Pepper Frittata

For a light and easy-to-make lunch or a quick informal supper with plenty of flavour and colour this frittata will certainly fit the bill. Serve it with a mixed salad to complement the crisp flavours of the fresh mint sprigs and red peppers. You can also make this a day in advance to take to a picnic or serve at a barbecue.

Serves 6–8

900g/2lb small new or salad potatoes
12 eggs
60ml/4 tbsp chopped fresh mint
60ml/4 tbsp olive oil
2 onions, chopped
4 garlic cloves, crushed
4 red (bell) peppers, seeded and
   coarsely chopped
salt and ground black pepper
mint sprigs and crisp bacon, to garnish

1 Cook the potatoes in their skins in a large pan of lightly salted boiling water until they are just tender. Drain and leave to cool slightly, then cut the potatoes into thick slices.

2 Whisk together half the eggs, mint and seasoning in a large bowl, then set aside. Heat 30ml/2 tbsp oil in a large frying pan that can be safely used under the grill (broiler).

3 Add half the onion, garlic, peppers and potatoes to the pan and cook, stirring occasionally, for 5 minutes.

4 Pour the beaten egg mixture into the frying pan and stir gently. Gently push the mixture towards the centre of the pan as it cooks to allow the uncooked liquid egg to run on to the base and cook completely. Continue to cook over a medium heat. Meanwhile, preheat the grill.

5 When the frittata is lightly set, place the pan under the hot grill for 2–3 minutes, or until the top is a light golden brown colour.

6 Make another frittata with the other half of the ingredients.

7 Serve hot or cold, cut into wedges piled high on a serving dish and garnished with mint and crisp bacon.

VARIATIONS

Lightly cooked broccoli florets, cut quite small, are delicious with or instead of (bell) peppers in this frittata. Coarsely chopped black olives also go well with both peppers and broccoli.

Energy 321kcal/1342kJ; Protein 15g; Carbohydrate 20g, of which sugars 8g; Fat 18g, of which saturates 4g; Cholesterol 348mg; Calcium 80mg; Fibre 4g; Sodium 145mg.

Risotto Frittata

Half omelette, half risotto, this makes a delightful and satisfying lunch. If possible, cook each frittata separately and preferably in a small, cast-iron pan, so that the eggs cook quickly underneath but stay moist on top. Or cook in one large pan and serve in wedges.

Serves 4

30–45ml/2–3 tbsp olive oil
1 small onion, finely chopped
1 garlic clove, crushed
1 large red (bell) pepper, seeded and
    cut into thin strips
150g/5oz/3/4 cup risotto rice
400–475ml/14–16fl oz/12/3–2 cups
    simmering vegetable stock
25–40g/1–11/2oz/2–3 tbsp butter
175g/6oz/21/2 cups button (white)
    mushrooms, thinly sliced
60ml/4 tbsp freshly grated
    Parmesan cheese
6–8 eggs
salt and ground black pepper

1 Heat 15ml/1 tbsp oil in a large frying pan. Add the onion and garlic and cook over a gentle heat, stirring occasionally, for 2–3 minutes, until the onion begins to soften but does not brown. Add the pepper and cook, stirring frequently, for 4–5 minutes, until softened.

2 Stir in the rice and cook gently for 2–3 minutes, stirring constantly, until the grains are evenly coated with oil.

3 Add a quarter of the vegetable stock and season with a little salt and pepper. Stir over a low heat until the stock has been completely absorbed. Continue to add more stock, a little at a time, allowing the rice to absorb the liquid completely before adding more. Continue cooking and adding the stock in this way, stirring constantly, until the rice is *al dente*. This will take about 20 minutes.

4 In a separate small pan, heat a little of the remaining oil and some of the butter. Add the mushrooms and cook quickly over a medium heat until golden. Transfer to a plate.

5 When the rice is tender, remove from the heat and stir in the cooked mushrooms and the Parmesan cheese.

6 Beat the eggs together with 40ml/ 8 tsp cold water and season well with salt and pepper. Heat the remaining oil and butter in an omelette pan and add the risotto mixture. Spread the mixture out in the pan, then immediately add the beaten eggs, tilting the pan so that the omelette cooks evenly. Cook over a moderately high heat for 1–2 minutes, then transfer to a warmed plate and serve in wedges.

COOK'S TIP
Don't be impatient while cooking the rice. Adding the stock gradually ensures that the rice has a wonderfully creamy consistency. It is important to stir the rice so that it absorbs the stock fully. By the time you have added three-quarters of the stock, you can stop stirring constantly, but must still do so frequently.

Energy 434kcal/1804kJ; Protein 19.5g; Carbohydrate 34.1g, of which sugars 3.6g; Fat 24.5g, of which saturates 9.5g; Cholesterol 314mg; Calcium 241mg; Fibre 1.4g; Sodium 311mg.

Chilli Cheese Tortilla with Tomato Salsa

Good warm or cold, this is like a quiche without the pastry base.

Serves 8

45ml/3 tbsp sunflower or olive oil
1 small onion, thinly sliced
2–3 green jalapeño chillies, sliced
200g/7oz cold cooked potato, sliced
120g/4¼oz/generous 1 cup grated Manchego, Mexican queso blanco or Monterey Jack cheese
6 eggs, beaten
salt and ground black pepper
fresh herbs, to garnish

For the salsa
500g/1¼ lb tomatoes, peeled, seeded and finely chopped
1 green chilli, seeded and finely chopped
2 garlic cloves, crushed
45ml/3 tbsp chopped fresh coriander (cilantro)
juice of 1 lime
2.5ml/½ tsp salt

1 Begin by making the salsa. Put the tomatoes in a bowl and add the chilli, garlic, coriander, lime juice and salt. Mix well, cover with clear film (plastic wrap) and set aside in a cool place.

2 To make the tortilla, heat half the oil in a large omelette pan. Add the onion and jalapeños and cook over a low heat, stirring occasionally, for 5 minutes, until softened. Add the sliced potato and cook for a further 5 minutes until lightly browned, taking care to keep the slices whole.

3 Transfer the vegetables to a warm plate. Wipe the pan with kitchen paper, then pour in the remaining oil. Heat well and return the vegetable mixture to the pan. Sprinkle the grated cheese evenly over the top.

4 Pour in the beaten eggs, making sure that they seep underneath the vegetables. Cook the tortilla over a low heat until set. Serve in wedges, garnished with fresh herbs, with the salsa on the side.

COOK'S TIP
If you cannot find the cheeses listed, use a medium Cheddar instead.

Energy 582kcal/2422kJ; Protein 43g; Carbohydrate 7g, of which sugars 3g; Fat 43g, of which saturates 13g; Cholesterol 1138mg; Calcium 297mg; Fibre 1g; Sodium 654mg.

Quesadillas

These cheese-filled tortillas are the Mexican equivalent of toasted sandwiches. Serve them hot or they will become chewy. If you are making them for a crowd, fill and fold the tortillas ahead of time, but only cook them to order.

Serves 8

400g/14oz mozzarella, Monterey Jack or mild Cheddar cheese
2 fresh fresno chillies (optional)
16 wheat flour tortillas, about 15cm/6in across
onion relish or tomato salsa, to serve

1 If using mozzarella cheese, it must be drained thoroughly and then patted dry and sliced into thin strips. Monterey Jack and Cheddar cheese should both be coarsely grated, as finely grated cheese will melt and ooze away when cooking. Set the cheese aside in a bowl.

2 If using the chillies, spear them on a long-handled metal skewer and roast them over the flame of a gas burner until the skin blisters and darkens. Do not let the flesh burn. Place the roasted chillies in a strong plastic bag and tie the top to keep the steam in. Set aside for 20 minutes for the skin to loosen.

VARIATIONS
Try spreading a thin layer of your favourite salsa on the tortillas before adding the cheese, or add some cooked chicken or prawns (shrimp) before folding the tortillas.

3 Remove the roasted chillies from the bag and carefully peel off the skin. Cut off the stalk, then slit the chillies and scrape out all the seeds. Cut the flesh into 16 even-sized thin strips.

4 Warm a large frying pan or griddle. Place one tortilla on the pan or griddle at a time, sprinkle about one sixteenth of the cheese on to one half and add a strip of chilli, if using. Fold the tortilla over the cheese and press the edges together gently to seal. Cook the filled tortilla for 1 minute, then turn over and cook the other side for 1 minute.

5 Remove the filled tortilla from the frying pan or griddle, cut it into three triangles or four strips and serve immediately while it is still hot, with the onion relish or tomato salsa.

Energy 372kcal/1559kJ; Protein 17.2g; Carbohydrate 37.4g, of which sugars 0.8g; Fat 17g, of which saturates 10.9g; Cholesterol 49mg; Calcium 438mg; Fibre 1.5g; Sodium 537mg.

Chicken Fajitas with Grilled Onions

Classic fajitas are fun to eat with
friends and make a good choice
for an informal supper.

Serves 6

finely grated rind of 1 lime and the
    juice of 2 limes
120ml/4fl oz/½ cup olive oil
1 garlic clove, finely chopped
2.5ml/½ tsp dried oregano
good pinch of dried red chilli flakes
5ml/1 tsp coriander seeds, crushed
6 chicken breast fillets
3 Spanish onions, thickly sliced
2 large red, yellow or orange (bell)
    peppers, seeded and cut into strips
30ml/2 tbsp chopped fresh
    coriander (cilantro)
salt and ground black pepper

For the tomato salsa

450g/1lb tomatoes, peeled, seeded
    and chopped
2 garlic cloves, finely chopped
1 small red onion, finely chopped
1–2 green chillies, seeded and chopped
finely grated rind of ½ lime
30ml/2 tbsp chopped fresh
    coriander (cilantro)
pinch of caster (superfine) sugar
2.5–5ml/½–1 tsp ground roasted
    cumin seeds

To serve

12–18 soft flour tortillas
guacamole
120ml/4fl oz/½ cup sour cream
crisp lettuce leaves
coriander (cilantro) sprigs and
    lime wedges

1 Mix the lime rind and juice, 75ml/
5 tbsp of the oil, the garlic, oregano,
chilli flakes and coriander seeds in an
ovenproof dish and season. Slash the
chicken skin several times and turn in
the mixture, then cover and set aside to
marinate for several hours.

2 To make the salsa, combine the
tomatoes, garlic, onion, chillies, lime
rind and chopped coriander. Season to
taste with salt, pepper, caster sugar
and cumin seeds. Set aside for about
30 minutes, then taste and adjust the
seasoning, adding more cumin and
sugar, if necessary.

3 Preheat the grill (broiler). Thread the
onion slices on to a skewer or place
them on a grill rack. Brush with 15ml/
1 tbsp of the remaining oil and season.
Grill (broil) until softened and slightly
charred in places. Preheat the oven to
200°C/400°F/Gas 6.

4 Cover the dish containing the
chicken and marinade and cook in the
oven for 20 minutes. Remove from
the oven, then grill (broil) for about
8–10 minutes, or until browned and
cooked right through.

5 Meanwhile, heat the remaining oil in
a large frying pan and cook the peppers
for about 10 minutes, or until softened
and browned in places. Add the grilled
onions and cook for 2–3 minutes.

6 Add the chicken cooking juices
and cook over a high heat, stirring
frequently, until the liquid evaporates.
Stir in the chopped coriander.

7 Heat the tortillas following the
instructions on the packet. Using a
sharp knife, cut the grilled chicken into
strips and transfer to a serving dish.
Place the onion and pepper mixture
and the salsa in separate dishes.

8 Serve the dishes of chicken, onions
and peppers and salsa with the tortillas,
guacamole, sour cream, lettuce and
coriander for people to help themselves.
Serve with lime wedges.

Energy 485kcal/2044kJ; Protein 26g; Carbohydrate 67.4g, of which sugars 15.3g; Fat 14.2g, of which saturates 3.8g; Cholesterol 60mg; Calcium 118mg; Fibre 4g; Sodium 53mg.

Tortilla Cones with Smoked Salmon and Soft Cheese

These simple yet sophisticated wraps are a must for serving with drinks or as part of a buffet.

Serves 4

115g/4oz/½ cup soft white
   (farmer's) cheese
30ml/2 tbsp coarsely chopped fresh dill
juice of 1 lemon
1 small red onion
15ml/1 tbsp drained bottled capers
30ml/2 tbsp extra virgin olive oil
30ml/2 tbsp coarsely chopped fresh flat
   leaf parsley
115g/4oz sliced smoked salmon
8 small wheat flour tortillas
salt and ground black pepper
lemon wedges, for squeezing

3 Cut the smoked salmon into short, thin strips and add to the red onion mixture. Toss to mix. Season to taste with plenty of pepper.

COOK'S TIP
You can use salted capers in this dish instead of the unsalted variety, but rinse them thoroughly before using.

4 Spread a little of the soft cheese mixture on each tortilla and top with the smoked salmon mixture.

5 Roll up the tortillas into cones and secure with wooden cocktail sticks (toothpicks). Arrange on a serving plate and add some lemon wedges, for squeezing. Serve immediately.

1 Place the soft cheese in a bowl and mix in half the chopped dill. Add a little salt and pepper and a dash of the lemon juice to taste. Reserve the remaining lemon juice in a separate mixing bowl.

2 Finely chop the red onion. Add the onion, capers and olive oil to the lemon juice in the mixing bowl. Add the chopped flat leaf parsley and the remaining dill and gently stir.

VARIATION
Tortilla cones can be filled with a variety of ingredients. Try soft cheese with red pesto and chopped sun-dried tomatoes, or mackerel pâté with slices of cucumber.

Energy 374kcal/1576kJ; Protein 16.6g; Carbohydrate 53.2g, of which sugars 3g; Fat 12g, of which saturates 3.6g; Cholesterol 22mg; Calcium 128mg; Fibre 2.9g; Sodium 783mg.

Seafood Pancakes

The combination of unsmoked and smoked haddock fillets imparts a wonderful flavour to the filling.

Serves 6

For the pancakes
115g/4oz/1 cup plain
   (all-purpose) flour
pinch of salt
1 egg plus 1 egg yolk
300ml/½ pint/1¼ cups milk
15ml/1 tbsp melted butter, plus extra
   for cooking
50–75g/2–3oz Gruyère cheese, grated
frisée lettuce, to serve

For the filling
225g/8oz smoked haddock fillet
225g/8oz fresh haddock fillet
300ml/½ pint/1¼ cups milk
150ml/¼ pint/⅔ cup single
   (light) cream
40g/1½ oz/3 tbsp butter
40g/1½ oz/¼ cup plain
   (all-purpose) flour
freshly grated nutmeg
2 hard-boiled eggs, chopped
salt and ground black pepper

1 To make the pancakes, sift the flour and salt into a bowl. Make a well in the centre and add the egg and yolk.

2 Whisk the egg, incorporating some of the flour. Gradually whisk in the milk, until the batter is smooth and has the consistency of thin cream. Stir in the measured melted butter.

3 Heat a small crêpe pan or omelette pan until hot, then rub around the inside of the pan with a pad of kitchen paper dipped in melted butter. Pour about 30ml/2 tbsp of the batter into the pan, then immediately tip the pan to coat the base evenly. Cook the pancake over a low to medium heat for about 30 seconds until the top is beginning to set and the underside is golden brown.

4 Flip the pancake over with a spatula and cook on the other side until it is lightly browned. Repeat with the remaining batter to make 12 pancakes, rubbing the pan with melted butter between each pancake. Stack the pancakes as you make them between sheets of baking parchment. Keep the pancakes warm on a plate set over a pan of simmering water.

5 To make the filling, put the haddock fillets in a pan. Add the milk and poach for 6–8 minutes, until tender. Lift out the fish and, when cool enough to handle, remove the skin and any bones. Reserve the milk.

6 Pour the single cream into a measuring jug (cup) then strain enough of the reserved milk into the jug to make the quantity up to 450ml/¾ pint/scant 2 cups in total.

7 Melt the butter in a pan, stir in the flour and cook gently, stirring constantly, for 1 minute. Gradually mix in the milk and cream mixture, stirring constantly to make a smooth sauce. Cook for 2–3 minutes, until thickened. Season with salt, black pepper and nutmeg. Coarsely flake the haddock and fold into the sauce with the eggs. Leave to cool.

8 Preheat the oven to 180°C/350°F/ Gas 4. Divide the filling among the pancakes. Fold the sides of each pancake into the centre, then roll them up to enclose the filling completely.

9 Butter six individual ovenproof dishes and then arrange two filled pancakes in each, or butter one large dish for all the pancakes. Brush the tops with melted butter and cook for 15 minutes. Sprinkle over the Gruyère and cook for a further 5 minutes, until warmed through. Serve hot with frisée lettuce leaves.

VARIATION
For a different, but no less delicious flavour, omit the smoked haddock and stir 225g/8oz cooked, peeled prawns (shrimp) or smoked oysters into the sauce with the fresh haddock in step 7.

Energy 393kcal/1647kJ; Protein 26.7g; Carbohydrate 25.4g, of which sugars 5.7g; Fat 21.2g, of which saturates 11.9g; Cholesterol 203mg; Calcium 273mg; Fibre 0.8g; Sodium 513mg.

Leek, Saffron and Mussel Tartlets

Serve these vividly coloured little tarts with cherry tomatoes and a few salad leaves, such as watercress, rocket and frisée.

Serves 6

*4 large yellow (bell) peppers, halved
    and seeded*
2kg/4½lb mussels
*large pinch of saffron threads
    (about 30)*
30ml/2 tbsp hot water
4 large leeks, sliced
60ml/4 tbsp olive oil
4 large (US extra large) eggs
*600ml/1 pint/2½ cups single
    (light) cream*
*60ml/4 tbsp finely chopped
    fresh parsley*
salt and ground black pepper
salad leaves, to serve

For the pastry
*450g/1lb/4 cups plain (all-
    purpose) flour*
5ml/1 tsp salt
250g/8oz/1 cup butter, diced
30–45ml/2–3 tbsp water

1 To make the pastry, mix together the flour, salt and butter. Using your fingertips, rub the butter into the flour until the mixture resembles fine breadcrumbs. Mix in the water and knead lightly to form a firm dough. Wrap the dough in clear film (plastic wrap) and chill for 30 minutes.

2 Grill (broil) the pepper halves, skin sides uppermost, until they are black. Place the peppers in a bowl, cover and leave for 10 minutes. When they are cool enough to handle, peel and cut the flesh into thin strips.

3 Scrub the mussel shells with a brush, rinse in cold running water and pull off the beards.

4 Preheat the oven to 190°C/375°F/ Gas 5. Roll out the pastry and use it to line 12 × 10cm/4in tartlet tins (muffin pans), 2.5cm/1in deep. Prick the bases all over with a fork and then line the sides with strips of foil.

5 Bake the pastry cases (pie shells) for 10 minutes. Remove the foil and bake for another 5–8 minutes, or until they are lightly coloured. Remove them from the oven. Reduce the temperature to 180°C/350°F/Gas 4.

6 Soak the saffron in the hot water for 10 minutes. Cook the leeks in the oil over a medium heat for 6–8 minutes until beginning to brown. Add the peppers and cook for 2 minutes.

7 Bring 2.5cm/1in depth of water to a rolling boil in a large pan and add 10ml/2 tsp salt. Discard any open mussels that do not shut when tapped sharply, then throw the rest into the pan. Cover and cook over a high heat, shaking the pan occasionally, for 3–4 minutes, or until the mussels open. Discard any mussels that do not open. Shell the remainder.

8 Beat the eggs, cream and saffron liquid together. Season and whisk in the parsley. Arrange the leeks, peppers and mussels in the cases, add the egg mixture and bake for 20–25 minutes, until just firm. Serve with salad leaves.

Energy 520kcal/2171kJ; Protein 16g; Carbohydrate 36g, of which sugars 6g; Fat 36g, of which saturates 19g; Cholesterol 173mg; Calcium 151mg; Fibre 4g; Sodium 478mg.

Quiche Lorraine

A classic quiche from eastern France that is perfect to serve at a relaxed lunch party. This recipe retains the traditional characteristics that are often forgotten in modern versions, namely very thin pastry, a really creamy and light, egg-rich filling and smoked bacon.

Serves 6–8

175g/6oz/1½ cups plain
    (all-purpose) flour, sifted
pinch of salt
115g/4oz/½ cup unsalted (sweet)
    butter, at room temperature, diced
3 eggs, plus 3 yolks
6 smoked streaky (fatty) bacon rashers
    (strips), rinds removed
300ml/½ pint/1¼ cups double
    (heavy) cream
25g/1oz/2 tbsp unsalted (sweet) butter
salt and ground black pepper

1 Place the flour, salt, butter and 1 egg yolk in a food processor and process until blended. Tip out on to a floured surface and bring the mixture together into a ball. Leave to rest for 20 minutes.

2 Lightly flour a deep 20cm/8in quiche tin (pan), and place it on a baking tray. Roll out the pastry and use to line the tin, trimming off any overhanging pieces. Press the pastry into the edges of the tin. If the pastry breaks up, just gently push it into shape. Chill for 20 minutes. Preheat the oven to 200°C/400°F/Gas 6.

3 Meanwhile, cut the bacon into thin strips and grill (broil) until the fat runs. Arrange the bacon in the pastry case. Beat together the cream, the remaining eggs and yolks and seasoning, and pour into the pastry case (pie shell).

4 Bake for 15 minutes, then reduce the heat to 180°C/350°F/Gas 4 and bake for a further 15–20 minutes. When the filling is puffed up and golden and the pastry is crisp, remove from the oven and top with knobs (pats) of butter. Stand for 5 minutes before serving.

Energy 670kcal/2775kJ; Protein 13g; Carbohydrate 23.7g, of which sugars 1.4g; Fat 58.9g, of which saturates 32.9g; Cholesterol 302mg; Calcium 94mg; Fibre 0.9g; Sodium 611mg.

Wild Mushroom and Fontina Tarts

Italian fontina cheese gives these tarts a creamy, nutty flavour.

Serves 4

25g/1oz/¹/₂ cup dried wild mushrooms
1 red onion, chopped
30ml/2 tbsp olive oil
2 garlic cloves, chopped
30ml/2 tbsp medium-dry sherry
1 egg
120ml/4fl oz/¹/₂ cup single (light) cream
25g/1oz fontina cheese, thinly sliced
salt and ground black pepper
rocket (arugula) leaves, to serve

For the pastry

115g/4oz/1 cup wholemeal
  (whole-wheat) flour
50g/2oz/4 tbsp unsalted (sweet) butter
25g/1oz/¹/₄ cup walnuts, roasted
  and ground
1 egg, lightly beaten

1 To make the pastry, sift the flour into a bowl and rub in butter with your fingertips until the mixture resembles fine breadcrumbs. Add the nuts then the egg and mix to a soft dough. Gather into a ball, wrap, then chill for 30 minutes.

2 Meanwhile, place the dried wild mushrooms in a bowl and add 300ml/ ½ pint/1¼ cups boiling water. Soak for 30 minutes. Drain well and reserve the liquid. Cook the onion in the oil for 5 minutes, then add the garlic and cook for about 2 minutes, stirring.

3 Add the soaked mushrooms and cook for 7 minutes over a high heat until the edges become crisp. Add the sherry and the reserved mushroom soaking liquid. Cook over a high heat for about 10 minutes, until the liquid has evaporated. Season to taste with salt and pepper and set aside to cool.

COOK'S TIPS

• You can prepare the pastry cases in advance, bake them blind for 10 minutes, then store in an airtight container for up to 2 days.
• Baking beans are small metal weights that help to prevent the pastry case (pie shell) from shrinking and blistering during the initial baking. You can, of course, use real dried beans that are kept especially for the purpose.

4 Preheat the oven to 200°C/400°F/ Gas 6. Lightly grease four 10cm/4in tartlet tins (muffin pans). Roll out the pastry on a lightly floured work surface and use to line the tart tins.

5 Prick the pastry bases all over with a fork, line with baking parchment and baking beans and bake blind for about 10 minutes. Remove the paper and the beans.

6 Whisk the egg and cream to mix, add to the mushroom mixture, then season to taste with salt and pepper. Spoon the filling into the pastry cases (pie shells), top with cheese slices and bake for 15–20 minutes, until the filling is set. Leave to cool slightly, then serve warm with rocket.

Energy 409kcal/1701kJ; Protein 10.2g; Carbohydrate 21.9g, of which sugars 2.3g; Fat 31g, of which saturates 13.4g; Cholesterol 143mg; Calcium 121mg; Fibre 2.3g; Sodium 199mg.

Leek and Onion Tartlets

Baking in individual tins makes for easier serving and they look attractive too.

Serves 6

25g/1oz/2 tbsp butter
1 onion, thinly sliced
2.5ml/¹/₂ tsp dried thyme
450g/1lb leeks, thinly sliced
50g/2oz/¹/₂ cup grated Gruyère or
    Emmenthal cheese
3 eggs
300ml/¹/₂ pint/1¹/₄ cups single
    (light) cream
pinch of freshly grated nutmeg
salt and ground black pepper
mixed salad leaves, to serve

For the pastry
175g/6oz/1¹/₃ cup plain
    (all-purpose) flour
75g/3oz/6 tbsp cold butter
1 egg yolk
30–45ml/2–3 tbsp cold water
2.5ml/¹/₂ tsp salt

1 To make the pastry, sift the flour into a bowl and add the butter. Using your fingertips, rub the butter into the flour until it resembles fine breadcrumbs. Make a well in the centre.

2 Beat together the egg yolk, water and salt, pour the mixture into the well and combine the flour and liquid until it begins to stick together. Form into a ball. Wrap in clear film, (plastic wrap) and chill for 30 minutes.

3 Butter six 10cm/4in tartlet tins (muffin pans). On a lightly floured surface, roll out the dough to about 3mm/¹/₈in thick, then using a 12.5cm/5in cutter, cut as many rounds as possible. Gently ease the rounds into the tins, pressing the pastry firmly into the base and sides. Gather up the trimmings, re-roll them and line the remaining tins. Prick the bases all over with a fork and chill in the refrigerator for 30 minutes.

4 Preheat the oven to 190°C/375°F/Gas 5. Line the pastry cases (pie shells) with foil and fill with baking beans. Place them on a baking sheet and bake for 6–8 minutes, until golden brown at the edges. Remove the foil and baking beans and bake for a further 2 minutes, until the bases appear dry. Transfer to a wire rack to cool. Reduce the oven temperature to 180°C/350°F/Gas 4.

5 Melt the butter in a large, heavy frying pan over a medium heat, then add the onion and thyme and cook, stirring occasionally, for 3–5 minutes until the onion is just softened.

6 Add the leeks and cook, stirring occasionally, for 10–12 minutes, until they are soft and tender. Divide the leek and onion mixture among the pastry cases and sprinkle each with cheese, dividing it evenly.

7 Beat the eggs with the cream and nutmeg in a medium bowl and season to taste with salt and pepper. Place the pastry cases on a baking sheet and pour in the egg mixture. Bake for 15–20 minutes, until set and golden.

8 Transfer the tartlets to a wire rack to cool slightly, then remove them from the tins and serve warm or at room temperature with salad leaves.

Energy 422kcal/1755kJ; Protein 11.5g; Carbohydrate 26.8g, of which sugars 3.9g; Fat 30.4g, of which saturates 17.7g; Cholesterol 200mg; Calcium 189mg; Fibre 2.7g; Sodium 215mg.

Vegetable Tarte Tatin

This upside-down tart combines Mediterranean vegetables with rice, garlic, onions and olives.

Serves 4

30ml/2 tbsp sunflower oil
25ml/1 1/2 tbsp olive oil
1 aubergine (eggplant),
    sliced lengthways
1 large red (bell) pepper, seeded and
    cut into long strips
5 tomatoes
2 red shallots, finely chopped
1–2 garlic cloves, crushed
150ml/1/4 pint/2/3 cup white wine
10ml/2 tsp chopped fresh basil
225g/8oz/2 cups cooked rice
40g/1 1/2oz/2/3 cup pitted black
    olives, chopped
350g/12oz puff pastry, thawed if frozen
ground black pepper
salad leaves, to serve

1 Preheat the oven to 190°C/375°F/Gas 5. Heat the sunflower oil with 15ml/1 tbsp of the olive oil. Add the aubergine slices and cook over a medium heat for 4–5 minutes on each side. Drain on kitchen paper.

COOK'S TIP
Modern varieties of aubergine no longer contain bitter juices that must be removed before cooking by salting. However, if you have time, it is still worth doing this because it helps to prevent them from soaking up large amounts of oil during cooking.

2 Add the pepper strips to the oil remaining in the pan, turning them to coat. Cover the pan with a lid or a sheet of foil and sweat the peppers over a moderately high heat for 5–6 minutes, stirring occasionally, until the pepper strips are soft and flecked with brown.

3 Slice two of the tomatoes and set them aside. Place the remaining tomatoes in a bowl, cover with boiling water and leave for 30 seconds, then drain and peel them. Cut them into quarters and remove the cores and seeds. Chop the tomato flesh coarsely.

4 Heat the remaining oil in the frying pan. Add the shallots and garlic and cook over a low heat, stirring occasionally, for 3–4 minutes, until softened but not browned. Then add the chopped tomatoes and cook, for a few minutes, until just softened. Stir in the white wine and basil and season with black pepper to taste. Bring to the boil, then remove the pan from the heat and stir in the cooked rice and black olives.

5 Arrange the tomato slices, the aubergine slices and the peppers in a single layer on the base of a heavy, 30cm/12in, shallow ovenproof dish. Spread the rice and tomato mixture evenly on top.

6 Roll out the pastry to a round slightly larger than the diameter of the dish and place on top of the rice, gently tucking the overlap down inside the dish.

7 Bake for 25–30 minutes, until the pastry is golden and risen. Leave to cool slightly, then invert the tart on to a large, warmed serving plate. Serve in slices, with some salad leaves.

VARIATION
Courgettes (zucchini) and mushrooms could be used as well as, or instead of, the aubergines (eggplants) and (bell) pepper. Alternatively, you could use strips of lightly browned chicken.

Energy 535kcal/2240kJ; Protein 8.2g; Carbohydrate 59.1g, of which sugars 8.8g; Fat 29.5g, of which saturates 1.2g; Cholesterol 0mg; Calcium 89mg; Fibre 2.6g; Sodium 521mg.

Dolmades

Stuffed vine leaves are a popular choice for a Greek mezze and will prove a great favourite at parties.

Serves 5–6

24–28 fresh young vine (grape)
  leaves, soaked
30ml/2 tbsp olive oil
1 large onion, finely chopped
1 garlic clove, crushed
225g/8oz/2 cups cooked long grain
  rice, or mixed white and wild rice
45ml/3 tbsp pine nuts
15ml/1 tbsp flaked (sliced) almonds
40g/1¹/₂oz/¹/₄ cup sultanas
  (golden raisins)
15ml/1 tbsp chopped fresh chives
15ml/1 tbsp finely chopped fresh mint
juice of ¹/₂ lemon
150ml/¹/₄ pint/²/₃ cup white wine
150ml/¹/₄ pint/²/₃ cup hot
  vegetable stock
salt and ground black pepper
fresh mint sprig, to garnish
garlic yogurt and pitta bread, to serve

1 Bring a large pan of water to the boil and cook the vine leaves for about 2–3 minutes. They will darken and go limp after about 1 minute and then simmering for a further minute or so will make sure that they are pliable. If you are using packet or canned leaves, place them in a bowl, cover with boiling water and leave for about 20 minutes, until the leaves can be separated easily. Rinse and dry well on kitchen paper.

2 Heat the oil in a small frying pan. Add the onion and garlic and cook over a low heat, stirring occasionally, for 3–4 minutes, until soft. Spoon the mixture into a large bowl and add the cooked rice. Stir to combine.

3 Stir in 30ml/2 tbsp of the pine nuts, the almonds, sultanas, chives and mint. Squeeze in the lemon juice. Season with salt and pepper to taste and mix well.

4 Set aside four large vine leaves. Lay a vine leaf on a clean work surface, veined side uppermost. Place a spoonful of filling near the stem, fold the lower part of the vine leaf over it and roll up, folding in the sides as you go. Stuff the rest of the vine leaves in the same way.

5 Line the base of a deep frying pan with the reserved vine leaves. Place the dolmades close together in the pan, seam side down, in a single layer. Pour over the wine and enough stock just to cover. Anchor the dolmades by placing a plate on top of them, then cover the pan and simmer gently for 30 minutes.

6 Transfer the dolmades to a plate. Leave to cool, then chill in the refrigerator. When ready to serve, garnish with the remaining pine nuts and the mint. Serve with a little garlic yogurt and some pitta bread.

COOK'S TIP

Dolmades are delicious served hot but be sure to sprinkle them with fresh lemon juice.

Energy 43kcal/181kJ; Protein 0.7g; Carbohydrate 6.7g, of which sugars 1.7g; Fat 1.1g, of which saturates 0.1g; Cholesterol 0mg; Calcium 12mg; Fibre 0.3g; Sodium 2mg.

Quail's Eggs in Aspic with Prosciutto

These impressive-looking eggs in jelly are so easy to make, and are great for summer eating. Serve them with salad leaves and some home-made mayonnaise on the side.

Serves 4

20g/³/₄oz aspic powder
45ml/3 tbsp dry sherry
12 quail's eggs
6 slices prosciutto
12 fresh coriander (cilantro) or flat leaf
  parsley leaves
salad leaves, to serve

1 Make up the aspic in a jug (pitcher) following the packet instructions but replace 45ml/3 tbsp water with the dry sherry, to give a greater depth of flavour. Leave the aspic in the refrigerator until it begins to thicken, but not set.

2 Put the quail's eggs in a pan of cold water and bring to the boil over a medium heat. Boil for 1½ minutes only, then pour off the hot water and leave in cold water until cold. This way, the yolks will be a little soft but the whites will be firm enough for you to shell the eggs easily when they are really cold.

3 Rinse 12 dariole moulds in cold water so that they are damp and place them on a tray. Cut the prosciutto into 12 pieces, then roll or fold so they will fit into the moulds.

4 Place a coriander or parsley leaf in the base of each mould, then put a shelled egg on top. As the jelly begins to thicken, pour in enough to nearly cover each egg, holding it steady. Then put the slice of prosciutto on the egg and pour in the rest of the jelly to fill each mould, so that when you turn them out the eggs will be sitting on the prosciutto.

5 Transfer the tray of moulds to a cold place and then leave for 3–4 hours, until completely set and cold. When ready to serve, run a knife blade around the top rim of the jelly to loosen. Dip the base of the moulds into warm, not hot, water and shake or tap gently until they appear loose. Invert on to small plates and serve with salad leaves.

Energy 31kcal/129kJ; Protein 3.9g; Carbohydrate 0.2g, of which sugars 0.2g; Fat 1.2g, of which saturates 0.3g; Cholesterol 36mg; Calcium 8mg; Fibre 0.1g; Sodium 97mg.

Cheese and Leek Sausages with Chilli and Tomato Sauce

These popular vegetarian sausages served with a spicy sauce flavoured with chilli and balsamic vinegar are bound to be a hit for an informal lunch or supper.

Serves 4

25g/1oz/2 tbsp butter
175g/6oz leeks, finely chopped
90ml/6 tbsp cold mashed potato
115g/4oz/2 cups fresh
    white breadcrumbs
150g/5oz/1¼ cups grated Caerphilly,
    Cheddar or Cantal cheese
30ml/2 tbsp chopped fresh parsley
5ml/1 tsp chopped fresh sage
    or marjoram
2 large (US extra large) eggs, beaten
good pinch of cayenne pepper
65g/2½oz/1 cup dry
    white breadcrumbs
vegetable oil, for shallow frying
salt and ground black pepper

For the sauce
30ml/2 tbsp olive oil
2 garlic cloves, thinly sliced
1 fresh red chilli, seeded and finely
    chopped, or a good pinch of dried
    red chilli flakes
1 small onion, finely chopped
500g/1¼lb tomatoes, peeled,
    seeded and chopped
a few fresh thyme sprigs
10ml/2 tsp balsamic vinegar or red
    wine vinegar
pinch of light muscovado
    (brown) sugar
15–30ml/1–2 tbsp chopped fresh
    marjoram or oregano

COOK'S TIP
These sausages are also delicious when they are served with a fruity chilli salsa and a watercress salad.

1 Melt the butter in a frying pan and cook the leeks for 4–5 minutes, or until softened but not browned. Mix with the mashed potato, fresh breadcrumbs, grated cheese, chopped parsley and sage or marjoram.

2 Add sufficient beaten egg (about two-thirds of the quantity) to bind the mixture together. Season well and add cayenne pepper to taste.

3 Pat or roll the mixture between dampened hands to form 12 sausage shapes. Dip in the remaining egg, then coat in the dry breadcrumbs. Chill the coated sausages.

4 Make the sauce. Heat the oil in a pan and cook the garlic, chilli and onion over a low heat for 3–4 minutes. Add the tomatoes, thyme and vinegar. Season with salt, pepper and sugar.

5 Cook the sauce for 40–50 minutes, or until considerably reduced. Remove the thyme and purée the sauce in a food processor or blender. Reheat with the marjoram or oregano and then adjust the seasoning.

6 Cook the sausages in shallow oil until golden brown on all sides. Drain on kitchen paper and serve with the sauce.

Energy 185kcal/771kJ; Protein 6g; Carbohydrate 13g, of which sugars 1g; Fat 12g, of which saturates 4g; Cholesterol 54mg; Calcium 101mg; Fibre 1g; Sodium 202mg.

Polpettes

Little fried mouthfuls of potato and tangy-sharp Greek feta cheese, flavoured with dill and lemon juice are ideal to serve for lunch or supper.

Serves 4

500g/1¼lb floury (mealy) potatoes
115g/4oz/1 cup feta cheese
4 spring onions (scallions), chopped
45ml/3 tbsp chopped fresh dill
1 egg, beaten
15ml/1 tbsp lemon juice
plain (all-purpose) flour, for dredging
45ml/3 tbsp olive oil
salt and ground black pepper
fresh dill sprigs and shredded spring
* onions (scallions), to garnish*
lemon wedges, to serve

1 Cook the potatoes in their skins in lightly salted, boiling water until soft. Drain and cool slightly, then chop them in half and peel while still warm.

COOK'S TIP
To save time, cook the polpettes in advance, cool and chill until required. Reheat in the oven before serving.

2 Place the potatoes in a bowl and mash until smooth. Crumble the feta cheese into the potatoes and add the spring onions, dill, egg and lemon juice and season with salt and pepper. (The cheese is salty, so taste before you add salt.) Stir well, until combined.

3 Cover and chill until firm. Divide the mixture into walnut-size balls, then flatten them slightly. Dredge with flour, shaking off the excess.

4 Heat the oil in a large frying pan and cook the polpettes, in batches, until golden brown on both sides. Drain on kitchen paper and serve hot, garnished with spring onions and sprigs of dill, and serve with lemon wedges.

Energy 230kcal/960kJ; Protein 8.4g; Carbohydrate 20.9g, of which sugars 2.3g; Fat 13.1g, of which saturates 5.3g; Cholesterol 68mg; Calcium 122mg; Fibre 1.4g; Sodium 446mg.

Crab Cakes with Tartare Sauce

Sweet crab meat is offset by a
piquant tartare sauce.

Serves 4

675g/1½lb fresh crab meat
1 egg, beaten
30ml/2 tbsp mayonnaise
15ml/1 tbsp Worcestershire sauce
15ml/1 tbsp sherry
30ml/2 tbsp chopped fresh parsley
15ml/1 tbsp chopped fresh chives
salt and ground black pepper
45ml/3 tbsp olive oil
salad leaves, chives and lemon, to garnish

For the sauce

1 egg yolk
15ml/1 tbsp white wine vinegar
30ml/2 tbsp Dijon mustard
250ml/8fl oz/1 cup vegetable oil
30ml/2 tbsp lemon juice
60ml/4 tbsp chopped spring
    onions (scallions)
30ml/2 tbsp chopped drained capers
60ml/4 tbsp chopped sour dill pickles
60ml/4 tbsp chopped fresh parsley

1 Carefully pick over the crab meat,
removing any stray pieces of shell or
cartilage. Keep the pieces of crab as
large as possible.

2 In a mixing bowl, combine the
beaten egg with the mayonnaise,
Worcestershire sauce, sherry, parsley
and chives. Season with a little salt and
lots of black pepper. Gently fold in the
crab meat.

3 Divide the mixture into eight equal
portions and gently form each one into
an oval patty. Place them on a baking
sheet between layers of baking
parchment and chill in the refrigerator
for at least 1 hour.

4 Meanwhile, make the sauce. In a
medium-size bowl, beat the egg yolk
with a wire whisk until smooth. Add
the vinegar and mustard, season with
salt and pepper to taste and whisk for
about 10 seconds to blend. Gradually
whisk in the oil.

5 Add the lemon juice, spring onions,
capers, pickles and parsley and mix
well. Check the seasoning. Cover with
clear film (plastic wrap) and chill.

6 Preheat the grill (broiler). Brush the
crab cakes with the olive oil. Place on
an oiled baking sheet, in one layer.

7 Grill (broil) 15cm/6in from the heat
until golden brown, about 5 minutes
on each side. Serve the crab cakes with
the tartare sauce, garnished with salad
leaves, chives and lemon.

COOK'S TIPS

• For easier handling and to make the
crab meat go further, add 50g/2oz/1 cup
fresh breadcrumbs and 1 more egg to the
crab mixture. Divide the mixture into
12 patties to serve six people.
• Fresh crab meat is widely available from
supermarkets and fish stores. You can
also buy freshly cooked whole crab and
remove the meat from the shell yourself.
If buying a whole crab, choose one that
feels heavy for its size. Shake it before
purchase to check whether it contains any
water. If it does, reject it. Most of the
white meat is found in the claws.

Energy 710kcal/2934kJ; Protein 33.8g; Carbohydrate 1.9g, of which sugars 1.7g; Fat 62.6g, of which saturates 8.1g; Cholesterol 225mg; Calcium 234mg; Fibre 0.2g; Sodium 1249mg.

Turkey Croquettes

Smoked turkey gives these crisp croquettes a distinctive flavour. Served with the tangy tomato sauce, crispy bread and salad they make a tasty fork supper.

Serves 4

450g/1lb potatoes, diced
3 eggs
30ml/2 tbsp milk
175g/6oz smoked turkey rashers (strips), finely chopped
2 spring onions (scallions), thinly sliced
115g/4oz/2 cups fresh white breadcrumbs
vegetable oil, for deep-frying
salt and ground black pepper

For the sauce

15ml/1 tbsp olive oil
1 onion, finely chopped
400g/14oz can tomatoes, drained
30ml/2 tbsp tomato purée (paste)
15ml/1 tbsp chopped fresh parsley

1 Boil the potatoes until tender. Drain and return the pan to a low heat to make sure all the excess water evaporates.

2 Mash the potatoes with two eggs and the milk. Season well with salt and pepper. Stir in the turkey rashers and spring onions. Chill for 1 hour.

3 To make the sauce heat the oil in a frying pan and cook the onion until softened. Add the tomatoes and tomato purée, stir and simmer for 10 minutes. Stir in the parsley and season. Keep the sauce warm.

4 Remove the potato mixture from the refrigerator and divide into eight pieces. Shape each piece into a sausage and dip in the remaining beaten egg and then the breadcrumbs.

5 Heat the vegetable oil in a pan or deep-fryer to 190°C/375°F or until a cube of day-old bread dropped into the hot oil browns in 45 seconds. Deep-fry the croquettes for 5 minutes, or until they are golden and crisp. Drain on kitchen paper. Reheat the sauce gently, if necessary, and serve with the freshly cooked croquettes.

Energy 404kcal/1698kJ; Protein 19.4g; Carbohydrate 47g, of which sugars 7.7g; Fat 16.7g, of which saturates 2.4g; Cholesterol 73mg; Calcium 93mg; Fibre 3.3g; Sodium 315mg.

Smoked Salmon and Rice Salad Parcels

Feta, cucumber and tomatoes give a Greek flavour to the salad in these parcels, a combination which goes well with the rice, especially if a little wild rice is added.

Serves 4

175g/6oz/scant 1 cup mixed wild rice
  and basmati rice
8 slices smoked salmon, total weight
  about 350g/12oz
10cm/4in piece of cucumber,
  finely diced
225g/8oz feta cheese, cubed
8 cherry tomatoes, quartered
30ml/2 tbsp mayonnaise
10ml/2 tsp fresh lime juice
15ml/1 tbsp chopped fresh chervil
salt and ground black pepper
lime slices and fresh chervil, to garnish

1 Cook the rice according to the instructions on the packet. Drain, tip into a bowl and leave to cool completely.

2 Line four ramekins with clear film (plastic wrap), then line each ramekin with two slices of smoked salmon, allowing the ends to overlap the edges of the dishes.

VARIATION
You can use other smoked fish in place of the salmon. Smoked trout is an obvious alternative, but you could also try trout, monkfish, freshwater eel or halibut, if you are able to find it.

3 Add the cucumber, cubes of feta and tomato quarters to the rice and stir in the mayonnaise, lime juice and chopped chervil. Mix together well. Season with salt and ground black pepper to taste.

4 Spoon the rice salad mixture into the salmon-lined ramekins. (Any leftover mixture can be used to make a separate rice salad.) Then carefully fold over the overlapping ends of the salmon so that the rice mixture is completely encased.

5 Chill the parcels in the refrigerator for 30–60 minutes, then invert each parcel on to a plate, using the clear film to ease them out of the ramekins. Carefully peel off the clear film, then garnish each parcel with slices of lime and a sprig of fresh chervil and serve.

COOK'S TIP
Wild rice is actually an aquatic grass and is quite expensive, as it is so difficult to harvest. However, a little goes a long way. You can buy packs of mixed wild and long grain rice in most supermarkets.

Energy 479kcal/2000kJ; Protein 34.6g; Carbohydrate 36.9g, of which sugars 1.9g; Fat 21.3g, of which saturates 9.3g; Cholesterol 76mg; Calcium 232mg; Fibre 0.3g; Sodium 2492mg.

Salmon Rillettes

This is an economical, but
delightful way of serving salmon.

Serves 6

350g/12oz salmon fillets
175g/6oz/³/₄ cup butter, softened
1 celery stick, finely chopped
1 leek, white part only, finely chopped
1 bay leaf
150ml/¹/₄ pint/²/₃ cup dry white wine
115g/4oz smoked salmon trimmings
generous pinch of ground mace
60ml/4 tbsp fromage frais
  (farmer's cheese)
salt and ground black pepper
salad leaves, to serve
brown bread or oatcakes, to serve

1 Lightly season the salmon fillets.
Melt 25g/1oz/2 tbsp of the butter in a
medium frying pan. Add the celery and
leek and cook over a low heat, stirring
occasionally, for about 5 minutes. Add
the salmon fillets and bay leaf and
pour the wine over. Cover and cook
for 15 minutes, until the fish is tender.

2 Strain the cooking liquid into a pan
and boil until reduced to 30ml/2 tbsp.
Cool. Meanwhile, melt 50g/2oz/4 tbsp
of the remaining butter and gently
cook the smoked salmon until it turns
pale pink. Leave to cool.

3 Remove the skin and any bones
from the salmon fillets. Flake the flesh
into a bowl and add the reduced,
cooled cooking liquid.

4 Beat in the remaining butter, with
the ground mace and the fromage
frais. Break up the cooked smoked
salmon trimmings and fold into the
salmon mixture with all the juices
from the pan. Taste and adjust the
seasoning if you need to.

5 Spoon the salmon mixture into a
dish or terrine and smooth the top
level. Cover with clear film (plastic
wrap) and chill.

COOK'S TIP
If you are preparing the rillettes ahead,
you can store the salmon mixture in the
refrigerator for up to 2 days.

6 To serve the salmon rillettes, shape
the mixture into oval quenelles using
two dessertspoons and arrange them
on individual plates with the salad
leaves. Serve the rillettes accompanied
by slices of brown bread or oatcakes,
if you like.

Energy 370kcal/1530kJ; Protein 17.2g; Carbohydrate 0.9g, of which sugars 0.7g; Fat 31.4g, of which saturates 16.5g; Cholesterol 98mg; Calcium 30mg; Fibre 0.4g; Sodium 568mg.

Pork and Bacon Rillettes with Onion Salad

These traditional potted meat rillettes make a great light meal.

Serves 8

1.8kg/4lb belly (side) of pork, boned and cut into cubes (reserve the bones)
450g/1lb rindless streaky (fatty) bacon, finely chopped
5ml/1 tsp salt
1.5ml/¼ tsp freshly ground black pepper
4 garlic cloves, finely chopped
2 fresh parsley sprigs
1 bay leaf
2 fresh thyme sprigs
1 fresh sage sprig
300ml/½ pint/1¼ cups water
crusty French bread, to serve

For the onion salad

1 small red onion, halved and thinly sliced
2 spring onions (scallions), cut into fine strips
2 celery sticks, cut into fine strips
15ml/1 tbsp freshly squeezed lemon juice
15ml/1 tbsp light olive oil
ground black pepper

1 Mix together the pork, bacon and salt in a bowl. Cover and leave for 30 minutes. Preheat the oven to 150°C/300°F/Gas 2. Stir the pepper and garlic into the meat. Tie the herbs together and add to the meat.

2 Spread the meat mixture in a roasting pan and pour in the water. Place the bones from the pork on top and cover tightly with foil. Cook for 3½ hours.

3 Discard the bones and herbs, and ladle the meat mixture into a metal sieve set over a large bowl. Leave the liquid to drain through into the bowl, then turn the meat into a shallow dish. Repeat until all the meat is drained. Reserve the liquid. Use two forks to pull the meat apart into fine shreds.

4 Line a 1.5 litre/2½ pint/6¼ cup terrine or deep, straight-sided dish with clear film (plastic wrap) and spoon in the shredded meat. Strain the reserved liquid and pour it over the meat. Leave to cool. Cover and chill in the refrigerator for at least 24 hours, or until set.

5 To make the onion salad, place the sliced onion, spring onions and celery in a bowl. Add the freshly squeezed lemon juice and light olive oil and toss gently. Season with a little freshly ground black pepper, but do not add any salt as the rillettes is well salted.

6 Serve the rillettes, cut into thick slices, on individual plates with a little onion salad and thick slices of crusty French bread.

Energy 735kcal/3056kJ; Protein 59g; Carbohydrate 2g, of which sugars 1g; Fat 55g, of which saturates 19g; Cholesterol 209mg; Calcium 47mg; Fibre 1g; Sodium 1255mg.

Smoked Salmon Pâté

Making this pâté in individual ramekins wrapped in extra smoked salmon gives a really special presentation. Taste the mousse as you are making it as some people prefer more lemon juice.

Serves 4

350g/12oz thinly sliced
   smoked salmon
150ml/¼ pint/⅔ cup double
   (heavy) cream
finely grated rind and juice of 1 lemon
salt and ground black pepper
Melba toast, to serve

1 Line four small ramekins with clear film (plastic wrap). Then line the dishes with 115g/4oz of the smoked salmon cut into strips long enough to flop over the edges.

2 In a food processor fitted with a metal blade, process the rest of the salmon with the cream, lemon rind and juice, salt and plenty of pepper.

COOK'S TIP

The quality of smoked salmon is variable. Atlantic salmon is vastly superior to Pacific. Traditional cold smoking over wood still produces the best results.

3 Pack the lined ramekins with the smoked salmon pâté and wrap over the loose strips of salmon. Cover with clear film and chill in the refrigerator for 30 minutes. Invert on to plates and serve with Melba toast.

Energy 311kcal/1293kJ; Protein 22.9g; Carbohydrate 0.8g, of which sugars 0.8g; Fat 24.1g, of which saturates 13.2g; Cholesterol 82mg; Calcium 36mg; Fibre 0g; Sodium 1654mg.

Potted **Salmon** with **Lemon** and **Dill**

This sophisticated dish would be ideal for a brunch party. It can be prepared a couple of days in advance and stored in the refrigerator, allowing you to concentrate on cooking any dishes that you plan to serve hot.

Serves 6

350g/12oz cooked salmon
150g/5oz/²⁄₃ cup butter, softened
rind and juice of 1 large lemon
10ml/2 tsp chopped fresh dill
salt and ground white pepper
75g/3oz/³⁄₄ cup flaked (sliced)
  almonds, coarsely chopped

1 Skin the salmon and remove and discard any bones. Flake the flesh into a bowl and then place in a food processor together with two-thirds of the butter, the lemon rind and juice and half the dill. Season to taste with plenty of salt and pepper. Process until the mixture is quite smooth and thoroughly combined.

2 Mix in the flaked almonds. Check the seasoning and pack the mixture into small ramekins.

3 Sprinkle the remaining dill over the top of each ramekin. Clarify the remaining butter and pour over each ramekin to make a seal. Chill. Serve with crudités or buttered brown bread.

Energy 370kcal/1531kJ; Protein 14.8g; Carbohydrate 1.2g, of which sugars 0.9g; Fat 34.1g, of which saturates 14.7g; Cholesterol 82mg; Calcium 64mg; Fibre 1.4g; Sodium 182mg.

Grilled Vegetable Terrine

A colourful, layered terrine, this dish uses all the vegetables that are associated with the Mediterranean.

Serves 6

2 large red (bell) peppers, quartered and seeded
2 large yellow (bell) peppers, quartered and seeded
1 large aubergine (eggplant), sliced lengthways
2 large courgettes (zucchini), sliced lengthways
90ml/6 tbsp olive oil
1 large red onion, thinly sliced
75g/3oz/¹/₂ cup raisins
15ml/1 tbsp tomato purée (paste)
15ml/1 tbsp red wine vinegar
400ml/14fl oz/1²/₃ cups tomato juice
30ml/2 tbsp powdered gelatine
fresh basil leaves, to garnish

For the dressing
90ml/6 tbsp extra virgin olive oil
30ml/2 tbsp red wine vinegar
salt and ground black pepper

1 Place the peppers skin side up under a hot grill (broiler) and cook until the skins are blackened. Transfer to a bowl and cover with a plate. Leave to cool.

2 Arrange the slices of aubergine and courgette on separate baking sheets. Brush them with a little olive oil and cook under the grill, turning them occasionally, until they are tender and golden brown.

3 Heat the remaining olive oil in a frying pan and add the sliced onion, raisins, tomato purée and red wine vinegar. Cook over a low heat, stirring occasionally, until the mixture is soft and syrupy. Set aside and leave to cool in the frying pan.

4 Line a 1.75 litre/3 pint/7½ cup terrine with clear film (plastic wrap). It helps if you lightly oil the terrine first. Leave a little clear film overhanging the sides of the container.

5 Pour half the tomato juice into a pan and sprinkle with the gelatine. Leave for 5 minutes to soften, then dissolve gently over a low heat, stirring to prevent any lumps from forming.

6 Place a layer of the grilled (broiled) red peppers in the base of the terrine and pour in enough of the tomato juice with gelatine to cover it.

COOK'S TIP
If you don't own a terrine, you can use a loaf tin (pan) instead. It will still need to be lined with clear film (plastic wrap).

7 Continue layering the vegetables, pouring tomato juice over each layer, finishing with a layer of red peppers. Add the remaining tomato juice to the pan and pour into the terrine. Give it a sharp tap, to disperse the juice. Cover and chill until set.

8 To make the dressing, whisk together the oil and vinegar, then season to taste. Turn out the terrine and remove the clear film. Serve in thick slices, drizzled with dressing and garnished with basil leaves.

VARIATION
Use orange and green (bell) peppers along with or in place of the red and yellow ones. Green beans, simply boiled first, would make a tasty addition, as would a colourful layer of peas or corn.

Energy 296kcal/1229kJ; Protein 3.5g; Carbohydrate 20.2g, of which sugars 19.7g; Fat 22.9g, of which saturates 3.4g; Cholesterol 0mg; Calcium 42mg; Fibre 3.8g; Sodium 169mg.

Roast Pepper Terrine

This terrine is perfect for all kinds of entertaining because it tastes better if made ahead. Prepare the salsa on the day of serving. Serve with Italian bread.

Serves 8

8 (bell) peppers (red, yellow
    and orange)
675g/1½lb/3 cups mascarpone
3 eggs, separated
30ml/2 tbsp each coarsely chopped
    flat leaf parsley and shredded basil
2 large garlic cloves, coarsely chopped
2 red, yellow or orange (bell) peppers,
    seeded and coarsely chopped
30ml/2 tbsp extra virgin olive oil
10ml/2 tsp balsamic vinegar
a few fresh basil sprigs
salt and ground black pepper

1 Place the whole peppers under a hot grill (broiler) for 8–10 minutes, turning them frequently, until blackened and charred. Then put into a plastic bag, tie the top and leave until cold before peeling and seeding them. Slice seven of the peppers lengthways into thin strips and reserve the eighth.

2 Put the mascarpone in a bowl with the egg yolks, parsley, basil and half the garlic. Season with salt and pepper to taste. Beat well. In a separate, grease-free bowl, whisk the egg whites to a soft peak, then fold into the cheese mixture until they are evenly incorporated.

3 Preheat the oven to 180°C/350°F/Gas 4. Line the base of a lightly oiled 900g/2lb loaf tin (pan). Put one-third of the cheese mixture in the tin and spread evenly, levelling the surface. Arrange half the pepper strips on top in an even layer. Repeat until all the cheese and pepper strips have been used, ending with a layer of the mascarpone mixture.

4 Cover the tin with foil and place in a roasting pan. Pour in boiling water to come halfway up the sides of the loaf tin. Bake for 1 hour. Remove from the oven and leave the terrine to cool in the water bath, then lift out and chill overnight in the refrigerator.

5 A few hours before serving, make the salsa. Place the remaining peeled pepper and fresh peppers in a food processor. Add the remaining garlic, oil and vinegar. Set aside a few basil leaves for garnishing and add the rest to the processor. Process until finely chopped. Tip the mixture into a bowl, season with salt and pepper to taste and mix well. Cover with clear film (plastic wrap) and chill in the refrigerator until ready to serve.

6 Turn out the terrine on to a chopping board, peel off the lining paper and slice thickly. Garnish with the reserved basil leaves and serve cold, with the sweet pepper salsa.

Energy 581kcal/2425kJ; Protein 21.9g; Carbohydrate 78.1g, of which sugars 74.6g; Fat 21.8g, of which saturates 9.8g; Cholesterol 107mg; Calcium 105mg; Fibre 18.9g; Sodium 74mg.

Asparagus and **Egg Terrine**

For a special occasion, this terrine is a delicious choice yet it is very light. Make the hollandaise sauce well in advance and warm through gently when required.

Serves 8

150ml/¼ pint/⅔ cup milk
150ml/¼ pint/⅔ cup double
  (heavy) cream
40g/1½oz/3 tbsp butter
40g/1½oz/3 tbsp plain
  (all-purpose) flour
75g/3oz herbed or garlic cream cheese
675g/1½ lb asparagus spears, cooked
vegetable oil, for brushing
2 eggs, separated
15ml/1 tbsp chopped fresh chives
30ml/2 tbsp chopped fresh dill
salt and ground black pepper
fresh dill sprigs, to garnish

For the orange hollandaise sauce
15ml/1 tbsp white wine vinegar
15ml/1 tbsp fresh orange juice
4 black peppercorns
1 bay leaf
2 egg yolks
115g/4oz/½ cup butter, melted and
  cooled slightly

1 Put the milk and cream into a small pan and heat to just below boiling point. Melt the butter in a medium pan, stir in the flour and cook over a low heat, stirring constantly, to a thick paste. Gradually stir in the milk, whisking as it thickens. Stir in the cream cheese, season to taste with salt and ground black pepper and leave to cool slightly.

2 Trim the asparagus to fit the width of a 1.2 litre/2 pint/5 cup loaf tin (pan) or terrine. Lightly oil the tin and then base line with baking parchment. Preheat the oven to 180°C/350°F/ Gas 4.

3 Beat the egg yolks into the sauce mixture. Whisk the whites until stiff and fold in with the chives, dill and seasoning. Layer the asparagus and egg mixture in the tin, starting and finishing with asparagus. Cover the top with foil.

4 Place the terrine in a roasting pan and half fill with hot water. Cook for 45–55 minutes, until firm.

5 When the terrine is just firm to the touch, remove from the oven and leave to cool, then chill.

6 To make the sauce, put the vinegar, orange juice, peppercorns and bay leaf in a small pan and heat gently until reduced by half.

7 Cool the sauce slightly, then whisk in the egg yolks, then the butter, with a balloon whisk over a very gentle heat. Season to taste with salt and pepper and continue whisking until thick. Keep the sauce warm over a pan of hot water.

8 Invert the terrine on to a serving dish, remove the paper and garnish with the dill. Cut into slices and pour over the warmed sauce.

Energy 359kcal/1483kJ; Protein 6.6g; Carbohydrate 7.1g, of which sugars 3.2g; Fat 34.1g, of which saturates 20.2g; Cholesterol 175mg; Calcium 87mg; Fibre 1.6g; Sodium 179mg.

Striped Fish Terrine

Serve this terrine cold or just warm, with a hollandaise sauce if you like.

Serves 8

15ml/1 tbsp sunflower oil
450g/1lb salmon fillet
450g/1lb sole fillets
3 egg whites
105ml/7 tbsp double (heavy) cream
15ml/1 tbsp finely chopped
  fresh chives
2.5ml/¹/₂ tsp grated nutmeg
juice of 1 lemon
115g/4oz/1 cup peas, cooked
5ml/1 tsp chopped fresh mint
salt and ground white pepper
thinly sliced cucumber, salad cress and
  whole fresh chives, to garnish

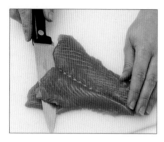

1 Grease a 1 litre/1¾ pint/4 cup loaf tin (pan) or terrine with the oil. Skin the salmon and sole fillets. Using a sharp knife, slice the salmon thinly; then cut it and the sole into long strips, 2.5cm/1in wide. Preheat the oven to 200°C/400°F/Gas 6.

2 Line the terrine neatly with alternate strips of salmon and sole, leaving the ends overhanging the edge. You should be left with about a third of the salmon and half the sole. Set aside until required.

COOK'S TIP
You can use fresh or frozen peas, but both must be cooked first.

3 In a clean grease-free bowl, whisk the egg whites with a pinch of salt until they form soft peaks. Place the reserved sole strips in a food processor and process until smooth. Spoon into a bowl, season with salt and ground white pepper, then fold in two-thirds of the egg whites, followed by two-thirds of the cream. Put half the mixture into a second bowl; stir in the chives. Add nutmeg to the first bowl.

4 Place the reserved salmon strips in the food processor and process until smooth. Scrape the purée into a bowl and add the lemon juice and seasoning. Fold in the remaining whisked egg whites, then the remaining cream.

5 Place the cooked peas and the mint in the food processor and process until smooth. Season the mixture to taste with salt and pepper and spread it over the base of the loaf tin or terrine, smoothing the surface with a spatula. Spoon over the sole with chives mixture and spread that layer evenly with a spatula.

6 Add the salmon mixture, then finish with the sole and nutmeg mixture, spreading them both evenly. Cover with the overhanging fish fillets and make a lid of oiled foil. Stand the loaf tin or terrine in a roasting pan and pour in enough boiling water to come halfway up the sides of the terrine.

7 Bake for 15–20 minutes, until the top fillets are just cooked and the mousse feels springy. Remove the foil, lay a wire rack over the top of the loaf tin or terrine and invert both rack and terrine on to a lipped baking sheet to catch the cooking juices that drain out. Keep these to make fish stock or soup.

8 Leaving the container in place, let the terrine stand for about 15 minutes, then turn it over again, invert it on to a serving dish and lift off the tin or terrine carefully. Serve warm, or chill in the refrigerator first and serve cold. Garnish with thinly sliced cucumber, salad cress and chives before serving.

VARIATION
While Dover sole has an incomparable flavour, you could also use the slightly less expensive lemon sole or, even more economically, substitute brill. Also known in some places as Torbay sole, this much underrated fish has an exquisite flavour.

Energy 248kcal/1030kJ; Protein 24g; Carbohydrate 2.2g, of which sugars 0.6g; Fat 15.9g, of which saturates 5.7g; Cholesterol 74mg; Calcium 51mg; Fibre 0.7g; Sodium 108mg.

Chicken and **Pork Terrine**

This elegant terrine is flecked with
parsley and green peppercorns,
which give it a lovely subtle flavour.

Serves 6–8

*225g/8oz rindless, streaky
   (fatty) bacon*
*375g/13oz skinless, boneless chicken
   breast portions*
15ml/1 tbsp lemon juice
225g/8oz lean minced (ground) pork
½ small onion, finely chopped
2 eggs, beaten
30ml/2 tbsp chopped fresh parsley
5ml/1 tsp salt
5ml/1 tsp green peppercorns, crushed
vegetable oil, for greasing
*salad leaves, radishes and lemon
   wedges, to serve*

1 Preheat the oven to 160°C/325°F/
Gas 3. Put the bacon on a board and
stretch it using the back of a knife
before arranging it in overlapping
slices over the base and sides of a
900g/2lb loaf tin (pan).

2 Cut 115g/4oz of the chicken into
strips about 10cm/4in long. Sprinkle
with lemon juice and set aside. Put the
rest of the chicken in a food processor
or blender with the minced pork and
the onion. Process until fairly smooth.

3 Add the eggs, parsley, salt and
peppercorns to the meat mixture
and process again briefly. Spoon half
the mixture into the loaf tin and then
level the surface.

4 Arrange the reserved chicken strips
on top, then spoon in the remaining
meat mixture and smooth the top.
Give the tin a couple of sharp taps on
the work surface to knock out any
pockets of air.

5 Cover the loaf tin with a piece of
oiled foil and put it in a roasting pan.
Pour in enough hot water to come
halfway up the sides of the loaf tin.
Bake for about 45–50 minutes, until
the terrine is firm.

6 Leave the terrine to cool in the tin
before turning out on to a plate and
chilling in the refrigerator.

7 Serve the terrine in slices, with salad
leaves, radishes and wedges of lemon
for squeezing.

COOK'S TIP

For a slightly sharper flavour, substitute
chopped fresh coriander (cilantro) for the
parsley. It goes particularly well with
the flavour of lemon.

Energy 191kcal/798kJ; Protein 22g; Carbohydrate 0.6g, of which sugars 0.4g; Fat 11.3g, of which saturates 3.8g; Cholesterol 115mg; Calcium 15mg; Fibre 0.1g; Sodium 417mg.

Turkey, Juniper and Peppercorn Terrine

This can be made several days in advance. If you prefer, arrange some of the pancetta and pistachio nuts as a layer in the middle of the terrine.

Serves 10–12

225g/8oz chicken livers, trimmed
450g/1lb minced (ground) turkey
450g/1lb minced (ground) pork
225g/8oz pancetta, cubed
50g/2oz/^{1}/2 cup shelled pistachio nuts, coarsely chopped
5ml/1 tsp salt
2.5ml/^{1}/2 tsp ground mace
2 garlic cloves, crushed
5ml/1 tsp drained green peppercorns in brine
5ml/1 tsp juniper berries
120ml/4fl oz/^{1}/2 cup dry white wine
30ml/2 tbsp gin
finely grated rind of 1 orange
8 large vine (grape) leaves in brine
vegetable oil, for greasing
pickle or chutney, to serve

1 Chop the chicken livers finely. Put them in a bowl and add the turkey, pork, pancetta, pistachio nuts, salt, mace and garlic. Mix well.

2 Lightly crush the peppercorns and juniper berries in a mortar with a pestle or with the end of a rolling pin and add them to the mixture. Stir in the wine, gin and orange rind. Cover with clear film (plastic wrap) and chill overnight to allow the flavours to mingle.

3 Preheat the oven to 160°C/325°F/Gas 3. Rinse the vine leaves under cold running water. Drain them thoroughly and pat dry. Lightly oil a 1.2 litre/2 pint/5 cup pâté terrine or loaf tin (pan). Line the terrine or tin with the vine leaves, letting the ends overhang the sides. Pack the meat mixture into the terrine or tin and fold the overhanging leaves over to enclose the filling completely. Brush the top lightly with a little oil.

4 Cover the terrine with its lid or the loaf tin with foil. Place it in a roasting pan and pour in boiling water to come halfway up the sides of the terrine. Bake for 1¾ hours, checking the level of the water occasionally, so that the roasting pan does not dry out.

5 Leave the terrine to cool, then pour off the surface juices. Cover with clear film (plastic wrap), then foil and place weights on top. Chill in the refrigerator overnight. Serve at room temperature with a pickle or chutney, such as spiced kumquats or red bell pepper and chilli jelly.

COOK'S TIP
A pâté terrine is usually made of cast iron, which is ideal for even cooking. Its traditional long shape makes it easier to cut the terrine into neat slices.

Energy 240kcal/1003kJ; Protein 25.3g; Carbohydrate 1.7g, of which sugars 1.5g; Fat 13.4g, of which saturates 4.1g; Cholesterol 153mg; Calcium 29mg; Fibre 0.8g; Sodium 316mg.

Hot Crab Soufflés

These delicious little soufflés must be served as soon as they are ready, so seat your guests at the table before taking the soufflés out of the oven.

Serves 6

50g/2oz/¼ cup butter
45ml/3 tbsp fine wholemeal
    (whole-wheat) breadcrumbs
4 spring onions (scallions),
    finely chopped
15ml/1 tbsp Malayan or mild Madras
    curry powder
25g/1oz/2 tbsp plain
    (all-purpose) flour
105ml/7 tbsp coconut milk or milk
150ml/¼ pint/⅔ cup whipping cream
4 egg yolks
225g/8oz white crab meat
mild green Tabasco sauce
6 egg whites
salt and ground black pepper

1 Use some of the butter to grease six ramekins or a 1.75 litre/3 pint/7½ cup soufflé dish. Sprinkle the breadcrumbs in the dishes or dish and roll them around to coat the base and sides completely, then tip out the excess breadcrumbs. Preheat the oven to 200°C/400°F/Gas 6.

2 Melt the remaining butter in a pan, add the spring onions and Malayan or mild Madras curry powder and cook over a low heat, stirring frequently, for about 1 minute, until softened. Stir in the flour and cook, stirring constantly, for 1 minute more.

3 Gradually add the coconut milk or milk and the cream, stirring constantly. Cook over a low heat, still stirring, until smooth and thick. Remove the pan from the heat, stir in the egg yolks, then the crab. Season to taste with salt, black pepper and Tabasco sauce.

4 In a clean grease-free bowl, whisk the egg whites with a pinch of salt until they are stiff. Using a metal spoon, stir one-third of the whites into the crab mixture to slacken, then fold in the remainder. Spoon into the dishes or dish.

5 Bake the soufflés until well risen, golden brown and just firm to the touch. Individual soufflés will take about 8 minutes, while a large, single soufflé will take 15–20 minutes. Serve immediately.

Twice-baked Gruyère and **Potato Soufflé**

This recipe can be prepared in advance and given its second baking just before you serve it up.

Serves 4

225g/8oz floury (mealy) potatoes
2 eggs, separated
175g/6oz/1½ cups grated
   Gruyère cheese
50g/2oz/½ cup self-raising
   (self-rising) flour
50g/2oz spinach leaves
butter, for greasing
salt and ground black pepper

1 Preheat the oven to 200°C/400°F/ Gas 6. Peel the potatoes and cook in lightly salted, boiling water for 20 minutes, until very tender. Drain well and mash with the egg yolks, using a potato masher or a fork.

2 Stir in half of the Gruyère cheese and all of the flour. Season to taste with salt and ground black pepper.

COOK'S TIP
Never attempt to mash potatoes with an electric mixer. It breaks down the starch and turns the potatoes into a sticky mess with the texture of wallpaper paste. Use a potato masher or fork to pound them by hand or a potato ricer which will produce an even, lump-free, fine mash.

3 Finely chop the spinach and fold into the potato mixture.

VARIATION
Try replacing the Gruyère with a crumbled blue cheese, such as Stilton or Shropshire Blue, which have a stronger flavour.

4 Whisk the egg whites in a clean. grease-free bowl until they form soft peaks. Fold a little of the egg white into the mixture to slacken it slightly, then, using a large spoon, fold the remaining egg white into the mixture.

5 Grease four large ramekins. Pour the mixture into the dishes and place on a baking sheet. Bake for 20 minutes. Remove the dishes from the oven and leave to cool.

6 Turn the soufflés out on to a baking sheet and sprinkle with the remaining cheese. Bake again for 5 minutes and serve immediately.

Energy 304kcal/1270kJ; Protein 16.7g; Carbohydrate 19g, of which sugars 1.2g; Fat 17.5g, of which saturates 10.4g; Cholesterol 138mg; Calcium 380mg; Fibre 1.2g; Sodium 376mg.

Leek Roulade with Cheese, Walnut and Sweet Pepper Filling

This roulade is easy to prepare and is ideal for brunch or a vegetarian main course, served with home-made tomato sauce.

Serves 6

butter or oil, for greasing
30ml/2 tbsp dry white breadcrumbs
75g/3oz/1 cup grated Parmesan cheese
50g/2oz/¼ cup butter
2 leeks, thinly sliced
40g/1½oz/⅓ cup plain
 (all-purpose) flour
250ml/8fl oz/1 cup milk
5ml/1 tsp Dijon mustard
1.5ml/¼ tsp freshly grated nutmeg
2 large (US extra large) eggs,
 separated, plus 1 egg white
2.5ml/½ tsp cream of tartar
salt and ground black pepper
rocket (arugula) and balsamic dressing,
 to serve

For the filling

2 large red (bell) peppers
350g/12oz/1½ cups ricotta cheese or
 soft goat's cheese
90g/3½oz/scant 1 cup chopped walnuts
4 spring onions (scallions), chopped
15g/½oz/½ cup fresh basil leaves

1 Grease and line a 30 × 23cm/ 12 × 9in Swiss roll tin (jelly roll pan) with baking parchment, then sprinkle with the breadcrumbs and 30ml/2 tbsp of the grated Parmesan. Preheat the oven to 190°C/375°F/Gas 5.

2 Melt the butter in a pan and cook the leeks for 5 minutes, until softened.

3 Stir in the flour and cook over a low heat, stirring constantly, for 2 minutes, then gradually stir in the milk. Cook for 3–4 minutes, stirring constantly to make a thick sauce.

4 Stir in the mustard and nutmeg and season with salt and plenty of pepper. Reserve 30–45ml/2–3 tbsp of the remaining Parmesan, then stir the rest into the sauce. Cool slightly.

5 Beat the egg yolks into the sauce. In a clean, grease-free bowl, whisk the egg whites and cream of tartar until stiff. Stir 2–3 spoonfuls of the whites into the leek mixture, then carefully fold in the remaining egg whites.

6 Pour the mixture into the tin and gently level it out using a spatula. Bake for 15–18 minutes, until risen and just firm to a light touch in the centre. If the roulade is to be served hot, increase the oven temperature to 200°C/400°F/ Gas 6 after removing the roulade.

7 Preheat the grill (broiler). Halve and seed the peppers, grill (broil) them, skin sides up, until black. Place in a bowl, cover and leave for 10 minutes. Peel and cut the flesh into strips. Mix the cheese, nuts and spring onions. Chop half the basil and stir into the mixture.

8 Sprinkle the remaining Parmesan on to a large sheet of baking parchment. Turn out the roulade on to it. Strip off the lining paper and allow the roulade to cool. Spread the cheese mixture over it and top with the red pepper strips. Sprinkle the remaining basil leaves over the top. Roll up the roulade and place on a platter. If serving hot, roll it on to a baking sheet, cover with a tent of foil and bake for 15–20 minutes. Serve with rocket and drizzle with dressing.

Energy 203kcal/845kJ; Protein 10g; Carbohydrate 11g, of which sugars 2g; Fat 14g, of which saturates 8g; Cholesterol 115mg; Calcium 177mg; Fibre 2g; Sodium 243mg.

Smoked **Fish** and **Asparagus Mousse**

This elegant mousse looks good with its studding of asparagus and smoked salmon. Serve a mustard and dill dressing separately if you like.

Serves 8

15ml/1 tbsp powdered gelatine
juice of 1 lemon
105ml/7 tbsp fish stock
50g/2oz/¼ cup butter, plus extra
*   for greasing*
2 shallots, finely chopped
225g/8oz smoked trout fillets
105ml/7 tbsp sour cream
225g/8oz/1 cup soft white
*   (farmer's) cheese*
1 egg white
12 spinach leaves, blanched
12 fresh asparagus spears,
*   lightly cooked*
115g/4oz smoked salmon, cut in strips
salt
shredded beetroot (beet) and beetroot
*   leaves, to garnish*

1 Sprinkle the gelatine over the lemon juice and leave until spongy. In a small pan, heat the fish stock, then add the soaked gelatine and stir to dissolve completely. Set aside. Melt the butter in a pan, add the shallots and cook gently until softened but not coloured.

2 Break up the smoked trout fillets and put them in a food processor with the shallots, sour cream, stock mixture and cheese. Process until smooth, then spoon into a bowl.

3 In a clean bowl, beat the egg white with a pinch of salt to soft peaks. Fold into the fish. Cover the bowl; chill for 30 minutes, or until starting to set.

4 Grease a 1 litre/1¾ pint/4 cup loaf tin (pan) or terrine with butter, then line it with the spinach leaves. Carefully spread half the trout mousse over the spinach-covered base, arrange the asparagus spears on top, then cover with the remaining trout mousse.

5 Arrange the smoked salmon strips lengthways on the mousse and fold over the overhanging spinach leaves. Cover with clear film (plastic wrap) and chill for 4 hours, until set. To serve, remove the clear film, turn out on to a serving dish and garnish with the shredded beetroot and leaves.

COOK'S TIP
Use a serrated knife with a fine-toothed blade to cut the mousse into neat slices.

Energy 174kcal/723kJ; Protein 15.8g; Carbohydrate 2.8g, of which sugars 2.6g; Fat 11g, of which saturates 6g; Cholesterol 58mg; Calcium 75mg; Fibre 0.8g; Sodium 432mg.

Risotto alla Milanese

This classic risotto is often served with the hearty veal stew, osso bucco, but it also makes a delicious light meal in its own right.

Serves 5–6

about 1.2 litres/2 pints/5 cups beef or
    chicken stock
good pinch of saffron threads
75g/3oz/6 tbsp butter
1 onion, finely chopped
275g/10oz/1½ cups risotto rice
75g/3oz/1 cup freshly grated
    Parmesan cheese
salt and ground black pepper

1 Bring the stock to the boil in a large pan, then reduce to a low simmer. Ladle a little hot stock into a small bowl. Add the saffron threads and set aside to infuse (steep).

2 Melt 50g/2oz/4 tbsp of the butter in a large, heavy pan until foaming. Add the onion and cook over a low heat, stirring occasionally, for about 3 minutes, until softened and translucent but not browned.

3 Add the rice. Stir until the grains are coated with butter and starting to swell and burst, then add a few ladlefuls of the hot stock, with the saffron liquid and salt and pepper to taste. Stir constantly over a low heat until all the stock has been absorbed. Add the remaining stock, a few ladlefuls at a time, allowing the rice to absorb all the liquid before adding more, and stirring constantly. After about 20–25 minutes, the rice should be just tender and the risotto golden yellow, moist and creamy.

4 Gently stir in about two-thirds of the grated Parmesan and the remaining butter. Heat through gently until the butter has melted, then taste and adjust the seasoning, if necessary. Transfer the risotto to a warmed serving bowl or platter and serve hot, with the remaining grated Parmesan served separately.

COOK'S TIP

Italians always cook with unsalted (sweet) butter.

Energy 397kcal/1650kJ; Protein 10.6g; Carbohydrate 46.8g, of which sugars 0.8g; Fat 18.3g, of which saturates 11.3g; Cholesterol 49mg; Calcium 204mg; Fibre 0.2g; Sodium 265mg.

Risotto with Four Cheeses

This is a very rich dish. Serve it with a light, dry sparkling white wine.

Serves 4–6

40g/1¹/₂oz/3 tbsp butter
1 small onion, finely chopped
1.2 litres/2 pints/5 cups chicken stock
350g/12oz/1³/₄ cups risotto rice
200ml/7fl oz/scant 1 cup dry
*   white wine*
50g/2oz/¹/₂ cup grated Gruyère cheese
50g/2oz/¹/₂ cup diced taleggio cheese
50g/2oz/¹/₂ cup diced
*   Gorgonzola cheese*
50g/2oz/²/₃ cup freshly grated
*   Parmesan cheese*
salt and ground black pepper
chopped fresh flat leaf parsley,
*   to garnish*

1 Melt the butter in a large, heavy pan or deep frying pan. Add the onion and cook over a low heat, stirring occasionally, for about 4–5 minutes, until softened and lightly browned. Meanwhile, pour the stock into a separate pan, bring to the boil, then lower the heat to a simmer.

2 Add the rice to the pan with the onion, stir until the grains are coated with butter and starting to swell and burst, then add the wine. Stir until it stops sizzling and most of it has been absorbed by the rice.

3 Pour in a little of the hot stock. Season with salt and ground black pepper to taste. Stir the rice over a low heat until all the stock has been absorbed.

4 Gradually add the remaining stock, a little at a time, allowing the rice to absorb the liquid before adding more, and stirring constantly. After about 20–25 minutes, the rice will be tender and the risotto will be creamy.

5 Turn off the heat under the pan, then add the Gruyère, taleggio, Gorgonzola and 30ml/2 tbsp of the Parmesan. Stir gently until the cheeses have melted, then taste and adjust the seasoning, if necessary. Spoon the risotto into a warm serving bowl and garnish with parsley. Serve the remaining Parmesan separately.

Energy 420kcal/1749kJ; Protein 13.7g; Carbohydrate 47.6g, of which sugars 0.8g; Fat 16.4g, of which saturates 10.4g; Cholesterol 45mg; Calcium 282mg; Fibre 0.1g; Sodium 355mg.

Pancakes with Leek, Chicory and Squash Stuffing

Serve a chunky tomato sauce with these melt-in-the-mouth pancakes.

Serves 8

225g/8oz/2 cups plain
  (all-purpose) flour
115g/4oz/1 cup yellow corn meal
5ml/1 tsp salt
5ml/1 tsp chilli powder
4 large (US extra large) eggs
900ml/1½ pint/3¾ cups milk
50g/2oz/4 tbsp butter, melted
vegetable oil, for greasing

For the filling
60ml/4 tbsp olive oil
900g/2lb butternut squash (peeled
  weight), seeded and diced
large pinch of dried red chilli flakes
4 large leeks, thickly sliced
5ml/1 tsp chopped fresh thyme
6 chicory (Belgian endive) heads, sliced
225g/8oz goat's cheese, cut into cubes
200g/7oz/1¾ cups walnuts, chopped
60ml/4 tbsp chopped fresh
  flat leaf parsley
50g/2oz/⅔ cup grated Parmesan cheese
90ml/6 tbsp melted butter or olive oil
salt and ground black pepper

1 Sift the flour, corn meal, salt and chilli powder into a bowl and make a well in the centre. Add the eggs and a little milk. Whisk together, gradually adding the remaining milk.

2 When ready to cook the pancakes, whisk the melted butter into the batter. Heat a lightly greased or oiled 18cm/7in heavy frying pan or crêpe pan. Pour about 60ml/4 tbsp batter into the pan and cook over a medium heat for 2–3 minutes, until set and lightly browned underneath. Turn and cook the pancake on the second side for 2–3 minutes. Lightly grease the pan after every second pancake.

3 To make the filling, heat the oil in a large frying pan. Add the squash and cook, stirring frequently, for about 10 minutes, until almost tender. Add the chilli flakes and cook, stirring, for 1–2 minutes. Stir in the leeks and thyme and cook for 4–5 minutes.

4 Add the chicory and cook, stirring frequently, for 4–5 minutes, until the leeks are cooked and the chicory is hot, but still has some bite. Cool slightly, then stir in the cheese, walnuts and parsley. Season to taste.

5 Preheat the oven to 200°C/400°F/Gas 6. Lightly grease an ovenproof dish. Spoon 30–45ml/2–3 tbsp filling on to each pancake. Roll or fold each pancake to enclose the filling, then place in the prepared dish.

6 Sprinkle the Parmesan over the pancakes and drizzle the melted butter or olive oil over. Bake for 10–15 minutes, until the cheese is bubbling. Serve hot.

Energy 800kcal/3327kJ; Protein 25g; Carbohydrate 53g, of which sugars 14g; Fat 56g, of which saturates 21g; Cholesterol 194mg; Calcium 476mg; Fibre 5g; Sodium 909mg.

Indian Mee Goreng

This colourful noodle dish is truly
international, combining Indian,
Chinese and Western ingredients.
In Singapore and Malaysia, it can
be bought from many street stalls.

Serves 6

450g/1lb fresh yellow egg noodles
115g/4oz fried or plain tofu
60–90ml/4–6 tbsp vegetable oil
2 eggs
30ml/2tbsp water
1 onion sliced
1 garlic clove, crushed
15ml/1 tbsp light soy sauce
30–45ml/2–3 tbsp tomato ketchup
15ml/1 tbsp chilli sauce (or to taste)
1 large cooked potato, diced
4 spring onions (scallions), shredded
1–2 fresh green chillies, seeded and
*   thinly sliced (optional)*

1 Bring a large pan of water to the
boil, add the fresh egg noodles and
cook for just 2 minutes. Drain the
noodles and immediately rinse them
under cold water to stop any further
cooking. Drain again and set aside.

COOK'S TIP

Nowadays, many supermarkets provide a
guide to the heat of the chillies on sale.
This is helpful, but not always completely
reliable, as even different pods from the
same plant may vary. As a general rule,
dark green chillies tend to be hotter than
pale green ones and pointed, thin chillies
hotter than larger, blunt ones.

2 If using fried tofu, cut each cube in
half, refresh it in a pan of boiling
water, then drain well Heat 30ml/
2 tbsp of the oil in a large frying pan.
If using using plain tofu, cut into
cubes, add to the pan and cook until
brown, then lift it out with a slotted
spoon and set aside.

3 Beat the eggs with the water. Add to
the the frying pan and cook without
stirring until just set. Flip over, cook the
other side briefly, then slide it out of
the pan, roll up and slice thinly into
narrow strips.

4 Heat the remaining oil in a wok. Add
the onion and garlic and stir-fry for
2–3 minutes. Add the drained noodles,
soy sauce, tomato ketchup and chilli
sauce. Toss well over medium heat for
2 minutes, then add the diced potato.
Reserve half the spring onions for the
garnish and stir the remainder into
the noodles with the chilli, if using,
and the tofu.

5 When hot, stir in the omelette strips.
Transfer to a hot platter and serve
immediately, garnished with the
remaining spring onions.

Energy 478kcal/2010kJ; Protein 16.8g; Carbohydrate 64.2g, of which sugars 5.1g; Fat 18.9g, of which saturates 3.2g; Cholesterol 86mg; Calcium 323mg; Fibre 2.9g; Sodium 466mg.

Black Pasta with Ricotta

This is designer pasta – which is coloured with squid or cuttlefish ink – at its most dramatic, the kind of dish you are most likely to see at a fashionable Italian restaurant. Serve it for a smart party supper – it will create a great talking point.

Serves 4

300g/11oz dried black pasta
60ml/4 tbsp ricotta cheese
60ml/4 tbsp extra virgin
* olive oil*
1 small fresh red chilli, seeded and
* finely chopped*
small handful of fresh basil leaves
salt and ground black pepper

1 Cook the pasta in a large pan of lightly salted, boiling water for about 8–10 minutes, until tender but still firm to the bite.

2 Meanwhile, put the ricotta in a bowl, season with salt and pepper to taste and use a little of the hot water from the pasta pan to mix it to a smooth, creamy consistency.

3 Drain the pasta. Heat the olive oil gently in a clean pan and add the pasta with the chilli and salt and pepper to taste. Toss quickly over a high heat to combine.

4 Divide the pasta equally among four warmed bowls, then top with the ricotta cheese. Sprinkle with the basil leaves and serve immediately. Each diner tosses their own portion of pasta and cheese.

VARIATION
If you prefer, use green spinach-flavoured pasta or red tomato-flavoured pasta in place of the black pasta. Alternatively, for an equally dramatic contrast, try magenta pasta, flavoured with beetroot (beet) or golden brown wild-mushroom pasta.

Paglia e Fieno with Walnuts and Gorgonzola

Cheese and nuts are popular ingredients for pasta sauces. The combination is very rich. The contrasting colours make this dish look particularly attractive. It needs no accompaniment other than wine – a dry white would be good.

Serves 4

25g/1oz/2 tbsp butter
5ml/1 tsp finely chopped fresh sage, or
* 2.5ml/1/2 tsp dried, plus fresh sage*
* leaves, to garnish (optional)*
115g/4oz/1 cup diced
* Gorgonzola cheese*
45ml/3 tbsp mascarpone
75ml/5 tbsp milk
275g/10oz dried paglia e fieno
50g/2oz/1/2 cup walnut halves, ground
30ml/2 tbsp freshly grated
* Parmesan cheese*
ground black pepper

1 Melt the butter in a large, heavy pan over a low heat, add the sage and stir it around. Sprinkle in the diced Gorgonzola and then add the mascarpone. Stir the ingredients with a wooden spoon until the cheeses are starting to melt. Pour in the milk and keep stirring.

2 Meanwhile, cook the pasta in a large pan of lightly salted, boiling water for about 8–10 minutes, until tender but still firm to the bite.

3 Sprinkle the walnuts and grated Parmesan into the cheese mixture and add plenty of black pepper. Continue to stir over a low heat until the mixture forms a creamy sauce. Do not let it boil or the nuts will taste bitter, and do not cook the sauce for longer than a few minutes or the nuts will begin to discolour it.

4 Drain the pasta, tip it into a warmed bowl, then add the sauce and toss well. Serve immediately, with more black pepper ground on top. Garnish with sage leaves, if using.

COOK'S TIP
To cook pasta to perfection, bring the pan of water back to the boil after adding it and time the cooking from that moment. Pasta needs to boil, not simmer, so do not turn the heat right down. Test the pasta for readiness by biting a small piece.

Pasta: Energy 387kcal/1631kJ; Protein 10.8g; Carbohydrate 56.5g, of which sugars 3.3g; Fat 14.7g, of which saturates 3.1g; Cholesterol 6mg; Calcium 49mg; Fibre 2.9g; Sodium 7mg.
Paglia: Energy 529kcal/2216kJ; Protein 20.7g; Carbohydrate 52.6g, of which sugars 3.9g; Fat 27.7g, of which saturates 12.4g; Cholesterol 48mg; Calcium 283mg; Fibre 2.4g; Sodium 481mg.

sensational soups

Sharing a large dish with a few accompaniments or dipping into a classic one-pot meal is a sure way of having a memorable no-fuss meal with friends.

Vichyssoise with **Watercress Cream**

Classic soups, such as this cold French version of leek and potato soup, will always remain firm favourites for dinner parties.

Serves 6

50g/2oz/¼ cup butter
1 onion, sliced
450g/1lb leeks, sliced
225g/8oz potatoes, sliced
750ml/1¼ pints/3 cups chicken stock
300ml/½ pint/1¼ cups milk
45ml/3 tbsp single (light) cream
salt and ground black pepper
fresh chervil, to garnish

For the watercress cream
1 bunch watercress, about 75g/3oz,
  stalks removed
small bunch of fresh chervil,
  finely chopped
150ml/¼ pint/⅔ cup double
  (heavy) cream
pinch of freshly grated nutmeg

1 Melt the butter in a pan. Add the onion and leeks, cover and cook gently for 10 minutes, stirring occasionally, until softened. Stir in the potatoes and stock, and bring to the boil. Reduce the heat and simmer for 20 minutes, or until the potatoes are tender. Cool slightly.

2 Process the soup in a food processor or blender until smooth, then press through a sieve into a clean pan.

3 Stir in the milk and single cream. Season the soup well and chill for at least 2 hours.

4 To make the watercress cream, process the watercress in a food processor or blender until finely chopped, then stir in the chervil and cream. Pour into a bowl and stir in the nutmeg with seasoning to taste.

5 Ladle the vichyssoise into bowls and spoon the watercress cream on top. Garnish with chervil and serve.

COOK'S TIP
The soup is also delicious served hot in winter, especially sprinkled with a little grated nutmeg.

Energy 362kcal/1494kJ; Protein 3g; Carbohydrate 11.1g, of which sugars 4g; Fat 34.2g, of which saturates 21.2g; Cholesterol 86mg; Calcium 51mg; Fibre 2.3g; Sodium 68mg.

Iced Melon Soup with Melon and Mint Sorbet

You can use different melons for the cool soup and ice sorbet to create a subtle contrast in flavour and colour. Try a combination of Charentais and Ogen or cantaloupe and piel de sapo. This soup is refreshing and ideal for formal and informal summer dinner parties, and *al fresco* dining.

Serves 6–8

2.25kg/5lb very ripe melon
45ml/3 tbsp orange juice
30ml/2 tbsp lemon juice
fresh mint leaves, to garnish

For the melon and mint
sorbet (sherbet)
25g/1oz/2 tbsp sugar
120ml/4fl oz/½ cup water
2.25kg/5lb very ripe melon
juice of 2 limes
30ml/2 tbsp chopped fresh mint

1 To make the melon and mint sorbet, put the sugar and water into a pan and heat gently until the sugar dissolves. Bring to the boil and simmer for 4–5 minutes, then leave to cool.

2 Halve the melon. Scrape out the seeds, then cut it into large wedges and cut the flesh out of the skin. It should weigh about 1.6kg/3½lb.

3 Process the melon flesh in a food processor or blender with the cooled syrup and lime juice.

4 If you are using an ice cream maker: stir in the mint and pour in the melon mixture. Churn, following the maker's instructions, or until the sorbet is smooth and firm. By hand: stir in the mint and pour the mixture into a freezerproof container. Freeze until icy at the edges. Transfer to a food processor and process until smooth. Repeat this process until the mixture is smooth and holding its shape, then freeze until firm.

5 To make the chilled melon soup, prepare the melon as in step 2 and process until smooth in a food processor or blender. Pour the purée into a bowl and stir in the orange and lemon juice. Place the soup in the refrigerator for 30–40 minutes, but do not chill it for too long as this will dull its flavour.

6 Ladle the soup into bowls and add a large scoop of the melon and mint sorbet to each. Garnish with mint leaves and serve immediately.

COOK'S TIP
The soup also looks impressive served in large wine glasses, with small balls of sorbet (sherbet) instead of large scoops. Keep the glasses cool by standing them in bowls filled with ice cubes.

Energy 106kcal/449kJ; Protein 2g; Carbohydrate 24g, of which sugars 24g; Fat 1g, of which saturates 0g; Cholesterol 0mg; Calcium 43mg; Fibre 3g; Sodium 91mg.

Chilled Asparagus Soup

This soup provides a delightful way to enjoy a favourite seasonal vegetable. Choose bright, crisp-looking asparagus with firm stalks.

Serves 6

900g/2lb fresh asparagus
60ml/4 tbsp butter or olive oil
175g/6oz/1½ cups sliced leeks or
  spring onions (scallions)
45ml/3 tbsp plain (all-purpose) flour
1.5 litres/2½ pints/6¼ cups chicken
  stock or water
120ml/4fl oz/½ cup single (light)
  cream or plain (natural) yogurt
salt and ground black pepper
15ml/1 tbsp minced (ground) fresh
  tarragon or chervil

3 Heat the butter or olive oil in a heavy pan. Add the leeks or spring onions and cook over a low heat, stirring occasionally, for 5–8 minutes, until softened and translucent.

4 Stir in the chopped asparagus stalks, cover and cook gently for a further 6–8 minutes.

5 Add the flour and stir well to blend. Cook for 3–4 minutes, uncovered, stirring constantly.

6 Gradually stir in the chicken stock or water and bring to the boil, stirring frequently, then reduce the heat and simmer for 30 minutes. Season to taste with salt and pepper.

7 Process the soup in a food processor or blender. If necessary, strain it through a fine sieve to remove any coarse fibres. Stir in the asparagus tips, most of the cream or yogurt, and the herbs. Cool, then chill well. Stir thoroughly before serving and check the seasoning. Garnish with the remaining cream or yogurt.

1 Cut the top 6cm/2½in off the asparagus spears. Blanch these tips in a small pan of boiling water for about 5–6 minutes, until they are just tender. Drain well. Cut each tip into two or three pieces, and set aside.

2 Trim the ends of the stalks, removing any brown or woody parts. Chop the asparagus stalks into 1cm/½in pieces.

COOK'S TIP
Chilled soups can require extra seasoning, so remember to check the taste just before you serve.

Energy 163kcal/676kJ; Protein 6.4g; Carbohydrate 10.2g, of which sugars 4.3g; Fat 11g, of which saturates 6.5g; Cholesterol 27mg; Calcium 82mg; Fibre 3.2g; Sodium 54mg.

Chilled Tomato and Sweet Pepper Soup

This recipe was inspired by the Spanish gazpacho, the difference being that this soup is cooked first, and then chilled.

Serves 4

2 red (bell) peppers, halved and seeded
45ml/3 tbsp olive oil
1 onion, finely chopped
2 garlic cloves, crushed
675g/1½ lb ripe well-flavoured tomatoes
150ml/¼ pint/⅔ cup red wine
600ml/1 pint/2½ cups chicken stock
salt and ground black pepper
chopped fresh chives, to garnish

For the croûtons
2 slices white bread, crusts removed
60ml/4 tbsp olive oil

1 Cut each red pepper half into quarters. Place skin side up on a grill (broiler) rack and cook until the skins are charred. Transfer to a bowl and cover with a plate or put into a plastic bag and seal.

2 Heat the oil in a large pan. Add the onion and garlic and cook over a low heat, stirring occasionally, for about 5 minutes, until soft. Meanwhile, remove the skin from the peppers and coarsely chop the flesh. Cut the tomatoes into chunks.

3 Add the peppers and tomatoes to the pan, then cover and cook gently for 10 minutes. Add the wine and cook for a further 5 minutes, then add the stock and season with salt and pepper to taste and continue to simmer for 20 minutes.

4 To make the croûtons, cut the bread into cubes. Heat the oil in a small frying pan, add the bread and cook, stirring and tossing frequently, until golden brown all over. Drain well on kitchen paper, leave to cool and then store in an airtight box until you are ready to serve.

5 Process the soup in a blender or food processor until smooth. Pour it into a clean glass or ceramic bowl, cover with clear film (plastic wrap) and leave to cool thoroughly before chilling in the refrigerator for at least 3 hours. When the soup is cold, taste and adjust the seasoning, if necessary.

6 Serve the soup in bowls, topped with the croûtons and garnished with chopped chives.

Energy 292kcal/1216kJ; Protein 3.4g; Carbohydrate 18.8g, of which sugars 11.8g; Fat 20.4g, of which saturates 3g; Cholesterol 0mg; Calcium 40mg; Fibre 3.5g; Sodium 92mg.

Gazpacho with Avocado Salsa

Tomatoes, cucumber and peppers form the basis of this classic, chilled soup. Add a spoonful of chunky, fresh avocado salsa and a sprinkling of croûtons for a delicious summer appetizer. This is quite a substantial soup, so follow with a light main course, such as grilled fish or chicken.

Serves 4–6

2 slices day-old bread
600ml/1 pint/2½ cups chilled water
1kg/2¼ lb tomatoes
1 cucumber
1 red (bell) pepper, seeded
  and chopped
1 fresh green chilli, seeded
  and chopped
2 garlic cloves, chopped
30ml/2 tbsp extra virgin olive oil
juice of 1 lime and 1 lemon
few drops Tabasco sauce
salt and ground black pepper
handful of fresh basil, to garnish
8–12 ice cubes, to serve

For the croûtons

2–3 slices day-old bread,
  crusts removed
1 garlic clove, halved
15–30ml/1–2 tbsp olive oil

For the avocado salsa

1 ripe avocado
5ml/1 tsp lemon juice
2.5cm/1in piece cucumber, diced
½ fresh red chilli, finely chopped

1 Make the soup first. Place the bread in a shallow bowl, add 150ml/¼ pint/⅔ cup of the chilled water and leave to soak for 5 minutes.

COOK'S TIP

For a superior flavour, choose Haas avocados with the rough-textured, almost black skins.

2 Meanwhile, place the tomatoes in a heatproof bowl; cover with boiling water. Leave for 30 seconds, then peel, seed and chop the flesh.

3 Thinly peel the cucumber, cut in half lengthways and scoop out the seeds with a teaspoon. Discard the seeds and chop the flesh.

4 Place the soaked bread, tomatoes, cucumber, red pepper, chilli, garlic, oil, citrus juices, Tabasco and 450ml/¾ pint/scant 2 cups chilled water in a food processor or blender. Blend until mixed but still chunky. Season with salt and pepper and chill well.

5 To make the croûtons, rub the slices of bread with the cut surface of the garlic clove. Cut the bread into cubes and place in a plastic bag with the olive oil. Seal the bag and shake until the bread cubes are coated with the oil. Heat a large non-stick frying pan and cook the croûtons over a medium heat until crisp and golden. Remove from the pan and drain thoroughly on kitchen paper. Store in an airtight box until ready to serve.

6 Just before serving make the avocado salsa. Halve the avocado and twist it apart, remove the stone (pit) with the point of the knife, then peel and dice the flesh. Toss the avocado in the lemon juice to prevent it from turning brown, then mix with the cucumber and chilli.

7 Ladle the soup into individual bowls, add the ice cubes, and top each bowl with a spoonful of avocado salsa. Garnish with the basil and hand around the croûtons separately.

Energy 164kcal/685kJ; Protein 3.5g; Carbohydrate 16.6g, of which sugars 7.9g; Fat 9.7g, of which saturates 1.7g; Cholesterol 0mg; Calcium 40mg; Fibre 3.1g; Sodium 112mg.

Cold Cucumber and Yogurt Soup

This refreshing cold soup uses the classic combination of cucumber and yogurt, with the added flavours of garlic and crunchy walnuts.

Serves 5–6

1 cucumber
4 garlic cloves
2.5ml/1/2 tsp salt
75g/3oz/3/4 cup walnut pieces
40g/11/2 oz day-old bread, torn into pieces
30ml/2 tbsp walnut or sunflower oil
400ml/14fl oz/12/3 cups sheep's or cow's yogurt
120ml/4fl oz/1/2 cup cold water or chilled still mineral water
5–10ml/1–2 tsp lemon juice
40g/11/2oz/scant 1/2 cup walnuts, chopped, to garnish
olive oil, for drizzling
fresh dill sprigs, to garnish

1 Cut the cucumber into two and peel one half of it. Dice the cucumber flesh and set aside.

2 Using a large pestle and mortar, crush the garlic and salt together well, then add the walnuts and bread.

3 When the mixture is smooth, add the walnut or sunflower oil slowly and combine well.

4 Transfer the walnut and bread mixture to a large bowl, then beat in the cow's or sheep's yogurt and the diced cucumber.

5 Add the cold water or mineral water and lemon juice to taste. Chill until ready to serve.

6 Ladle the soup into chilled soup bowls to serve. Garnish with the chopped walnuts, drizzling a little olive oil over them, and with sprigs of dill.

COOK'S TIP
If you prefer your soup smooth, purée it in a food processor or blender before serving.

Energy 220kcal/910kJ; Protein 6.9g; Carbohydrate 9.2g, of which sugars 5.9g; Fat 17.6g, of which saturates 1.9g; Cholesterol 1mg; Calcium 155mg; Fibre 0.9g; Sodium 92mg.

Chilled Prawn and Cucumber Soup

If you've never served a chilled soup before, this is the one to try first. Delicious and light, it's the perfect way to celebrate summer.

Serves 4

25g/1oz/2 tbsp butter
2 shallots, finely chopped
2 garlic cloves, crushed
1 cucumber, peeled, seeded and diced
300ml/$\frac{1}{2}$ pint/1$\frac{1}{4}$ cups milk
225g/8oz cooked peeled prawns
    (shrimp)
15ml/1 tbsp each finely chopped fresh
    mint, dill, chives and chervil
300ml/$\frac{1}{2}$ pint/1$\frac{1}{4}$ cups whipping cream
salt and ground white pepper

For the garnish
30ml/2 tbsp crème fraîche (optional)
4 large, cooked prawns (shrimp),
    peeled with tails intact
chopped fresh chives and dill

1 Melt the butter in a pan. Add the shallots and garlic and cook over a low heat, stirring occasionally, for about 4 minutes, until soft but not coloured. Add the cucumber and cook the vegetables gently, stirring frequently, until tender.

2 Stir in the milk, bring almost to the boil, then lower the heat and simmer for 5 minutes. Tip the soup into a blender or food processor and process until very smooth. Season to taste with salt and ground white pepper.

3 Pour the soup into a bowl and set aside to cool. When cool, stir in the prawns, chopped herbs and the whipping cream. Cover the bowl with clear film (plastic wrap) and chill in the refrigerator for at least 2 hours.

4 To serve, ladle the soup into four individual bowls and top each portion with a spoonful of crème fraîche, if using. Place a prawn over the edge of each bowl. Garnish the soup with the chives and dill.

VARIATIONS
• For a change try fresh or canned crab meat or cooked, flaked salmon fillet instead of the prawns.
• If crème fraîche is not available, use sour cream.
• Garnish the soup with a sprinkling of salmon or sea trout roe or, for a truly special occasion, a little caviar.

Energy 439kcal/1817kJ; Protein 18.9g; Carbohydrate 7.5g, of which sugars 7.1g; Fat 37.2g, of which saturates 23.1g; Cholesterol 255mg; Calcium 212mg; Fibre 0.5g; Sodium 245mg.

Hot-and-sour Soup

This light and invigorating soup is traditionally served at the start of a formal Thai meal.

Serves 4

2 carrots
900ml/1 1/2 pints/3 3/4 cups
   vegetable stock
2 Thai chillies, seeded and thinly sliced
2 lemon grass stalks, each cut into
   3 pieces
4 kaffir lime leaves
2 garlic cloves, finely chopped
4 spring onions (scallions), thinly sliced
5ml/1 tsp sugar
juice of 1 lime
45ml/3 tbsp chopped fresh
   coriander (cilantro)
salt
130g/4 1/2 oz/1 cup Japanese tofu,
   sliced

1 To make carrot flowers, cut each carrot in half crossways, then, using a sharp knife, cut four V-shaped channels lengthways. Slice the carrots into thin rounds and set aside.

COOK'S TIPS

• Kaffir lime leaves have a distinctive citrus flavour. The fresh leaves can be bought from Asian stores, and some supermarkets now sell them dried.
• Before using lemon grass stalks, remove and discard the tough outer layers.
• Thai chillies are notorious for their intense heat, so if you prefer a milder flavour, use only one.

2 Pour the vegetable stock into a large pan. Reserve 2.5ml/1/2 tsp of the chillies and add the rest to the pan with the lemon grass, lime leaves, garlic and half the spring onions. Bring to the boil, then reduce the heat and simmer for 20 minutes. Strain the stock and discard the flavourings.

3 Return the stock to the pan, add the reserved chillies and spring onions, the sugar, lime juice and coriander and season with salt to taste.

4 Simmer for 5 minutes, then add the carrot flowers and tofu slices, and cook the soup for a further 2 minutes, until the carrot is just tender. Ladle into warm bowls and serve hot.

Energy 43kcal/180kJ; Protein 3.4g; Carbohydrate 3.9g, of which sugars 3.6g; Fat 1.7g, of which saturates 0.2g; Cholesterol 0mg; Calcium 202mg; Fibre 1.4g; Sodium 13mg.

Pear and **Watercress Soup**

The pears in the soup are complemented beautifully by Stilton croûtons.

Serves 6

1 bunch watercress
4 pears, sliced
900ml/1½ pints/3¾ cups
   chicken stock
120ml/4fl oz/½ cup double
   (heavy) cream
juice of 1 lime
salt and ground black pepper

For the croûtons
25g/1oz/2 tbsp butter
15ml/1 tbsp olive oil
200g/7oz/3 cups cubed stale bread
150g/5oz/1 cup chopped Stilton

1 Reserve about one-third of the watercress leaves. Place the rest of the leaves and stalks in a pan with the pear slices, stock and a little salt and pepper. Simmer gently for about 15–20 minutes. Set aside some of the reserved watercress leaves for garnishing, then add the rest of the leaves to the soup. Process in a blender or food processor until smooth.

2 Put the mixture into a bowl and stir in the cream and the lime juice to mix the flavours thoroughly. Season again to taste. Pour all the soup back into a pan and reheat, stirring gently until warmed through.

3 To make the croûtons, melt the butter and oil in a frying pan. Add the bread cubes and cook, stirring and tossing them frequently, until golden brown. Drain well on kitchen paper.

4 Spread them out on a baking sheet, sprinkle the cheese over them and heat under a hot grill (broiler) until bubbling. Reheat the soup and pour into bowls. Divide the croûtons and the reserved watercress leaves among them and serve immediately.

Energy 371kcal/1547kJ; Protein 9.9g; Carbohydrate 26.9g, of which sugars 11.3g; Fat 25.4g, of which saturates 14.9g; Cholesterol 60mg; Calcium 168mg; Fibre 3g; Sodium 411mg.

Baby Carrot and Fennel Soup

Sweet tender carrots find their
moment of glory in this delicately
spiced soup. Fennel provides a very
subtle aniseed flavour.

Serves 4

50g/2oz/4 tbsp butter
1 small bunch spring onions
(scallions), chopped
150g/5oz fennel bulb, chopped
1 celery stick, chopped
450g/1lb new carrots, grated
2.5ml/¹/₂ tsp ground cumin
150g/5oz new potatoes, diced
1.2 litres/2 pints/5 cups chicken or
vegetable stock
60ml/4 tbsp double (heavy) cream
salt and ground black pepper
60ml/4 tbsp chopped fresh parsley,
to garnish

1 Melt the butter in a large pan and
add the spring onions, fennel, celery,
carrots and cumin. Cover and cook
over a low heat for about 5 minutes,
or until soft.

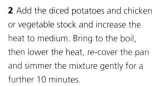

COOK'S TIP
For convenience, you can prepare the
soup in advance and freeze, in portions if
you like, before adding the cream,
seasoning and parsley.

2 Add the diced potatoes and chicken
or vegetable stock and increase the
heat to medium. Bring to the boil,
then lower the heat, re-cover the pan
and simmer the mixture gently for a
further 10 minutes.

3 Purée the soup in the pan with a
hand-held blender. Stir in the cream
and season to taste with salt and
pepper. Ladle into individual soup
bowls and garnish with chopped
parsley. Serve immediately.

Energy 244kcal/1010kJ; Protein 2.5g; Carbohydrate 16.8g, of which sugars 10.6g; Fat 19g, of which saturates 11.7g; Cholesterol 47mg; Calcium 62mg; Fibre 4.4g; Sodium 122mg.

Broccoli Soup with Garlic Toast

This is an Italian recipe, originating from Rome. For the best flavour and brightest colour, use the freshest broccoli you can find.

Serves 6

675g/1½ lb broccoli spears
1.75 litres/3 pints/7½ cups chicken or
    vegetable stock
30ml/2 tbsp fresh lemon juice
salt and ground black pepper
freshly grated Parmesan cheese
    (optional), to serve

For the garlic toast
6 slices white bread
1 large garlic clove, halved

1 Using a small sharp knife, peel the broccoli stems, starting from the base of the stalks and pulling gently up towards the florets. (The peel comes off very easily.) Chop the broccoli into small chunks.

2 Bring the stock to the boil in a large pan over a medium heat. Add the chopped broccoli, lower the heat and simmer for 30 minutes, or until soft.

COOK'S TIP
As this is an Italian recipe, choose a really good-quality Parmesan cheese, if you are using it. The very best is Italy's own Parmigiano-Reggiano. Alternatively, as it is Roman, substitute Pecorino Romano, which is made from sheep's milk. Both should be freshly grated.

3 Remove the pan from the heat and leave the soup to cool slightly, then transfer about half of it to a blender or food processor. Process to a smooth purée. Return the puréed soup to the pan and mix it into the rest of the soup. Stir in lemon juice and season to taste with salt and pepper.

4 Just before serving, gently reheat the soup to just below boiling point. Toast the bread, rub with the cut surfaces of the garlic and cut into quarters. Place three or four pieces of toast in the base of each soup plate. Ladle on the soup. Serve immediately, with grated Parmesan cheese if you like.

Energy 98kcal/413kJ; Protein 7.2g; Carbohydrate 14.6g, of which sugars 2.4g; Fat 1.5g, of which saturates 0.2g; Cholesterol 0mg; Calcium 91mg; Fibre 3.4g; Sodium 139mg.

Split Pea Soup

This tasty winter soup is a perfect for informal entertaining.

Serves 4–6

25g/1oz/2 tbsp butter
1 large onion, chopped
1 large celery stalk with leaves, chopped
2 carrots, chopped
1 smoked gammon (cured ham)
 knuckle, 450g/1lb
2 litres/3½ pints/8½ cups water
350g/12oz/1½ cups split peas
30ml/2 tbsp chopped fresh parsley,
 plus extra to garnish
2.5ml/½ tsp dried thyme
1 bay leaf
about 30ml/2 tbsp lemon juice
salt and ground black pepper

3 After 2 hours, once the split peas are very tender, remove the gammon knuckle from the soup. Leave it to cool slightly, then, with a sharp knife, remove the skin and cut the meat from the bones. Discard the skin and bones, then cut the meat into chunks as evenly sized as possible.

4 Return the chunks of gammon to the soup. Remove and discard the bay leaf. Taste and adjust the seasoning with more lemon juice, salt and pepper, if necessary.

5 Ladle the soup into warm bowls and serve, sprinkled with fresh parsley.

1 Melt the butter in a large, heavy pan. Add the onion, celery and carrots and cook over a medium heat, stirring occasionally, until softened.

2 Add all the rest of the ingredients to the pan. Bring to the boil, cover the pan, then lower the heat and simmer gently for 2 hours.

Energy 244kcal/1033kJ; Protein 17.2g; Carbohydrate 35.2g, of which sugars 3.4g; Fat 4.8g, of which saturates 2.5g; Cholesterol 19mg; Calcium 40mg; Fibre 3.5g; Sodium 254mg.

Corn Soup

This is a simple to make, yet very flavoursome soup. It is sometimes made with sour cream and cream cheese. Poblano chillies may be added, but these are rather difficult to locate outside Mexico. However, you may be able to find them in cans.

Serves 4

30ml/2 tbsp corn oil
1 onion, finely chopped
1 red (bell) pepper, seeded
    and chopped
450g/1lb corn kernels, thawed
    if frozen
750ml/1¼ pints/3 cups chicken stock
250ml/8fl oz/1 cup single (light) cream
salt and ground black pepper
½ red (bell) pepper, seeded and finely
    diced, to garnish

1 Heat the oil in a frying pan. Add the onion and red pepper and cook over a low heat, stirring occasionally, for about 5 minutes, until softened but not browned. Add the corn and cook for 2 minutes.

2 Carefully tip the contents of the pan into a food processor or blender. Process until the mixture is smooth, scraping down the sides and adding a little of the stock, if necessary.

3 Transfer the mixture to a clean pan and stir in the stock. Season to taste with salt and pepper, bring to a simmer and cook for 5 minutes.

4 Gently stir in the cream. Serve the soup hot or chilled, with the diced red pepper sprinkled over. If serving hot, reheat gently after adding the cream, but do not allow the soup to boil.

Courgette Soup

This soup is so simple – in terms of ingredients and preparation. It would provide an elegant start to a dinner party.

Serves 4

30ml/2 tbsp butter
1 onion, finely chopped
450g/1lb young courgettes (zucchini),
    trimmed and chopped
750ml/1¼ pints/3 cups chicken stock
120ml/4fl oz/½ cup single (light)
    cream, plus extra to serve
salt and ground black pepper

1 Melt the butter in a large, heavy pan. Add the onion and cook over a low heat, stirring occasionally, for about 5 minutes, until it is softened but not browned. Add the courgettes and cook, stirring occasionally, for about 1–2 minutes.

2 Add the chicken stock. Bring to the boil over a medium heat and then simmer for about 5 minutes, or until the courgettes are just tender.

COOK'S TIPS
• Always use the smallest courgettes (zucchini) available, as these have the best flavour.
• Be careful to prevent the soup from boiling once you have added the cream. Single (light) cream has a tendency to curdle if it is overheated.

3 Strain the stock into a clean pan, saving the vegetable solids in the sieve. Place the solids in a food processor and process until smooth, then add them to the pan. Season to taste with salt and pepper.

4 Stir the cream into the soup and heat through very gently without allowing it to come to the boil. Ladle into warm bowls and serve the soup immediately with a little extra cream swirled in to garnish.

Corn: Energy 218kcal/914kJ; Protein 4.2g; Carbohydrate 27.4g, of which sugars 12.8g; Fat 11g, of which saturates 4.5g; Cholesterol 17mg; Calcium 39mg; Fibre 2.2g; Sodium 237mg.
Courgette: Energy 139kcal/575kJ; Protein 3.3g; Carbohydrate 3.9g, of which sugars 3.5g; Fat 12.4g, of which saturates 7.7g; Cholesterol 33mg; Calcium 60mg; Fibre 1.2g; Sodium 56mg.

Tomato and Blue Cheese Soup with Bacon

As blue cheese is rather salty, it is important to use unsalted stock for this flavoursome soup.

Serves 4

1.3kg/3lb ripe tomatoes, peeled, quartered and seeded
2 garlic cloves, crushed
30ml/2 tbsp vegetable oil or butter
1 leek, chopped
1 carrot, chopped
1 litre/1¾ pints/4 cups unsalted chicken stock
115g/4oz Danish blue cheese, crumbled
45ml/3 tbsp whipping cream
several large fresh basil leaves, or 1–2 fresh parsley sprigs
salt and ground black pepper
175g/6oz bacon, cooked and crumbled, to garnish

1 Preheat the oven to 200°C/400°F/Gas 6. Spread out the tomato quarters in an ovenproof dish. Sprinkle with the garlic and some salt and ground black pepper. Place in the oven and bake for 35 minutes.

2 Heat the oil or butter in a large pan. Add the leek and carrot and season lightly with salt and pepper. Cook over a low heat, stirring frequently, for about 10 minutes, or until softened.

COOK'S TIP

Don't be tempted to use unripe tomatoes for this soup, as their lack of sweetness and flavour will spoil it.

3 Stir in the chicken stock and baked tomatoes. Bring to the boil, lower the heat, cover and simmer for 20 minutes.

VARIATION

Danish blue cheese, also known as Danablu, has a very sharp, almost metallic taste, which some people dislike intensely, while others love it. If you prefer, you could use a milder blue cheese, such as Dolcelatte or Bleu de Causses.

4 Add the blue cheese, cream and basil or parsley. Remove from the heat and leave to cool slightly, then transfer the soup to a food processor or blender and process until smooth, working in batches if necessary. Taste and adjust the seasoning, if you like.

5 If necessary, reheat the soup, but do not let it boil. Ladle into warmed bowls and sprinkle the crumbled bacon over.

Energy 354kcal/1473kJ; Protein 16.4g; Carbohydrate 12.6g, of which sugars 12.3g; Fat 26.8g, of which saturates 12.1g; Cholesterol 57mg; Calcium 186mg; Fibre 4.5g; Sodium 1061mg.

Fresh Tomato Soup

Intensely flavoured sun-ripened tomatoes need little embellishment in this fresh-tasting soup. If you buy from the supermarket, choose the juiciest looking ones and add the amount of sugar and vinegar necessary, depending on their natural sweetness.

Serves 6

1.3–1.6kg/3–3¹/₂ lb ripe tomatoes
400ml/14fl oz/1²/₃ cups chicken or
    vegetable stock
45ml/3 tbsp sun-dried tomato paste
30–45ml/2–3 tbsp balsamic vinegar
10–15ml/2–3 tsp caster
    (superfine) sugar
small handful of basil leaves
salt and ground black pepper
basil leaves, to garnish
toasted cheese croûtes and crème
    fraîche, to serve

1 Plunge the tomatoes into boiling water for 30 seconds, then refresh in cold water. Peel off the skins and quarter the tomatoes. Put them in a large, heavy pan and pour over the chicken or vegetable stock. Bring just to the boil, reduce the heat, cover and simmer the mixture gently for about 10 minutes, until the tomatoes are thickened and pulpy.

COOK'S TIP
This Italian soup may be left to cool and then chilled in the refrigerator before serving in a hot day.

2 Stir in the tomato paste, vinegar, sugar and basil. Season with salt and pepper, then cook gently, stirring, for 2 minutes. Process the soup in a blender or food processor, then return to the pan and reheat gently.

3 Serve in bowls topped with one or two toasted cheese croûtes and a spoonful of crème fraîche, garnished with basil leaves.

Energy 49kcal/210kJ; Protein 1.9g; Carbohydrate 9.5g, of which sugars 9.5g; Fat 0.7g, of which saturates 0.2g; Cholesterol 0mg; Calcium 19mg; Fibre 2.4g; Sodium 38mg.

French Onion and Morel Soup

French onion soup is appreciated for its light beefy taste. There are few improvements to be made to this classic soup, but a few richly scented morel mushrooms will impart a worthwhile flavour.

Serves 4

50g/2oz/4 tbsp unsalted (sweet) butter, plus extra for spreading
15ml/1 tbsp vegetable oil
3 onions, sliced
900ml/1½ pints/3¾ cups beef stock
75ml/5 tbsp Madeira or sherry
8 dried morel mushrooms
4 slices French bread
75g/3oz Gruyère, Beaufort or Fontina cheese, grated
30ml/2 tbsp chopped fresh parsley

1 Melt the butter with the oil in a large frying pan, then add the sliced onions and cook over a low heat for 10–15 minutes, until the onions are a rich mahogany brown colour.

2 Transfer the browned onions to a large pan, pour in the beef stock, add the Madeira or sherry and the dried morels, then simmer for 20 minutes.

4 Ladle the soup into four flameproof bowls, float the cheese-topped toasts on top and grill (broil) until they are crisp and brown and the cheese is bubbling. Alternatively, grill the cheese-topped toast, then place one slice in each warmed soup bowl before ladling the hot soup over it. The toast will float to the surface.

3 Preheat the grill (broiler) to medium and toast the French bread on both sides, until golden brown. Spread one side with butter and heap with the grated cheese.

5 Sprinkle over the chopped fresh parsley and serve immediately.

COOK'S TIP
The flavour and richness of this soup will improve with keeping. Store in the refrigerator for up to 5 days.

Energy 304kcal/1263kJ; Protein 8.8g; Carbohydrate 22.6g, of which sugars 8g; Fat 20.1g, of which saturates 10.9g; Cholesterol 45mg; Calcium 225mg; Fibre 2.8g; Sodium 349mg.

Spanish Garlic Soup

This is a simple and satisfying soup, made with one of the most popular ingredients in the Mediterranean region – garlic.

Serves 4

30ml/2 tbsp olive oil
4 large garlic cloves, peeled
4 slices French bread, 5mm/¹/₄ in thick
15ml/1 tbsp paprika
1 litre/1³/₄ pints/4 cups beef stock
1.5ml/¹/₄ tsp ground cumin
pinch of saffron threads
4 eggs
salt and ground black pepper
chopped fresh parsley, to garnish

1 Preheat the oven to 230°C/450°F/ Gas 8. Heat the oil in a large pan. Add the whole garlic cloves and cook over a low heat until golden. Remove with a slotted spoon and set aside.

2 Add the bread to the pan and cook on both sides until golden. Remove from the pan and set aside.

3 Add the paprika to the pan and cook for a few seconds, stirring constantly. Stir in the beef stock, cumin and saffron, then add the reserved fried garlic, crushing the cloves with the back of a wooden spoon. Season with salt and ground black pepper to taste then cook over a low heat for about 5 minutes.

4 Ladle the soup into four individual ovenproof bowls and gently break an egg into each one. Place the slices of fried French bread on top of the eggs and place the bowls in the oven for about 3–4 minutes, or until the eggs are just set. Sprinkle with chopped fresh parsley to garnish and serve the soup immediately.

COOK'S TIP
Use home-made beef stock for the best flavour or buy prepared stock from your supermarket – you'll find it in the chilled counter. Never use stock (bouillon) cubes as most of them contain too much salt.

Energy 253kcal/1061kJ; Protein 11.8g; Carbohydrate 26.5g, of which sugars 1.5g; Fat 12g, of which saturates 2.5g; Cholesterol 190mg; Calcium 82mg; Fibre 2g; Sodium 318mg.

Tortellini Chanterelle Broth

The savoury-sweet quality of chanterelle mushrooms combines well in a simple broth with spinach-and-ricotta-filled tortellini. The addition of a little sherry creates a lovely warming effect.

Serves 4

1.2 litres/2 pints/5 cups chicken stock
75ml/5 tbsp dry sherry
175g/6oz fresh chanterelle
  mushrooms, trimmed and sliced, or
  15g/¹/₂ oz/¹/₂ cup dried chanterelles
350g/12oz fresh spinach and ricotta
  tortellini, or 175g/6oz dried
chopped fresh parsley, to garnish

1 Bring the chicken stock to the boil, add the dry sherry and fresh or dried mushrooms and simmer over a low heat for 10 minutes.

2 Cook the tortellini according to the packet instructions.

3 Drain the tortellini, add to the stock and mushroom mixture, then ladle the broth into four warmed soup bowls, making sure each contains the about same proportions of tortellini and mushrooms. Garnish with the chopped parsley and serve immediately.

Energy 204kcal/859kJ; Protein 7.6g; Carbohydrate 23.4g, of which sugars 1.5g; Fat 4.3g, of which saturates 0.1g; Cholesterol 0mg; Calcium 106mg; Fibre 1.6g; Sodium 185mg.

Cream of **Mushroom Soup** with **Goat's Cheese Crostini**

Classic cream of mushroom soup is still a firm favourite, especially with the addition of crisp and garlicky croûtes with tangy goat's cheese.

Serves 6

25g/1oz/2 tbsp butter
1 onion, chopped
1 garlic clove, chopped
450g/1lb/6 cups chestnut or brown
   cap (cremini) mushrooms, some
   whole, some coarsely chopped
15ml/1 tbsp plain (all-purpose) flour
45ml/3 tbsp dry sherry
900ml/1½ pints/3¾ cups
   vegetable stock
150ml/¼ pint/⅔ cup double
   (heavy) cream
salt and ground black pepper
fresh chervil sprigs, to garnish

For the crostini
15ml/1 tbsp olive oil, plus extra
   for brushing
1 shallot, chopped
115g/4oz/2 cups button (white)
   mushrooms, finely chopped
15ml/1 tbsp chopped fresh parsley
6 brown cap (cremini) mushrooms
6 slices baguette
1 small garlic clove
115g/4oz/1 cup soft goat's cheese

1 Melt the butter. Cook the onion and garlic for 5 minutes. Add the mushrooms, cover, cook for 10 minutes.

2 Add the flour and cook, stirring, for 1 minute. Stir in the dry sherry and stock and bring to the boil, then simmer for 15 minutes. Cool slightly, then process the mixture in a food processor or blender until smooth.

3 Meanwhile, prepare the crostini. Heat the oil in a small pan. Add the shallot and button mushrooms, and cook for 8–10 minutes, until softened. Drain well and transfer to a food processor or blender. Add the fresh parsley and process the mushroom mixture until finely chopped.

4 Preheat the grill (broiler). Brush the brown cap mushrooms with oil and grill (broil) for 5–6 minutes.

5 Toast the slices of baguette, rub with the garlic and put a spoonful of cheese on each. Top the grilled mushrooms with the mushroom mixture and place on the crostini.

6 Return the soup to the pan and stir in the cream. Season, then reheat gently. Ladle the soup into six bowls. Float a crostini in the centre of each and garnish with chervil.

Energy 312kcal/1297kJ; Protein 8g; Carbohydrate 17g, of which sugars 3g; Fat 24g, of which saturates 14g; Cholesterol 57mg; Calcium 123mg; Fibre 4g; Sodium 631mg.

Spinach and Rice Soup

Use very fresh, young spinach leaves in the preparation of this light and fresh-tasting soup.

Serves 4

675g/1¹/₂ lb fresh spinach, washed
45ml/3 tbsp extra virgin olive oil
1 small onion, finely chopped
2 garlic cloves, finely chopped
1 small fresh red chilli, seeded and
*   finely chopped*
115g/4oz/generous 1 cup risotto rice
1.2 litres/2 pints/5 cups
*   vegetable stock*
salt and ground black pepper
60ml/4 tbsp grated Pecorino cheese

1 Place the spinach in a large pan with just the water that clings to its leaves after washing. Add a large pinch of salt. Heat gently until the spinach has wilted, then remove from the heat and drain, reserving any liquid.

2 Either chop the spinach finely using a large knife or place it in a food processor and process briefly to a fairly coarse purée.

COOK'S TIP
Pecorino, made from sheep's milk, has a slightly sharper taste than its cow's-milk counterpart, Parmesan. However, if you cannot find it, use Parmesan instead.

VARIATION
Substitute young Swiss chard leaves or sorrel for the spinach if you like.

3 Heat the oil in a large pan. Add the onion, garlic and chilli and cook over a low heat, stirring occasionally, for 4–5 minutes, until softened. Stir in the rice until well coated, then pour in the stock and reserved spinach liquid. Bring to the boil, lower the heat and simmer for 10 minutes. Add the spinach, with salt and ground black pepper to taste. Cook for a further 5–7 minutes, until the rice is tender. Check the seasoning and adjust if necessary. Serve immediately with the Pecorino cheese.

Energy 293kcal/1215kJ; Protein 13g; Carbohydrate 26.8g, of which sugars 3.4g; Fat 14.7g, of which saturates 4.4g; Cholesterol 15mg; Calcium 476mg; Fibre 3.8g; Sodium 400mg.

Vermicelli Soup

The inclusion of fresh coriander adds a piquancy to this soup and complements the tomato flavour.

Serves 4

30ml/2 tbsp olive or corn oil
50g/2oz vermicelli
1 onion, coarsely chopped
1 garlic clove, chopped
450g/1lb tomatoes, peeled, seeded
   and coarsely chopped
1 litre/1¾ pints/4 cups chicken stock
1.5ml/¼ tsp sugar
15ml/1 tbsp finely chopped fresh
   coriander (cilantro), plus extra
   to garnish
salt and ground black pepper
25g/1oz/¼ cup freshly grated
   Parmesan cheese, to serve

1 Heat the oil in a large, heavy frying pan. Add the vermicelli and cook over a medium heat until golden brown. Take care not to let the strands burn. Remove the vermicelli with a slotted spoon or tongs and drain well on kitchen paper.

2 Place the onion, garlic and tomatoes in a food processor or blender and process until smooth. Return the frying pan to the heat. When the oil is hot again, add the vegetable purée to the pan. Cook, stirring constantly to prevent sticking, for about 5 minutes, or until thick.

3 Transfer the purée to a pan. Add the vermicelli and pour in the stock. Stir in the sugar and season to taste with salt and pepper. Stir in the coriander, bring to the boil, then lower the heat, cover the pan and simmer the soup gently, until the vermicelli is tender.

4 Ladle the soup into warmed bowls, sprinkle with chopped fresh coriander and serve immediately. Offer the grated Parmesan cheese separately.

COOK'S TIP
Vermicelli will burn very easily, so move it about constantly in the frying pan with a wooden spoon and remove it from the heat the moment it has turned a golden brown colour.

Energy 141kcal/589kJ; Protein 4.4g; Carbohydrate 13.3g, of which sugars 3.5g; Fat 7.9g, of which saturates 2.2g; Cholesterol 6mg; Calcium 86mg; Fibre 1.1g; Sodium 79mg.

Spinach and Tofu Soup

This soup is really delicious. If fresh spinach is not in season, watercress or lettuce can be used instead.

Serves 4

1 cake tofu, 7.5cm/3in sq. and
   2.5cm/1in thick
115g/4oz spinach leaves
750ml/1¼ pints/3 cups
   vegetable stock
15ml/1 tbsp light soy sauce
salt and ground black pepper

1 Rinse the tofu then cut into 12 small pieces, each about 5mm/¼in thick. Wash the spinach leaves and cut them into small pieces.

2 Pour the vegetable stock into a wok or large, heavy pan and bring to a rolling boil over a medium heat. Add the pieces of tofu and the soy sauce, stir carefully without breaking up the tofu, bring back to the boil, then lower the heat and simmer gently for about 2 minutes.

3 Add the pieces of spinach, and simmer for a further 1–2 minutes. Skim the surface of the soup to remove any foam and to make it clear, then season with salt and ground black pepper to taste. Ladle the soup into warm bowls or a tureen and serve immediately.

Energy 55kcal/231kJ; Protein 7.6g; Carbohydrate 1.4g, of which sugars 1.1g; Fat 2.2g, of which saturates 0.3g; Cholesterol 25mg; Calcium 352mg; Fibre 1.3g; Sodium 300mg.

Fish Soup with Rouille

Making this soup is simplicity itself, yet the flavour suggests it is the product of painstaking preparation and complicated cooking. Rouille, a spicy Provençal paste, makes a colourful addition.

Serves 6

1kg/2¹⁄₄lb mixed fish, skinned
30ml/2 tbsp olive oil
1 onion, chopped
1 carrot, chopped
1 leek, chopped
2 large ripe tomatoes, chopped
1 red (bell) pepper, seeded
  and chopped
2 garlic cloves, peeled
150g/5oz/²⁄₃ cup tomato purée (paste)
1 large fresh bouquet garni,
  containing 3 parsley sprigs, 3 small
  celery sticks and 3 bay leaves
300ml/¹⁄₂ pint/1¹⁄₄ cups dry white wine
salt and ground black pepper

For the rouille

2 garlic cloves, coarsely chopped
5ml/1 tsp coarse salt
1 thick slice of white bread, crust
  removed, soaked in water and then
  squeezed dry
1 fresh red chilli, seeded and
  coarsely chopped
45ml/3 tbsp olive oil
salt
pinch of cayenne pepper (optional)

For the garnish

12 slices of baguette, toasted in
  the oven
50g/2oz/¹⁄₂ cup finely grated
  Gruyère cheese

COOK'S TIP

Any firm fish, such as monkfish, sea bass or snapper, can be used for this recipe, but avoid oily types. If you use whole fish, include the heads, which enhance the flavour of the soup.

1 Cut the fish into 7.5cm/3in chunks, removing any obvious bones. Heat the olive oil in a large, heavy pan, then add the chunks of fish, onion, carrot, leek, tomatoes, red pepper and garlic. Stir gently over a medium heat until the vegetables begin to colour.

2 Add the tomato purée, bouquet garni and white wine, then pour in just enough cold water to cover the mixture. Season well with salt and pepper and bring to just below boiling point, then lower the heat so that the soup is barely simmering, cover and cook for 1 hour.

3 Meanwhile, make the rouille. Put the garlic and coarse salt in a mortar and crush to a paste with a pestle. Add the soaked bread and chilli and pound until smooth, or process in a food processor to a purée.

4 Whisk in the olive oil, a drop at a time to begin with, to make a smooth, shiny sauce that resembles mayonnaise in consistency. Season to taste with salt and add a pinch of cayenne if you like. Set aside.

5 Lift out and discard the bouquet garni. Process the soup, in batches, in a food processor, then strain through a fine sieve into a clean pan, pushing the solids through with a ladle.

6 Reheat the soup but do not allow it to boil. Taste and adjust the seasoning, if necessary, and ladle into individual bowls. Top each with two slices of toasted baguette, a spoonful of rouille and some grated Gruyére.

Energy 554kcal/2334kJ; Protein 42.7g; Carbohydrate 56.8g, of which sugars 11.4g; Fat 15.2g, of which saturates 3.7g; Cholesterol 85mg; Calcium 210mg; Fibre 4.7g; Sodium 748mg.

Salmon Chowder

This salmon version of a traditional fish chowder is quite exquisite.

Serves 4–6

20g/³/₄oz/1¹/₂ tbsp butter or margarine
1 onion, minced (ground)
1 leek, minced (ground)
50g/2oz/¹/₂ cup minced (ground)
   bulb fennel
60ml/4 tbsp plain (all-purpose) flour
1.5 litres/2¹/₂ pints 6¹/₄ cups fish stock
225g/8oz potatoes, cut into 1cm/¹/₂in
   cubes (about 2 medium-size potatoes)
salt and ground black pepper
450g/1lb boneless, skinless salmon,
   cut into 2cm/³/₄in cubes
175ml/6fl oz/³/₄ cup milk
120ml/4fl oz/¹/₂ cup whipping cream
30ml/2 tbsp chopped fresh dill

4 Add the cubed salmon and then simmer for about 3–5 minutes, until just cooked through and tender. The salmon cubes should remain intact, not fall apart.

5 Stir in the milk, cream and dill. Cook until just warmed through, but do not allow the soup to boil. Taste and adjust the seasoning, if necessary, then ladle into warm bowls and serve.

1 Melt the butter or margarine in a large, heavy pan. Add the onion, leek and fennel and cook over a medium heat, stirring occasionally, for about 5–8 minutes, until all the vegetables are softened.

2 Stir in the flour. Reduce the heat to low and cook, stirring constantly to prevent any lumps forming, for 3 minutes.

3 Gradually stir in the stock and add potatoes. Season to taste with salt and ground black pepper. Bring to the boil, then reduce the heat, cover and simmer for about 20 minutes, until the potatoes are tender.

Energy 301kcal/1253kJ; Protein 18.3g; Carbohydrate 13g, of which sugars 3.8g; Fat 19.9g, of which saturates 8.6g; Cholesterol 67mg; Calcium 83mg; Fibre 1.5g; Sodium 78mg.

Cappuccino of **Puy Lentils, Lobster** and **Tarragon**

Here is a really impressive soup to start a dinner party with. Adding ice-cold butter a little at a time is the secret of whipping up the good froth that gives the soup its clever cappuccino effect.

Serves 6

450–675g/1–1½lb live lobster
150g/5oz/⅔ cup Puy lentils
1 carrot, halved
1 celery stick, halved
1 small onion, halved
1 garlic clove
1 bay leaf
large bunch of tarragon, tied firmly
1 litre/1¾ pints/4 cups fish stock
120ml/4fl oz/½ cup double
*   (heavy) cream*
25g/1oz/2 tbsp butter, finely diced and
*   chilled until ice cold*
salt and ground black pepper
fresh tarragon sprigs,
*   to garnish*

1 Bring a large stockpot of water to the boil. Lower the live lobster into the water and cover the pan. Cook for 15–20 minutes, then drain the lobster and leave to cool.

2 Put the Puy lentils in a large pan and pour in enough cold water to cover. Add the carrot, celery, onion, garlic and herbs. Bring the water to the boil and simmer for 20 minutes.

3 Drain the lentils and discard the herbs and vegetables. Process the lentils in a food processor until smooth. Set aside.

4 Break the claws off the lobster, crack them open and remove all the meat from inside. Break off the tail, split it open and remove the meat. Cut all the meat into bitesize pieces.

5 Pour the fish stock into a large clean pan and bring to the boil. Lightly stir in the lentil purée and cream, but do not mix too much at this point otherwise you will not be able to create the frothy effect. The mixture should still be quite watery in places. Season well.

6 Using either a hand-held blender or electric beater, whisk the soup mixture, adding the butter, one piece at a time, until it is very frothy.

7 Divide the lobster meat among the bowls and carefully pour in the soup. Garnish with sprigs of tarragon and serve immediately.

COOK'S TIP

Instead of adding the live lobster to the pan, kill it first by freezing it overnight. Cook from frozen, allowing 30 minutes in the boiling water. The other way of killing lobster is by stabbing it in the back of the head, where the tail shell meets the head.

Energy 241kcal/1005kJ; Protein 13g; Carbohydrate 14g, of which sugars 2g; Fat 15g, of which saturates 9g; Cholesterol 66mg; Calcium 51mg; Fibre 0g; Sodium 325mg.

dinner party appetizers

These tempting first courses are all visually
appealing and perfect for setting the right
tone at the beginning of a special meal.

Pears and Stilton

This is a traditional English dish and a marriage made in heaven. The flavours and textures of pears and cheese are simply superb together.

Serves 4

4 ripe pears, lightly chilled
75g/3oz blue Stilton
50g/2oz curd (farmer's) cheese
ground black pepper
watercress sprigs, to garnish

For the dressing
45ml/3 tbsp light olive oil
15ml/1 tbsp lemon juice
10ml/2 tsp toasted poppy seeds
salt and ground black pepper

1 First make the dressing, place the olive oil and lemon juice, poppy seeds and seasoning to taste in a screw-top jar and then shake together vigorously until emulsified.

COOK'S TIPS
• Comice pears are a good choice for this dish, being very juicy and aromatic. For a dramatic colour contrast, select the excellent sweet and juicy Red Williams or Red Bartletts.
• You can mix the cheese filling in advance and store, covered with clear film (plastic wrap) in the refrigerator. Similarly, mix the dressing ahead of time, but bring it to room temperature to serve. However, don't halve the pears until just before serving or the flesh will discolour, becoming an unappetizing brown.

2 Cut the pears in half lengthways, then scoop out the cores and cut away the calyx from the rounded end.

3 Place the Stilton and curd cheese in a bowl and beat together, then season with a little pepper and beat lightly again. Divide this mixture among the cavities in the pears.

4 Shake the dressing to mix it again, then spoon it over the pears. Serve garnished with some watercress sprigs.

VARIATION
Stilton is the classic British blue cheese, but you could use Blue Cheshire or even a non-British cheese, such as Gorgonzola or Roquefort, if you like.

Energy 243kcal/1007kJ; Protein 7.2g; Carbohydrate 15.5g, of which sugars 15.5g; Fat 17.2g, of which saturates 6.4g; Cholesterol 21mg; Calcium 109mg; Fibre 3.5g; Sodium 208mg.

Asparagus with **Raspberry Dressing**

Asparagus and raspberries complement each other. The sauce gives this appetizer a real zing.

Serves 4

675g/1 1/2lb thin asparagus spears
30ml/2 tbsp raspberry vinegar
2.5ml/1/2 tsp salt
5ml/1 tsp Dijon mustard
25ml/1 1/2 tbsp sunflower oil
30ml/2 tbsp sour cream or
    natural (plain) yogurt
ground white pepper
175g/6oz/1 cup fresh raspberries

1 Fill a large wide frying pan or wok with water 10cm/4in deep and bring to the boil.

4 Using a fish slice or metal spatula, carefully remove the asparagus bundles from the frying pan or wok and immerse them in cold water to stop any further cooking. Drain, then untie the bundles. Pat the spears dry with kitchen paper. Chill the asparagus in the refrigerator for at least 1 hour.

5 Put the vinegar and salt into a bowl and stir with a fork until the salt has dissolved. Stir in the Dijon mustard. Gradually stir in the oil until it is blended. Add the sour cream or yogurt and season with pepper to taste.

6 To serve, arrange the asparagus on individual plates, dividing the spears equally, and drizzle the dressing across the middle of them. Garnish with the fresh raspberries.

COOK'S TIP
Adding Dijon or other mustard to salad dressings not only provides flavour, but also helps the oil and vinegar mixture to combine and emulsify.

2 Trim off the tough ends of the asparagus spears. If you like, remove the "scales" on the stems, using a vegetable peeler.

3 Tie the asparagus spears into two bundles. Lower the bundles into the boiling water and cook for about 2 minutes, until just tender.

Energy 104kcal/431kJ; Protein 5.8g; Carbohydrate 5.8g, of which sugars 5.6g; Fat 6.5g, of which saturates 1.6g; Cholesterol 5mg; Calcium 64mg; Fibre 4g; Sodium 43mg.

Tomato and Courgette Timbales

Timbales are baked savoury custards typical of the south of France, and mainly made with light vegetables. This combination is delicious as an appetizer. It can be served warm or cool.

Serves 4

butter, for greasing
2 courgettes (zucchini), about
*   175g/6oz*
2 firm, ripe vine tomatoes, sliced
2 eggs plus 2 egg yolks
45ml/3 tbsp double (heavy) cream
15ml/1 tbsp fresh tomato sauce or
*   passata (bottled strained tomatoes)*
10ml/2 tsp chopped fresh basil or
*   oregano or 5ml/1 tsp dried oregano*
salt and ground black pepper
salad leaves, to serve

1 Preheat the oven to 180°C/350°F/ Gas 4. Lightly butter four large ramekins. Trim the courgettes, then cut them into thin slices. Put them into a steamer and steam over boiling water for 4–5 minutes.

2 Drain the courgette slices well in a colander, then layer them in the prepared ramekins alternating with the sliced tomatoes.

3 Whisk together the eggs, cream, tomato sauce or passata and basil or oregano in a bowl. Season to taste with salt and pepper.

4 Pour the egg mixture into the ramekins. Place them in a roasting pan and half fill the pan with hot water. Bake the ramekins for 20–30 minutes, until the custard is just firm.

5 Cool slightly, then run a knife blade around the rims of the ramekins and carefully turn out on to small plates. Serve with salad leaves.

COOK'S TIP
Don't overcook the timbales or the texture of the savoury custard will become rubbery.

Energy 72kcal/299kJ; Protein 5.1g; Carbohydrate 2.7g, of which sugars 2.5g; Fat 4.7g, of which saturates 1.3g; Cholesterol 146mg; Calcium 35mg; Fibre 1g; Sodium 55mg.

Lemon, Thyme and Bean Stuffed Mushrooms

Portabello mushrooms have a rich flavour and a meaty texture that go well with this fragrant herb-and-lemon stuffing. The garlicky pine nut accompaniment is a traditional Middle Eastern dish with a smooth, creamy consistency similar to that of hummus.

Serves 4–6

200g/7oz/1 cup dried or 400g/14oz/
*   2 cups drained, canned aduki beans*
45ml/3 tbsp olive oil, plus extra
*   for brushing*
1 onion, finely chopped
2 garlic cloves, crushed
30ml/2 tbsp fresh chopped thyme or
*   5ml/1 tsp dried*
8 large field mushrooms, such as
*   portabello mushrooms, stalks*
*   finely chopped*
50g/2oz/1 cup fresh wholemeal
*   (whole-wheat) breadcrumbs*
juice of 1 lemon
185g/6¹/₂ oz/³/₄ cup crumbled
*   goat's cheese*
salt and ground black pepper

For the pine nut sauce
50g/2oz/¹/₂ cup pine nuts, toasted
50g/2oz/1 cup cubed white bread
2 garlic cloves, chopped
200ml/7fl oz/scant 1 cup milk
45ml/3 tbsp olive oil
15ml/1 tbsp chopped fresh parsley, to
*   garnish (optional)*

1 If using dried beans, place them in a bowl, add cold water to cover and leave to soak overnight, then drain and rinse well. Place the beans in a pan, add enough water to cover and bring to the boil. Boil vigorously for 10 minutes, then reduce the heat, cook for about 30 minutes, until tender, then drain. If using canned beans, rinse under cold running water, drain well, then set aside.

2 Preheat the oven to 200°C/400°F/ Gas 6. Heat the oil in a large, heavy frying pan. Add the onion and garlic and cook, stirring occasionally, for about 5 minutes, until softened. Add the thyme and the mushroom stalks and cook for a further 3 minutes, stirring occasionally, until tender.

3 Stir in the beans, breadcrumbs and lemon juice, season well with salt and pepper, then cook for 2 minutes, until heated through. Mash two-thirds of the beans with a fork or potato masher, leaving the remaining beans whole.

4 Brush an ovenproof dish and the base and sides of the mushrooms with olive oil, then top each one with a spoonful of the bean mixture. Place the mushrooms in the dish, cover with foil and bake for 20 minutes.

5 Remove the foil. Top each mushroom with some of the goat's cheese and bake for a further 15 minutes, or until the goat's cheese is melted and bubbly and the mushrooms are tender.

6 To make the pine nut sauce, place all the ingredients in a food processor or blender and process or blend until smooth and creamy. Add more milk if the mixture appears too thick. Sprinkle with parsley, if using, and serve with the stuffed mushrooms.

Energy 403kcal/1680kJ; Protein 17g; Carbohydrate 25.8g, of which sugars 5.8g; Fat 26.5g, of which saturates 8g; Cholesterol 31mg; Calcium 158mg; Fibre 5.8g; Sodium 572mg.

Hard-boiled Eggs with Tuna Sauce

The combination of eggs and tasty tuna mayonnaise makes a nourishing first course that is quick and easy to prepare.

Serves 6

6 large (US extra large) eggs
200g/7oz can tuna in olive oil
3 anchovy fillets
15ml/1 tbsp capers, drained
lemon juice
30ml/2 tbsp olive oil
salt and ground black pepper
drained capers and anchovy fillets, to
    garnish (optional)

For the mayonnaise

1 egg yolk, at room temperature
5ml/1 tsp Dijon mustard
5ml/1 tsp white wine vinegar or
    lemon juice
150ml/¼ pint/⅔ cup olive oil

1 Cook the eggs in a pan of boiling water for 12–14 minutes. Drain and rinse under cold water. Shell carefully and set aside.

2 Make the mayonnaise by whisking the egg yolk, Dijon mustard and white wine vinegar or lemon juice together in a small bowl. Whisk in the olive oil, a few drops at a time to begin with, until 45–60ml/3–4 tbsp of the oil have been incorporated. Pour in the remaining oil in a slow, steady stream, whisking constantly until thickened and fully incorporated.

3 Place the tuna with its oil, the anchovies, capers, lemon juice and olive oil in a blender or a food processor. Process until smooth.

4 Fold the tuna and anchovy mixture into the mayonnaise. Season with black pepper, and extra salt if necessary. Chill for at least 1 hour.

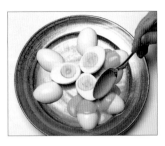

5 To serve, cut the eggs in half lengthways. Arrange them on a serving platter. Spoon over the sauce, and garnish with capers and anchovy fillets, if using. Serve the eggs chilled.

COOK'S TIP

If hard-boiled eggs are left to cool in their shells, the yolks will discolour.

Energy 223kcal/933kJ; Protein 19.3g; Carbohydrate 9.1g, of which sugars 0.6g; Fat 12.6g, of which saturates 3g; Cholesterol 304mg; Calcium 69mg; Fibre 0.6g; Sodium 310mg.

Salmon Cakes with Butter Sauce

Salmon fish cakes make a real treat for the start of a dinner party. They are also economical as you could use any small tail pieces which are on special offer from your local fish store or supermarket.

Makes 6

225g/8oz salmon tail piece, cooked
30ml/2 tbsp chopped fresh parsley
2 spring onions (scallions), chopped
grated rind and juice of 1/2 lemon
225g/8oz mashed potato (not too soft)
1 egg
50g/2oz/1 cup fresh white breadcrumbs
75g/3oz/6 tbsp butter, plus extra for
*   frying (optional)*
oil, for frying (optional)
salt and ground black pepper
courgette (zucchini) and carrot slices
*   and coriander (cilantro), to garnish*

1 Remove and discard all the skin and bones from the fish and mash or flake the flesh well.

2 Place the fish in a bowl and add the fresh parsley, onions and 5ml/1 tsp of the lemon rind, then season with salt and plenty of black pepper.

3 Gently work in the mashed potato and then, with lightly dampened hands, shape the mixture into six rounds, triangles or croquettes. Place the salmon cakes on a platter and chill them in the refrigerator for 20 minutes to firm up.

4 Preheat the grill (broiler). Beat the egg in a shallow dish and spread out the breadcrumbs.When chilled, coat the salmon cakes well in egg and then in the breadcrumbs. Grill (broil) gently for 5 minutes on each side, or until golden, or fry in butter and oil.

5 To make the butter sauce, melt the butter, whisk in the remaining lemon rind, the lemon juice, 15–30ml/ 1–2 tbsp water and season to taste with salt and pepper. Simmer for a few minutes, whisking, and serve with the hot fish cakes, garnished with slices of courgette and carrot and a sprig of fresh coriander.

Energy 188kcal/782kJ; Protein 9.5g; Carbohydrate 6.2g, of which sugars 0.7g; Fat 14.1g, of which saturates 6.8g; Cholesterol 68mg; Calcium 36mg; Fibre 0.9g; Sodium 101mg.

Prawn, Egg and Avocado Mousses

A light and creamy mousse with lots of chunky texture and a great mix of flavours.

Serves 6

a little olive oil
juice and rind of 1 lemon
1 sachet gelatine
60ml/4 tbsp good-quality mayonnaise
60ml/4 tbsp chopped fresh dill
5ml/1 tsp anchovy essence (extract)
5ml/1 tsp Worcestershire sauce
1 large avocado, ripe but just firm
4 hard-boiled eggs, shelled
  and chopped
175g/6oz/1 cup cooked peeled prawns
  (shrimp), coarsely chopped if large
250ml/8fl oz/1 cup double (heavy) or
  whipping cream, lightly whipped
2 egg whites, whisked
salt and ground black pepper
fresh dill or parsley sprigs, to garnish
warm bread or toast, to serve

1 Prepare six small ramekins. Lightly grease the dishes with olive oil, then wrap a greaseproof (wax) paper collar around the top of each and secure with tape. This makes sure that you can fill the dishes as high as you like, and the extra mixture will be supported while it is setting. The mousses will look really dramatic when you remove the paper. Alternatively, prepare just one medium soufflé dish.

2 Put the lemon juice into a small, heatproof bowl, stir in 15ml/1 tbsp hot water and sprinkle over the gelatine. Leave for 5 minutes, until spongy, then set the bowl over hot water, until clear, stirring occasionally. Leave to cool slightly, then blend in the lemon rind, mayonnaise, dill, anchovy essence and Worcestershire sauce.

3 Cut the avocado in half, twist to separate and remove the stone (pit) with the point of the knife. In a medium bowl mash the avocado flesh, then mix in the eggs and prawns. Stir in the gelatine mixture and then fold in the cream and egg whites. Season to taste with salt and pepper. When evenly blended, spoon into the ramekins or soufflé dish and chill for 3–4 hours.

4 Garnish with the dill or parsley and serve the mousse with bread or toast.

COOK'S TIP
Other fish can make a good alternative to prawns (shrimp). Try substituting the same quantity of smoked trout or salmon, or cooked crab meat.

Energy 371kcal/1535kJ; Protein 14g; Carbohydrate1g, of which sugars 1g; Fat 35g, of which saturates 16g; Cholesterol 301mg; Calcium 82mg; Fibre 0g; Sodium 626mg.

Sea Trout Mousse

This deliciously creamy mousse makes a little sea trout go a long way. It is equally good made with salmon if sea trout is unavailable. Serve with crisp Melba toast or triangles of lightly toasted pitta bread.

Serves 6

250g/9oz sea trout fillet
120ml/4fl oz/¹⁄₂ cup fish stock
2 gelatine leaves, or 15ml/1 tbsp
*   powdered gelatine*
juice of ¹⁄₂ lemon
30ml/2 tbsp dry sherry or dry vermouth
30ml/2 tbsp freshly grated Parmesan
300ml/¹⁄₂ pint/1¹⁄₄ cups whipping cream
2 egg whites
15ml/1 tbsp sunflower oil, for greasing
salt and ground white pepper

For the garnish
5cm/2in piece cucumber, with peel,
*   thinly sliced and halved*
fresh dill or chervil

1 Put the sea trout in a large, shallow pan. Pour in the fish stock and heat gently to simmering point. Poach the fish for about 3–4 minutes, until it is lightly cooked. Carefully strain the stock into a jug (pitcher) and leave the sea trout to cool slightly.

2 Add the gelatine to the reserved hot stock and stir well until it has dissolved completely. Cover and set aside until required.

3 When the sea trout is cool enough to handle, remove and discard the skin and any stray bones, then flake the flesh. Pour the stock into a food processor or blender. Process briefly, then gradually add the flaked sea trout, lemon juice, sherry or vermouth and Parmesan through the feeder tube, continuing to process the mixture until it is smooth. Scrape into a large bowl and leave to cool completely.

4 Lightly whip the cream in a bowl, then fold it into the cold trout mixture. Season to taste with salt and pepper, then cover with clear film (plastic wrap) and chill until the mousse is just starting to set. It should have the consistency of mayonnaise.

5 In a clean, grease-free bowl, beat the egg whites with a pinch of salt until they form soft peaks. Then using a large metal spoon or rubber spatula, stir about one-third of the egg whites into the sea trout mixture to slacken it slightly, then carefully fold in the remainder.

6 Lightly grease six ramekins or similar individual serving dishes. Divide the mousse equally among the prepared dishes and level the surface. Place in the refrigerator for 2–3 hours, until set. Just before serving, arrange a few slices of cucumber and a small herb sprig on top of each mousse and, finally, sprinkle over a little chopped dill or chervil.

Energy 241kcal/999kJ; Protein 12.3g; Carbohydrate 1.8g, of which sugars 1.8g; Fat 20g, of which saturates 14.5g; Cholesterol 9mg; Calcium 104mg; Fibre 0.1g; Sodium 127mg.

Salmon and Scallop Brochettes

With their delicate colours and really superb flavour, these skewers make the perfect first course.

Serves 4

8 lemon grass stalks
225g/8oz salmon fillet, skinned
8 shucked queen scallops, with their corals if possible
8 baby (pearl) onions, blanched
1/2 yellow (bell) pepper, seeded and cut into 8 squares
25g/1oz/2 tbsp butter
juice of 1/2 lemon
salt, ground white pepper and paprika

For the sauce

30ml/2 tbsp dry vermouth
50g/2oz/1/4 cup butter
5ml/1 tsp chopped fresh tarragon

1 Preheat the grill (broiler) to medium-high. Cut off the top 7.5–10cm/3–4in of each lemon grass stalk to make "skewers" for the brochettes. Reserve the bulb ends for another dish. Cut the salmon fillet into twelve 2cm/3/4in cubes. Thread the salmon cubes, scallops, corals if available, onions and pepper squares on to the lemon grass stalks and arrange the brochettes in a grill pan.

2 Melt the butter in a small pan, add the lemon juice and a pinch of paprika and then brush all over the brochettes. Grill (broil) the skewers for about 2–3 minutes on each side, turning and basting the brochettes every minute, until the fish and scallops are just cooked, but are still very juicy. Transfer to a platter and keep hot while you make the tarragon butter sauce.

3 To make the sauce, pour the dry vermouth and the leftover cooking juices from the brochettes into a pan, bring to the boil and boil fiercely to reduce by half. Lower the heat, add the butter and melt, then stir in the chopped fresh tarragon and season with salt and ground white pepper. Pour the tarragon butter sauce over the brochettes and serve.

Energy 321kcal/1336kJ; Protein 23.5g; Carbohydrate 4.8g, of which sugars 2.7g; Fat 22.4g, of which saturates 11.1g; Cholesterol 92mg; Calcium 36mg; Fibre 0.6g; Sodium 231mg.

Coquilles St Jacques

A classic French first course that calls for the best quality scallops possible to produce a truly wonderful result. Select firm, white shellfish and check that they have not previously been frozen before buying them to avoid their being watery and flabby. You will need eight scallop shells to serve this dish.

Serves 8

900g/2lb potatoes, chopped
115g/4oz/¹/₂ cup butter
8 large or 16 small scallops
250ml/8fl oz/1 cup fish stock
fresh dill sprigs, to garnish
grilled (broiled) lemon wedges, to serve

For the sauce
50g/2oz/4 tbsp butter
50g/2oz/¹/₂ cup plain (all-purpose) flour
600ml/1 pint/2¹/₂ cups milk
60ml/4 tbsp single (light) cream
250g/8oz/2 cups grated mature (sharp)
    Cheddar cheese
salt and ground black pepper

1 Preheat oven to 200°C/400°F/Gas 6. Place the chopped potatoes in a large pan, cover with lightly salted water and boil for 15 minutes, or until tender. Drain and mash with the butter.

2 Spoon the mixture into a piping (pastry) bag fitted with a star nozzle. Pipe the potatoes around the outside of a cleaned scallop shell. Repeat the process, making eight in total.

3 Simmer the scallops in the fish stock for about 3 minutes, or until just firm. Do not allow the stock to boil but poach the scallops gently, otherwise they will become tough and rubbery. Drain and slice the scallops thinly. Set them aside.

4 To make the sauce, melt the butter in a small pan, add the flour and cook over a low heat, stirring constantly, for a couple of minutes, gradually add the milk and cream, stirring constantly, and cook until thickened.

5 Stir in the cheese and cook until melted. Season to taste with salt and pepper. Spoon a little sauce in the base of each shell. Divide the scallops between the shells and then pour the remaining sauce over the scallops.

6 Bake the scallops for 10 minutes, or until golden. Garnish with dill and serve with grilled lemon wedges.

Energy 466kcal/1948kJ; Protein 24.2g; Carbohydrate 28.8g, of which sugars 5.7g; Fat 28.6g, of which saturates 18.3g; Cholesterol 103mg; Calcium 342mg; Fibre 1.3g; Sodium 496mg.

Grilled Scallops with Brown Butter

This is a very striking dish as the scallops are served on the half shell, still sizzling from the grill. Reserve it for a special occasion – and special guests.

Serves 4

50g/2oz/¹/₄ cup unsalted (sweet)
*   butter, diced*
8 scallops, prepared on the half shell
15ml/1 tbsp chopped fresh parsley
salt and ground black pepper
lemon wedges, to serve

COOK'S TIP

If you can't get hold of scallops in their shells, you can use shelled, fresh scallops if you cook them on the day of purchase. Avoid frozen scallops, as they have a flabby texture.

1 Preheat the grill (broiler) to high. Melt the butter in a small pan over a medium heat. Continue to heat it gently until it is pale golden brown. Remove the pan from the heat immediately – the butter must not be allowed to burn. Arrange the scallops in their half shells in a single layer in a large casserole or a shallow roasting pan. Brush a little of the brown butter over them.

2 Grill (broil) the scallops for 4 minutes – it will not be necessary to turn them. Pour over the remaining brown butter, then season with a little salt and pepper and sprinkle the parsley over them. Serve immediately, with lemon wedges for squeezing over.

Fried Squid

The squid is simply dusted in flour and dipped in egg before being fried, so the coating is light and does not mask the flavour.

Serves 2

115g/4oz prepared squid, cut
*   into rings*
30ml/2 tbsp seasoned plain
*   (all-purpose) flour*
1 egg
30ml/2 tbsp milk
olive oil, for frying
sea salt, to taste
lemon wedges, to serve

VARIATION

For a crisper coating, dust the rings in flour, then dip them in batter instead of this simple egg and flour coating.

1 Toss the squid rings in the seasoned flour in a bowl or strong plastic bag. Beat the egg and milk together in a shallow bowl. Heat the oil in a large, heavy frying pan.

COOK'S TIP

Keep the squid warm in the oven while you cook the rest.

2 Dip the floured squid rings, one at a time, into the egg mixture, shaking off any excess liquid. Add to the hot oil, in batches if necessary, and cook for 2–3 minutes on each side, until evenly golden all over.

3 Drain the fried squid on kitchen paper, then sprinkle with salt. Transfer to a small warm plate and serve with the lemon wedges.

Scallops: Energy 186kcal/776kJ; Protein 17.9g; Carbohydrate 3g, of which sugars 0.4g; Fat 11.5g, of which saturates 6.8g; Cholesterol 62mg; Calcium 49mg; Fibre 0.6g; Sodium 215mg.
Squid: Energy 646kcal/2724kJ; Protein 90.9g; Carbohydrate 19.1g, of which sugars 1g; Fat 23.7g, of which saturates 4.8g; Cholesterol 1350mg; Calcium 126mg; Fibre 0.5g; Sodium 655mg.

Scallop-stuffed Roast Peppers with **Pesto**

Serve these scallop-and-pesto-filled sweet red peppers with Italian bread, such as ciabatta or focaccia, to mop up the garlicky juices.

Serves 4

4 squat red (bell) peppers
2 large garlic cloves, cut into
  thin slivers
60ml/4 tbsp olive oil
4 shelled scallops
45ml/3 tbsp pesto sauce
salt and ground black pepper
freshly grated Parmesan cheese, to serve
salad leaves and basil sprigs, to garnish

1 Preheat the oven to 180°C/350°F/Gas 4. Cut the peppers in half lengthways, through their stalks. Scrape out and discard the cores and seeds. Wash the pepper shells and pat dry with kitchen paper.

2 Put the peppers, cut side up, in an oiled roasting pan. Divide the slivers of garlic equally among them and sprinkle with salt and ground black pepper to taste. Then spoon the olive oil into the peppers and roast for 40 minutes.

VARIATION
You could also prepare this dish using red pesto sauce, which is made with sun-dried tomatoes.

3 Using a sharp knife, carefully cut each of the shelled scallops in half horizontally to make two flat discs, each with a piece of coral. When cooked, remove the peppers from the oven and place a scallop half in each pepper half. Then top the scallops with the pesto sauce.

4 Return the roasting pan to the oven and roast for 10 minutes more. Transfer the peppers to individual serving plates, sprinkle with grated Parmesan and garnish each plate with a few salad leaves and basil sprigs. Serve warm.

COOK'S TIP
Scallops are available from most fishmongers and supermarkets with fresh fish counters. Never cook scallops for longer than the time stated in the recipe or they will be tough and rubbery. The orange-coloured corals – scallop roe – are regarded by many as a delicacy, although in the United States and some other countries they are usually discarded.

Energy 285kcal/1186kJ; Protein 18.6g; Carbohydrate 16.7g, of which sugars 13.8g; Fat 16.3g, of which saturates 4.3g; Cholesterol 35mg; Calcium 168mg; Fibre 3.8g; Sodium 222mg.

Marinated Asparagus and Langoustines

For an even more extravagant treat, you could make this attractive salad with medallions of fresh lobster. For a slightly more economical version, use large prawns, allowing six per serving.

Serves 4

16 langoustines
16 fresh asparagus spears, trimmed
2 carrots
30ml/2 tbsp olive oil
1 garlic clove, peeled
salt and ground black pepper
4 fresh tarragon sprigs and some
   chopped fresh tarragon, to garnish

For the dressing
30ml/2 tbsp tarragon vinegar
120ml/4fl oz/¹/₂ cup olive oil

1 Peel the langoustines and keep the discarded parts for making shellfish stock. Set the tail meat aside.

2 Steam the asparagus over a pan of boiling salted water until just tender, but still a little crisp. Refresh under cold water, drain well and place in a shallow dish.

3 Peel the carrots and cut into fine julienne shreds. Cook in a pan of lightly salted, boiling water for about 3 minutes, until tender but still retaining some crunch. Drain, refresh under cold water and drain again. Add to the asparagus.

4 Make the dressing. Whisk the tarragon vinegar with the olive oil in a jug (pitcher). Season to taste with salt and pepper. Pour the dressing over the asparagus and carrots, cover and set aside to marinate.

5 Heat the oil with the garlic in a frying pan until very hot. Add the langoustines and sauté quickly until just heated through. Discard the garlic.

6 Arrange four asparagus spears and a quarter of the carrots on each of four individual plates. Drizzle over the dressing remaining in the dish and top each portion with four langoustine tails. Top with the tarragon sprigs and sprinkle the chopped tarragon on top. Serve immediately.

COOK'S TIP
Langoustines are also known as Dublin Bay prawns, Norway lobster and, when sold already peeled, scampi. Most of the langoustines we buy have been cooked at sea, a necessary act because the flesh deteriorates rapidly after death. Bear this in mind when you cook the shellfish. Because it has already been cooked, it will need to be only lightly sautéed until heated through. If you are lucky enough to buy live langoustines, kill them quickly by immersing them in boiling water, then sauté until cooked through.

Energy 409kcal/1691kJ; Protein 15g; Carbohydrate 1g, of which sugars 1g; Fat 38g, of which saturates 6g; Cholesterol 168mg; Calcium 80mg; Fibre 1g; Sodium 961mg.

Tiger Prawns with **Mint, Dill** and **Lime**

A wonderful combination – mint, dill and lime blend together to make a magical concoction to flavour succulent tiger prawns that will delight everyone who tries it.

Serves 4

4 large sheets filo pastry
75g/3oz/$\frac{1}{3}$ cup butter
16 large tiger prawns (jumbo shrimp), cooked and peeled
15ml/1 tbsp chopped fresh mint, plus extra to garnish
15ml/1 tbsp chopped fresh dill
juice of 1 lime
8 cooked unpeeled tiger prawns (jumbo shrimp) and lime wedges, to serve

1 Keep the sheets of filo pastry covered with a dry, clean dishtowel to keep them moist. Melt the butter in a small pan over a low heat, then remove the pan from the heat. Cut one sheet of filo pastry in half widthways and brush with some of the melted butter. Place one half on top of the other.

2 Preheat the oven to 230°C/450°F/ Gas 8. Cut the tiger prawns in half down the back of the prawn and remove the dark vein.

3 Place four prawns in the centre of the double layer of filo pastry and sprinkle a quarter of the mint, dill and lime juice over the top. Fold over the sides, brush with butter and roll up to make a parcel.

4 Make three more parcels in the same way. Place all the parcels, join side down, on a lightly greased baking sheet. Bake for 10 minutes, or until golden. Serve immediately, garnished with whole tiger prawns, lime wedges and extra chopped mint.

Energy 246kcal/1024kJ; Protein 11.1g; Carbohydrate 15g, of which sugars 0.7g; Fat 16.1g, of which saturates 9.9g; Cholesterol 137mg; Calcium 94mg; Fibre 1.2g; Sodium 213mg.

Prawn Cocktail

There is no nicer appetizer than a good, fresh prawn cocktail – and nothing nastier than one in which soggy prawns swim in a thin, vinegary sauce embedded in limp lettuce. This recipe shows just how good a prawn cocktail can be.

Serves 6

60ml/4 tbsp double (heavy) cream,
* lightly whipped*
60ml/4 tbsp mayonnaise, preferably
* home-made*
60ml/4 tbsp tomato ketchup
5–10ml/1–2 tsp Worcestershire sauce
juice of 1 lemon
1/2 cos or romaine lettuce
450g/1lb/4 cups cooked peeled
* prawns (shrimp)*
salt, ground black pepper and paprika
6 large whole cooked unpeeled prawns
* (shrimp), to garnish (optional)*
thinly sliced brown bread and lemon
* wedges, to serve*

1 Mix together the whipped cream, mayonnaise and ketchup in a bowl. Add Worcestershire sauce to taste. Stir in enough lemon juice to make a really tangy cocktail sauce.

VARIATION
You can also use this mixture for filling vol-au-vents, cold puff pastry cases, to serve as appetizers, canapés or party snacks. The prawns (shrimp) should be chopped before they are mixed with the sauce. Fill the cases just before serving, otherwise they will become soggy and liable to collapse.

2 Finely shred the lettuce and fill six individual glasses one-third full. Gently stir the prawns into the sauce, then taste and adjust the seasoning, if necessary. Spoon the prawn mixture generously over the lettuce.

3 If you like, drape a whole cooked prawn over the edge of each glass (see Cook's Tip). Sprinkle each of the cocktails with ground black pepper and some paprika. Serve the cocktails immediately, with thinly sliced brown bread and butter and lemon wedges for squeezing over.

COOK'S TIP
To prepare the garnish, remove the heads and peel the body shells from the prawns, including the legs, and leave the tail "fan" for decoration.

Energy 194kcal/805kJ; Protein 13.9g; Carbohydrate 4.2g, of which sugars 4g; Fat 13.6g, of which saturates 4.6g; Cholesterol 167mg; Calcium 80mg; Fibre 0.4g; Sodium 384mg.

Mussels and Clams with Lemon Grass

Lemon grass has an incomparable flavour and is excellent used with a medley of seafood.

Serves 6

1.8–2kg/4–4¹/₂ lb fresh mussels
450g/1lb baby clams, washed
120ml/4fl oz/¹/₂ cup dry white wine
1 bunch spring onions
   (scallions), chopped
2 lemon grass stalks, chopped
6 kaffir lime leaves, chopped
10ml/2 tsp Thai green curry paste
200ml/7fl oz/scant 1 cup coconut cream
30ml/2 tbsp chopped fresh
   coriander (cilantro)
salt and ground black pepper
whole garlic chives, to garnish

1 Scrub the mussels and pull off the beards. Discard any that are broken or stay open when tapped.

2 Put the wine, spring onions, lemon grass, lime leaves and curry paste in a pan. Simmer over a low heat until the wine has almost evaporated.

COOK'S TIPS
• Buy a few extra mussels just in case there are any which have to be discarded.
• Small, smooth-shelled clams just need rinsing in cold water, but the larger, rough-shelled varieties should be well scrubbed. Like mussels, discard any with broken shells or that are open and do not shut immediately when sharply tapped with a knife.

3 Add the mussels and clams to the pan, cover with a tight-fitting lid and steam the shellfish over a high heat, shaking the pan occasionally, for about 5–6 minutes, until all the shells have opened.

4 Using a slotted spoon, transfer the mussels and clams to a warmed serving bowl and keep hot. Discard any shellfish that remain closed. Strain the cooking liquid through a sieve lined with muslin (cheesecloth) into a clean pan. Set over a low heat and simmer to reduce the quantity to about 250ml/8fl oz/1 cup.

5 Stir in the coconut cream and coriander and season with salt and pepper to taste. Heat through. Pour the sauce over the seafood and serve immediately, garnished with whole garlic chives.

Energy 177kcal/745kJ; Protein 21.8g; Carbohydrate 1.9g, of which sugars 1.2g; Fat 7.8g, of which saturates 5.3g; Cholesterol 58mg; Calcium 212mg; Fibre 0.3g; Sodium 594mg.

Prosciutto with **Potato Rémoulade**

Lime juice brings a contemporary twist to this cream-enriched version of the classic piquant rémoulade dressing. It is best made when the new season's asparagus is available.

Serves 8

*4 potatoes, each weighing about
    350g/12oz, quartered lengthways
300ml/¹⁄₂ pint/1¹⁄₄ cup mayonnaise
300ml/¹⁄₂ pint/1¹⁄₄ cup double
    (heavy) cream
10–15ml/2–3 tsp Dijon mustard
juice of 1 lime
60ml/4 tbsp olive oil
24 prosciutto slices
900g/2lb asparagus spears, halved
salt and ground black pepper
50g/2oz wild rocket (arugula),
    to garnish
extra virgin olive oil, to serve*

1 Put the potatoes in a pan. Add water to cover and bring to the boil. Add salt, then simmer for about 15 minutes, or until the potatoes are tender, but do not let them get too soft. Drain thoroughly and leave to cool, then cut into long, thin strips.

2 Beat together the mayonnaise, cream, mustard, lime juice and seasoning in a large bowl. Add the potatoes and stir carefully to coat them with the dressing.

3 Heat the oil in a griddle or frying pan and cook the prosciutto, in batches, until crisp and golden. Remove with a slotted spoon, draining each piece well.

4 Cook the asparagus in the olive oil remaining in the pan for 3 minutes, or until tender and golden.

5 Put a generous spoonful of potato rémoulade on each plate and top with several slices of prosciutto. Add the asparagus and garnish with rocket. Serve immediately, offering olive oil to drizzle over.

VARIATION
Use a mixture of potatoes and celeriac instead of all potatoes. For an inexpensive salad, use mixed root vegetables and omit the asparagus, adding fresh or roasted cherry tomatoes instead.

Energy 740kcal/3064kJ; Protein 13g; Carbohydrate 34g, of which sugars 5g; Fat 62g, of which saturates 20g; Cholesterol 95mg; Calcium 65mg; Fibre 5g; Sodium 708mg.

Stuffed Garlic Mushrooms with Prosciutto

Field mushrooms can vary greatly in size. Try to find similar-sized specimens with undamaged edges.

Serves 4

8 field (portabello) mushrooms
15g/¹/₂oz/¹/₄ cup dried ceps, bay boletus or saffron milk-caps, soaked in warm water for 20 minutes
75g/3oz/6 tbsp unsalted (sweet) butter
1 onion, chopped
1 garlic clove, crushed
75g/3oz/³/₄ cup fresh breadcrumbs
1 egg
75ml/5 tbsp chopped fresh parsley
15ml/1 tbsp chopped fresh thyme
salt and ground black pepper
115g/4oz prosciutto di Parma or San Daniele, thinly sliced
fresh parsley, to garnish

1 Preheat the oven to 190°C/375°F/ Gas 5. Carefully break off the stems of the field mushrooms, without damaging the caps. Set the caps aside. Finely chop the stems. Drain the dried mushrooms and chop finely.

2 Melt half the butter in a large, heavy frying pan until foaming. Add the onion and cook over a low heat, stirring occasionally, for 6–8 minutes, until softened but not coloured.

3 Add the garlic, dried mushroom and chopped mushroom stems to the pan and cook, stirring occasionally, for about 2–3 minutes.

4 Transfer the mixture to a bowl, add the breadcrumbs, egg, parsley and thyme and season to taste with salt and pepper. Melt the remaining butter in a small pan and generously brush over the reserved mushroom caps. Arrange the mushroom caps on a baking sheet and spoon in the filling. Bake for 20–25 minutes, until they are well browned and tender.

5 Top each mushroom with a slice of prosciutto, garnish with parsley and serve immediately.

COOK'S TIPS

• Garlic mushrooms can be easily prepared in advance ready to go into the oven when your guests arrive.

• Fresh breadcrumbs can be made and then frozen. They can be taken from the freezer as they are required and do not need to be thawed first.

• Prosciutto is a dry-cured ham and opinions on whether Parma or San Daniele ham is superior differ. You could also use Jambon de Bayonne, Lomo Ahumado or Smithfield ham.

Energy 323kcal/1356kJ; Protein 14g; Carbohydrate 18g, of which sugars 3g; Fat 22g, of which saturates 12g; Cholesterol 101mg; Calcium 73mg; Fibre 4g; Sodium 748mg.

Grilled Asparagus with Salt-cured Ham

Serve this classic Spanish tapas when asparagus is plentiful and not too expensive.

Serves 4

6 slices of Serrano ham
12 asparagus spears
15ml/1 tbsp olive oil
sea salt and coarsely ground
    black pepper

COOK'S TIP
If you can't find Serrano ham, the best variety of which is called Jamón de Jabugo, you can use Italian prosciutto or Portuguese presunto instead.

1 Preheat the grill (broiler) to high. Cut each slice of ham lengthways in half and wrap one half around each of the asparagus spears.

2 Brush the ham and asparagus lightly with oil and season to taste with salt and pepper. Place on the grill rack. Grill (broil), turning frequently but carefully with tongs, for 5–6 minutes, until the asparagus is tender but still firm. Serve immediately.

Energy 183kcal/760kJ; Protein 11g; Carbohydrate 0g, of which sugars 0g; Fat 15g, of which saturates 5g; Cholesterol 41mg; Calcium 9mg; Fibre 2g; Sodium 756mg.

dinner party and festive main courses

Classic dishes are sure winners for dinner parties
and celebrations, especially with a clever twist
of seasoning or a contemporary garnish.

Tempura

This flavourful Japanese dish of crunchy battered vegetables and crispy squid rings is served with a piquant dipping sauce. Tempura can be cooked at the table over a special spill-proof spirit burner making it ideal for a party.

Serves 4

2 medium aubergines (eggplants)
4 red (bell) peppers, seeded
500g/1¼ lb/5 cups plain (all-purpose)
   flour, plus extra for dusting
8 baby squid, cut into rings
400g/14oz green beans, trimmed
24 mint sprigs
oil, for deep-frying
4 egg yolks
1 litre/1¾ pints/4 cups iced water
10ml/2 tsp salt
gari (Japanese pickled ginger) or grated
   fresh root ginger, and grated mooli
   (daikon) or pink radishes, to serve

For the dipping sauce
400ml/14fl oz/1⅔ cups water
90ml/6 tbsp mirin or sweet sherry
20g/½oz bonito flakes (see Cook's Tip)
90ml/6 tbsp soy sauce

1 To make the dipping sauce, mix the sauce ingredients together in a pan, bring to the boil and then strain into serving saucers and leave to cool.

COOK'S TIP

If you cannot get hold of bonito flakes, an acceptable substitute would be to use 200ml/7fl oz/scant 1 cup fish stock instead of the water to make the dipping sauce.

VARIATIONS

• Any seafood is suitable for cooking in a tempura batter. Try mussels, clams, prawns (shrimp) or scallops, or slices of salmon, cod, tuna or haddock.
• Cauliflower, broccoli, and mangetouts (snow peas) work well, too.

2 Cut the aubergine and peppers into fine julienne strips using a sharp knife or a mandolin. Put the flour for dusting into a plastic bag and add the squid. Shake the bag to coat the squid with a little flour, then place on a serving dish. Repeat with the vegetables and mint.

3 When you are ready to serve, heat the oil for deep-frying in a wok or deep pan to 190°C/375°F or until a cube of day-old bread dropped into the hot oil browns in 45 seconds. Transfer the wok or pan to a burner at the table. Never leave it unattended.

4 When ready to eat, beat the egg yolks and the iced water together. Tip in the flour and salt, and stir briefly. It is important that the tempura is lumpy and not mixed to a smooth batter.

5 Each diner dips the food into the batter and then immediately into the hot oil, using chopsticks, long fondue forks or wire baskets. Deep-fry for about 2 minutes, or until crisp.

6 Serve the tempura dipped in the sauce and accompanied by gari or ginger and mooli or radishes.

Energy 767kcal/3234kJ; Protein 38g; Carbohydrate 114g, of which sugars 16g; Fat 21g, of which saturates 4g; Cholesterol 472mg; Calcium 274mg; Fibre 13g; Sodium 1136mg.

Swiss Cheese Fondue with Vegetables

This classic, richly flavoured fondue is traditionally served with cubes of bread, but here it is updated with herbed vegetable dippers and toasted garlic croûtes.

Serves 4–6

2 French batons or 1 baguette
1–2 garlic cloves, halved
1 small head broccoli, divided
   into florets
1 small head cauliflower, divided
   into florets
200g/7oz mangetouts (snow peas)
   or green beans, trimmed
115g/4oz baby carrots, trimmed,
   or 2 medium carrots, cut into wedges
250ml/8fl oz/1 cup dry white wine
115g/4oz/1 cup grated Gruyère cheese
250g/9oz/2¼ cups grated
   Emmenthal cheese
15ml/1tbsp cornflour (cornstarch)
30ml/2tbsp Kirsch
freshly grated nutmeg
salt and ground black pepper

For the dressing
30ml/2 tbsp extra virgin olive oil
rind and juice of 2 lemons
25g/1oz/1 cup chopped fresh parsley
25g/1oz/1 cup chopped fresh mint
1 red chilli, seeded and finely chopped

1 Cut the batons or baguette on the diagonal into 1cm/½in slices, then toast on both sides. Rub one side of each slice with the cut side of a garlic clove, if you like, and transfer to a platter.

2 Blanch the vegetables for 2 minutes in a large pan of lightly salted, boiling water, then place them in a large bowl. While they are hot, add all the dressing ingredients, season and toss together.

3 Rub the inside of the fondue pot with the cut side of a garlic clove. Pour in the white wine and heat gently on the stove. Gradually add the grated cheeses to the pot, stirring constantly until melted. Mix the cornflour with the Kirsch and add to the pot, then stir until thickened.

4 Season with salt, ground black pepper and grated nutmeg to taste. When the fondue is hot and smooth, but not boiling, transfer to a burner at the table. Do not leave unattended.

5 Each diner dips the vegetables and toasted bread into the fondue.

VARIATIONS
• Use fresh chopped basil instead of mint.
• Use crunchy, fresh vegetables such as pink radishes, mushrooms, baby corn and red or yellow (bell) peppers.

Energy 363kcal/1518kJ; Protein 19g; Carbohydrate 27g, of which sugars 9g; Fat 20g, of which saturates 10g; Cholesterol 42mg; Calcium 507mg; Fibre 5g; Sodium 501mg.

Peppers filled with Spiced Vegetables

Indian spices season the potato and aubergine stuffing in these colourful baked peppers. They are good with plain rice and a lentil dhal, or a salad, Indian breads and a cucumber or mint and yogurt raita.

Serves 6

6 large evenly shaped red or yellow
   (bell) peppers
500g/1¼lb waxy potatoes
1 small onion, chopped
4–5 garlic cloves, chopped
5cm/2in piece fresh root
   ginger, chopped
1–2 fresh green chillies, seeded
   and chopped
105ml/7 tbsp water
90–105ml/6–7 tbsp groundnut
   (peanut) oil
1 aubergine (eggplant), cut into
   1cm/½in dice
10ml/2 tsp cumin seeds
5ml/1 tsp kalonji (nigella) seeds
2.5ml/½ tsp ground turmeric
5ml/1 tsp ground coriander
5ml/1 tsp ground toasted cumin seeds
pinch of cayenne pepper
about 30ml/2 tbsp lemon juice
salt and ground black pepper
30ml/2 tbsp chopped fresh coriander
   (cilantro), to garnish

2 Bring a large pan of lightly salted water to the boil. Add the peppers and cook for 5–6 minutes. Drain and leave upside down in a colander.

3 Cook the potatoes in lightly salted, boiling water for 10–12 minutes, until just tender. Drain, cool and peel, then cut into 1cm/½in dice.

4 Put the onion, garlic, ginger and green chillies in a food processor or blender with 60ml/4 tbsp of the water and process to a purée.

5 Heat 45ml/3 tbsp of the oil in a large, deep frying pan and cook the aubergine over a medium heat, stirring occasionally, until browned on all sides. Remove from the pan and set aside. Add another 30ml/2 tbsp of the oil to the pan and cook the diced potatoes until lightly browned. Remove from the pan and set aside.

6 If necessary, add another 15ml/1 tbsp oil to the pan, then add the cumin and kalonji seeds. Cook briefly until the seeds darken, then add the turmeric, coriander and ground cumin. Cook for 15 seconds. Stir in the onion and garlic purée and cook, scraping the pan with a spatula, until it begins to brown.

7 Return the potatoes and aubergines to the pan, season with salt, pepper and 1–2 pinches of cayenne. Add the remaining water and 15ml/1 tbsp lemon juice and then cook, stirring, until the liquid evaporates. Preheat the oven to 190°C/375°F/Gas 5.

8 Fill the peppers with the potato mix and place on a lightly greased baking tray. Brush the peppers with a little oil and bake for 30–35 minutes, until the peppers are cooked. Leave to cool, then sprinkle with a little more lemon juice, garnish with the coriander and serve.

1 Cut the tops off the red or yellow peppers then remove and discard the seeds. Cut a thin slice off the base of the peppers, if necessary, to make them stand upright.

Energy 260kcal/1085kJ; Protein 4g; Carbohydrate 26g, of which sugars 12g; Fat 16g, of which saturates 3g; Cholesterol 0mg; Calcium 34mg; Fibre 6g; Sodium 19mg.

Goat's Cheese Soufflé

The mellow flavour of roasted garlic pervades this simple, but elegant soufflé. Balance this rich dish with a crisp green salad, including peppery leaves.

Serves 6–8

4 large heads of garlic
6 fresh thyme sprigs
30ml/2 tbsp olive oil
475ml/16fl oz/2 cups milk
2 fresh bay leaves
4 × 1cm/½in thick onion slices
4 cloves
115g/4oz/½ cup butter
75g/3oz/⅔ cup plain (all-purpose)
    flour, sifted
cayenne pepper
6 eggs, separated, plus 1 egg white
300g/11oz goat's cheese, crumbled
115g/4oz/1⅓ cups freshly grated
    Parmesan cheese
5–10ml/1–2 tsp chopped fresh thyme
5ml/1 tsp cream of tartar
salt and ground black pepper

1 Preheat the oven to 180°C/350°F/Gas 4. Place the garlic and thyme sprigs on a piece of foil. Sprinkle with the oil and close the foil around the garlic, then bake for about 1 hour, until the garlic is soft. Leave to cool.

2 Squeeze the garlic out of its skin. Discard the thyme and garlic skins, then purée the garlic flesh with the oil.

3 Meanwhile, place the milk, bay leaves, onion slices and cloves in a medium pan. Bring to the boil, then remove from the heat. Cover and leave to stand for 30 minutes.

4 Melt 75g/3oz/6 tbsp of the butter in another pan. Stir in the flour and cook gently for 2 minutes, stirring. Reheat and strain the milk, then gradually stir it into the flour and butter.

5 Cook the sauce very gently for 10 minutes, stirring frequently. Season with salt, pepper and a pinch of cayenne. Cool slightly. Preheat the oven to 200°C/400°F/Gas 6.

6 Beat the egg yolks into the sauce, one at a time. Then beat in the goat's cheese, all but 30ml/2 tbsp of the Parmesan and the chopped thyme. Use the remaining butter to grease a large soufflé dish (1 litre/1¾ pints/4 cups) or eight ramekins (about 125ml/4fl oz/½ cup).

7 Whisk the egg whites and cream of tartar in a clean, grease-free bowl until firm, but not dry. Stir 90ml/6 tbsp of the egg whites into the sauce, then gently, but thoroughly, fold in the remainder using a rubber spatula.

8 Pour the mixture into the prepared dish or dishes. Run a knife around the edge of each dish, pushing the mixture away from the rim. Sprinkle with the reserved Parmesan.

9 Place the dish or dishes on a baking sheet and cook for 25–30 minutes for a large soufflé or 20 minutes for small soufflés. The mixture should be risen and firm to a light touch in the centre; it should not wobble excessively when given a light push. Serve immediately.

COOK'S TIP

Whisked egg whites give a soufflé its characteristic airy texture. But the lightness can be destroyed if they are folded in too roughly. Fold whites in using a rubber spatula and a cutting and scooping action. Turn the bowl a little after each stroke.

Energy 563kcal/2339kJ; Protein 28.8g; Carbohydrate 16.5g, of which sugars 5.8g; Fat 42.9g, of which saturates 24.1g; Cholesterol 294mg; Calcium 422mg; Fibre 0.7g; Sodium 710mg.

Potato and Leek Filo Pie

This filo pastry pie, filled with a wonderful mixture of potatoes, leeks, cheese, cream and herbs, makes an attractive and unusual centrepiece for a vegetarian buffet. Serve it cold, together with a choice of different salads.

Serves 8

800g/1¾lb new potatoes, sliced
400g/14oz leeks (trimmed weight)
75g/3oz/6 tbsp butter
15g/½ oz/¼ cup finely chopped
* fresh parsley*
60ml/4 tbsp chopped mixed fresh
* herbs, such as chervil, chives,*
* a little tarragon and basil*
12 sheets filo pastry, thawed if frozen
150g/5oz white Cheshire, Lancashire
* or Sonoma Jack cheese, sliced*
2 garlic cloves, finely chopped
250ml/8fl oz/1 cup double
* (heavy) cream*
2 large (US extra large) egg yolks
salt and ground black pepper

1 Preheat the oven to 190°C/375°F/ Gas 5. Cook the potatoes in lightly salted, boiling water for 3–4 minutes, then drain and set aside.

2 Thinly slice the leeks. Melt 25g/1oz/ 2 tbsp of the butter in a frying pan and cook the leeks gently over a low heat, stirring occasionally, until softened. Remove from the heat and season with pepper and stir in half the parsley and half the mixed herbs.

3 Melt the remaining butter. Line a 23cm/9in loose-based metal cake tin (pan) with six sheets of filo pastry, brushing each layer with melted butter. Allow the edges of the filo pastry to overhang the tin.

4 Layer the potatoes, leeks and cheese in the tin, sprinkling a few herbs and the garlic between the layers. Season.

5 Flip the overhanging pastry over the filling and cover with another two sheets of filo pastry, tucking in the sides to fit, and brush with melted butter as before. Cover the pie loosely with foil and bake for 35 minutes. (Keep the remaining pastry covered with a plastic bag and a damp cloth.)

6 Meanwhile beat the cream, egg yolks and remaining herbs together. Make a hole in the centre of the pie and gradually pour in the eggs and cream.

7 Arrange the remaining pastry on top, teasing it into swirls and folds, then brush with melted butter.

8 Reduce the oven temperature to 180°C/350°F/Gas 4 and bake the pie for another 25–30 minutes, or until the top is golden and crisp. Leave to cool before serving.

COOK'S TIP

To make a spicy tomato sauce to serve with the pie, cook 1 chopped onion in 15ml/ 1 tbsp olive oil for 3 minutes, add 1 chopped garlic clove and cook for 2 minutes. Stir in 400g/14oz can chopped tomatoes and 5ml/1 tsp hot chilli powder. Simmer for 15–20 minutes, or until thickened.

VARIATIONS

• Reduce the quantity of leeks to 225g/ 8oz. Cook 1kg/2¼lb washed spinach leaves in a covered pan over a high heat for 3–4 minutes, gently shaking the pan frequently. Drain, chop and mix with the cooked leeks.
• Reduce the quantity of leeks to 225g/ 8oz. Blanch 450g/1lb small broccoli florets in boiling water for 1 minute. Drain and add to the leeks.
• For a punchy flavour, use Stilton or Danish blue cheese instead of white cheese. Crumble the cheese rather than slicing it.

Energy 468kcal/1948kJ; Protein 10.7g; Carbohydrate 33g, of which sugars 3.5g; Fat 33.1g, of which saturates 20g; Cholesterol 137mg; Calcium 225mg; Fibre 3.2g; Sodium 218mg.

Tofu and Vegetable Thai Curry

Traditional Thai ingredients – chillies, galangal, lemon grass and kaffir lime leaves – give this vegetarian curry a wonderfully fragrant aroma. It makes an excellent main course when served with boiled jasmine rice or noodles.

Serves 8

350g/12oz tofu, drained
90ml/6 tbsp dark soy sauce
30ml/2 tbsp sesame oil
10ml/2 tsp chilli sauce
5cm/2in piece fresh root ginger,
    finely grated
450g/1lb cauliflower
450g/1lb broccoli
60ml/4 tbsp vegetable oil
2 onions, peeled and sliced
750ml/1¼ pints/3 cups coconut milk
300ml/½ pint/1¼ cups water
2 red (bell) peppers, seeded
    and chopped
350g/12oz green beans, halved
225g/8oz/3 cups shiitake or button
    (white) mushrooms, halved
shredded spring onions (scallions),
    to garnish
boiled jasmine rice or noodles,
    to serve

For the curry paste
4 chillies, seeded and chopped
2 lemon grass stalks, chopped
5cm/2in piece fresh galangal, chopped
4 kaffir lime leaves
20ml/4 tsp ground coriander
a few fresh coriander (cilantro) sprigs,
    including the stalks

1 Cut the drained tofu into 2.5cm/1in cubes and place in an ovenproof dish. Mix together the soy sauce, sesame oil, chilli sauce and ginger and pour over the tofu. Toss gently, then marinate for at least 2 hours or overnight, turning and basting the tofu occasionally.

2 To make the curry paste, blend the chopped chillies, lemon grass, galangal, kaffir lime leaves, ground and fresh coriander in a food processor for a few seconds. Add 90ml/6 tbsp water and process to a thick paste.

3 Preheat the oven to 190°C/375°F/ Gas 5. Using a sharp knife cut the cauliflower and broccoli into florets and cut any stalks into thin slices.

4 Heat the vegetable oil in a frying pan, add the sliced onions and cook gently for about 8 minutes, or until soft and lightly browned. Stir in the curry paste and the coconut milk. Add the water and bring to the boil.

5 Stir in the red peppers, green beans, cauliflower and broccoli. Transfer to a casserole. Cover and place in the oven.

6 Stir the tofu and marinade, then place the dish in the top of the oven and cook for 30 minutes. Add the marinade mixture and mushrooms to the curry. Reduce the oven temperature to 180°C/ 350°F/Gas 4 and cook for 15 minutes, or until the vegetables are tender. Garnish the curry with shredded spring onions. Serve immediately with boiled jasmine rice or noodles.

Energy 210kcal/873kJ; Protein 11g; Carbohydrate 15.1g, of which sugars 13.3g; Fat 12g, of which saturates 1.8g; Cholesterol 0mg; Calcium 328mg; Fibre 5g; Sodium 927mg.

Malaysian Seafood Stew

This Malaysian stew of fish, seafood and vegetables with noodles is wonderfully tasty. If you prefer a hot and spicy version, add a little chilli powder instead of some of the paprika.

Serves 8–10

4 medium-hot fresh red
   chillies, seeded
6–8 garlic cloves
10ml/2 tsp mild paprika
20ml/4 tsp fermented shrimp paste
45ml/3 tbsp chopped fresh root
   ginger or galangal
500g/1 ¼ lb small red shallots
50g/2oz fresh coriander (cilantro),
   preferably with roots
90ml/6 tbsp groundnut (peanut) oil
10ml/2 tsp fennel seeds, crushed
4 fennel bulbs, cut into
   thin wedges
1.2 litres/2 pints/5 cups fish stock
600g/1 lb 6oz thin vermicelli
   rice noodles
900ml/1 ½ pints/3¾ cups coconut milk
juice of 2–4 limes
60–90ml/4–6 tbsp Thai fish sauce
900g/2lb firm white fish fillet, such as
   monkfish, halibut or snapper
900g/2lb large raw prawns (shrimp)
   (about 40), shelled and deveined
bunch of fresh basil
4 spring onions (scallions),
   thinly sliced

1 Process the chillies, garlic, paprika, shrimp paste, ginger or galangal and four shallots to a paste in a food processor, blender or spice grinder. Remove the roots and stems from the coriander and add them to the paste; chop and reserve the coriander leaves. Add 30ml/2 tbsp of the groundnut oil to the paste and process again until fairly smooth.

2 Heat the remaining oil in a large pan or stockpot. Add the remaining shallots, the fennel seeds and fennel wedges. Cook until lightly browned, then add 90ml/6 tbsp of the paste and stir-fry for about 2 minutes. Pour in the fish stock and bring to the boil. Reduce the heat and simmer for 8–10 minutes.

3 Meanwhile, cook the vermicelli rice noodles according to the instructions on the packet. Drain and set aside.

4 Pour the coconut milk into the pan of shallots, stirring constantly to prevent them from sticking, then add the juice of two limes, with 60ml/4 tbsp of the fish sauce. Stir well to combine. Bring to a simmer and taste, adding more of the curry paste, lime juice or fish sauce as necessary.

5 Cut the fish into chunks and add to the pan. Cook for 3–4 minutes, then add the prawns and cook until they turn pink. Chop most of the basil and add to the pan with the reserved chopped coriander leaves.

6 Divide the noodles equally among 8–10 bowls, then ladle in the stew. Sprinkle with spring onions and the remaining basil leaves and serve.

Fillets of Sea Bream in Filo Pastry

Any firm fish fillets can be used for this dish. Each little parcel is a meal in itself and can be prepared several hours in advance, which makes them ideal for entertaining.

Serves 8

16 small waxy salad potatoes
400g/14oz sorrel, stalks removed
60ml/4 tbsp olive oil
32 sheets of filo pastry, thawed
  if frozen
8 sea bream fillets, about 175g/6oz
  each, scaled but not skinned
115g/4oz/½ cup butter, melted
250ml/8fl oz/1 cup fish stock
475ml/16fl oz/2 cups double
  (heavy) cream
salt and ground black pepper
finely diced red (bell) pepper, to garnish

1 Preheat the oven to 200°C/400°F/ Gas 6. Cook the salad potatoes in lightly salted, boiling water for about 15–20 minutes, or until just tender. Drain and set aside to cool.

2 Shred half the sorrel leaves by piling up six or eight at a time, rolling them up like a fat cigar and cutting them with a sharp knife, into very fine slices: shake these out.

3 Thinly slice the potatoes lengthways. Brush a baking tray with a little oil. Lay a sheet of filo pastry on the tray, brush it with oil then lay a second sheet crossways over the first. Repeat with two more sheets. Arrange one-eighth of the sliced potatoes in the centre of the pastry, season well and add one-eighth of the shredded sorrel. Lay a bream fillet on top, skin side up. Season to taste again.

4 Loosely fold the filo pastry up and over to make a neat parcel. Make seven more parcels in the same way. Place on the baking tray and brush them with half the butter. Bake for 20 minutes, or until the filo has fully puffed up and is golden brown.

5 Meanwhile, make the sorrel sauce. Heat the remaining butter in a small pan, add the reserved sorrel and cook until it wilts. Stir in the fish stock and cream. Heat almost to boiling point, stirring constantly. Season and keep hot. Serve the fish parcels garnished with red pepper and offer the sauce separately in its own bowl.

Energy 00kcal/00kJ; Protein 00g; Carbohydrate 00g, of which sugars 00g; Fat 00g, of which saturates 00g; Cholesterol 00mg; Calcium 00mg; Fibre 00g; Sodium 00mg.

Malaysian Prawn Laksa

This spicy prawn and noodle stew tastes just as good when made with fresh crab meat or any flaked cooked fish.

Serves 3–4

115g/4oz rice vermicelli or stir-fry
    rice noodles
15ml/1 tbsp vegetable or groundnut
    (peanut) oil
600ml/1 pint/2¹/₂ cups fish stock
400ml/14fl oz/1²/₃ cups thin
    coconut milk
30ml/2 tbsp Thai fish sauce
¹/₂ lime
16–24 cooked peeled prawns (shrimp)
salt and cayenne pepper
60ml/4 tbsp chopped fresh coriander
    (cilantro), to garnish

For the spicy paste
2 lemon grass stalks, finely chopped
2 fresh red chillies, seeded
    and chopped
2.5cm/1in piece fresh root ginger,
    peeled and sliced
2.5ml/¹/₂ tsp dried shrimp paste
2 garlic cloves, chopped
2.5ml/¹/₂ tsp ground turmeric
30ml/2 tbsp tamarind paste

1 Cook the rice vermicelli or noodles in a large pan of lightly salted, boiling water according to the instructions on the packet. Tip into a large sieve or colander, then rinse under cold water to stop any further cooking and drain. Set aside and keep warm.

2 To make the spicy paste, place the lemon grass, chillies, ginger, shrimp paste, garlic, turmeric and tamarind paste in a mortar and pound with a pestle until smooth. Alternatively, if you prefer, put all the ingredients in a food processor or blender and then process until a smooth paste is formed.

3 Heat the oil in a large pan, add the spicy paste and cook over a low heat, stirring constantly, for a few moments to release all the flavours, but be careful not to let it burn.

4 Add the fish stock and coconut milk and bring to the boil. Stir in the Thai fish sauce, then simmer for 5 minutes. Season with salt and cayenne to taste, adding a squeeze of lime juice. Add the prawns and heat through gently for a few seconds.

5 Divide the noodles among three or four soup plates. Pour the soup over, making sure that each portion includes an equal number of prawns. Garnish with the chopped coriander and serve piping hot.

Energy 423kcal/1775kJ; Protein 20g; Carbohydrate 62g, of which sugars 10g; Fat 10g, of which saturates 2g; Cholesterol 18mg; Calcium 101mg; Fibre 1g; Sodium 751mg.

Red Chicken Curry with Bamboo Shoots

Bamboo shoots have a lovely crunchy texture and make a delightful, contrasting texture to the chicken in this Thai curry. It is perfect served with jasmine rice.

Serves 6

1 litre/1¾ pints/4 cups coconut milk
30ml/2 tbsp red curry paste
450g/1lb skinless chicken breast fillets, cut into bitesize pieces
30ml/2 tbsp Thai fish sauce
15ml/1 tbsp sugar
225g/8oz canned whole bamboo shoots, rinsed, drained and sliced
5 kaffir lime leaves, torn
salt and ground black pepper
chopped fresh red chillies and kaffir lime leaves, to garnish

For the red curry paste
5ml/1tsp roasted coriander seeds
2.5ml/½ tsp roasted cumin seeds
6–8 fresh red chillies, seeded and chopped
4 shallots, thinly sliced
2 garlic cloves, chopped
15ml/1 tbsp fresh galangal, peeled and chopped
2 lemon grass stalks, chopped
4 fresh coriander (cilantro) roots
10 black peppercorns
pinch of ground cinnamon
5ml/1 tsp ground turmeric
2.5ml/½ tsp shrimp paste
5ml/1 tsp salt
30 ml/2 tbsp vegetable oil

1 To make the red curry paste, put all the ingredients except the oil into a mortar or food processor and pound or process to a paste. Add the oil, a little at a time, mixing or processing well after each addition. If you are not using the paste immediately, transfer it to a jar and keep in the refrigerator until you are ready to use it. For a hotter paste, add a few chilli seeds.

2 Pour half of the coconut milk into a wok or large pan over a medium heat. Bring to the boil, stirring constantly, with large cooking chopsticks or a spoon until it has separated.

3 Add the red curry paste and cook the mixture for 2–3 minutes. Stir the paste constantly to prevent it from sticking to the base of the pan.

4 Add the chicken pieces, fish sauce and sugar to the pan. Stir well, then cook for 5–6 minutes, or until the chicken changes colour and is cooked through. Continue to stir during cooking to prevent the mixture from sticking to the base of the pan and to cook the chicken evenly.

5 Pour the remaining coconut milk into the pan, then add the sliced bamboo shoots and torn kaffir lime leaves. Bring back to the boil over a medium heat, stirring constantly to prevent the mixture from sticking, then taste and add salt and pepper if necessary.

6 To serve, spoon the curry into a warmed serving dish and garnish with chopped chillies and kaffir lime leaves.

COOK'S TIP
Preparing a double or larger quantity of paste in a food processor or blender makes the blending of the ingredients easier and the paste will be smoother. Store surplus curry paste in the freezer.

VARIATIONS
• For green curry paste, process 12–15 green chillies, 2 chopped lemon grass stalks, 3 sliced shallots, 2 garlic cloves, 15ml/1 tbsp chopped galangal, 4 chopped kaffir lime leaves, 2.5ml/½ tsp grated kaffir rind, 5ml/1 tsp each of chopped coriander (cilantro) root, salt, roasted coriander seeds, roasted cumin seeds and shrimp paste, 15ml/1 tbsp sugar, 6 black peppercorns and 15ml/1 tbsp vegetable oil until a paste forms.
• For yellow curry paste, process 6–8 yellow chillies, 1 chopped lemon grass stalk, 2 sliced shallots, 4 garlic cloves, 15ml/1 tbsp chopped fresh root ginger, 5ml/1 tsp ground cinnamon, 15ml/1 tbsp light brown sugar and 30ml/2 tbsp vegetable oil until a paste forms.
• Use turkey or pork instead of chicken.

Energy 255kcal/1077kJ; Protein 29.5g; Carbohydrate 18g, of which sugars 16.9g; Fat 7.8g, of which saturates 1.5g; Cholesterol 79mg; Calcium 92mg; Fibre 0.9g; Sodium 1104mg.

Herb-crusted Rack of Lamb with Puy Lentils

This roast is easy to prepare, yet impressive when served – the perfect choice when entertaining.

Serves 8

4 × 6-bone racks of lamb, chined
115g/4oz/2 cups fresh
    white breadcrumbs
4 large garlic cloves, crushed
40g/1½ oz chopped mixed fresh herbs,
    such as rosemary, thyme, flat leaf
    parsley and marjoram, plus extra
    sprigs to garnish
115g/4oz/½ cup butter, melted
salt and ground black pepper

For the Puy lentils

2 red onions, chopped
60ml/4 tbsp olive oil
2 × 400g/14oz cans Puy or green
    lentils, rinsed and drained
2 × 400g/14oz cans
    chopped tomatoes
60ml/4 tbsp chopped fresh parsley

1 Preheat the oven to 220°C/425°F/ Gas 7. Trim off any excess fat from the racks of lamb, and season well with salt and ground black pepper.

2 Mix together the breadcrumbs, garlic, herbs and butter and press on to the fat-sides of the lamb. Place in a roasting pan and roast for 25 minutes. Cover with foil and leave to stand for 5 minutes before carving.

COOK'S TIP

Boiled or steamed new potatoes and broccoli are good accompaniments.

3 To make the Puy lentils, cook the onion in the olive oil until softened. Add the lentils and tomatoes and cook gently for 5 minutes, or until the lentils are piping hot. Stir in the parsley and season to taste.

4 Cut each rack of lamb in half and serve with the lentils. Garnish with the extra herb sprigs.

VARIATION

Add the grated rind of 1 lemon and 30ml/2 tbsp finely chopped walnuts to the crumb mixture.

Energy 639kcal/2673kJ; Protein 51.5g; Carbohydrate 28.2g, of which sugars 1.9g; Fat 36.4g, of which saturates 16.7g; Cholesterol 171mg; Calcium 89mg; Fibre 4.9g; Sodium 294mg.

Moussaka

Layers of minced lamb, aubergines, tomatoes and onions are topped with a creamy yogurt and cheese sauce in this delicious, authentic eastern Mediterranean recipe. Serve with a simple, mixed leaf, green salad.

Serves 8

900g/2lb aubergines (eggplants)
300ml/½ pint/1¼ cups olive oil
2 large onions, chopped
4–6 garlic cloves, finely chopped
1.3kg/3lb lean minced (ground) lamb
30ml/2 tbsp plain (all-purpose) flour
2 × 400g/14oz cans
　chopped tomatoes
60ml/4 tbsp chopped mixed fresh
　herbs, such as parsley, marjoram
　and oregano
salt and ground black pepper

For the topping
600ml/1 pint/2½ cups natural
　(plain) yogurt
4 eggs
50g/2oz feta cheese, crumbled
50g/2oz/⅔ cup grated Parmesan cheese

1 Cut the aubergines into thin slices and layer them in a colander, sprinkling each layer with salt. Cover them with a plate and a weight, then leave to drain for about 30 minutes. Drain and rinse well to remove all traces of salt, then pat dry with kitchen paper.

2 Heat 90ml/6 tbsp of the olive oil in a large, heavy pan. Cook the chopped onion and garlic until softened, but not coloured. Add the lamb and cook over a high heat, stirring frequently, until lightly browned.

3 Stir in the flour until mixed, then stir in the tomatoes, herbs and seasoning. Bring to the boil, reduce the heat and simmer gently for 20 minutes.

4 Meanwhile, heat a little of the remaining oil in a large frying pan. Add as many aubergine slices as can be laid in the pan, then cook until golden on both sides. Set the cooked aubergines aside. Heat more oil and continue cooking the aubergines, in batches, adding oil as necessary.

5 Preheat the oven to 180°C/350°F/Gas 4. Arrange half the aubergine slices in a large, shallow ovenproof dish or divide among two smaller dishes.

6 Top the aubergine slices with about half of the meat and tomato mixture, then add the remaining aubergine slices. Spread the remaining meat mixture over the aubergines.

7 Beat together the yogurt and eggs, mix in the feta and Parmesan cheeses, and spread the mixture over the meat.

8 Transfer the moussaka to the oven and bake for 35–40 minutes, or until golden and bubbling.

Energy 588kcal/2445kJ; Protein 37.9g; Carbohydrate 14.8g, of which sugars 3.7g; Fat 40.9g, of which saturates 18.2g; Cholesterol 206mg; Calcium 379mg; Fibre 2.4g; Sodium 506mg.

Tagine of **Lamb** with **Couscous**

A tagine is a classic Moroccan stew which is traditionally served with couscous. Its warm and fruity flavourings create a rich and sumptuous sauce that is perfect for serving at winter evening dinner parties.

Serves 6

*1kg/2¼lb lean boneless lamb,
 such as shoulder or neck fillet
25g/1oz/2 tbsp butter
15ml/1 tbsp sunflower oil
1 large onion, chopped
2 garlic cloves, chopped
2.5cm/1in piece fresh root ginger,
 peeled and finely chopped
1 red (bell) pepper, seeded
 and chopped
900ml/1½ pints/3¾ cups lamb stock
 or water
250g/9oz/generous 1 cup
 ready-to-eat prunes
juice of 1 lemon
15ml/1 tbsp clear honey
1.5ml/¼ tsp saffron threads
1 cinnamon stick, broken in half
50g/2oz/½ cup flaked (sliced)
 almonds, toasted
salt and ground black pepper*

To serve
*450g/1lb/2⅔ cups couscous
25g/1oz/2 tbsp butter
30ml/2 tbsp chopped fresh
 coriander (cilantro)*

1 Trim the lamb and cut it into 2.5cm/1in cubes. Heat the butter and oil in a large flameproof casserole until foaming. Add the onion, garlic and ginger and cook, stirring occasionally, until softened but not coloured.

2 Add the lamb and red pepper and mix well. (The meat is not sealed in batches over high heat for an authentic tagine.) Pour in the stock or water.

3 Add the prunes, lemon juice, honey, saffron threads and cinnamon. Season to taste with salt and pepper and stir well. Bring to the boil, then reduce the heat and cover the casserole. Simmer for 1½–2 hours, stirring occasionally, or until the meat is melt-in-the-mouth tender.

4 Meanwhile, cook the couscous according to packet instructions, usually by placing in a large bowl and pouring in boiling water to cover the "grains" by 2.5cm/1in. Stir well, then cover and leave to stand for 5–10 minutes. The couscous absorbs the water and swells to become tender and fluffy. Stir in the butter, chopped fresh coriander and seasoning to taste.

5 Taste the stew for seasoning and add more salt and pepper if necessary. Pile the couscous into a large, warmed serving dish or on to individual warmed bowls or plates. Ladle the stew on to the couscous and sprinkle the toasted flaked almonds over the top.

Energy 652kcal/2716kJ; Protein 35.2g; Carbohydrate 30.9g, of which sugars 26g; Fat 44.2g, of which saturates 16.4g; Cholesterol 141mg; Calcium 97mg; Fibre 5.4g; Sodium 223mg.

Beef Carbonade

This rich, dark stew of beef, cooked slowly with lots of onions, garlic and beer, is a classic one-pot casserole from the north of France and Belgium. Serve with roasted potatoes, if you like.

Serves 6

45ml/3 tbsp vegetable oil
3 onions, sliced
45ml/3 tbsp plain (all-purpose) flour
2.5ml/½ tsp mustard powder
1kg/2¼lb stewing beef, such as shin
*   (shank) or chuck, cut into large cubes*
2–3 garlic cloves, finely chopped
300ml/½ pint/1¼ cups dark beer
*   or ale*
150ml/¼ pint/⅔ cup water
5ml/1 tsp dark brown sugar
1 fresh thyme sprig
1 fresh bay leaf
1 piece celery stick
salt and ground black pepper

For the topping
50g/2oz/¼ cup butter
1 garlic clove, crushed
15ml/1 tbsp Dijon mustard
45ml/3 tbsp chopped fresh parsley
6–12 slices baguette or ficelle loaf

1 Preheat the oven to 160°C/325°F/ Gas 3. Heat 30ml/2 tbsp of the oil in a frying pan and cook the onions over a low heat until softened. Remove from the pan and set aside.

2 Meanwhile, mix together the flour and mustard and season. Toss the beef in the flour. Add the remaining oil to the pan and heat over a high heat. Brown the beef all over, then transfer it to a casserole.

COOK'S TIP
When making more than double the quantity, limit the garlic cloves to 8 in total, otherwise the flavour is too strong.

3 Reduce the heat and return the onions to the pan. Add the garlic, cook, then add the beer or ale, water and sugar. Tie the thyme and bay leaf together and add to the pan with the celery. Bring to the boil, stirring, then season.

4 Pour the sauce over the beef and mix. Cover, then place in the oven for 2½ hours. Check the beef to make sure that it is not too dry, adding water, if necessary. Test for tenderness, allowing an extra 30–40 minutes cooking time.

5 To make the topping, cream the butter together with the garlic, mustard and 30ml/2 tbsp of the parsley. Spread the butter thickly over the bread.

6 Increase the oven temperature to 190°C/375°F/Gas 5. Taste and season the casserole, then arrange the bread slices, buttered side uppermost, on top. Bake for 20–25 minutes, until the bread is browned. Sprinkle the remaining parsley over the top and serve.

Energy 530kcal/2217kJ; Protein 42g; Carbohydrate 36g, of which sugars 7g; Fat 25g, of which saturates 9g; Cholesterol 123mg; Calcium 96mg; Fibre 4g; Sodium 483mg.

Lasagne with Three Cheeses

Mozzarella, ricotta and Parmesan cheeses make this lasagne rich and filling. Pasta meals such as these are always popular with adults and children alike so they make good fare for gatherings of family and friends.

Serves 6–8

25g/1oz/2 tbsp butter
15ml/1 tbsp olive oil
225–250g/8–9oz/2–2¼ cups button (white) mushrooms, quartered
30ml/2 tbsp chopped fresh flat leaf parsley
250–350ml/8–12fl oz/1–1½ cups hot beef stock
9–12 fresh or no pre-cook dried lasagne sheets
450g/1lb/2 cups ricotta cheese
1 large (US extra large) egg
3 × 130g/4½oz packets mozzarella cheese, drained and thinly sliced
115g/4oz/1⅓ cups freshly grated Parmesan cheese
salt and ground black pepper

For the bolognese sauce
45ml/3 tbsp olive oil
1 onion, finely chopped
1 small carrot, finely chopped
1 celery stick, finely chopped
2 garlic cloves, finely chopped
400g/14oz minced (ground) beef
120ml/4fl oz/½ cup red wine
200ml/7fl oz/scant 1 cup passata (bottled, strained tomatoes)
15ml/1 tbsp tomato purée (paste)
5ml/1 tsp dried oregano
15ml/1 tbsp chopped fresh flat leaf parsley
350ml/12fl oz/1½ cups beef stock
8 baby Italian tomatoes (optional)
salt and ground black pepper

VARIATION
Grated mature (sharp) Cheddar cheese can be used instead of the grated Parmesan.

1 Preheat the oven to 190°C/375°F/ Gas 5. Melt the butter in the oil in a frying pan. Add the mushrooms, with salt and pepper to taste, and toss over a medium to high heat for 5–8 minutes, until the mushrooms are tender and quite dry. Remove the pan from the heat and stir in the parsley.

2 To make the bolognese sauce, heat the oil in a large pan, add the chopped vegetables and cook over a low heat, stirring frequently, for 5–7 minutes.

3 Add the minced beef and cook for 5 minutes, stirring frequently. Stir in the wine and mix well.

4 Cook for 1–2 minutes, then add the passata, tomato purée, herbs and 60ml/4 tbsp of the stock. Season with salt and pepper to taste. Stir well and bring to the boil.

5 Cover the pan, and cook over a low heat for 30 minutes, adding more stock as necessary and stirring occasionally. Add the fresh tomatoes, if using, and simmer for 5–10 minutes more.

6 Stir in enough hot beef stock to make the sauce quite runny. (This is particularly important if using the no pre-cook sheets of dried lasagne).

7 Stir in the mushroom and parsley mixture, then spread about a quarter of this sauce over the base of an ovenproof dish. Cover with three or four sheets of lasagne.

8 Beat together the ricotta and egg in a bowl, with salt and pepper to taste, then spread about a third of the mixture over the lasagne sheets. Cover with a third of the mozzarella slices, then sprinkle with about a quarter of the grated Parmesan.

9 Repeat these layers twice, using half the remaining bolognese sauce each time, and finishing with the remaining Parmesan cheese.

10 Bake for 30–40 minutes, or until the cheese topping is golden brown and bubbling. Leave the lasagne to stand for about 10 minutes before serving straight from the dish.

Energy 533kcal/2226kJ; Protein 32.5g; Carbohydrate 29.7g, of which sugars 3.1g; Fat 32.4g, of which saturates 18.7g; Cholesterol 121mg; Calcium 370mg; Fibre 1.4g; Sodium 402mg.

Beef Wellington

Tender fillet of beef baked in puff pastry makes a sophisticated main course for a formal dinner. Start preparing the dish well in advance to allow time for the meat to cool before it is wrapped in the pastry.

Serves 6

1.5kg/3¼lb fillet (tenderloin) of beef
45ml/3 tbsp sunflower oil
115g/4oz/1½ cups mushrooms, chopped
2 garlic cloves, crushed
175g/6oz smooth liver pâté
30ml/2 tbsp chopped fresh parsley
400g/14oz puff pastry
beaten egg, to glaze
salt and ground black pepper
fresh flat leaf parsley, to garnish

1 Tie the fillet of beef at regular intervals with string so that it stays in a neat shape during cooking.

2 Heat 30ml/2 tbsp of the sunflower oil in a large frying pan, and cook the beef over a high heat for about 10 minutes, until brown on all sides. Transfer to a roasting pan, bake for 20 minutes. Leave to cool.

3 Heat the remaining oil in a frying pan and cook the mushrooms and garlic for about 5 minutes. Beat the mushroom mixture into the pâté with the parsley, season well. Set aside to cool.

4 Roll out the pastry into a sheet large enough to enclose the beef, plus a strip to spare. Trim off the spare pastry, trim the other edges to neaten. Spread the pâté mix down the middle of the pastry. Untie the beef and lay it on the pâté.

5 Preheat the oven to 220°C/425°F/ Gas 7. Brush the edges of the pastry with beaten egg and fold it over the meat to enclose it in a neat parcel. Place the parcel on a baking sheet with the join in the pastry underneath. Cut leaf shapes from the reserved pastry. Brush the parcel with egg, garnish with pastry leaves. Chill for 10 minutes.

6 Bake the Beef Wellington for 50–60 minutes, covering it loosely with foil after about 30 minutes to prevent the pastry from burning. Serve cut into thick slices garnished with parsley.

Energy 511kcal/2131kJ; Protein 41.7g; Carbohydrate 19.3g, of which sugars 1.2g; Fat 30.6g, of which saturates 7.2g; Cholesterol 128mg; Calcium 41mg; Fibre 0.4g; Sodium 320mg.

Boeuf Bourguignonne

This classic French dish of beef cooked in Burgundy style with red wine, small pieces of bacon, baby onions and mushrooms, is a favourite choice for a dinner party.

Serves 6

175g/6oz rindless streaky (fatty) bacon
   rashers (strips), chopped
900g/2lb lean braising steak
30ml/2 tbsp plain (all-purpose) flour
45ml/3 tbsp sunflower oil
25g/1oz/2 tbsp butter
12 baby (pearl) onions
2 garlic cloves, crushed
175g/6oz/2⅓ cups mushrooms, sliced
450ml/¾ pint/scant 2 cups red wine
150ml/¼ pint/⅔ cup beef stock
   or consommé
1 bay leaf
2 sprigs each of fresh thyme, parsley
   and marjoram
salt and ground black pepper
creamed potatoes and celeriac,
   to serve

1 Preheat the oven to 160°C/325°F/ Gas 3. Heat a large flameproof casserole, then add the bacon and cook, stirring occasionally, until the fat runs and the cooked pieces are crisp and golden brown.

2 Meanwhile, cut the meat into 2.5cm/ 1in cubes. Season the flour and use to coat the meat. Use a slotted spoon to remove the bacon from the casserole and set aside. Add the oil and heat, then brown the beef, in batches, and set aside with the bacon (cooking too much at once reduces the temperature of the oil drastically).

3 Add the butter to the fat remaining in the casserole. Cook the onions and garlic until just starting to colour, then add the mushrooms and cook for a further 5 minutes. Replace the bacon and meat, and stir in the wine and stock or consommé. Tie the bay leaf, thyme, parsley and marjoram together into a bouquet garni and add to the casserole.

4 Cover and cook in the oven for 1½ hours, or until the meat is tender, stirring once or twice. Season to taste and serve the casserole with creamy mashed root vegetables, such as celeriac and potatoes.

Energy 460kcal/1912kJ; Protein 40g; Carbohydrate 6g, of which sugars 1g; Fat 31g, of which saturates 10g; Cholesterol 124mg; Calcium 24mg; Fibre 1g; Sodium 540mg.

Seared Tuna Steaks with Red Onion Salsa

Red onions are ideal for this salsa, not only for their mild and sweet flavour, but also because they look so appetizing. Salad, rice or bread and a bowl of thick yogurt flavoured with chopped fresh herbs are good accompaniments.

Serves 8

8 tuna steaks, about 175–200g/
  6–7oz each
10ml/2 tsp cumin seeds, toasted
  and crushed
pinch of dried red chilli flakes
grated rind and juice of 2 limes
60–75ml/4–5 tbsp extra virgin
  olive oil
salt and ground black pepper
lime wedges and fresh coriander
  (cilantro) sprigs, to garnish

For the salsa

2 small red onions, finely chopped
400g/14oz red or yellow cherry
  tomatoes, coarsely chopped
2 avocados, peeled, stoned, (pitted)
  and chopped
4 kiwi fruit, peeled and chopped
2 fresh red chillies, seeded and
  finely chopped
25g/1oz/¹⁄₂ cup chopped fresh
  coriander (cilantro)
12 fresh mint sprigs, leaves
  only, chopped
10–15ml/2–3 tsp Thai fish sauce
about 10ml/2 tsp muscovado
  (molasses) sugar

1 Wash the tuna steaks and pat dry with kitchen paper. Sprinkle with half the cumin, the dried chilli flakes, salt, pepper and half the lime rind. Rub in 60ml/4 tbsp of the oil and set aside in a dish for about 30 minutes.

COOK'S TIP
The spicy fruity salsa also goes well with salmon steaks cooked on the barbecue.

2 Meanwhile, make the salsa. Mix the onions, tomatoes, avocados, kiwi fruit, fresh chilli, chopped coriander and mint. Add the remaining cumin, the rest of the lime rind and half the lime juice. Add the Thai fish sauce and sugar to taste. Set aside for 15–20 minutes, then add more Thai fish sauce, lime juice and olive oil if required.

3 Heat a griddle. Cook the tuna, allowing about 2 minutes on each side for rare tuna or a little longer for a medium result.

4 Serve the tuna steaks garnished with lime wedges and coriander sprigs. Serve the salsa separately or spoon it next to the tuna.

Energy 463Kcal/1935kJ; Protein 46g; Carbohydrate 9g, of which sugars 7g; Fat 27g, of which saturates 5g; Cholesterol 53mg; Calcium 64mg; Fibre 2.6g; Sodium 0.3g.

Lobster Thermidor

One of the classic French dishes, lobster thermidor makes a little lobster go a long way. It is best to use large lobsters rather than small ones, as they will contain a higher proportion of flesh and the meat will be sweeter.

Serves 6

3 large lobsters, about 800g–1kg/
   1¾–2¼lb, boiled
120ml/4fl oz/½ cup brandy
75g/3oz/6 tbsp butter
6 shallots, finely chopped
350g/12oz/4½ cups button (white)
   mushrooms, thinly sliced
50ml/3 tbsp plain (all-purpose) flour
350ml/12fl oz/1½ cups fish stock
350ml/12fl oz/1½ cups double
   (heavy) cream
15ml/1 tbsp Dijon mustard
6 egg yolks, beaten
120ml/9 tbsp dry white wine
115g/4oz/1⅓ cups freshly grated
   Parmesan cheese
salt, ground black pepper and
   cayenne pepper
steamed rice and salad leaves, to serve

1 Split each lobster in half lengthways; crack the claws. Discard the stomach sac, and keep the coral for another dish. Keeping each half-shell intact, extract the meat from the tail and claws, then cut into large dice. Place in a shallow dish and sprinkle over the brandy. Cover and set aside. Wipe and dry the half-shells and set them aside.

2 Melt the butter in a pan and cook the shallots over a low heat until soft. Add the mushrooms and cook until just tender, stirring constantly. Stir in the flour and a pinch of cayenne pepper; cook, stirring, for 2–3 minutes. Gradually add the stock, stirring until the sauce boils and thickens.

3 Stir in the cream and mustard and continue to cook until the sauce is smooth and thick. Season to taste with salt, black pepper and cayenne. Pour half the sauce on to the egg yolks, stir well and return the mixture to the pan. Stir in the wine. Taste and adjust the seasoning, being generous with the cayenne pepper.

4 Preheat the grill (broiler) to medium-high. Stir the diced lobster and the brandy into the sauce. Arrange the lobster half-shells in a grill pan and divide the mixture among them. Sprinkle with Parmesan and place under the grill until browned. Serve with the rice and salad leaves.

Energy 859kcal/3573kJ; Protein 56g; Carbohydrate 9.8g, of which sugars 2g; Fat 59.6g, of which saturates 33.8g; Cholesterol 536mg; Calcium 488mg; Fibre 1.2g; Sodium 976mg.

Baked Salmon with Watercress Sauce

A whole baked salmon makes a stunning centrepiece for a buffet. Baking it in foil is easier than poaching and yet the flesh has a similar melting quality. If you decorate the fish with thin slices of cucumber it will add a delicate touch to its appearance.

Serves 6–8

2–3kg/4½–6½lb salmon, cleaned
   with head and tail left on
3–5 spring onions (scallions),
   thinly sliced
1 lemon, thinly sliced
1 cucumber, thinly sliced
fresh dill sprigs, to garnish
lemon wedges, to serve
salt and ground black pepper

For the sauce
3 garlic cloves, chopped
200g/7oz watercress leaves,
   finely chopped
40g/1½oz/¾ cup finely chopped
   fresh tarragon
300g/11oz mayonnaise
15–30ml/1–2 tbsp freshly squeezed
   lemon juice
200g/7oz/scant 1 cup unsalted
   (sweet) butter

1 Preheat the oven to 180°C/350°F/ Gas 4. Rinse the salmon and lay it on a large piece of foil. Stuff the fish with the sliced spring onions and layer the lemon slices inside and around the fish, then sprinkle with salt and pepper.

2 Loosely fold the foil around the fish and fold the edges over to seal. Bake for about 1 hour.

3 Remove the fish from the oven and leave it to stand, still wrapped in the foil, for about 15 minutes. Then unwrap the foil parcel and leave the salmon to cool.

4 When the fish is cool, carefully lift it on to a large plate, still covered with lemon slices. Cover the fish tightly with clear film (plastic wrap) and chill for several hours in the refrigerator.

5 Use a blunt knife to lift up the edge of the skin and carefully peel the skin away from the flesh, avoiding tearing the flesh. Pull out any fins at the same time. Carefully turn over the salmon and repeat on the other side. Leave the head on for serving, if you wish. Discard the skin.

6 Arrange the cucumber slices in overlapping rows along the length of the fish, so that they look like large fish scales.

7 To make the sauce, put the garlic, watercress, tarragon, mayonnaise and lemon juice in a food processor or blender or a bowl, and process or mix well to combine.

8 Melt the butter, then add to the watercress mixture, a little at a time, processing or stirring, until the butter has been incorporated and the sauce is thick and smooth. Cover and chill before serving.

9 Serve the fish, garnished with dill and lemon wedges, and the watercress sauce alongside.

COOK'S TIP
Do not prepare the sauce more than a few hours ahead of serving as the watercress will discolour it.

VARIATION
If you prefer to poach the fish rather than baking it, you will need to use a fish kettle. Place the salmon on the rack, in the kettle. Cover with cold water and bring to a simmer, cook for 5–10 minutes per 450g/1lb until tender.

Energy 515kcal/2133kJ; Protein 25.5g; Carbohydrate 0.7g, of which sugars 0.6g; Fat 45.6g, of which saturates 14g; Cholesterol 114mg; Calcium 67mg; Fibre 0.4g; Sodium 275mg.

Celebration Paella

This paella is a marvellous mixture of some of the finest Spanish ingredients and makes a colourful one-pot party dish.

Serves 6–8

6–8 large raw prawns (shrimp), peeled, or 12–16 smaller raw prawns
450g/1lb fresh mussels
90ml/6 tbsp white wine
150g/5oz green beans, cut into 2.5cm/1in lengths
115g/4oz/1 cup frozen broad (fava) beans
6 small skinless chicken breast fillets, cut into large pieces
30ml/2 tbsp plain (all-purpose) flour, seasoned with salt and pepper
about 90ml/6 tbsp olive oil
150g/5oz pork fillet (tenderloin), cut into bitesize pieces
2 onions, chopped
2–3 garlic cloves, crushed
1 red (bell) pepper, seeded and sliced
2 ripe tomatoes, peeled, seeded and chopped
900ml/1½ pints/3¾ cups well-flavoured chicken stock
good pinch of saffron threads, dissolved in 30ml/2 tbsp hot water
350g/12oz/1¾ cups Spanish rice or risotto rice
225g/8oz chorizo, sliced
115g/4oz/1 cup frozen peas
6–8 stuffed green olives, thickly sliced
salt and ground black pepper

COOK'S TIP
Ideally, you should use a paella pan for this recipe and the paella should not be stirred during cooking. However, you may find that the rice cooks in the centre but not around the outside. To make sure it cooks evenly stir occasionally, or cook the paella on the bottom of a preheated 190°C/375°F/Gas 5 oven for about 15–18 minutes.

1 Make a shallow cut down the centre of the curved back of each of the large prawns. Pull out the black veins with a cocktail stick (toothpick) or your fingers, then rinse the prawns thoroughly and set them aside.

2 Scrub the mussel shells with a stiff brush and rinse thoroughly under cold running water. Scrape off any barnacles and remove the "beards" with a small knife. Rinse well. Discard any mussels that are open and do not close when sharply tapped.

3 Place the mussels in a large pan with the wine, bring to the boil, then cover the pan tightly and cook, shaking the pan occasionally, for 3–4 minutes, or until the mussels have opened. Drain, reserving the liquid and discarding any mussels that remain closed.

4 Briefly cook the green beans and broad beans in separate pans of boiling water for 2–3 minutes. Drain. As soon as the broad beans are cool enough to handle, pop the bright green inner beans out of their skins.

5 Dust the chicken with the seasoned flour. Heat half the oil in a paella pan or frying pan and cook the chicken until browned all over. Transfer to a plate. Cook the prawns briefly, adding more oil if needed, use a slotted spoon to transfer them to a plate. Heat a further 30ml/2 tbsp of the oil in the pan and brown the pork. Transfer to a plate.

6 Heat the remaining oil and cook the onions and garlic for 3–4 minutes, or until golden brown. Add the red pepper, cook for 2–3 minutes, then add the chopped tomatoes and cook until the mixture is fairly thick.

7 Stir in the chicken stock, the reserved mussel liquid and the saffron liquid. Season well with salt and pepper and bring to the boil. When the liquid is bubbling, add the rice. Stir once, then add the chicken pieces, pork, prawns, beans, chorizo and peas. Cook over a moderately high heat for 12 minutes, then lower the heat and cook for 8–10 minutes more, until all the liquid has been absorbed.

8 Add the mussels and olives and cook for a further 3–4 minutes to heat through. Remove the pan from the heat, cover with a clean, damp dishtowel and leave the paella to stand for 10 minutes before serving straight from the pan.

Roasted Stuffed Turkey

Serve this classic roast with stuffing balls, bacon rolls, roast potatoes, vegetables and gravy.

Serves 8

4.5kg/10lb oven-ready turkey, with giblets, thawed, if frozen
1 large onion, peeled and studded with 6 whole cloves
50g/2oz/¼ cup butter, softened
10 chipolata sausages
salt and ground black pepper

For the stuffing

225g/8oz rindless streaky (fatty) bacon, chopped
1 large onion, finely chopped
450g/1lb pork sausage meat (bulk sausage)
25g/1oz/⅓ cup rolled oats
30ml/2 tbsp chopped fresh parsley
10ml/2 tsp dried mixed herbs
1 large (US extra large) egg, beaten
115g/4oz/1 cup ready-to-eat dried apricots, finely chopped

For the gravy

25g/1oz/¼ cup plain (all-purpose) flour
450ml/¾ pint/scant 2 cups giblet stock

1 Preheat the oven to 200°C/400°F/ Gas 6. To make the stuffing, cook the bacon and onion over a gentle heat in a frying pan until the bacon is crisp and the onion is tender but not browned. Transfer to a large bowl and add the remaining stuffing ingredients. Season well and mix to combine.

2 Stuff the neck end of the turkey only, tucking the flap of skin under and securing it with a small skewer or stitching it in place with a thread. Do not overstuff the turkey or the skin will burst during cooking. Reserve any remaining stuffing and set aside.

3 Put the onion studded with cloves in the body cavity of the turkey and tie the legs together with string to hold them in place. Weigh the stuffed bird and calculate the cooking time: allow 15 minutes per 450g/1lb plus an extra 15 minutes. Place the turkey in a large roasting pan.

4 Brush the turkey with the butter and season well with salt and pepper. Cover it loosely with foil and cook it for 30 minutes. Baste the turkey with the pan juices. Then lower the oven temperature to 180°C/350°F/Gas 4 and cook for the remainder of the calculated cooking time. Baste the turkey every 30 minutes or so and check for any small bubbles of fat, pricking them with a fork to release the fat from the skin.

5 Remove the foil from the turkey for the last hour of cooking and baste. With wet hands, shape the remaining stuffing into small balls or pack it into a greased ovenproof dish. Cook in the oven for 20 minutes, or until golden brown and crisp. About 20 minutes before the end of cooking, put the chipolata sausages into an ovenproof dish and put them in the oven. The turkey is cooked if the juices run clear when the thickest part of the thigh is pierced with a skewer.

6 Transfer the turkey to a serving plate, cover it with foil and let it stand for 15 minutes before carving. To make the gravy, spoon off the fat from the roasting pan, leaving the meat juices. Blend in the flour and cook on the stove for 2 minutes. Gradually stir in the stock and bring to the boil. Check the seasoning. Pour into a sauce boat.

7 To serve the turkey, remove the skewer and pour any juices into the gravy. Surround the turkey with chipolata sausages and stuffing and carve it at the table.

Energy 761kcal/3174kJ; Protein 63.9g; Carbohydrate 43.4g, of which sugars 7.6g; Fat 36.9g, of which saturates 12.5g; Cholesterol 235mg; Calcium 68mg; Fibre 1.5g; Sodium 272mg.

Turkey and Cranberry Pie

This is ideal for using up leftovers and the cranberries add a tart layer to this attractive pie. It needs to be made the day before, and it can even be frozen in advance.

Serves 8

450g/1lb pork sausage meat
  (bulk sausage)
450g/1lb/2 cups minced (ground) pork
15ml/1 tbsp ground coriander
15ml/1 tbsp mixed dried herbs
finely grated rind of 2 large oranges
10ml/2 tsp grated fresh root ginger or
  2.5ml/½ tsp ground ginger
450g/1lb turkey breast fillets, skinned
115g/4oz/1 cup fresh cranberries
salt and ground black pepper

For the pastry
450g/1lb/4 cups plain (all-purpose) flour
5ml/1 tsp salt
150g/5oz/10 tbsp white cooking fat
150ml/¼ pint/⅔ cup mixed milk
  and water

To finish
1 egg, beaten
300ml/½ pint/1¼ cups aspic jelly, made
  up as packet instructions

1 Preheat the oven to 180°C/350°F/ Gas 4. Place a large baking tray in the oven to preheat. In a large bowl, mix together the sausage meat, minced pork, coriander, mixed dried herbs, orange rind and ginger with plenty of salt and ground black pepper.

2 To make the pastry, put the flour into a large bowl with the salt. Heat the fat in a small pan with the milk and water until just beginning to boil. Set aside and leave to cool slightly.

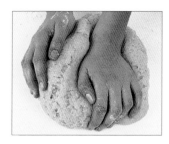

3 Using a spoon, stir the liquid into the flour until a stiff dough forms. Turn on to a work surface and knead until smooth. Cut one-third off the dough for the lid, wrap it in clear film (plastic wrap), and keep it in a warm place.

4 Roll out the large piece of dough on a floured surface and line the base and sides of a well-greased 20cm/8in loose-based, springform cake tin (pan). Work the dough while it is warm, as it will crack and break if it is left to get cold.

5 Thinly slice the turkey fillets and put between two pieces of clear film and flatten with a rolling pin to a 3mm/⅛in thickness. Spoon half the pork mixture into the base of the tin, pressing it into the edges. Cover with half of the turkey slices and then the cranberries, followed by the remaining turkey and finally the rest of the pork mixture.

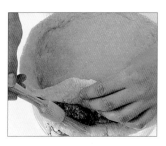

6 Roll out the rest of the dough and cover the filling, trimming any excess and sealing the edges with beaten egg. Make a steam hole in the lid and decorate with pastry trimmings. Brush with beaten egg. Bake for 2 hours. Cover the pie with foil if it gets too brown. Place the pie on a wire rack to cool. When cold, use a funnel to fill the pie with aspic jelly. Leave to set for a few hours before unmoulding the pie.

COOK'S TIPS
• Stand the springform pan on a baking tray with a shallow rim to catch any juices that may seep from the pie during baking.
• Leave the pie to cool in the pan until the pastry has firmed up slightly before transferring it to a wire rack.

Energy 670kcal/2801kJ; Protein 38.1g; Carbohydrate 50.8g, of which sugars 4.1g; Fat 36.2g, of which saturates 13.9g; Cholesterol 119mg; Calcium 155mg; Fibre 2.5g; Sodium 558mg.

Duck with **Plum Sauce**

This is an updated version of an old English dish, which is quite quick to prepare and cook, and ideal formal dinner party fare. Make it when plums are in season, when they will be ripe and juicy.

Serves 8

8 duck quarters
2 large red onions, finely chopped
1kg/2¼lb ripe plums, stoned (pitted)
    and quartered
60ml/4 tbsp redcurrant jelly
salt and ground black pepper

COOK'S TIP
It is important that the plums used in this dish are very ripe, otherwise the mixture will be too dry and the sauce will be extremely tart.

1 Prick the duck skin all over with a fork to release the fat during cooking and help give a crisp result, then place the portions in a heavy frying pan, skin sides down.

2 Cook the duck pieces for 10 minutes on each side, or until golden brown and cooked right through. Remove the duck from the frying pan using a slotted spoon, and keep warm.

3 Pour away all but 30ml/2 tbsp of the duck fat, then stir-fry the onion for 5 minutes, or until golden. Add the plums and cook, stirring frequently, for a further 5 minutes. Add the redcurrant jelly and mix well.

4 Replace the duck portions and cook for a further 5 minutes, or until thoroughly reheated. Season with salt and pepper to taste before serving.

Energy 608kcal/2515kJ; Protein 15.1g; Carbohydrate 17.4g, of which sugars 17g; Fat 53.5g, of which saturates 14.5g; Cholesterol 0mg; Calcium 35mg; Fibre 2.2g; Sodium 102mg.

Wild Duck with Olives

Compared to farmed duck, wild duck, which has a brilliant flavour, is worth the extra expense for a special occasion meal. They are often quite small birds, so allow two pieces per portion. Mashed parsnips and green vegetables are good accompaniments.

Serves 4

2 wild ducks, weighing about 1.5kg/
   3¼lb, each cut into 4 portions
2 onions, chopped
2 carrots, chopped
4 celery sticks, chopped
6 garlic cloves, sliced
2 bottles red wine
600ml/1 pint/2½ cups well-flavoured
   game stock
handful of fresh thyme leaves
5ml/1 tsp arrowroot
450g/1lb/4 cups pitted green olives
225g/8oz passata (bottled
   strained tomatoes)
salt and ground black pepper

1 Preheat the oven to 220°C/425°F/ Gas 7. Season the duck portions generously with salt and ground black pepper and place them in a large flameproof casserole.

2 Roast the duck portions for 25–30 minutes, then remove the casserole from the oven. Use a slotted spoon to remove the duck from the casserole, reserving the cooking fat, and set aside. Reduce the oven temperature to 160°C/325°F/Gas 3.

3 Carefully transfer the casserole to the stove and heat the duck fat until it is sizzling. Add the chopped onions, carrots, celery sticks and garlic cloves, and cook for 10 minutes, or until the vegetables have softened. Pour in the red wine and boil until it has reduced by about half.

4 Add the stock and thyme leaves, then replace the duck portions in the casserole. Bring to the boil, skim the surface, then cover the casserole and place in the oven for about 1 hour, or until the duck is tender. Remove the duck portions and keep warm.

5 Skim the excess fat from the cooking liquid, strain it and return it to the casserole, then bring it to the boil. Skim the liquid again, if necessary.

VARIATION

Process 225g/8oz canned tomatoes in a blender and use instead of the passata.

6 Mix the arrowroot to a thin paste with a little cold water and whisk it into the simmering sauce. Add the olives and passata and replace the duck, then cook, uncovered, for 15 minutes. Check the seasoning and serve.

Energy 386kcal/1608kJ; Protein 30g; Carbohydrate 13g, of which sugars 9g; Fat 24g, of which saturates 5g; Cholesterol 125mg; Calcium 134mg; Fibre 8g; Sodium 2969mg.

Roast Goose with Caramelized Apples

Tender goose served with sweet apples makes this a perfect celebration main course.

Serves 8

4.5–5.5kg/10–12lb goose, with giblets, thawed, if frozen
salt and ground black pepper

For the apple and nut stuffing
225g/8oz/1 cup prunes
150ml/¼ pint/⅔ cup port or red wine
675g/1½ lb cooking apples, peeled, cored and cubed
1 large onion, chopped
4 celery sticks, sliced
15ml/1 tbsp mixed dried herbs
finely grated rind of 1 orange
goose liver, chopped
450g/1lb pork sausage meat (bulk sausage)
115g/4oz/1 cup chopped pecan nuts
2 eggs

For the caramelized apples
50g/2oz/¼ cup butter
60ml/4 tbsp redcurrant jelly
30ml/2 tbsp red wine vinegar
9 small eating apples, peeled and cored

For the gravy
30ml/2 tbsp plain (all-purpose) flour
600ml/1 pint/2½ cups giblet stock
juice of 1 orange

1 Soak the prunes in the port or red wine for 24 hours. Stone (pit) and cut each prune into four. Reserve the liquid.

2 The next day, mix the prunes with all the remaining stuffing ingredients and season well. Moisten with half the reserved port or red wine.

3 Preheat the oven to 200°C/400°F/ Gas 6. Stuff the neck-end of the goose, tucking the flap of skin under and securing it with a small skewer. Remove the excess fat from the cavity and pack it with the stuffing. Tie the legs together to hold them in place.

4 Weigh the stuffed goose to calculate the cooking time: allow 15 minutes for each 450g/1lb plus an extra 15 minutes. Put the bird on a rack in a roasting pan and rub the skin with salt. Prick the skin all over to help the fat run out. Roast for 30 minutes, then reduce the heat to 180°C/350°F/Gas 4 and roast for the remaining cooking time. Occasionally check and pour off any fat produced during cooking into a bowl. The goose is cooked when the juices run clear when the thickest part of the thigh is pierced with a skewer. Pour a little cold water over the breast halfway through the cooking time to crisp up the skin.

5 Meanwhile, prepare the apples. Melt the butter, redcurrant jelly and vinegar in a small roasting pan or a shallow ovenproof dish. Put in the apples, baste them well and cook in the oven for 15–20 minutes. Baste the apples halfway through the cooking time. Do not cover them or they will collapse.

6 Lift the goose on to a serving dish and let it stand for 15 minutes before carving. Pour off the excess fat from the roasting pan, leaving any sediment in the base. Stir in the flour, cook gently until brown, and then blend in the stock. Bring to the boil, add the remaining reserved port, orange juice and seasoning. Simmer gently for 2–3 minutes. Strain into a gravy boat.

7 Surround the goose with the caramelized apples and spoon over the redcurrant glaze. Serve with the gravy.

COOK'S TIP
Do not overestimate the yield from a goose – the bird often looks big but there is a lot of fat and not too much meat on it for its size.

Energy 822kcal/3437kJ; Protein 54.8g; Carbohydrate 44.1g, of which sugars 21.8g; Fat 48.7g, of which saturates 0.9g; Cholesterol 0mg; Calcium 87mg; Fibre 3.1g; Sodium 486mg.

Glazed Poussins

Golden poussins make an impressive main course. Serve them with traditional roast accompaniments or a refreshing side salad.

Serves 6

75g/3oz/6 tbsp butter
15ml/1 tbsp mixed (pumpkin pie) spice
45ml/3 tbsp clear honey
grated rind and juice of 3 clementines
6 poussins, each weighing
  about 450g/1lb
1 large onion, finely chopped
2 garlic cloves, chopped
25ml/1½ tbsp plain (all-purpose) flour
75ml/2½ fl oz/⅓ cup Marsala
450ml/¾ pint/scant 2 cups
  chicken stock
bunch of fresh coriander (cilantro),
  to garnish

VARIATION

You can stuff each poussin, before roasting, with a quartered clementine.

1 Preheat the oven to 220°C/425°F/ Gas 7. To make the glaze, heat the butter, mixed spice, honey and clementine rind and juice until the butter has melted, stirring to mix well. Remove from the heat.

2 Place the poussins in a large roasting pan, brush them with the glaze, then roast for 40 minutes. Brush with any remaining glaze and baste occasionally with the pan juices during cooking. Transfer the poussins to a serving platter, cover with foil and leave to stand for 10 minutes.

3 Skim off all but 15ml/1 tbsp of the fat from the roasting pan. Add the onion and garlic to the juices in the pan and cook on the stove, stirring occasionally, until beginning to brown. Stir in the flour, then gradually pour in the Marsala, followed by the stock, whisking constantly. Bring to the boil and simmer for 3 minutes to make a smooth, rich gravy.

4 Transfer the poussins to warm plates or leave on the serving platter and garnish with coriander. Serve at once, offering the gravy separately.

Energy 681kcal/2837kJ; Protein 51g; Carbohydrate 14g, of which sugars 10g; Fat 47g, of which saturates 16g; Cholesterol 288mg; Calcium 43mg; Fibre 1g; Sodium 450mg.

Medallions of **Venison** with **Herbed Horseradish Dumplings**

Venison is lean and full-flavoured, and tastes simply wonderful with these piquant dumplings.

Serves 8

1.2 litres/2 pints/5 cups venison stock
250ml/8fl oz/1 cup port
30ml/2 tbsp sunflower oil
8 medallions of venison, about
  175g/6oz each
chopped fresh parsley, to garnish
steamed baby vegetables, to serve

For the dumplings
150g/5oz/1¼ cup self-raising
  (self-rising) flour
75g/3oz beef suet (US chilled
  grated shortening)
30ml/2 tbsp chopped mixed herbs
10ml/2 tsp creamed horseradish
90–120ml/6–8 tbsp water

1 First make the dumplings: mix the flour, suet and herbs and make a well in the centre. Add the horseradish and water, then mix to make a soft but not sticky dough. Shape the dough into walnut-size balls and chill in the refrigerator for up to 1 hour.

2 Boil the venison stock in a pan until reduced by half. Add the port and continue boiling until reduced again by half, then pour the reduced stock into a frying pan. Heat the stock until it is simmering and add the dumplings. Poach them for 5–10 minutes, or until risen and cooked through. Use a slotted spoon to remove the dumplings.

COOK'S TIP
Serve a variety of steamed vegetables with the venison such as carrots, courgettes (zucchini) and turnips.

3 Smear the sunflower oil over a non-stick griddle, heat until very hot. Add the venison, cook for 2–3 minutes on each side. Place the venison medallions on warmed serving plates and pour the sauce over. Serve with the dumplings and vegetables, garnished with parsley.

VARIATION
Beef fillet (tenderloin) medallions can be used instead of the venison. Replace the venison stock with beef stock.

Energy 363kcal/1528kJ; Protein 41g; Carbohydrate 16g, of which sugars 1g; Fat 16g, of which saturates 7g; Cholesterol 95mg; Calcium 50mg; Fibre 1g; Sodium 394mg.

Rich Game Pie

Smart enough for a formal wedding buffet but also terrific for a stylish picnic, this rich game pie looks spectacular when baked in a fluted raised pie mould. Some specialist kitchen stores hire the moulds so you can avoid the expense of purchasing one; alternatively a 20cm/8in round deep, loose-based tin can be used. Serve the pie garnished with salad leaves.

Serves 10

25g/1oz/2 tbsp butter
1 onion, finely chopped
2 garlic cloves, finely chopped
900g/2lb mixed boneless game meat, such as skinless pheasant and/or pigeon (US squab) breast, venison and rabbit, diced
30ml/2 tbsp chopped mixed fresh herbs, such as parsley, thyme and marjoram
salt and ground black pepper

For the pâté
50g/2oz/¼ cup butter
2 garlic cloves, finely chopped
450g/1lb chicken livers, rinsed, trimmed and chopped
60ml/4 tbsp brandy
5ml/1 tsp ground mace

For the pastry
675g/1½lb/6 cups strong white bread flour
5ml/1 tsp salt
115ml/3½fl oz/scant ½ cup milk
115ml/3½fl oz/scant ½ cup water
115g/4oz/½ cup white cooking fat, diced
115g/4oz/½ cup butter, diced
beaten egg, to glaze

For the jelly
300ml/½ pint/1¼ cups game or beef consommé
2.5ml/½ tsp powdered gelatine

1 Melt the butter in a small pan until foaming, then add the onion and garlic, and cook until softened but not coloured. Remove from the heat and mix with the diced game meat and the chopped mixed herbs. Season well, cover and chill.

2 To make the pâté, melt the butter in a pan until foaming. Add the garlic and chicken livers and cook until the livers are just browned. Remove the pan from the heat and stir in the brandy and mace. Process the mixture in a blender or food processor until smooth, then set aside and leave to cool completely.

3 To make the pastry, sift the flour and salt into a bowl and make a well in the centre. Place the milk and water in a pan. Add the white cooking fat and butter and heat gently until melted, then bring to the boil and remove from the heat as soon as the mixture begins to bubble. Pour the hot liquid into the well in the flour and beat until smooth. Cover and leave until the dough is cool enough to handle.

4 Preheat the oven to 200°C/400°F/Gas 6. Roll out two-thirds of the pastry and use to line a 23cm/9in raised pie mould. Press the pastry into the flutes and around the edge. Patch any thin areas with offcuts (scraps) from the top edge. Spoon in half the mixture and press it down evenly. Add the pâté and then top with the remaining game.

5 Roll out the remaining pastry to form a lid. Brush the edge of the pastry lining the tin with a little water and cover the pie with the pastry lid. Trim off excess pastry from around the edge. Pinch the edges together to seal in the filling. Make two holes in the centre of the lid and glaze with egg. Use pastry trimmings to roll out leaves to garnish the pie. Brush with egg.

6 Bake the pie for 20 minutes, then cover it with foil and cook for a further 10 minutes. Reduce the oven temperature to 150°C/300°F/Gas 2. Glaze the pie again with beaten egg and cook for a further 1½ hours, with the top covered loosely with foil.

7 Remove the pie from the oven and leave it to stand for 15 minutes. Increase the oven temperature to 200°C/400°F/Gas 6. Stand the tin on a baking sheet and remove the sides. Quickly glaze the sides of the pie with beaten egg and cover the top with foil, then cook for a final 15 minutes to brown the sides. Leave to cool completely, then chill the pie overnight.

8 To make the jelly, heat the game or beef consommé in a small pan until just beginning to bubble, whisk in the gelatine until dissolved and leave to cool until just setting. Using a small funnel, carefully pour the jellied consommé into the holes in the pie. Chill until set. This pie will keep in the refrigerator for up to 3 days.

Energy 731kcal/3058kJ; Protein 44g; Carbohydrate 54.3g, of which sugars 2.5g; Fat 32g, of which saturates 17.9g; Cholesterol 223mg; Calcium 163mg; Fibre 2.3g; Sodium 444mg.

Fillet of Beef with Ratatouille

This succulent beef is served cold with a colourful garlicky ratatouille.

Serves 8

675–900g/1½–2lb fillet (tenderloin)
of beef
45ml/3 tbsp olive oil
300ml/½ pint/1¼ cups aspic jelly, made
up as packet instructions

For the marinade

30ml/2 tbsp sherry
30ml/2 tbsp olive oil
30ml/2 tbsp soy sauce
10ml/2 tsp grated fresh root ginger
2 garlic cloves, crushed

For the ratatouille

60ml/4 tbsp olive oil
1 onion, sliced
2–3 garlic cloves, crushed
1 large aubergine (eggplant), cubed
1 small red (bell) pepper, seeded
and sliced
1 small green (bell) pepper, seeded
and sliced
1 small yellow (bell) pepper, seeded
and sliced
225g/8oz courgettes (zucchini), sliced
450g/1lb tomatoes, peeled
15ml/1 tbsp chopped fresh mixed herbs
30ml/2 tbsp French dressing
salt and ground black pepper

1 Mix all the marinade ingredients together and pour over the beef. Cover the dish with clear film (plastic wrap) and leave for 30 minutes.

2 Preheat the oven to 220°C/425°F/ Gas 7. Using a large slotted spoon, lift the beef out of the marinade and pat it dry with kitchen paper. Heat the oil in a frying pan until smoking hot and then brown the beef all over to seal it.

3 Transfer the beef to a roasting pan and roast for 10–15 minutes, basting it occasionally with the marinade. Lift the beef out on to a large plate and leave it to cool.

4 Meanwhile, for the ratatouille, heat the oil in a large casserole and cook the onion and garlic over a low heat, until tender, without letting the onions become brown. Add the aubergine cubes to the casserole and cook for a further 5 minutes, until soft.

5 Add the sliced peppers and the courgettes and cook for 2 minutes more. Then add the tomatoes and chopped herbs, and season well with salt and pepper. Cook for a few minutes longer. Turn the ratatouille into a dish and set aside to cool. Drizzle with a little French dressing.

6 Slice the beef fillet and arrange overlapping slices on a large serving platter. Brush the slices of beef with a little cold aspic jelly that is just on the point of setting.

7 Leave the beef until the aspic jelly has set completely, then brush the slices with a second coat. Spoon the cooled ratatouille around the beef slices on the platter and serve immediately.

COOK'S TIP

Ratatouille is a traditional French recipe that is at its best when made with the choicest fresh ingredients. It makes a wonderful side dish for a buffet or can be eaten as a snack or as a vegetarian filling for jacket potatoes.

VARIATIONS

• Instead of marinating the beef in soy sauce and ginger, add 15ml/1 tbsp chopped fresh marjoram to the mixture, increase the quantity of sherry to 60ml/ 4 tbsp and add 15ml/1 tbsp crushed juniper berries.
• Use pork instead of beef and increase the roasting time to 20–30 minutes.

Energy 250kcal/1043kJ; Protein 21.9g; Carbohydrate 7.7g, of which sugars 7.2g; Fat 14.8g, of which saturates 4.4g; Cholesterol 51mg; Calcium 28mg; Fibre 2.7g; Sodium 66mg.

Cider-glazed Ham

A succulent gammon joint with a sweet cider glaze that looks impressive and tastes wonderful. Served with a zesty cranberry sauce, it would be ideal for a Christmas or Thanksgiving buffet.

Serves 8–10

2kg/4½lb middle gammon (smoked or cured ham) joint
1 large or 2 small onions
about 30 whole cloves
3 bay leaves
10 black peppercorns
1.3 litres/2¼ pints/5⅔ cups medium-dry (hard) cider
45ml/3 tbsp soft light brown sugar
bunch of flat leaf parsley, to garnish

For the sauce
350g/12oz/3 cups cranberries
175g/6oz/¾ cup soft light brown sugar
grated rind and juice of 2 clementines
30ml/2 tbsp port

1 Weigh the gammon joint and calculate the cooking time: allow 20 minutes per 450g/1lb, then place it in a large casserole or pan. Stud the onion or onions with 5–10 of the cloves and add to the casserole or pan with the bay leaves and peppercorns.

VARIATION
Use clear honey in place of the soft brown sugar for the glaze and serve the gammon with redcurrant sauce or jelly instead of the cranberry sauce.

2 Add 1.2 litres/2 pints/5 cups of the cider and enough water to just cover the gammon. Heat until simmering and then carefully skim off the scum that rises to the surface using a large spoon. Start timing the cooking from the moment the stock begins to simmer.

3 Cover with a lid or foil and simmer gently for the calculated time. Towards the end of the cooking time, preheat the oven to 220°C/425°F/Gas 7.

4 Heat the sugar and remaining cider in a pan; stir until the sugar has dissolved. Simmer for 5 minutes to make a dark, sticky glaze. Remove the pan from the heat and leave to cool for 5 minutes.

COOK'S TIPS
• A large stock pot or preserving pan can be used for cooking the gammon.
• Leave the gammon until it is just cool enough to handle before removing the rind. Snip off the string, then carefully slice off the rind, leaving a thin, even layer of fat. Use a narrow-bladed, sharp knife for the best results.

5 Lift the gammon out of the casserole or pan with a slotted spoon and a large fork. Carefully and evenly, cut off the rind, then score the fat into a neat diamond pattern. Place the gammon in a roasting pan or ovenproof dish.

6 Press a clove into the centre of each diamond, then carefully spoon over the glaze. Bake for 20–25 minutes, or until the fat is brown, glistening and crisp.

7 Simmer all the sauce ingredients in a heavy pan for 15–20 minutes, stirring frequently. Pour into a jug (pitcher).

8 Serve the ham hot or cold, garnished with parsley and with the cranberry sauce accompaniment.

Energy 368kcal/1541kJ; Protein 39.6g; Carbohydrate 15.2g, of which sugars 15.2g; Fat 16.9g, of which saturates 5.6g; Cholesterol 52mg; Calcium 25mg; Fibre 0.6g; Sodium 1982mg.

stylish salads

A repertoire of exciting salads is every cook's

standby for colourful first courses,

refreshing side dishes or buffet pizzazz.

Pear and Parmesan Salad

This is great when pears are at their seasonal best. Try Packhams or Comice when plentiful, drizzled with a poppy-seed dressing and topped with shavings of Parmesan.

Serves 4

4 just-ripe dessert pears
50g/2oz piece Parmesan cheese
watercress, to garnish
water biscuits (crackers) or rye bread,
*   to serve (optional)*

For the dressing

30ml/2 tbsp extra virgin olive oil
15ml/1 tbsp sunflower oil
30ml/2 tbsp cider vinegar or white
*   wine vinegar*
2.5ml/1/2 tsp soft light brown sugar
good pinch of dried thyme
15ml/1 tbsp poppy seeds
salt and ground black pepper

1 Cut the pears in quarters and remove the cores. Cut each pear quarter in half lengthways and arrange them on four small serving plates. Peel the pears if you wish, though they look more attractive unpeeled.

COOK'S TIP

Always buy Parmesan cheese in a piece. It will keep for months in the refrigerator. If you have bought a large piece, freeze half of it. You can, in fact, make Parmesan shavings and grate it from frozen.

2 Make the dressing. Whisk the olive oil, sunflower oil, vinegar, sugar, thyme and seasoning in a bowl, then tip in the poppy seeds. Trickle over the pears. Garnish with watercress and shave Parmesan over the top. Serve with water biscuits or rye bread, if you like.

VARIATION

Blue cheeses and pears also have an affinity. Stilton, Dolcelatte, Gorgonzola or Danish blue are all good substitutes. Allow about 200g/7oz and cut into wedges or cubes.

Energy 193kcal/804kJ; Protein 5.4g; Carbohydrate 15.7g, of which sugars 15.7g; Fat 12.5g, of which saturates 3.7g; Cholesterol 13mg; Calcium 167mg; Fibre 3.3g; Sodium 141mg.

Melon and Prosciutto Salad

Sections of cool fragrant melon wrapped with slices of air-dried ham make a delicious salad appetizer. If strawberries are in season, serve with a savoury-sweet strawberry salsa and watch it disappear.

Serves 4

1 large cantaloupe, Charentais or
Galia melon
175g/6oz prosciutto or Serrano ham,
thinly sliced

For the salsa

225g/8oz/2 cups strawberries
5ml/1 tsp caster (superfine) sugar
30ml/2 tbsp sunflower oil
15ml/1 tbsp orange juice
2.5ml/¹/₂ tsp finely grated orange rind
2.5ml/¹/₂ tsp finely grated fresh
root ginger
salt and ground black pepper

2 For the salsa, hull the strawberries and cut them into large dice. Place in a small mixing bowl with the sugar and crush very lightly to release the juices. Add the sunflower oil, orange juice, orange rind and grated ginger. Season with a little salt and plenty of ground black pepper.

3 Arrange the melon slices on a serving plate, lay the prosciutto or Serrano ham over the top and then serve with a bowl of salsa, handed around separately.

1 Halve the melon, scoop out the seeds with a spoon and discard. Cut the rind away with a paring knife, then slice the melon thickly. Chill in the refrigerator until ready to serve.

Energy 207kcal/859kJ; Protein 9g; Carbohydrate 10g, of which sugars 10g; Fat 15g, of which saturates 4g; Cholesterol 23mg; Calcium 42mg; Fibre 2g; Sodium 690mg.

Moroccan Orange, Onion and Olive Salad

This is a refreshing salad to add to a selection of buffet dishes.

Serves 6

5 large oranges
90g/3½oz/scant 1 cup black olives
1 red onion, thinly sliced
1 large fennel bulb, thinly sliced,
  feathery tops reserved
15ml/1 tbsp chopped fresh mint, plus
  a few extra sprigs to garnish
15ml/1 tbsp chopped fresh coriander
  (cilantro), plus extra to garnish
60ml/4 tbsp olive oil
10ml/2 tsp lemon juice
2.5ml/½ tsp ground toasted
  coriander seeds
2.5ml/½ tsp orange flower water
salt and ground black pepper

1 Peel the oranges with a sharp knife, making sure that you remove all the white pith, and cut them into 5mm/¼in slices. Remove any pips (seeds) and work over a bowl to catch all the orange juice. Set the juice aside for adding to the salad dressing.

2 Pit the olives, if you like. In a bowl, toss the orange slices, onion and fennel together with the olives, chopped fresh mint and coriander.

3 Make the dressing: in a bowl or jug (pitcher), whisk together the olive oil, 15ml/1 tbsp of the reserved fresh orange juice and the lemon juice. Add the ground toasted coriander seeds and season to taste with a little salt and pepper. Whisk thoroughly to mix.

4 Toss the dressing into the salad, cover and leave to stand in a cool place for 30–60 minutes.

5 To serve, drain off any excess dressing and place the salad in a serving dish or bowl. Sprinkle with the chopped herbs and reserved fennel tops, and sprinkle with the orange flower water.

Tomato, Mozzarella and Red Onion Salad with Basil and Caper Dressing

Sweet tomatoes and the heady scent of basil capture the essence of summer in this simple salad.

Serves 8

10 large ripe tomatoes
4 small packets mozzarella di bufala
  cheese, drained and sliced
2 small red onions, chopped
fresh basil and parsley sprigs, to garnish

For the dressing
1 small garlic clove, peeled
25g/1oz/1 cup fresh basil
60ml/4 tbsp chopped fresh flat
  leaf parsley
45ml/3 tbsp salted capers, rinsed
5ml/1 tsp mustard
150ml/¼ pint/⅔ cup extra virgin
  olive oil
15ml/1tbsp balsamic vinegar
salt and ground black pepper

1 First make the dressing. Put the garlic, basil, parsley, half the capers and the mustard in a food processor or blender and process briefly to chop. Then, with the motor running, gradually pour in the olive oil through the feeder tube to make a smooth purée with a dressing consistency. Add the balsamic vinegar to taste and season with ground black pepper. Alternatively, the dressing can be made by pounding the ingredients in a mortar and adding the oil by hand.

2 Slice the tomatoes thinly. Arrange the tomato and mozzarella slices overlapping alternately on a large plate. Sprinkle the onion over the top and season with a little pepper.

3 Drizzle the dressing over the salad, then sprinkle a few basil leaves, parsley sprigs and the remaining capers on top.

4 Leave the salad to marinate for 10–15 minutes for the flavours to develop before serving.

Moroccan: Energy 177kcal/740kJ; Protein 3g; Carbohydrate 16g, of which sugars 15g; Fat 12g, of which saturates 2g; Cholesterol 0mg; Calcium 111mg; Fibre 5g; Sodium 368mg.
Tomato: Energy 307kcal/1272kJ; Protein 9g; Carbohydrate 8g, of which sugars 7g; Fat 27g, of which saturates 8g; Cholesterol 22mg; Calcium 166mg; Fibre 3g; Sodium 205mg.

Tricolour Salad

A popular salad, this dish depends for its success on the quality of its ingredients. Mozzarella di bufala is the best cheese to serve uncooked. Whole ripe plum tomatoes give up their juice to blend with extra virgin olive oil for a natural dressing.

Serves 4

300g/11oz mozzarella di bufala
cheese, thinly sliced
8 large plum tomatoes, sliced
1 large avocado
about 15 basil leaves or a small
handful of flat leaf parsley leaves
90–120ml/6–8 tbsp extra virgin olive oil
ground black pepper
ciabatta and sea salt flakes, to serve

1 Arrange the mozzarella cheese slices and tomato slices randomly on four salad plates. Crush over a few good pinches of sea salt flakes. This will help to draw out some of the juices from the plum tomatoes. Cover with clear film (plastic wrap), set aside in a cool place and leave to marinate for about 30 minutes.

2 Just before serving, cut the avocado in half lengthways, using a large, sharp knife and twist the halves to separate them. Lift out the stone (pit) with the point of the knife and remove the peel.

3 Carefully slice the avocado flesh crossways into half moons, or cut it into large chunks if that is easier.

4 Place the avocado slices on the salad, then sprinkle with the basil or parsley. Drizzle over the olive oil, add a little more salt if you like and season well with black pepper. Serve the salad at room temperature, with chunks of crusty Italian ciabatta or other country bread for mopping up the dressing.

Energy 480kcal/1992kJ; Protein 16g; Carbohydrate 9g, of which sugars 9g; Fat 42g, of which saturates 14g; Cholesterol 44mg; Calcium 296mg; Fibre 4g; Sodium 323mg.

Green Bean and Sweet Red Pepper Salad

Serrano chillies are very fiery so be cautious about their use.

Serves 4

350g/12oz cooked green beans
2 red (bell) peppers, seeded
2 spring onions (scallions), chopped
1 or more drained pickled serrano
  chillies, rinsed, seeded and chopped
1 iceberg lettuce, coarsely shredded
olives, to garnish

For the dressing
45ml/3 tbsp red wine vinegar
135ml/9 tbsp olive oil
salt and ground black pepper

1 Cut the cooked green beans into quarters and chop the peppers. Combine the beans, peppers, spring onions and chillies in a bowl.

2 Make the salad dressing. Pour the red wine vinegar into a bowl or jug (pitcher). Add salt and ground black pepper to taste, then gradually whisk in the olive oil until well combined. Alternatively, combine the vinegar and oil in a screw-top jar, add salt and pepper to taste, close the lid and shake vigorously to mix.

COOK'S TIPS
Although jars of pickled chillies may be labelled "mild" or "hot", as opposed to "very hot", do not assume that you have the same tolerance to their heat as the people in the country that pickled them.

3 Pour the salad dressing over the prepared vegetables and toss lightly together to mix and coat thoroughly. Set aside at room temperature until you are ready to serve.

4 Line a large serving platter with the shredded iceberg lettuce leaves and arrange the salad vegetables attractively on top. Garnish with the olives and serve immediately.

Energy 362kcal/1498kJ; Protein 3g; Carbohydrate 10g, of which sugars 8g; Fat 34g, of which saturates 5g; Cholesterol 0mg; Calcium 85mg; Fibre 3g; Sodium 63mg.

Roasted Tomato and **Mozzarella Salad**

Roasting the tomatoes brings out their sweetness and adds a new dimension to this salad. Make the basil oil just before serving to retain its fresh flavour and lovely vivid colour.

Serves 4

olive oil, for brushing
6 large plum tomatoes
2 fresh mozzarella cheese balls, cut
    into 8–12 slices
salt and ground black pepper
fresh basil leaves, to garnish

For the basil oil
25 fresh basil leaves
60ml/4 tbsp extra virgin olive oil
1 garlic clove, crushed

1 Preheat the oven to 200°C/400°F/ Gas 6 and brush a baking sheet with olive oil. Cut the tomatoes in half lengthways and remove and discard the seeds. Place the tomato halves, skin side down, on the baking sheet, brush with a little oil and roast for about 20 minutes, or until the tomatoes are very tender but still retain their shape.

2 Meanwhile, make the basil oil. Place the basil leaves, olive oil and garlic in a food processor or blender and process until smooth. You will need to scrape down the sides once or twice to make sure that the mixture is processed properly. Transfer to a bowl, cover with clear film (plastic wrap) and chill until required.

3 For each serving, place the tomato halves on top of two or three slices of mozzarella and drizzle over the basil oil. Season to taste with salt and pepper. Garnish with fresh basil leaves and serve immediately.

Mixed Herb Salad with **Toasted Mixed Seeds**

This simple salad is the perfect antidote to a rich, heavy meal, as it contains fresh herbs that can ease the digestion. Balsamic vinegar adds a rich, sweet taste to the dressing, but red or white wine vinegar could be used instead.

Serves 4

90g/3¹/₂oz/4 cups mixed salad leaves
50g/2oz/2 cups mixed salad herbs,
    such as coriander (cilantro),
    parsley, basil, chervil and
    rocket (arugula)
45ml/3 tbsp pumpkin seeds
45ml/3 tbsp sunflower seeds

For the dressing
60ml/4 tbsp extra virgin olive oil
15ml/1 tbsp balsamic vinegar
2.5ml/¹/₂ tsp Dijon mustard
salt and ground black pepper

1 To make the dressing, combine the ingredients in a bowl or screw-top jar. Mix with a small whisk or fork, or shake well, until completely combined.

2 Put the salad leaves and herb leaves in a large bowl. Toss with your fingers to mix together.

3 Toast the pumpkin and sunflower seeds in a dry frying pan over a medium heat for about 2 minutes, until golden, tossing frequently to prevent them from burning. Leave the seeds to cool slightly before sprinkling them over the salad.

4 Pour the dressing over the salad and toss with your hands until the leaves are well coated, then serve.

Tomato: Energy 207kcal/860kJ; Protein 12.5g; Carbohydrate 3.9g, of which sugars 3.9g; Fat 15.8g, of which saturates 9.1g; Cholesterol 36mg; Calcium 235mg; Fibre 1.3g; Sodium 258mg.
Herb: Energy 142kcal/585kJ; Protein 3.6g; Carbohydrate 3.1g, of which sugars 2.7g; Fat 12.9g, of which saturates 2.1g; Cholesterol 2mg; Calcium 216mg; Fibre 4.4g; Sodium 82mg.

Orange and Red Onion Salad with Cumin

Cumin and mint give this refreshing salad a typically Middle Eastern flavour. Choose small seedless oranges.

Serves 6

6 oranges
2 red onions
15ml/1 tbsp cumin seeds
5ml/1 tsp coarsely ground
    black pepper
15ml/1 tbsp chopped fresh mint
90ml/6 tbsp olive oil
salt

To serve
fresh mint sprigs
black olives

1 Slice the oranges thinly, working over a bowl to catch any juice. Then, holding each orange slice in turn over the bowl, cut round with scissors to remove the peel and pith. Slice the onions thinly and separate the rings.

2 Arrange the orange and onion slices in layers in a shallow dish, sprinkling each layer with cumin seeds, black pepper, chopped mint, olive oil and salt to taste. Pour over any orange juice collected when slicing the oranges.

3 Cover the salad with clear film (plastic wrap) and set aside to marinate in a cool place for about 2 hours. Just before serving, sprinkle the salad with the mint sprigs and black olives.

Spanish Salad with Olives and Capers

Make this refreshing salad in the summer when tomatoes are sweet and full of flavour. The dressing gives it a lovely tang.

Serves 4

4 tomatoes
1/2 cucumber
1 bunch spring onions
1 bunch purslane or watercress, washed
8 pimiento-stuffed olives
30ml/2 tbsp drained capers

For the dressing
30ml/2 tbsp red wine vinegar
5ml/1 tsp paprika
2.5ml/1/2 tsp ground cumin
1 garlic clove, crushed
75ml/5 tbsp olive oil
salt and ground black pepper

1 To peel the tomatoes, place them in a heatproof bowl, add boiling water to cover and leave for 1 minute. Lift the tomatoes out with a slotted spoon and plunge into a bowl of cold water. Leave for 1 minute, then drain. Slip the skins off the tomatoes and dice the flesh finely. Put in a salad bowl.

2 Peel the cucumber, dice it finely and add it to the tomatoes. Trim and chop half the spring onions, add them to the salad bowl and mix lightly.

3 Break the purslane or watercress into small sprigs. Add to the tomato mixture, with the olives and capers.

4 To make the dressing, mix the wine vinegar, paprika, cumin and garlic in a bowl. Whisk in the oil and season with salt and pepper to taste. Pour the dressing over the salad and toss lightly to coat. Serve with the remaining spring onions on the side.

Orange: Energy 161kcal/672kJ; Protein 2g; Carbohydrate 14.1g, of which sugars 13.2g; Fat 11.2g, of which saturates 1.6g; Cholesterol 0mg; Calcium 76mg; Fibre 2.7g; Sodium 8mg.
Spanish: Energy 179kcal/739kJ; Protein 3g; Carbohydrate 6.2g, of which sugars 6g; Fat 16g, of which saturates 2.4g; Cholesterol 0mg; Calcium 74mg; Fibre 3g; Sodium 303mg.

Warm Broad Bean and Feta Salad

This recipe is loosely based on a typical medley of fresh-tasting Greek salad ingredients – broad beans, tomatoes and feta cheese. It's delicious, served warm or cold.

Serves 4–6

900g/2lb broad (fava) beans, shelled,
*   or 350g/12oz shelled frozen broad*
*   (fava) beans*
60ml/4 tbsp olive oil
75g/3oz plum tomatoes, halved, or
*   quartered if large*
4 garlic cloves, crushed
115g/4oz firm feta cheese, cut into
*   large, even-size chunks*
45ml/3 tbsp chopped fresh dill, plus
*   extra to garnish*
12 black olives
salt and ground black pepper

1 Cook the fresh or frozen broad beans in lightly salted, boiling water until just tender. Drain and refresh under cold water, then set aside.

2 Meanwhile, heat the olive oil in a large, heavy frying pan and add the tomatoes and garlic. Cook over a medium heat, turning occasionally, until the tomatoes are beginning to colour, but not collapse.

3 Add the feta cheese to the pan and toss the ingredients together for 1 minute. Mix with the drained beans, dill, olives and salt and pepper. Serve garnished with chopped dill.

COOK'S TIP
Much of the feta cheese commonly available is made from cow's, rather than the traditional sheep's milk. Try to find the authentic cheese for this recipe.

Halloumi and Grape Salad

In Eastern Europe, firm salty halloumi cheese is often served fried for breakfast or supper. In this recipe for an unusual salad, it's tossed with sweet, juicy grapes which really complement its distinctive sweet and salty flavour.

Serves 4

150g/5oz mixed green salad leaves
75g/3oz seedless green grapes
75g/3oz seedless black grapes
250g/9oz halloumi cheese
45ml/3 tbsp olive oil
fresh young thyme leaves or dill,
*   to garnish*

For the dressing
60ml/4 tbsp olive oil
15ml/1 tbsp lemon juice
2.5ml/½ tsp caster (superfine) sugar
salt and ground black pepper
5ml/1 tsp chopped fresh thyme or dill

1 To make the dressing, mix together the olive oil, lemon juice and sugar in a bowl. Season to taste with salt and ground black pepper. Stir in the thyme or dill and set aside.

2 Toss together the salad leaves and the green and black grapes, then transfer to a large serving plate.

COOK'S TIP
If the cheese goes cold before it is served, it will become rubbery.

3 Thinly slice the halloumi cheese. Heat the oil in a large frying pan. Add the cheese and cook briefly until it turns golden on the underside. Turn the cheese with a fish slice or metal spatula and cook the other side.

4 Arrange the cheese over the salad. Pour over the dressing and garnish with thyme or dill. Serve immediately.

Bean: Energy 172kcal/715kJ; Protein 7.8g; Carbohydrate 7.5g, of which sugars 1.4g; Fat 12.5g, of which saturates 3.9g; Cholesterol 13mg; Calcium 108mg; Fibre 4.2g; Sodium 469mg.
Halloumi: Energy 362kcal/1497kJ; Protein 12.1g; Carbohydrate 6.4g, of which sugars 6.4g; Fat 32.2g, of which saturates 11.4g; Cholesterol 36mg; Calcium 242mg; Fibre 0.6g; Sodium 249mg.

Potato Salad with Curry Plant Mayonnaise

Potato salad can be made well in advance and is therefore a useful dish for serving as an unusual appetizer or accompaniment at a party. Its popularity means that there are very rarely any leftovers to be cleared away at the end of the day.

Serves 6

1kg/2¹/₄lb new potatoes
300ml/¹/₂ pint/1¹/₄ cups mayonnaise
6 curry plant leaves, coarsely chopped
salt and ground black pepper
mixed lettuce leaves or other salad
   leaves, to serve

1 Wash, but do not peel the potatoes. Place them in a pan of lightly salted water, cover and bring to the boil, then lower the heat and simmer gently for about 15 minutes, or until tender. Drain well, place in a large bowl and leave to cool slightly.

2 Mix the mayonnaise with the curry plant leaves and season with black pepper to taste. Stir the dressing into the potatoes while they are still warm. Leave to cool completely, then serve on a bed of mixed lettuce leaves or other assorted salad leaves.

Energy 474kcal/1967kJ; Protein 4.1g; Carbohydrate 29.1g, of which sugars 4.2g; Fat 38.7g, of which saturates 6g; Cholesterol 38mg; Calcium 37mg; Fibre 2.4g; Sodium 246mg.

Panzanella Salad

If sliced, juicy tomatoes layered with day-old bread sounds strange for a salad, don't be deceived – it's quite delicious. A popular Italian salad, this dish is ideal for entertaining.

Serves 4–6

*4 thick slices day-old bread, either
    white, brown or rye
1 small red onion
450g/1lb ripe tomatoes, thinly sliced
115g/4oz mozzarella cheese,
    thinly sliced
5ml/1 tbsp fresh basil, shredded, or
    fresh marjoram
120ml/4fl oz/1/2 cup extra virgin
    olive oil
45ml/3 tbsp balsamic vinegar
juice or 1 small lemon
salt and ground black pepper
pitted and sliced black olives or salted
    capers, to garnish*

1 Dip the bread briefly in a shallow dish of cold water, then carefully squeeze out the excess water. Arrange the bread in the base of a shallow salad bowl.

2 Thinly slice the onion, then soak the slices in a separate bowl of cold water for about 10 minutes while you prepare the other ingredients. This helps to reduce the astringency of the onion, so that it does not overpower the other flavours. Drain and reserve.

3 Layer the tomatoes, cheese, onion, basil or marjoram in the salad bowl, seasoning well with salt and pepper in between each layer. Sprinkle the salad with the olive oil, balsamic vinegar and lemon juice.

4 Top with the olives or capers. Cover with clear film (plastic wrap) and chill the salad in the refrigerator for at least 2 hours, or overnight, if possible.

Energy 237kcal/987kJ; Protein 6.3g; Carbohydrate 15.4g, of which sugars 3.5g; Fat 17.1g, of which saturates 4.5g; Cholesterol 11mg; Calcium 105mg; Fibre 1.3g; Sodium 213mg.

New York Deli Coleslaw

The key to a good coleslaw is a zesty dressing and an interesting selection of vegetables. Serve at barbecues, picnics or buffets.

Serves 6–8

1 large white or green cabbage, very thinly sliced
3–4 carrots, coarsely grated
½ red (bell) pepper, chopped
½ green (bell) pepper, chopped
1–2 celery sticks, finely chopped or 5–10ml/1–2 tsp celery seeds
1 onion, chopped
2–3 handfuls of raisins or sultanas (golden raisins)
45ml/3 tbsp white wine vinegar or cider vinegar
60–90ml/4–6 tbsp sugar
175–250ml/6–8fl oz/ ¾–1 cup mayonnaise
salt and ground black pepper

1 Put the cabbage, carrots, peppers, celery or celery seeds, onion, and raisins or sultanas in a salad bowl and mix to combine well. Add the vinegar and sugar to taste. Season with salt and pepper and toss together. Leave to stand for about 1 hour.

COOK'S TIP
The salad can be prepared beforehand to the end of step 1 and chilled overnight. Next day, it can be dressed with the mayonnaise before serving.

2 Stir enough mayonnaise into the salad to bind the ingredients lightly together. Taste the salad for seasoning and sweet-and-sour flavour, adding more sugar, salt and pepper if necessary. Chill for about 1 hour.

3 Drain off any excess liquid that has formed before serving.

VARIATION
Use low-fat crème fraîche for a lighter dressing.

Potato Salad with Egg, Mayonnaise and Olives

This version of potato salad includes a mustard mayonnaise, chopped eggs and green olives.

Serves 6–8

1kg/2¼lb waxy salad potatoes, cleaned
1 red, brown or white onion, finely chopped
2–3 celery sticks, finely chopped
60–90ml/4–6 tbsp chopped parsley
15–20 pimiento-stuffed olives, halved
3 hard-boiled eggs, chopped
60ml/4 tbsp extra virgin olive oil
60ml/4 tbsp white wine vinegar
15–30ml/1–2 tbsp mild or wholegrain mustard
celery seeds, to taste (optional)
175–250ml/6–8fl oz/ ¾–1 cup mayonnaise
salt and ground black pepper
paprika, to garnish

1 Cook the potatoes in a pan of lightly salted boiling water until tender. Drain, return to the pan and leave for 2–3 minutes to cool and dry a little.

2 When the potatoes are cool enough to handle but still warm, cut them into chunks and place in a salad bowl.

VARIATION
Instead of potatoes, use 400g/14oz cooked macaroni.

3 Sprinkle the potatoes with salt and pepper, then add the onion, celery, parsley, olives and the chopped eggs to the salad bowl.

4 In a jug (pitcher), combine the olive oil, vinegar, mustard and celery seeds, if using. Pour over the salad and toss to combine thoroughly. Add enough mayonnaise to bind the salad together. Chill for about 1 hour before serving, sprinkled with a little paprika.

Coleslaw: Energy 215kcal/891kJ; Protein 1.6g; Carbohydrate 15.1g, of which sugars 14.6g; Fat 16.8g, of which saturates 2.6g; Cholesterol 16mg; Calcium 46mg; Fibre 2.3g; Sodium 115mg.
Potato: Energy 323kcal/1343kJ; Protein 5.2g; Carbohydrate 21.5g, of which sugars 2.7g; Fat 24.7g, of which saturates 4g; Cholesterol 88mg; Calcium 49mg; Fibre 2g; Sodium 149mg.

Goat's Cheese Salad

Goat's cheese has a strong, tangy flavour, so choose robust salad leaves to accompany it.

Serves 4

30ml/2 tbsp olive oil
4 slices of French bread,
*   1cm/1/2 in thick*
8 cups mixed salad leaves, such as
*   frisée lettuce, radicchio and red oak*
*   leaf, torn in small pieces*
4 firm goat's cheese rounds, about
*   50g/2oz each, rind removed*
1 yellow or red (bell) pepper, seeded
*   and finely diced*
1 small red onion, thinly sliced
45ml/3 tbsp chopped fresh parsley
30ml/2 tbsp chopped fresh chives

For the dressing
30ml/2 tbsp white wine vinegar
1.5ml/1/4 tsp salt
5ml/1 tsp wholegrain mustard
75ml/5 tbsp olive oil
ground black pepper

1 To make the dressing, mix the vinegar and salt in a bowl or jug (pitcher), stirring with a fork until the salt has dissolved. Stir in the mustard. Gradually whisk in the olive oil until blended. Season to taste with pepper and set aside until needed.

2 Preheat the grill (broiler). Heat the oil in a frying pan. Add the bread slices and cook for about 1 minute, until the undersides are golden. Turn and cook on the other side for about 30 seconds more. Drain well on kitchen paper and set aside.

3 Place the salad leaves in a bowl. Add 45ml/3 tbsp of the dressing and toss to coat well. Divide the dressed leaves among four salad plates.

4 Place the goat's cheeses, cut sides up, on a baking sheet and grill (broil) for about 1–2 minutes, until bubbling and golden.

COOK'S TIP
Cheese made entirely from goat's milk is usually labelled "pure" or, if French, "chèvre". Milder cheeses are made with a mixture of cow's and goat's milk.

5 Set a goat's cheese on each slice of bread and place in the centre of each plate. Sprinkle the diced pepper, red onion, parsley and chives over the salad. Drizzle with the remaining dressing and serve.

Caesar Salad

This is a well-known and much enjoyed salad invented by a chef called Caesar Cardini. Be sure to use crisp lettuce and add the very soft eggs at the last minute.

Serves 6

175ml/6fl oz/³⁄₄ cup salad oil,
preferably olive oil
115g/4oz French or Italian bread, cut
in 2.5cm/1in cubes
1 large garlic clove, crushed with the
flat side of a knife
1 cos or romaine lettuce
2 eggs, boiled for 1 minute
120ml/4fl oz/¹⁄₂ cup lemon juice
50g/2oz/²⁄₃ cup freshly grated
Parmesan cheese
6 canned anchovy fillets, drained and
finely chopped (optional)
salt and ground black pepper

1 Heat 50ml/2fl oz/¹⁄₄ cup of the oil in a large frying pan. Add the bread cubes and garlic. Cook over a medium heat, stirring and turning constantly, until the bread cubes are golden brown all over. Drain well on kitchen paper. Discard the garlic.

2 Tear large lettuce leaves into smaller pieces. Put all the lettuce in a bowl.

3 Add the remaining oil to the lettuce and season with salt and plenty of ground black pepper. Toss well to coat the leaves.

4 Break the eggs on top. Sprinkle with the lemon juice. Toss thoroughly again to combine.

5 Add the Parmesan cheese and anchovies, if using. Toss gently to mix.

6 Sprinkle the fried bread cubes on top and serve immediately.

VARIATIONS

• To make a tangier dressing mix 30ml/ 2 tbsp white wine vinegar, 15ml/1 tbsp Worcestershire sauce, 2.5ml/¹⁄₂ tsp mustard powder, 5ml/1 tsp sugar, salt and pepper in a screw-top jar, then add the oil and shake well.

• If you are worried about the safety of eating very lightly cooked eggs, you can substitute quartered hard-boiled eggs. However, the dressing will not be as creamy without the runny egg yolk.

COOK'S TIP

Do not boil the eggs for longer than 1 minute. The whites should be milky, while the yolks remain raw.

Energy 198kcal/824kJ; Protein 5.6g; Carbohydrate 13.8g, of which sugars 1.7g; Fat 13.8g, of which saturates 2.1g; Cholesterol 50mg; Calcium 64mg; Fibre 0.9g; Sodium 400mg.

Avocado and Smoked Fish Salad

Avocado and smoked fish make a good combination, and flavoured with herbs and spices, create a delectable and elegant salad.

Serves 4

15g/¹/₂oz/1 tbsp butter
  or margarine
¹/₂ onion, thinly sliced
5ml/1 tsp mustard seeds
225g/8oz smoked mackerel, flaked
30ml/2 tbsp chopped fresh
  coriander (cilantro)
2 firm tomatoes, peeled
  and chopped
15ml/1 tbsp lemon juice

For the salad
2 avocados, halved, stoned (pitted)
  and peeled
¹/₂ cucumber
15ml/1 tbsp lemon juice
2 firm tomatoes
1 green chilli
salt and ground black pepper

1 Melt the butter or margarine in a heavy frying pan, add the onion and mustard seeds and cook over a low heat, stirring occasionally, for about 5 minutes, until the onion is soft but not browned.

2 Add the flaked mackerel, chopped coriander, tomatoes and lemon juice and cook over a low heat for about 2–3 minutes. Remove the pan from the heat and leave to cool.

COOK'S TIP

Although smoked mackerel has a very distinctive flavour, smoked haddock or cod can also be used in this salad, or a mixture of mackerel and haddock. For a speedy salad when time is short, canned tuna makes an easy and convenient substitute.

3 To make the salad, thinly slice the avocados and cucumber. Place them together in a bowl and sprinkle with the lemon juice to prevent the avocado flesh from discolouring.

4 Slice the tomatoes and seed and finely chop the chilli.

5 Place the fish mixture in the centre of a serving plate.

6 Arrange the avocado slices, cucumber and tomatoes decoratively around the outside of the fish mixture. Alternatively, spoon a quarter of the fish mixture on to each of four individual serving plates and divide the avocados, cucumber and tomatoes equally among them. Then sprinkle with the chopped chilli, season with a little salt and ground black pepper and serve immediately.

Energy 386kcal/1596kJ; Protein 12.8g; Carbohydrate 4.6g, of which sugars 3.1g; Fat 35.2g, of which saturates 8.6g; Cholesterol 67mg; Calcium 32mg; Fibre 3.4g; Sodium 455mg.

Salade Niçoise

Made with the freshest ingredients, this classic Provençal salad makes a simple yet unbeatable summer dish. Serve with country-style bread and chilled white wine for a Mediterannean treat.

Serves 4–6

115g/4oz green beans
1 tuna steak, about 175g/6oz
olive oil, for brushing
115g/4oz mixed salad leaves
1/2 small cucumber, thinly sliced
4 ripe tomatoes, quartered
50g/2oz can anchovies, drained and
   halved lengthways
4 hard-boiled eggs, quartered
1/2 bunch radishes, trimmed
50g/2oz/1/2 cup small black olives
salt and ground black pepper
flat leaf parsley, to garnish

For the dressing
90ml/6 tbsp virgin olive oil
2 garlic cloves, crushed
15ml/1 tbsp white wine vinegar
salt and ground black pepper

1 To make the dressing, whisk together the oil, garlic and vinegar in a bowl, then season to taste with salt and pepper.

2 Preheat the grill (broiler). Brush the tuna steak with olive oil and season with salt and black pepper. Grill (broil) for 3–4 minutes on each side, until cooked through. Set aside to cool.

3 Trim and halve the green beans. Cook them in a pan of boiling water for 2 minutes, until only just tender, then drain, refresh under cold water and leave to cool.

4 Mix together the salad leaves, sliced cucumber, tomatoes and green beans in a large, shallow bowl. Flake the cooled tuna steak with your fingers or two forks.

5 Sprinkle the tuna, anchovies, eggs, radishes and olives over the salad. Pour over the dressing and toss together lightly. Serve garnished with parsley.

COOK'S TIP
For an authentic touch, use black Nice olives and Nice mesclun – a mixture of frisée lettuce, lamb's lettuce, dandelion, rocket (arugula), chervil, purslane, young spinach leaves and oak leaf lettuce.

Energy 217kcal/902kJ; Protein 12.3g; Carbohydrate 3.4g, of which sugars 3.2g; Fat 17.4g, of which saturates 3.2g; Cholesterol 135mg; Calcium 50mg; Fibre 1.7g; Sodium 256mg.

Smoked Trout Pasta Salad

The little pasta shells catch the trout, creating tasty mouthfuls.

Serves 8

15g/¹/₂oz/1 tbsp butter
175g/6oz/1 cup minced (ground)
  bulb fennel
6 spring onions (scallions), 2 minced
  (ground) and the rest thinly sliced
225g/8oz skinless smoked trout
  fillets, flaked
45ml/3 tbsp chopped fresh dill
120ml/4fl oz/¹/₂ cup mayonnaise
10ml/2 tsp fresh lemon juice
30ml/2 tbsp whipping cream
450g/1lb/4 cups small pasta shells
salt and ground black pepper
fresh dill sprigs, to garnish

1 Melt the butter in a small pan. Add the fennel and minced spring onions and cook for 3–5 minutes. Transfer to a large bowl and cool slightly.

2 Add the sliced spring onions, trout, dill, mayonnaise, lemon juice and cream. Season to taste with salt and pepper and mix.

3 Bring a large pan of lightly salted water to the boil. Add the pasta, bring back to the boil and cook for about 8–10 minutes, until tender but still firm to the bite. Drain thoroughly and leave to cool.

4 Add the pasta to the vegetable and trout mixture and toss to coat evenly. Taste and adjust the seasoning, if necessary. Serve the salad lightly chilled or at room temperature, garnished with sprigs of dill.

Energy 369kcal/1548kJ; Protein 14.5g; Carbohydrate 42.7g, of which sugars 2.8g; Fat 16.8g, of which saturates 4g; Cholesterol 29mg; Calcium 31mg; Fibre 2.3g; Sodium 613mg.

Crab Salad with Rocket

Garnish these salads with strips of lemon rind, if you like.

Serves 8

8 dressed crabs
2 red (bell) peppers, seeded
 and chopped
2 small red onions, finely chopped
60ml/4 tbsp fresh coriander (cilantro)
60ml/4 tbsp drained capers
grated rind and juice of 3 lemons
Tabasco sauce, to taste
salt and ground black pepper

For the salad
75g/3oz rocket (arugula) leaves
60ml/4 tbsp sunflower oil
30ml/2 tbsp fresh lime juice

1 Remove all the white and brown meat from the crab. Put it into a large mixing bowl with the chopped peppers, onions and coriander. Add the capers, lemon rind and juice, and toss gently to mix everything thoroughly together. Season with a few drops of Tabasco sauce, according to taste, and a little salt and pepper.

2 To make the salad, wash the rocket leaves and pat them dry on kitchen paper. Divide among eight plates. Mix together the oil and lime juice in a small bowl. Dress the rocket leaves with the oil and lime juice.

3 Pile the crab salad on top and serve garnished with lemon rind strips.

Energy 121kcal/501kJ; Protein 6.4g; Carbohydrate 1.9g, of which sugars 1.8g; Fat 9.8g, of which saturates 1.5g; Cholesterol 32mg; Calcium 66mg; Fibre 1g; Sodium 232mg.

Thai Prawn Salad with Garlic Dressing and Frizzled Shallots

In this intensely flavoured salad, sweet prawns and mango are partnered with a sweet-sour garlic dressing heightened with the hot taste of chilli. The crisp frizzled shallots are a traditional addition to Thai salads.

Serves 4–6

675g/1½lb raw prawns (shrimp),
    shelled and deveined with tails on
finely shredded rind of 1 lime
½ fresh red chilli, seeded and chopped
30ml/2 tbsp olive oil, plus extra
    for brushing
1 ripe but firm mango
2 carrots, cut into long thin shreds
10cm/4in piece cucumber, sliced
1 red onion, halved and thinly sliced
a few fresh coriander (cilantro) sprigs
a few fresh mint sprigs
45ml/3 tbsp roasted peanuts, chopped
4 shallots, sliced and fried until crisp in
    30ml/2 tbsp peanut (groundnut) oil
salt and ground black pepper

For the dressing

1 large garlic clove, chopped
10–15ml/2–3 tsp caster
    (superfine) sugar
juice of 2 limes
15–30ml/1–2 tbsp Thai fish sauce
1 red chilli, seeded
5–10ml/1–2 tsp light rice vinegar

1 Place the prawns in a glass or china dish with the lime rind and chilli. Spoon the oil over them and season. Toss well and leave to marinate for 30 minutes.

2 For the dressing, place the garlic in a mortar with 10ml/2 tsp caster sugar and pound until smooth, then work in the juice of 1½ limes and 15ml/1 tbsp of the Thai fish sauce.

3 Transfer to a jug (pitcher). Finely chop half the chilli and add to the dressing. Taste and add more sugar, juice, fish sauce and the vinegar to taste.

COOK'S TIP

To devein prawns, make a shallow cut down the back of the prawn using a small, sharp knife. Using the tip of the knife, lift out the thin, black vein, then rinse the prawn under cold water.

4 Peel and stone (pit) the mango, then cut it into very fine strips.

5 Toss together the mango, carrots, cucumber and onion, and half the dressing. Arrange on plates or in bowls.

6 Heat a ridged, cast-iron griddle pan or heavy frying pan until very hot. Brush with a little oil, then sear the prawns for 2–3 minutes on each side, until they turn pink and are patched with brown on the outside. Arrange the prawns on the salads.

7 Sprinkle the remaining dressing over the salads and sprinkle the sprigs of coriander and mint over. Finely shred the remaining chilli and sprinkle it over the salads with the peanuts and crisp-fried shallots. Serve immediately.

Energy 292kcal/1222kJ; Protein 33.5g; Carbohydrate 13.4g, of which sugars 11.8g; Fat 11.9g, of which saturates 2g; Cholesterol 329mg; Calcium 160mg; Fibre 2.7g; Sodium 596mg.

Wilted Spinach and Bacon Salad

The hot dressing in this salad wilts the spinach and provides a taste sensation.

Serves 6

450g/1lb fresh young spinach leaves
25ml/1½ tbsp vegetable oil
225g/8oz bacon rashers (strips)
60ml/4 tbsp red wine vinegar
60ml/4 tbsp water
20ml/4 tsp caster (superfine) sugar
5ml/1 tsp mustard powder
8 spring onions (scallions), thinly sliced
6 radishes, thinly sliced
2 hard-boiled eggs, coarsely grated
salt and ground black pepper

1 Pull any coarse stalks from the spinach leaves and rinse well. Put the leaves in a large salad bowl.

VARIATION
For extra flavour, use hard-boiled duck eggs instead of hen's eggs.

2 Heat the oil in a frying pan and cook the bacon until crisp and brown. Remove with tongs and drain well on kitchen paper. Reserve the cooking fat in the pan. Chop the bacon and set aside until needed.

3 Combine the vinegar, water, sugar, mustard, and salt and ground black pepper in a bowl and stir until smoothly blended. Add to the fat in the frying pan and stir to mix. Bring the dressing to the boil over a medium heat, stirring constantly.

4 Pour the hot dressing evenly over the spinach leaves. Sprinkle the bacon, spring onions, radishes and eggs over, and toss, then serve.

Energy 161kcal/667kJ; Protein 10.7g; Carbohydrate 5.3g, of which sugars 5.2g; Fat 10.9g, of which saturates 3.2g; Cholesterol 83mg; Calcium 148mg; Fibre 1.9g; Sodium 708mg.

Mushroom Salad with Prosciutto

Pancake ribbons create a lovely light texture to this salad. Use whatever edible wild mushrooms you can find, or substitute interesting cultivated varieties if you need to.

Serves 4

40g/1 1/2 oz/3 tbsp unsalted
   (sweet) butter
450g/1lb assorted wild and cultivated
   mushrooms such as chanterelles,
   ceps, bay boletus, oyster, field
   (portabello) and Paris mushrooms,
   trimmed and sliced
60ml/4 tbsp Madeira or sherry
juice of 1/2 lemon
1/2 oak leaf lettuce
1/2 frisée lettuce
30ml/2 tbsp walnut oil
salt and ground black pepper

For the pancake and ham ribbons
25g/1oz/3 tbsp plain (all-purpose) flour
75ml/5 tbsp milk
1 egg
60ml/4 tbsp freshly grated
   Parmesan cheese
60ml/4 tbsp chopped fresh herbs such
   as parsley, thyme, marjoram or chives
salt and ground black pepper
butter, for frying
175g/6oz prosciutto, thickly sliced

1 To make the pancakes, blend the flour and the milk. Beat in the egg, cheese, herbs and some seasoning. Heat the butter in a frying pan and pour enough of the mixture to coat the base. When the batter has set, turn the pancake over and cook until firm.

2 Turn out and cool. Roll up the pancake and slice to make 1cm/1/2in ribbons. Cook the remaining batter the same way and cut the ham into similar sized ribbons. Toss with the pancake ribbons. Set aside.

3 Gently soften the mushrooms in the butter for 6–8 minutes, until the moisture has evaporated. Add the Madeira or sherry and lemon juice and season to taste.

4 Toss the salad leaves in the oil and arrange on four plates. Place the prosciutto and pancake ribbons in the centre, spoon on the mushrooms and serve immediately.

Energy 307kcal/1277kJ; Protein 17.5g; Carbohydrate 8.2g, of which sugars 3.2g; Fat 21.2g, of which saturates 9g; Cholesterol 105mg; Calcium 192mg; Fibre 2.1g; Sodium 730mg.

eating
outdoors

Discover great dishes for making barbecues

and *al fresco* eating as delicious and easy

as they are fun and informal.

Country Pasta Salad

Colourful, tasty and nutritious, this is the ideal pasta salad for a picnic.

Serves 6

300g/11oz/2¾ cups dried fusilli
150g/5oz green beans, trimmed and
cut into 5cm/2in lengths
1 potato, about 150g/5oz, diced
200g/7oz baby tomatoes, halved
2 spring onions (scallions),
finely chopped
90g/3½oz/scant 1¼ cups diced or
coarsely shaved Parmesan cheese
6–8 pitted black olives, cut into rings
15–30ml/1–2 tbsp capers, to taste

For the dressing
90ml/6 tbsp extra virgin olive oil
15ml/1 tbsp balsamic vinegar
15ml/1 tbsp chopped fresh flat
leaf parsley
salt and ground black pepper

1 Cook the pasta in lightly salted boiling water for 8–10 minutes, until tender. Drain in a colander, rinse under cold running water, then shake the colander to remove as much water as possible. Leave to drain and dry, shaking the colander occasionally so that it does not stick.

2 Cook the beans and diced potato in a pan of lightly salted, boiling water for 5–6 minutes, or until tender. Drain and leave to cool.

3 To make the dressing, put all the ingredients in a large bowl with salt and pepper to taste and whisk well until thoroughly combined.

4 Add the baby tomatoes, spring onions, Parmesan, olive rings and capers to the dressing, then the cold pasta, beans and potato. Toss well to mix all the ingredients. Cover the salad and leave to stand for about 30 minutes. Season to taste with salt and pepper before serving.

Energy 381kcal/1600kJ; Protein 13.3g; Carbohydrate 44.4g, of which sugars 3.8g; Fat 18g, of which saturates 5g; Cholesterol 15mg; Calcium 212mg; Fibre 2.9g; Sodium 341mg.

Salad with **Watermelon** and **Feta Cheese**

The combination of sweet and juicy watermelon with salty feta cheese was inspired by the Turkish tradition of eating watermelon with salty white cheese in the hot summer months. It is ideal for barbecues and picnics.

Serves 6–8

30–45ml/2–3 tbsp extra virgin olive oil
juice of ½ lemon
5ml/1 tsp vinegar of choice
sprinkling of fresh thyme
pinch of ground cumin
4 large slices of watermelon, chilled
1 frisée lettuce, core removed
130g/4½oz feta cheese, preferably
* sheep's milk feta, cut into*
* bitesize pieces*
handful of lightly toasted
* pumpkin seeds*
handful of sunflower seeds
10–15 black olives

1 Pour the extra virgin olive oil, lemon juice and vinegar into a bowl or jug (pitcher). Add the fresh thyme and ground cumin, and whisk until well combined. Set the dressing aside until you are ready to serve the salad.

2 Cut the rind off the watermelon and remove as many seeds as possible.

COOK'S TIP
Use plump black Mediterranean olives, such as kalamata, for this recipe or other shiny, dry-cured black olives.

3 Cut the flesh into bitesize triangular-shaped chunks.

4 Put the lettuce leaves in a bowl, pour over the dressing and toss together. Arrange the leaves on a serving dish or individual plates and add the watermelon, feta cheese, pumpkin and sunflower seeds and black olives. Serve the salad immediately.

VARIATION
Use Galia, cantaloupe or Charentais melon instead of the watermelon.

Energy 256kcal/1066kJ; Protein 7.7g; Carbohydrate 12.9g, of which sugars 11.6g; Fat 19.7g, of which saturates 6.2g; Cholesterol 23mg; Calcium 165mg; Fibre 1.4g; Sodium 616mg.

Peruvian Salad

This really is a spectacular-looking salad. If you serve it in a deep, glass salad bowl, the guests can then see the various layers of rice and green salad leaves, topped by the bright colours of the peppers, corn, eggs and olives.

Serves 8

450g/1lb/4 cups cooked long grain
   brown or white rice
30ml/2 tbsp chopped fresh parsley
2 red (bell) peppers
2 onions, sliced
olive oil, for sprinkling
250g/9oz green beans, halved
115g/4oz/²⁄₃ cup baby corn
8 quail's eggs, hard-boiled
75g/3oz Serrano ham, cut into
   thin slices (optional)
2 small avocados
lemon juice, for sprinkling
150g/5oz mixed salad leaves
30ml/2 tbsp capers
about 20 stuffed olives, halved

For the dressing
2 garlic cloves, crushed
120ml/4fl oz/½ cup olive oil
90ml/6 tbsp sunflower oil
60ml/4 tbsp lemon juice
90ml/6 tbsp natural (plain) yogurt
5ml/1 tsp mustard
5ml/1 tsp granulated sugar
salt and ground black pepper

1 Make the dressing by placing all the ingredients in a bowl and whisking with a fork until smooth. Alternatively, shake the ingredients together in a screw-top jar.

COOK'S TIP
To hard-boil quail's eggs, place them in a pan of simmering water, bring the water back to simmering point and cook for 4 minutes. Drain the eggs and rinse in cold water, then shell.

2 Put the cooked rice into a large bowl and spoon in half the dressing. Add the chopped parsley, stir well and set aside.

3 Cut the peppers in half, remove the seeds and pith, then place the halves, cut side down, in a small roasting pan. Add the onion rings. Sprinkle with a little olive oil, place the pan under a hot grill (broiler) and grill (broil) for 5–6 minutes, or until the peppers blacken and blister and the onion turns golden. You may need to stir the onion once or twice so that it cooks evenly.

4 Stir the onion into the rice. Put the peppers in a bowl, cover and leave until cool. Peel the peppers and cut the flesh into thin strips.

5 Cook the green beans in boiling water for 2 minutes, then add the corn and cook for 1–2 minutes more, until tender. Drain both vegetables, refresh them under cold water, then drain again. Place in a large mixing bowl and add the red pepper strips, quail's eggs and ham, if using.

6 Peel each avocado, remove the stone (pit), and cut the flesh into slices or chunks. Sprinkle with the lemon juice. Put the salad leaves in a separate bowl, add the avocado and mix lightly. Arrange the salad on top of the rice.

7 Stir about 45ml/3 tbsp of the remaining dressing into the green bean and pepper mixture. Pile this on top of the salad.

8 Sprinkle the capers and stuffed olives on top and serve the salad with the remaining dressing.

VARIATION
Use couscous instead of rice. Place in a bowl and cover with 2.5cm/1in boiling water. Leave to stand for 10–15 minutes.

Energy 415kcal/1726kJ; Protein 9.1g; Carbohydrate 52.8g, of which sugars 6.6g; Fat 18.5g, of which saturates 3.2g; Cholesterol 48mg; Calcium 77mg; Fibre 3.3g; Sodium 417mg.

Egg and Fennel Tabbouleh with Nuts

Tabbouleh is a Middle Eastern salad of steamed bulgur wheat, flavoured with lots of parsley, mint and garlic. It goes very well with almost all barbecue dishes, especially chicken.

Serves 4

250g/9oz/1¼ cups bulgur wheat
4 small (US medium) eggs
1 fennel bulb
1 bunch spring onions
   (scallions), chopped
25g/1oz/½ cup sun-dried
   tomatoes, sliced
45ml/3 tbsp chopped fresh parsley
30ml/2 tbsp chopped fresh mint
75g/3oz/½ cup black olives
60ml/4 tbsp olive oil, preferably Greek
   or Spanish
30ml/2 tbsp garlic oil
30ml/2 tbsp lemon juice
salt and ground black pepper

1 Place the bulgur wheat in a bowl, cover with boiling water and leave to soak for 15 minutes. Transfer to a metal sieve, place over a pan of boiling water, cover and steam for 10 minutes. Spread out on a metal tray and leave to cool while you cook the eggs and fennel.

2 Hard-boil the eggs for 8 minutes. Cool under running water, shell and quarter. Alternatively, using an egg slicer, slice them but not quite all the way through.

3 Halve and then thinly slice the fennel. Boil in salted water for 6 minutes, drain and cool under running water.

4 Combine the egg quarters, fennel, spring onions, sun-dried tomatoes, parsley, mint and olives with the bulgur wheat. If you have sliced the eggs, arrange them on top of the salad. Dress the tabbouleh with olive oil, garlic oil and lemon juice. Season well with salt and pepper.

COOK'S TIP
Small whole eggs, such as gull, quail, plover or guinea fowl, would also be good in this dish.

Energy 624kcal/2587kJ; Protein 13.4g; Carbohydrate 49.3g, of which sugars 1.5g; Fat 42.2g, of which saturates 6.6g; Cholesterol 190mg; Calcium 97mg; Fibre 1.9g; Sodium 83mg.

Tortilla Wrap with Tabbouleh and Avocado

To be successful, tabbouleh needs lemon juice, plenty of fresh herbs and lots of freshly ground black pepper.

Serves 6

175g/6oz/1 cup bulgur wheat
30ml/2 tbsp chopped fresh mint
30ml/2 tbsp chopped fresh flat
*   leaf parsley*
1 bunch spring onions
*   (scallions), sliced*
1/2 cucumber, diced
50ml/2fl oz/1/4 cup extra virgin olive oil
juice of 1 large lemon
1 ripe avocado, stoned (pitted), peeled
*   and diced*
juice of 1/2 lemon
1/2 red chilli, seeded and sliced
1 garlic clove, crushed
1/2 red (bell) pepper, seeded and
*   finely diced*
salt and ground black pepper
4 wheat tortillas, to serve
flat leaf parsley, to garnish (optional)

1 To make the tabbouleh, place the bulgur wheat in a large heatproof bowl and pour over enough boiling water to cover. Leave for 30 minutes until the grains are tender but still retain a little resistance to the bite. Drain thoroughly in a sieve, then tip back into the bowl.

2 Add the mint, parsley, spring onions and cucumber to the bulgur wheat and mix thoroughly. Blend together the olive oil and lemon juice in a jug (pitcher) and pour over the tabbouleh, season to taste with salt and pepper and toss well to mix. Cover with clear film (plastic wrap) and chill in the refrigerator for 30 minutes to allow the flavours to mingle.

COOK'S TIP
The soaking time for bulgur wheat can vary. For the best results, follow the instructions on the packet and taste the grain every now and again to check whether it is tender enough.

3 To make the avocado mixture, place the avocado in a bowl and add the lemon juice, chilli and garlic. Season to taste with salt and pepper and mash with a fork to form a smooth purée. Stir in the red pepper.

4 Warm the tortillas in a dry frying pan and serve either flat, folded or rolled up with the tabbouleh and avocado mixture. Garnish with parsley, if using.

Energy 259kcal/1081kJ; Protein 5.1g; Carbohydrate 35g, of which sugars 1.9g; Fat 11.5g, of which saturates 1.9g; Cholesterol 0mg; Calcium 55mg; Fibre 1.7g; Sodium 52mg.

Summer Vegetables with Yogurt Pesto

3 Slice the fennel bulbs and the red onions into thick wedges, using a sharp kitchen knife.

4 Prepare the barbecue. Stir the yogurt and pesto lightly together in a bowl, to make a marbled sauce. Spoon the yogurt pesto into a serving bowl, cover and set aside.

5 Arrange the vegetables on the hot barbecue, brush generously with olive oil and sprinkle with plenty of salt and ground black pepper.

Chargrilled summer vegetables make a meal on their own, or are delicious served as a Mediterranean-style accompaniment to grilled meats and fish.

Serves 8

4 small aubergines (eggplants)
4 large courgettes (zucchini)
2 red (bell) peppers
2 yellow (bell) peppers
2 fennel bulbs
2 red onions
300ml/½ pint/1¼ cups Greek
* (US strained plain) yogurt*
90ml/6 tbsp pesto
olive oil, for brushing
salt and ground black pepper

1 Cut the aubergines into 1cm/½in slices. Sprinkle with salt and leave to drain for about 30 minutes. Rinse well in cold running water and pat dry.

2 Use a sharp kitchen knife to cut the courgettes in half lengthways. Cut the peppers in half, removing the seeds but leaving the stalks in place.

6 Cook the vegetables until golden brown and tender, turning occasionally. The aubergines and peppers will take 6–8 minutes to cook, the courgettes, onion and fennel 4–5 minutes. Serve the vegetables as soon as they are cooked, with the yogurt pesto.

COOK'S TIP

Baby vegetables are excellent for cooking whole on the barbecue, so look for baby aubergines (eggplants) and (bell) peppers, in particular. There's no need to salt the aubergines if they are small.

Energy 107kcal/447kJ; Protein 5.7g; Carbohydrate 13g, of which sugars 12.1g; Fat 4g, of which saturates 1g; Cholesterol 2mg; Calcium 133mg; Fibre 4.5g; Sodium 56mg.

Aubergine and **Smoked Mozzarella Rolls**

Slices of grilled aubergine are stuffed with smoked mozzarella, tomato and fresh basil to make an attractive hors-d'oeuvre.

Serves 4

1 large aubergine (eggplant)
45ml/3 tbsp olive oil, plus extra for
*   drizzling (optional)*
165g/5¹/₂ oz smoked mozzarella
*   cheese, cut into 8 slices*
2 plum tomatoes, each cut into
*   4 even slices*
8 large basil leaves
balsamic vinegar, for
*   drizzling (optional)*
salt and ground black pepper

1 Cut the aubergine lengthways into 10 thin slices and discard the two outermost slices. Sprinkle the slices with salt and set them aside for 20 minutes. Rinse well under cold running water to remove all traces of salt, then drain and pat dry with kitchen paper.

2 Prepare the barbecue or preheat the grill (broiler) and line the rack with foil. Place the aubergine slices on the rack and brush liberally with oil. Cook for 8–10 minutes until tender and golden, turning once.

3 Remove the aubergine slices from the heat, then place a slice of mozzarella, a slice of tomato and a basil leaf in the centre of each aubergine slice, and season to taste. Fold the aubergine over the filling and return to the heat, seam side down, until heated through and the mozzarella begins to melt. Serve drizzled with olive oil and a little balsamic vinegar, if using.

Energy 196kcal/814kJ; Protein 8.5g; Carbohydrate 2.7g, of which sugars 2.6g; Fat 17g, of which saturates 7g; Cholesterol 24mg; Calcium 158mg; Fibre 1.5g; Sodium 169mg.

Chicken Liver Pâté with Garlic

This smooth pâté is indulgent and absolutely delicious. Start preparation the day before so that the flavour can develop fully.

Serves 6–8

225g/8oz/1 cup unsalted (sweet) butter
400g/14oz chicken livers, chopped
45–60ml/3–4 tbsp Madeira
3 large shallots, chopped
2 large garlic cloves, finely chopped
5ml/1 tsp finely chopped fresh thyme
pinch of ground allspice
30ml/2 tbsp double (heavy)
   cream (optional)
salt and ground black pepper
small fresh bay leaves or fresh thyme
   sprigs, to garnish
toast and small pickled gherkins,
   to serve

1 Melt 75g/3oz/6 tbsp butter in a small pan over a low heat, then leave it to bubble gently until it is clear. Pour off the clarified butter into a bowl.

2 Melt 40g/1½oz/3 tbsp butter in a frying pan and cook the chicken livers for 4–5 minutes, or until browned. Stir frequently to make sure that the livers cook evenly. Do not overcook them or they will be tough.

3 Add 45ml/3 tbsp Madeira and set it alight, then scrape the contents of the pan into a food processor or blender.

4 Melt 25g/1oz/2 tbsp butter in the pan over a low heat and cook the shallots for 5 minutes, or until soft. Add the garlic, thyme and allspice and cook for another 2–3 minutes. Add this mixture to the livers with the remaining butter and cream, if using, then process until smooth.

5 Add about 7.5ml/1½ tsp each of salt and black pepper and more Madeira to taste. Scrape the pâté into a serving dish and place a few bay leaves or thyme sprigs on top. Melt the clarified butter, if necessary, then pour it over the pâté. Cool and chill the pâté for 4 hours or overnight.

VARIATIONS
• Cognac, Armagnac or port can be used instead of Madeira.
• Use duck livers instead of chicken and add 2.5ml/½ tsp grated orange rind.
• Use chopped fresh tarragon instead of the thyme.

Energy 263kcal/1088kJ; Protein 14.1g; Carbohydrate 0.9g, of which sugars 0.7g; Fat 22.6g, of which saturates 10.3g; Cholesterol 352mg; Calcium 20mg; Fibre 0.1g; Sodium 175mg.

Herbed Liver Pâté Pie

Serve this highly flavoured pâté with a glass of Pilsner beer for a change from wine.

Serves 10

675g/1¹/₂ lb minced (ground) pork
350g/12oz pork liver
350g/12oz/2 cups diced cooked ham
1 small onion, finely chopped
30ml/2 tbsp chopped fresh parsley
5ml/1 tsp German mustard
30ml/2 tbsp Kirsch
5ml/1 tsp salt
beaten egg, for sealing and glazing
25g/1oz sachet (envelope) aspic jelly
250ml/8fl oz/1 cup boiling water
ground black pepper
mustard, crusty bread and dill pickles,
  to serve

For the pastry
450g/1lb/4 cups plain
  (all-purpose) flour
pinch of salt
275g/10oz/1¹/₄ cups butter
2 eggs plus 1 egg yolk
30ml/2 tbsp water

1 Preheat the oven to 200°C/400°F/ Gas 6. To make the pastry, sift the flour and salt and rub in the butter. Beat the eggs, egg yolk and water, add to the dry ingredients and mix.

2 Knead the dough briefly until smooth. Roll out two-thirds on a lightly floured surface and use to line a 10 × 25cm/4 × 10in hinged loaf tin (pan). Trim any excess dough.

3 Process half the pork and all of the liver until fairly smooth. Stir in the remaining minced pork, ham, onion, parsley, mustard, Kirsch, salt and black pepper to taste.

4 Spoon the filling into the tin and level the surface.

5 Roll out the remaining pastry on the lightly floured surface and use it to top the pie, brushing the edges with some of the beaten egg to seal. Decorate with the pastry trimmings and brush with the remaining beaten egg to glaze. Using a fork, make three or four holes in the top, for the steam to escape during cooking.

6 Bake for 40 minutes, then reduce the oven temperature to 180°C/350°F/ Gas 4 and cook for a further hour. Cover the pastry with foil if the top begins to brown too much. Leave the pie to cool in the tin.

7 Make up the aspic jelly, using the boiling water or according to the packet instructions. Stir to dissolve, then leave to cool.

8 Make a small hole near the edge of the pie with a skewer, then pour in the aspic through a greaseproof paper funnel. Chill in the refrigerator for at least 2 hours before slicing and serving the pie with mustard, crusty bread and dill pickles.

Energy 576kcal/2407kJ; Protein 32.9g; Carbohydrate 36g, of which sugars 1.6g; Fat 33.7g, of which saturates 18.1g; Cholesterol 273mg; Calcium 87mg; Fibre 1.5g; Sodium 888mg.

Summer Herb Ricotta Flan

Infused with aromatic herbs, this flan makes a delightful picnic dish.

Serves 8

olive oil, for greasing and glazing
800g/1³/₄lb/3½ cups ricotta cheese
75g/3oz/1 cup grated Parmesan cheese
3 eggs, separated
60ml/4 tbsp torn fresh basil leaves
60ml/4 tbsp chopped fresh chives
45ml/3 tbsp fresh oregano leaves
2.5ml/½ tsp paprika
salt and ground black pepper
fresh herb leaves, to garnish

For the tapenade
400g/14oz/3½ cups pitted black olives,
    rinsed and halved, reserving a few
    whole to garnish (optional)
5 garlic cloves, crushed
75ml/5 tbsp olive oil

1 Preheat the oven to 180°C/350°F/ Gas 4 and lightly grease a 23cm/9in springform cake tin (pan) with oil. Mix together the ricotta cheese, Parmesan and egg yolks in a food processor or blender. Add the herbs and seasoning, and blend until smooth and creamy.

2 Whisk the egg whites in a large bowl until they form soft peaks. Gently fold the egg whites into the ricotta cheese mixture using a rubber spatula, taking care not to knock out too much air. Spoon the ricotta mixture into the prepared tin and smooth the top.

3 Bake for 1 hour 20 minutes, or until the flan is risen and the top is golden. Remove from the oven and brush lightly with olive oil, then sprinkle with paprika. Leave the flan to cool before removing it from the pan.

4 Make the tapenade by placing the olives and garlic in a food processor or blender and process until finely chopped. Gradually add the olive oil and blend to a coarse paste, then transfer to a serving bowl. Garnish the flan with fresh herbs leaves and serve with the tapenade.

VARIATION
Sprinkle 25g/1oz chopped, drained sun-dried tomatoes over the flan as a garnish.

Red Onion and Goat's Cheese Pastries

These attractive little pastries are ideal for picnics and buffets and couldn't be easier to make. Serve simply with a mixed green salad dressed with balsamic vinegar and extra virgin olive oil.

Serves 8

30ml/2 tbsp olive oil
900g/2lb red onions, sliced
60ml/4 tbsp fresh thyme or
    20ml/4 tsp dried
30ml/2 tbsp balsamic vinegar
850g/1lb 14oz ready-rolled puff pastry
225g/8oz/1 cup goat's cheese, cubed
2 eggs, beaten
salt and ground black pepper
fresh thyme sprigs,
    to garnish (optional)
mixed green salad leaves and
    cherry tomatoes, to serve

1 Heat the olive oil in a large heavy frying pan, add the sliced red onions and cook over a gentle heat for about 10 minutes, or until softened, stirring occasionally with a wooden spoon to prevent them from browning.

2 Add the thyme, seasoning and balsamic vinegar, and cook the onions for a further 5 minutes. Remove the frying pan from the heat and leave to cool.

3 Preheat the oven to 220°C/425°F/ Gas 7. Unroll the puff pastry and using a 15cm/6in plate as a guide, cut out eight equal rounds. Place the pastry rounds on dampened baking sheets and, using the point of a sharp knife, score a border, 2cm/¾in inside the edge of each round.

4 Divide the onions among the pastry rounds and top with the cubes of goat's cheese. Brush the edge of each round with beaten egg and bake for 25–30 minutes, until golden. Garnish with the fresh thyme, if using. Serve with the salad leaves and tomatoes.

VARIATION
Ring the changes by spreading the pastry base with 45ml/3 tbsp pesto or tapenade (see recipe above) before you add the onion filling.

Flan: Energy 730kcal/3021kJ; Protein 32.7g; Carbohydrate 8.6g, of which sugars 6.7g; Fat 63g, of which saturates 26.7g; Cholesterol 245mg; Calcium 335mg; Fibre 4g; Sodium 2512mg.
Pastries: Energy 494kcal/2051kJ; Protein 13.2g; Carbohydrate 38.9g, of which sugars 11.3g; Fat 31.7g, of which saturates 16g; Cholesterol 100mg; Calcium 172mg; Fibre 3.2g; Sodium 307mg.

Herbed Greek Pies

Mixed fresh herbs give these
little pies a delicate flavour.

Makes 8

115g/4oz/1 cup plain (all-purpose) flour
50g/2oz/4 tbsp butter, diced
15–25ml/1–1½ tbsp water

For the filling
45–60ml/3–4 tbsp tapenade or
 sun-dried tomato paste
1 large (US extra large) egg
100g/3¾oz/scant ½ cup thick Greek
 (US strained plain) yogurt
90ml/6 tbsp milk
1 garlic clove, crushed
30ml/2 tbsp chopped mixed herbs,
 such as thyme, basil and parsley
salt and ground black pepper

1 To make the pastry, mix together the
flour, a pinch of salt and the butter.
Using the fingertips or a pastry blender,
rub the butter into the flour until the
mixture resembles fine breadcrumbs.
Mix in the water using a round-bladed
knife and knead lightly to form a
firm dough. Wrap the dough in clear
film (plastic wrap) and chill in the
refrigerator for 30 minutes.

2 Preheat the oven to 190°C/375°F/
Gas 5. Roll out the pastry thinly and cut
out eight rounds using a 7.5cm/3in
cutter. Line deep patty tins (muffin
pans) with the pastry rounds, then
line each one with a piece of baking
parchment. Bake blind for 15 minutes.
Remove the baking parchment and
cook for a further 5 minutes, or until
the cases are crisp.

3 To make the filling, spread a little
tapenade or tomato paste in the base of
each pastry case. Whisk together the egg,
yogurt, milk, garlic, herbs and seasoning.
Spoon into the pastry cases and bake
for 25–30 minutes, or until the filling is
just firm and the pastry golden. Leave
the pies to cool slightly before carefully
removing from the tins and serving.

Tomato and Black Olive Tart

This delicious tart has a fresh, rich
Mediterranean flavour and is ideal
for picnics and buffets. Using a
rectangular tin makes the tart
easier to transport and divide
into portions.

Serves 8

250g/9oz/1 cup plain (all-purpose)
 flour, plus extra for dusting
2.5ml/½ tsp salt
130g/4½oz/1 cup butter, diced
45ml/3 tbsp water

For the filling
3 eggs, beaten
300ml/½ pint/1¼ cups milk
30ml/2 tbsp chopped fresh herbs,
 such as parsley, marjoram or basil
6 firm plum tomatoes
75g/3oz ripe Brie
about 16 black olives, pitted
salt and ground black pepper

1 Preheat the oven to 190°C/375°F/
Gas 5. To make the pastry, mix together
the flour, salt and butter. Using your
fingertips or a pastry blender, rub the
butter into the flour until the mixture
resembles fine breadcrumbs. Mix in
the water and knead lightly to form a
firm dough. Roll out the pastry thinly
on a lightly floured surface. Line a
28 × 18cm/11 × 7in loose-based
rectangular flan tin (quiche pan),
trimming off any overhanging edges.

2 Line the pastry case with baking
parchment and baking beans, and
bake blind for 15 minutes. Remove the
baking parchment and baking beans
and bake for a further 5 minutes, or
until the base is crisp.

VARIATION
This tart is delicious made with other
cheeses. Try slices of Gorgonzola or
Camembert for a slightly stronger flavour.

3 To make the filling, beat the eggs
with the milk, seasoning and herbs.
Slice the tomatoes and olives and cube
the cheese. Add to the prepared flan
case (pie shell). Then pour over the
egg mixture.

4 Transfer the tart carefully to the oven
and bake for about 40 minutes, or until
the filling is just firm and turning
golden. Serve the tart warm or cold,
cut into slices.

Pies: Energy 193kcal/806kJ; Protein 5.2g; Carbohydrate 18.8g, of which sugars 3.7g; Fat 11.4g, of which saturates 3.8g; Cholesterol 50mg; Calcium 93mg; Fibre 0.9g; Sodium 190mg.
Tart: Energy 436kcal/1815kJ; Protein 5.9g; Carbohydrate 37.4g, of which sugars 5.8g; Fat 31.1g, of which saturates 1.5g; Cholesterol 0mg; Calcium 77mg; Fibre 1.5g; Sodium 542mg.

Roasted Vegetable and Garlic Sausage Loaf

Stuffed with cured meat and roasted vegetables, this crusty cob loaf makes a colourful centrepiece for a casual summer lunch or picnic. Serve with fresh green salad leaves.

Serves 6

1 large cob loaf
2 red (bell) peppers, quartered
    and seeded
1 large leek, sliced
90ml/6 tbsp olive oil
175g/6oz green beans, blanched
    and drained
75g/3oz garlic sausage, sliced
2 eggs, hard-boiled and quartered
115g/4oz/1 cup cashew nuts, toasted
75g/3oz/⅓ cup soft white (farmer's)
    cheese with garlic and herbs
salt and ground black pepper

1 Preheat the oven to 220°C/425°F/ Gas 7. Slice the top off the loaf using a large serrated knife and set it aside, then cut out the soft centre, leaving the crust intact. Stand the crusty shell on a baking sheet.

COOK'S TIP

Do not throw away the soft centre of the loaf. It can be made into breadcrumbs and frozen for use in another recipe.

2 Put the red peppers and sliced leek into a roasting pan with the olive oil and cook for 25–30 minutes, turning occasionally, or until the peppers have softened.

3 Spoon half of the pepper and leek mixture into the base of the loaf shell, pressing it down firmly with the back of a spoon. Add the green beans, garlic sausage slices, egg quarters and cashew nuts, packing the layers down well. Season each layer with salt and ground black pepper to taste before adding the next. Dot the soft cheese with garlic and herbs over the filling and top with the remaining pepper and leek mixture.

4 Replace the top of the loaf and bake it for 15–20 minutes, or until the filling is warmed through. Serve, cut into wedges or slices.

VARIATION

You can use a variety of different-shaped loaves, such as a large, uncut white or wholemeal (whole-wheat) sandwich loaf, for this recipe. Hollow out the loaf and fill as above, then cut into slices.

Energy 575kcal/2402kJ; Protein 18g; Carbohydrate 51g, of which sugars 8g; Fat 35g, of which saturates 8g; Cholesterol 98mg; Calcium 141mg; Fibre 6g; Sodium 628mg.

Potato Skewers with **Mustard Dip**

When potatoes are cooked on the barbecue, they have a great flavour and crisp skin. Try these delicious kebabs served with a thick, garlic-rich dip for an unusual start to a meal.

Serves 6

1kg/2¹/₄ lb small new potatoes
200g/7oz shallots, halved
30ml/2 tbsp olive oil
15ml/1 tbsp sea salt

For the dip
4 garlic cloves, crushed
2 egg yolks
30ml/2 tbsp lemon juice
300ml/¹/₂ pint/1¹/₄ cups extra virgin
   olive oil
10ml/2 tsp wholegrain mustard
salt and ground black pepper

1 Prepare the barbecue or preheat the grill (broiler). To make the dip place the garlic, egg yolks and lemon juice in a blender or a food processor fitted with a metal blade and process for just a few seconds until the mixture is smooth and combined.

2 Keep the blender or food processor motor running and add the oil very gradually, pouring it in a thin stream, until the mixture forms a thick, glossy cream. Transfer to a bowl, add the mustard and stir to combine, then season to taste with salt and pepper. Cover with clear film (plastic wrap) and chill until ready to use.

3 Par-boil the potatoes in their skins in a pan of boiling water for 5 minutes. Drain well and then thread them on to metal skewers alternating with the shallot halves.

4 Brush the skewers with olive oil and sprinkle with sea salt. Cook on the barbecue or grill (broil) for about 10–12 minutes, turning occasionally. Serve with the mustard dip.

COOK'S TIPS
• Only early or "new" potatoes and salad potatoes have the firmness necessary to stay on the skewer.
• Lightly oil the skewers before threading the potatoes and shallots to make the process easier.

Energy 488kcal/2024kJ; Protein 4.3g; Carbohydrate 29.5g, of which sugars 4.1g; Fat 40g, of which saturates 6.1g; Cholesterol 65mg; Calcium 28mg; Fibre 2.2g; Sodium 49mg.

Ceviche

You can use any firm-fleshed fish for this South American dish, provided that is perfectly fresh. The fish is "cooked" by the action of the acidic lime juice.

Serves 6

675g/1½ lb halibut, turbot, sea bass or
  salmon fillets, skinned
juice of 3 limes
1–2 fresh red chillies, seeded and very
  finely chopped
15ml/1 tbsp olive oil
salt

For the garnish
1 ripe avocado
4 large firm tomatoes, peeled, seeded
  and diced
15ml/1 tbsp lemon juice
30ml/2 tbsp olive oil
30ml/2 tbsp fresh coriander
  (cilantro) leaves

1 Cut the fish into strips measuring about 5 × 1cm/2 × ½in. Lay these in a shallow, non-metallic dish and pour over the lime juice, turning the fish strips to coat them all over in the juice. Cover with clear film (plastic wrap) and leave for 1 hour.

2 Meanwhile, prepare the garnish. Cut the avocado in half lengthways and twist to separate the halves. Remove the stone (pit) with the point of the knife, then peel and finely dice the flesh.

3 Place the avocado in a bowl and add the tomatoes, lemon juice and olive oil and mix gently. Cover with clear film and set aside.

4 Season the fish with salt and sprinkle over the chillies. Drizzle with the olive oil. Toss the fish in the mixture, then replace the cover. Leave to marinate in the refrigerator for 15–30 minutes more. To serve, divide the avocado and tomato garnish among six plates. Arrange the ceviche, then sprinkle with coriander.

Energy 293Kcal/1235kJ; Protein 40g; Carbohydrate 16g, of which sugars 14g; Fat 8g, of which saturates 1g; Cholesterol 220mg; Calcium 137mg; Fibre 1.9g; Sodium 1.1g.

Three-colour Fish Kebabs

Don't leave the fish to marinate for more than an hour. The lemon juice will start to break down the fibres of the fish after this time.

Serves 4

120ml/4fl oz/¹/₂ cup olive oil
finely grated rind and juice of
    1 large lemon
5ml/1 tsp crushed chilli flakes
350g/12oz monkfish fillet, skinned
    and cubed
350g/12oz swordfish fillet, skinned
    and cubed
350g/12oz thick salmon fillet or
    steak, skinned and cubed
2 red, yellow or orange
    (bell) peppers, seeded and
    cut into squares
30ml/2 tbsp finely chopped
    fresh flat leaf parsley
salt and ground black pepper

For the sweet tomato and
chilli salsa
225g/8oz ripe tomatoes,
    finely chopped
1 garlic clove, crushed
1 fresh red chilli, seeded
    and chopped
45ml/3 tbsp extra virgin olive oil
15ml/1 tbsp lemon juice
15ml/1 tbsp finely chopped
    fresh flat leaf parsley
pinch of sugar

1 Put the oil in a large, shallow glass or china dish and add the lemon rind and juice, the chilli flakes and pepper to taste. Whisk well to combine, then add all the fish chunks and turn gently to coat them evenly.

2 Add the pepper squares, stir, then cover with clear film (plastic wrap) and leave to marinate in a cool place for 1 hour, turning the fish occasionally with a slotted spoon.

3 Prepare the barbecue or preheat the grill (broiler) to medium. Thread the chunks of fish and pepper squares on to eight oiled metal skewers, reserving the marinade.

4 Cook the skewers on the barbecue or under the grill, turning once, for 5–8 minutes, until the fish is tender and light golden brown.

5 Meanwhile, make the salsa by mixing the tomatoes, garlic, chilli, olive oil, lemon juice, parsley and sugar in a bowl. Season to taste.

6 Heat the reserved marinade in a small pan to boiling point, then remove the pan from the heat and stir in the parsley and season with salt and pepper to taste.

7 Transfer the kebabs to warm plates, spoon the marinade over them and serve immediately, accompanied by the salsa.

VARIATION
Use tuna instead of swordfish, if you like. It has a similar meaty texture and will be equally successful.

Energy 715Kcal/2976kJ; Protein 50g; Carbohydrate 12g, of which sugars 11g; Fat 52g, of which saturates 8g; Cholesterol 92mg; Calcium 56mg; Fibre 3.4g; Sodium 0.3g.

Moroccan Grilled Fish Brochettes

Serve these delicious skewers with strips of red peppers, potatoes and aubergine slices, which can also be cooked on the barbecue. Accompany them with warm, soft flour tortillas.

Serves 6

5 garlic cloves, chopped
2.5ml/½ tsp paprika
2.5ml/½ tsp ground cumin
2.5–5ml/½–1 tsp salt
2–3 pinches of cayenne pepper
60ml/4 tbsp olive oil
30ml/2 tbsp lemon juice
30ml/2 tbsp chopped fresh coriander
    (cilantro) or parsley
675g/1½ lb firm-fleshed white fish,
    such as haddock, halibut, sea bass or
    snapper, cut into 2.5–5cm/
    1–2in cubes
3–4 green (bell) peppers, cut into
    2.5–5cm/1–2in pieces
2 lemon wedges, to serve

1 Put the garlic, paprika, cumin, salt, cayenne pepper, oil, lemon juice and coriander or parsley in a large bowl and mix together.

2 Add the fish and toss to coat. Leave to marinate for at least 30 minutes, and preferably 2 hours, at room temperature, or chill overnight.

COOK'S TIP
If you are using wooden skewers, soak them in cold water for 30 minutes before using to stop them burning.

3 Thread the fish cubes and pepper pieces alternately on to six wooden or metal skewers.

4 About 40 minutes before you are going to cook the brochettes, prepare and light the barbecue. It will be ready when the flames subside and the coals have turned white and grey.

5 Grill the brochettes on the barbecue for 2–3 minutes on each side, or until the fish is tender and lightly browned. Serve with lemon wedges.

Energy 276kcal/1157kJ; Protein 33.3g; Carbohydrate 8g, of which sugars 7.6g; Fat 12.5g, of which saturates 1.9g; Cholesterol 61mg; Calcium 34mg; Fibre 2g; Sodium 118mg.

Grilled Squid Stuffed with Feta Cheese

A large, fresh leafy salad or a vegetable dish, such as fresh green beans with tomato sauce could be served with the grilled squid.

Serves 8

8 medium squid, total weight
    about 900g/2lb
8–12 finger-length slices of feta cheese
175ml/6fl oz/³⁄₄ cup olive oil
4 garlic cloves, crushed
6–8 fresh marjoram sprigs, leaves
    removed and chopped
salt and ground black pepper
lemon wedges, to serve

1 To prepare the squid, wash it carefully. If there is any ink on the body, rinse it off so that you can see what you are doing. Holding the body firmly, pull away the head and tentacles. If the ink sac is still intact, remove it. Either keep it for cooking or discard it.

2 Pull out all the innards, including the long transparent stick or "quill". Peel off and discard the thin purple skin on the body, but keep the two small fins on the sides, if you like. Slice the head across just under the eyes, severing the tentacles. Discard the rest of the squid's head. Squeeze the tentacles at the head end to push out the round beak in the centre. Throw this away. Rinse the body sac inside and out and the tentacles very thoroughly under cold running water. Drain well and pat dry on kitchen paper.

3 Lay the squid bodies and tentacles in a large shallow dish that will hold them in a single layer. Tuck the pieces of cheese between the squid.

4 To make the marinade, pour the olive oil into a jug (pitcher) or bowl and whisk in the fresh garlic and marjoram sprigs. Season to taste with salt and pepper. Pour the marinade over the squid and the cheese, then cover with foil and leave in a cool place to marinate for 2–3 hours to allow the flavours to develop, turning once.

5 Insert one or two pieces of cheese and a few bits of marjoram from the marinade into each squid and place them in a lightly oiled grill (broiler) pan or tray. Thread the tentacles on to wooden skewers that have been soaked in water for half an hour (this prevents them from burning).

6 Preheat the grill (broiler) to a low setting or prepare a barbecue. Cook the stuffed squid for about 6 minutes, then turn them over. Cook them for 1–2 minutes more, then add the skewered tentacles. Cook them for 2 minutes on each side, until they start to scorch. Serve the stuffed squid with the tentacles and a few lemon wedges.

COOK'S TIP
Tentacles are often left whole for frying, but can be chopped into short lengths.

Energy 512kcal/2133kJ; Protein 43g; Carbohydrate 4g, of which sugars 1g; Fat 36g, of which saturates 11g; Cholesterol 541mg; Calcium 215mg; Fibre 0g; Sodium 968mg.

Scallops Wrapped in Prosciutto

Cook these lovely skewers on the barbecue for *al fresco* summer dining. Serve with lime wedges for a sharper flavour.

Serves 4

24 shucked medium-size scallops,
   corals removed
lemon juice
8–12 prosciutto slices, cut lengthways
   into 2 or 3 strips
olive oil, for brushing
ground black pepper
lemon wedges, to serve

1 Prepare the barbecue in advance or preheat the grill (broiler) when you make the skewers.

2 Sprinkle the scallops with lemon juice. Wrap a strip of prosciutto around each scallop. Thread them on to eight metal or wooden skewers.

3 Brush the wrapped scallops with olive oil. Arrange the skewers on a baking sheet if you are going to grill (broil) them. Cook for 3–5 minutes on each side, or until the scallops have just turned opaque. Be careful not to overcook them or they will become tough and inedible.

4 Set two skewers on each of four warmed serving plates. Sprinkle the scallops with freshly ground black pepper and serve immediately with lemon wedges for squeezing over.

COOK'S TIP
Use a short sturdy knife to prise scallop shells open and to cut the roof muscle and the muscle under the skirt. Discard the membrane, organs and gristle at the side of the white meat. Set the coral aside for another dish, if you like. Rinse the scallops well under cold running water and pat dry with kitchen paper.

Energy 162kcal/677kJ; Protein 20g; Carbohydrate 3g, of which sugars 0g; Fat 8g, of which saturates 2g; Cholesterol 46mg; Calcium 22mg; Fibre 0g; Sodium 511mg.

Italian Prawn Skewers

Parsley and lemon are all that is required to create a lovely tiger prawn dish. Grill them or cook on the barbecue for an informal *al fresco* summer appetizer.

Serves 4

900g/2lb raw tiger prawns (jumbo
   shrimp), peeled
60ml/4 tbsp olive oil
45ml/3 tbsp vegetable oil
75g/3oz/1¼ cups very fine
   dry breadcrumbs
1 garlic clove, crushed
15ml/1 tbsp chopped fresh parsley
salt and ground black pepper
lemon wedges, to serve

1 Slit the prawns down their backs and remove the dark vein with the point of the knife. Rinse in cold water and pat dry on kitchen paper.

2 Put the olive oil and vegetable oil in a large bowl and add the prawns, mixing them to coat evenly. Add the breadcrumbs, garlic and parsley and season with salt and pepper. Toss the prawns thoroughly, to give them an even coating of breadcrumbs. Cover and leave to marinate for 1 hour.

3 Thread the tiger prawns on to four metal or wooden skewers, curling them up slightly as you work, so that the tails are skewered neatly and securely in the middle.

4 Prepare the barbecue or preheat the grill (broiler). Cook the skewers for about 2 minutes on each side, until the breadcrumbs are golden. Serve with lemon wedges.

Energy 563kcal/2356kJ; Protein 45g; Carbohydrate 34g, of which sugars 1g; Fat 28g, of which saturates 4g; Cholesterol 439mg; Calcium 237mg; Fibre 2.5g; Sodium 859mg.

Clams with **Chilli** and **Yellow Bean Sauce**

This delicious Thai-inspired dish is simple to prepare. It can be made in a matter of minutes so will not keep you away from your guests for very long.

Serves 4–6

1kg/2¼ lb fresh clams
30ml/2 tbsp vegetable oil
4 garlic cloves, finely chopped
15ml/1 tbsp grated fresh root ginger
4 shallots, finely chopped
30ml/2 tbsp yellow bean sauce
6 fresh red chillies, seeded
  and chopped
15ml/1 tbsp Thai fish sauce
pinch of granulated sugar
handful of fresh basil leaves, plus extra
  to garnish

1 Wash and scrub the clams. Heat the oil in a wok or large frying pan. Add the garlic and ginger and stir-fry over a medium heat for 30 seconds, then add the shallots and stir-fry for a further minute.

2 Add the clams to the pan. Using a fish slice or spatula, turn them a few times to coat all over with the oil. Stir in the yellow bean sauce and half the chopped red chillies.

3 Continue to cook, stirring frequently, for 5–7 minutes, or until all the clams are open. Discard any that remain shut. You may need to add a splash of water. Adjust the seasoning with the fish sauce and a little sugar.

4 Finally add the basil leaves and stir to mix. Transfer the clams to individual bowls or a serving platter. Garnish with the remaining red chillies and basil leaves. Serve immediately.

Energy 94kcal/393kJ; Protein 11.6g; Carbohydrate 2.4g, of which sugars 0.6g; Fat 4.3g, of which saturates 0.6g; Cholesterol 45mg; Calcium 75mg; Fibre 0.7g; Sodium 998mg.

Barbecue Chicken

A fragrant marinade of Thai spices and coconut milk gives this chicken a superb flavour. It makes ideal party food for outdoor eating with a difference.

Serves 6

1 chicken, about 1.5kg/3¼lb, cut into
   8–10 pieces
lime wedges and fresh red chillies,
   to garnish

For the marinade

2 lemon grass stalks, roots removed
2.5cm/1in piece fresh root ginger,
   peeled and thinly sliced
6 garlic cloves, coarsely chopped
4 shallots, coarsely chopped
½ bunch coriander (cilantro)
   roots, chopped
15ml/1 tbsp palm sugar
120ml/4fl oz/½ cup coconut milk
30ml/2 tbsp Thai fish sauce
30ml/2 tbsp light soy sauce

2 Place the chicken pieces in a fairly deep dish, pour the marinade over them and stir to mix well, turning the chicken pieces over to coat thoroughly. Cover the dish with clear film (plastic wrap) and leave in a cool place to marinate for at least 4 hours or in the refrigerator overnight.

3 Prepare the barbecue. Cook the chicken over the barbecue for 20–30 minutes, or until the pieces are cooked and golden brown. Turn the pieces and brush with the marinade once or twice during cooking. Transfer to a serving platter and garnish with lime wedges and red chillies to serve.

1 To make the marinade, cut off the lower 5cm/2in of the lemon grass stalks and chop them coarsely. Put into a food processor or blender along with all the other marinade ingredients and process until the mixture has reached a smooth consistency.

COOK'S TIP

You can buy coconut milk fresh, in cans or cartons, or use 50g/2oz creamed coconut, available in packets, and dissolve in 120ml/4fl oz/½ cup warm water.

Energy 572kcal/2376kJ; Protein 46.5g; Carbohydrate 9.4g, of which sugars 8.2g; Fat 38.8g, of which saturates 11.3g; Cholesterol 240mg; Calcium 42mg; Fibre 0.7g; Sodium 222mg.

Lamb Tikka

Creamy yogurt and ground nuts go wonderfully with the spices in these little Indian meatballs.

Makes about 20

450g/1lb lamb fillet
2 spring onions (scallions), chopped

For the marinade
350ml/12fl oz/1½ cups yogurt
15ml/1 tbsp ground almonds, cashew
   nuts or peanuts
15ml/1 tbsp vegetable oil
2–3 garlic cloves, finely chopped
juice of 1 lemon
5ml/1 tsp garam masala or curry powder
2.5ml/½ tsp ground cardamom
1.5ml/¼ tsp cayenne pepper
15–30ml/1–2 tbsp chopped fresh mint

1 To prepare the marinade, put all the ingredients in a bowl and stir well to mix. Reserve about 120ml/4fl oz/½ cup of the mixture in a separate bowl to use as a dipping sauce.

2 With a sharp knife, cut the lamb fillet into small pieces and put in the bowl of a food processor with the spring onions. Process, using the pulse action, until the meat is finely chopped. Add 30–45ml/2–3 tbsp of the marinade and process again.

3 Test to see if the mixture holds together by pinching a little between your fingertips. Add a little more marinade if necessary, but do not make the mixture too wet and soft.

4 With moistened palms, form the meat mixture into slightly oval-shaped balls, measuring about 4cm/1½in long, and arrange them in a shallow dish. Spoon over the remaining marinade, cover with clear film (plastic wrap) and chill the meatballs in the refrigerator for 8–10 hours or overnight.

5 Preheat the grill (broiler) and line a baking sheet with foil. Thread each meatball on to a skewer and arrange on the baking sheet. Grill (broil) for 4–5 minutes, turning the skewers occasionally, until crisp and golden on all sides. Serve with the reserved marinade as a dipping sauce.

Energy 438kcal/1827kJ; Protein 34.4g; Carbohydrate 7.8g, of which sugars 7.7g; Fat 30.3g, of which saturates 10.4g; Cholesterol 128mg; Calcium 74mg; Fibre 2.3g; Sodium 162mg.

Turkey Patties

Minced turkey makes deliciously light patties, which are ideal for summer meals. Serve the patties in split and toasted buns or between thick pieces of crusty bread, with chutney, salad leaves and chunky fries or potato wedges.

Serves 6

675g/1½lb minced (ground) turkey
1 small red onion, finely chopped
grated rind and juice of 1 lime
small handful of fresh thyme leaves
15–30ml/1–2 tbsp olive oil
salt and ground black pepper

1 Mix together the turkey, onion, lime rind and juice, thyme and seasoning. Cover and chill for up to 4 hours to allow the flavours to infuse (steep), then divide the mixture into six equal portions and shape into round patties.

2 Preheat a griddle. Brush the patties with oil, then place them on the griddle and cook for 10–12 minutes. Turn the patties over, brush with more oil and cook for 10–12 minutes on the second side, or until cooked through.

Energy 141kcal/596kJ; Protein 24.8g; Carbohydrate 0.8g, of which sugars 0.6g; Fat 4.4g, of which saturates 1.1g; Cholesterol 69mg; Calcium 15mg; Fibre 0.2g; Sodium 62mg.

Lamb Burgers with Red Onion and Tomato Relish

A sharp-sweet red onion relish works well with burgers based on Middle-Eastern style lamb. The burgers can be made a day ahead and chilled. Serve them with pitta bread and tabbouleh or a crisp green salad.

Serves 8

50g/2oz/⅓ cup bulgur wheat
1kg/2¼lb lean minced (ground) lamb
2 small red onions, finely chopped
4 garlic cloves, finely chopped
2 fresh green chillies, seeded and
    finely chopped
10ml/2 tsp ground toasted cumin seeds
5ml/1 tsp ground sumac
25g/1oz/½ cup chopped fresh flat
    leaf parsley
60ml/4 tbsp chopped fresh mint
olive oil, for frying
salt and ground black pepper

For the relish

4 red (bell) peppers, halved
    and seeded
4 red onions, cut into 5mm/¼in
    thick slices
150ml/¼ pint/⅔ cup olive oil
700g/1lb 9oz cherry tomatoes, chopped
1 fresh red or green chilli, seeded and
    finely chopped (optional)
60ml/4 tbsp chopped fresh mint
60ml/4 tbsp chopped fresh parsley
30ml/2 tbsp chopped fresh oregano
    or marjoram
5ml/1 tsp ground toasted cumin seeds
5ml/1 tsp ground sumac
juice of 1 lemon
caster (superfine) sugar, to taste

1 Pour 300ml/½ pint/1¼ cups hot water over the bulgur wheat in a bowl and leave to stand for 15 minutes, then drain in a sieve and squeeze out the excess moisture.

2 Place the bulgur wheat in a bowl and add the minced lamb, onion, garlic, chilli, cumin, sumac, parsley and mint. Mix the ingredients thoroughly together by hand, then season with 10ml/2 tsp salt and plenty of black pepper and mix again. Form the mixture into 16 small burgers and set aside while you make the relish.

3 Grill (broil) the peppers, skin side up, until the skin chars and blisters. Place in a bowl, cover with clear film (plastic wrap) and leave to stand until cool. Peel off the skin, dice and place in a bowl.

4 Brush the onions with 30ml/2 tbsp oil and grill for 5 minutes on each side, until browned. Cool, then chop.

5 Add the onions, tomatoes, chilli (if using) to taste, the mint, parsley, oregano or marjoram and half of the cumin and sumac to the peppers. Stir in the remaining oil and 30ml/2 tbsp of the lemon juice. Season with salt, pepper and sugar and leave to stand for 20–30 minutes.

6 Prepare a barbecue or heat a heavy frying pan or griddle over a high heat and grease with olive oil. Cook the burgers for about 5–6 minutes on each side, or until just cooked at the centre.

7 While the burgers are cooking, taste the relish and adjust the seasoning, adding more salt, pepper, sugar, chilli, cumin, sumac and lemon juice to taste. Serve the burgers as soon as they are cooked, with the relish.

Energy 538kcal/2232kJ; Protein 28g; Carbohydrate 19g, of which sugars 11g; Fat 40g, of which saturates 11g; Cholesterol 94mg; Calcium 65mg; Fibre 4g; Sodium 92mg.

Skewered Lamb with Red Onion Salsa

This summery tapas dish is ideal for outdoor eating, although, if the weather fails, the skewers can be grilled rather than barbecued. The simple salsa makes a refreshing accompaniment – make sure that you use a mild-flavoured red onion that is fresh and crisp, and a tomato which is ripe and full of flavour.

Serves 4

225g/8oz lean lamb, cubed
2.5ml/½ tsp ground cumin
5ml/1 tsp paprika
15ml/1 tbsp olive oil
salt and ground black pepper

For the salsa
1 red onion, very thinly sliced
1 large tomato, seeded and chopped
15ml/1 tbsp red wine vinegar
3–4 fresh basil or mint leaves,
    coarsely torn
small mint leaves, to garnish

1 Place the cubes of lamb in a bowl and add the cumin, paprika and olive oil and season with plenty of salt and pepper. Toss thoroughly until the lamb is coated with the spices.

2 Cover the bowl with clear film (plastic wrap) and set aside in a cool place for several hours, or in the refrigerator overnight, so that the lamb absorbs the flavours of the spices.

3 Thread the lamb cubes on to four small skewers – if using wooden skewers, soak them first in cold water for about 30 minutes to prevent them from burning during cooking.

4 To make the salsa, put the sliced onion, tomato, red wine vinegar and torn basil or mint leaves in a small bowl and stir together until thoroughly combined. Season to taste with salt, garnish with mint, then set aside while you cook the lamb skewers.

5 Cook the skewers over the barbecue or under a preheated grill (broiler), turning frequently, for 5–10 minutes, until the lamb is well browned but still slightly pink in the centre. Serve immediately, with the salsa.

Energy 135kcal/563kJ; Protein 11.4g; Carbohydrate 2g, of which sugars 1.6g; Fat 9.2g, of which saturates 3.4g; Cholesterol 43mg; Calcium 10mg; Fibre 0.5g; Sodium 51mg.

Garlic and Chilli Marinated Beef with Corn-crusted Onion Rings

Fruity, smoky and mild Mexican chillies combine well with garlic in this marinade for grilled steak.

Serves 8

40g/1½oz large mild dried red chillies, such as mulato or pasilla
4 garlic cloves, plain or smoked, finely chopped
10ml/2 tsp ground toasted cumin seeds
10ml/2 tsp dried oregano
120ml/4fl oz/½ cup olive oil
8 beef steaks, rump (round) or rib-eye, 175–225g/6–8oz each
salt and ground black pepper

For the onion rings
4 onions, sliced into rings
475ml/16fl oz/2 cups milk
175g/6oz/1½ cup coarse corn meal
5ml/1 tsp dried red chilli flakes
10ml/2 tsp ground toasted cumin seeds
10ml/2 tsp dried oregano
vegetable oil, for deep-frying

1 Cut the stalks from the chillies and discard the seeds. Toast the chillies in a dry frying pan for 2–4 minutes. Place them in a bowl, cover with warm water and leave to soak for 20–30 minutes. Drain and reserve the water.

2 Process the chillies to a paste with the garlic, cumin, oregano and oil in a food processor. Add a little soaking water, if needed. Season with pepper.

3 Wash and dry the steaks, drizzle the chilli paste all over them and leave to marinate for up to 12 hours.

4 To make the onion rings, soak the onions in the milk for 30 minutes. Mix the corn meal, chilli, cumin and oregano and season to taste.

5 Heat the oil for deep-frying to 160–180°C/325–350°F, or until a cube of day-old bread turns brown in about 60 seconds.

6 Drain the onion rings and dip each one into the corn meal mixture, coating it thoroughly. Deep-fry for 2–4 minutes, or until browned and crisp. Do not overcrowd the pan, but cook in batches. Lift the onion rings out of the pan with a slotted spoon and drain on kitchen paper.

7 Heat a barbecue or griddle. Season the steaks with salt and cook for about 4 minutes on each side for a medium result.

Energy 428kcal/1787kJ; Protein 44.2g; Carbohydrate 17.4g, of which sugars 3g; Fat 20g, of which saturates 5.4g; Cholesterol 91mg; Calcium 51mg; Fibre 0.8g; Sodium 136mg.

diva desserts

Make sure that your guests leave the party on a high
note after sampling one (or more!) of these
superlative, mouthwatering sweet dishes.

Mint Chocolate Meringues

Omit the alcohol and these mini meringues are perfect for a child's birthday party.

Makes about 50

2 egg whites
115g/4oz/generous ½ cup caster
  (superfine) sugar
50g/2oz chocolate mint
  sticks, chopped
(unsweetened) cocoa powder,
  sifted (optional)

For the filling
150ml/¼ pint/⅔ cup double (heavy)
  or whipping cream
5–10ml/1–2 tsp crème de menthe,
  or mint essence (extract)

1 Preheat the oven to 110°C/225°F/ Gas ¼. Line two or three baking sheets with baking parchment. Whisk the egg whites until stiff, then gradually whisk in the sugar until it is thick and glossy.

2 Fold in the chopped mint sticks and then place teaspoons of the mixture on the prepared baking sheets.

3 Bake for 1 hour, or until crisp. Remove from the oven and leave to cool, then dust with cocoa, if using.

4 To make the filling whip the cream until it stands in soft peaks and stir in the crème de menthe or mint essence. Use the cream to sandwich the meringues together in pairs just before serving.

Energy 30kcal/125kJ; Protein 0g; Carbohydrate 3g, of which sugars 3g; Fat 2g, of which saturates 1g; Cholesterol 4mg; Calcium 2mg; Fibre 0g; Sodium 3mg.

Chocolate Truffles

These irresistible, melt-in-the-mouth truffles will make a dainty addition to the buffet table as a dessert or as an after-dinner treat. Use a good quality chocolate with a high percentage of cocoa solids to give a real depth of flavour.

Makes 20–30

175ml/6fl oz/¾ cup double
    (heavy) cream
1 egg yolk, beaten
275g/10oz plain (semisweet)
    Belgian chocolate, chopped
25g/1oz/2 tbsp unsalted
    butter, cut into pieces
30–45ml/2–3 tbsp brandy (optional)

For the coatings
(unsweetened) cocoa powder
finely chopped pistachio nuts
    or hazelnuts
400g/14oz plain (semisweet), milk
    or white chocolate, or a mixture

1 Bring the cream to the boil, then remove the pan from the heat and beat in the egg yolk. Add the chocolate, then stir until melted and smooth. Stir in the butter and the brandy, if using, then pour into a bowl and leave to cool. Cover and chill in the refrigerator for 6–8 hours.

COOK'S TIP
Chocolate truffles will delight guests at a drinks party – serve them with coffee to follow all the savoury bites.

2 Line a large baking sheet with baking parchment. Using a very small ice cream scoop or two teaspoons, form the chocolate mixture into 20–30 balls and place on the parchment. Chill if the mixture becomes too soft.

3 To coat the truffles with cocoa, sift some powder into a small bowl, drop in the truffles, one at a time, and roll to coat well. To coat them with nuts, roll the truffles in finely chopped pistachio nuts or hazelnuts.

4 To coat with chocolate, freeze the truffles for at least 1 hour. In a small bowl, melt the plain, milk or white chocolate over a pan of barely simmering water, stirring until melted and smooth, then leave to cool slightly.

5 Using a fork, dip the frozen truffles into the cooled chocolate, one at a time, tapping the fork on the edge of the bowl to shake off the excess. Place on a baking sheet lined with baking parchment and chill. If the melted chocolate thickens, reheat until smooth. All the truffles can be stored, well wrapped, in the refrigerator for up to 10 days.

Energy 160kcal/669kJ; Protein 2g; Carbohydrate 15g, of which sugars 14g; Fat 11g, of which saturates 6g; Cholesterol 18mg; Calcium 12mg; Fibre 0g; Sodium 11mg.

Tropical Scented Red and Orange Fruit Salad

This fresh fruit salad, with its bright colour and exotic flavour, is perfect after a rich, heavy meal or on the buffet table. It is also a refreshing dish to serve at a summer picnic or barbecue.

Serves 4–6

350–400g/12–14oz/3–3½ cups
  strawberries, hulled and halved
3 oranges, peeled and segmented
3 small blood oranges, peeled
  and segmented
1–2 passion fruit
120ml/4fl oz/½ cup dry white wine
sugar, to taste

1 Put the strawberries and oranges into a serving bowl. Halve the passion fruit and spoon the flesh into the bowl.

COOK'S TIP
Omit the white wine if you like and replace with orange or tropical juice.

2 Pour the wine over the fruit and add sugar to taste. Toss gently and then chill until ready to serve.

VARIATION
Other fruit that can be added include pear, kiwi fruit and banana.

Energy 80kcal/339kJ; Protein 2.1g; Carbohydrate 15.3g, of which sugars 15.3g; Fat 0.2g, of which saturates 0g; Cholesterol 0mg; Calcium 74mg; Fibre 3.1g; Sodium 12mg.

Fig, Port and Clementine Sundaes

These exotic sundaes will make an ideal finale to a rich meal. The fresh flavours of figs and clementines contrast beautifully with the warm spices and port.

Serves 6

6 clementines
30ml/2 tbsp clear honey
1 cinnamon stick, halved
15ml/1 tbsp light muscovado
    (brown) sugar
60ml/4 tbsp port
6 fresh figs
about 500ml/17fl oz/2¼ cups orange
    sorbet (sherbet)

1 Finely grate the rind from two clementines and put it in a small, heavy pan. Cut the peel off the clementines, then slice the flesh thinly. Add the honey, cinnamon, sugar and port to the rind. Heat gently until the sugar has dissolved, to make a syrup.

2 Put the clementine slices in a heatproof bowl and pour over the syrup. Cool completely, then chill.

3 Slice the figs thinly and add to the clementines and syrup, tossing the ingredients together gently. Leave to stand for 10 minutes, then discard the cinnamon stick.

4 Arrange half the fig and clementine slices around the sides of six serving glasses. Half fill the glasses with scoops of sorbet. Arrange the remaining fruit slices around the sides of the glasses, then pile more sorbet into the centre. Pour over the port syrup and serve.

COOK'S TIP
A variety of different types of fresh figs are available. Dark purple skinned figs have a deep red flesh; the yellowy-green figs have a pink flesh and green skinned figs have an amber coloured flesh. All types can be eaten, complete with the skin, simply as they are or baked and served with Greek (US strained plain) yogurt and honey for a quick dessert. When they are ripe, you can split them open with your fingers to reveal the soft, sweet flesh full of edible seeds.

Energy 282kcal/1205kJ; Protein 3.7g; Carbohydrate 66.5g, of which sugars 66.5g; Fat 0.9g, of which saturates 0g; Cholesterol 0mg; Calcium 173mg; Fibre 5.4g; Sodium 50mg.

Passion Fruit Crème Caramels with Dipped Physalis

The aromatic flavour of the fruit permeates these crème caramels, which are perfect for a dinner party.

Serves 8

375g/13oz/generous 1¾ cups caster (superfine) sugar
150ml/¼ pint/⅔ cup water
8 passion fruit
8 physalis
6 eggs plus 2 egg yolks
300ml/½ pint/1¼ cups double (heavy) cream
300ml/½ pint/1¼ cups full-cream (whole) milk

1 Place 300g/11oz/1½ cups of the caster sugar in a heavy pan. Add the water and heat the mixture gently until the sugar has dissolved. Increase the heat and boil until the syrup turns a dark golden colour.

2 Meanwhile, cut each passion fruit in half. Scoop out the seeds from the passion fruit into a sieve set over a bowl. Press the seeds against the sieve to extract all their juice. Spoon a few of the seeds into each of eight 150ml/¼ pint/⅔ cup ramekins. Reserve the passion fruit juice.

3 Peel back the papery casing from each physalis and dip the orange berries into the caramel. Place on a sheet of baking parchment and set aside. Pour the remaining caramel carefully into the ramekins.

4 Preheat the oven to 150°C/300°F/Gas 2. Whisk the eggs, egg yolks and remaining sugar in a bowl. Whisk in the cream and milk, then the passion fruit juice. Strain through a sieve into each ramekin, then place the ramekins in a baking tin (pan). Pour in hot water to come halfway up the sides of the dishes and bake for 40–45 minutes, or until just set.

5 Remove the custards from the tin and leave to cool, then cover and chill them for 4 hours before serving. Run a knife between the edge of each ramekin and the custard and invert each, in turn, onto a dessert plate. Shake the ramekins firmly to release the custards before lifting them off the desserts. Decorate each with a dipped physalis.

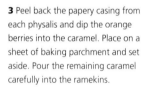

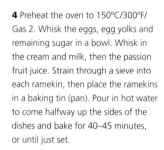

Energy 163kcal/681kJ; Protein 3g; Carbohydrate 18g, of which sugars 18g; Fat 9g, of which saturates 5g; Cholesterol 94mg; Calcium 34mg; Fibre 0g; Sodium 32mg.

Crème Brûlée

This dessert actually originated in the English city of Cambridge, but has become associated with France and is widely eaten there.

Serves 6

1 vanilla pod (bean)
1 litre/1¾ pints/4 cups double
(heavy) cream
6 egg yolks
90g/3½oz/½ cup caster
(superfine) sugar
30ml/2 tbsp orange liqueur (optional)
75g/3oz/⅓ cup soft light brown sugar

1 Preheat the oven to 150°C/300°F/ Gas 2. Place six 120ml/4fl oz/½ cup ramekins in a roasting pan and set aside until required.

2 With a small sharp knife, split the vanilla pod lengthways and scrape the black seeds into a medium pan. Add the cream and bring just to the boil over a medium heat, stirring constantly. Remove from the heat and cover. Set aside for 15–20 minutes.

VARIATION
You can omit the liqueur if you like. You could also substitute almond liqueur, such as Amaretto, if you prefer the flavour.

COOK'S TIP
To test if the custards are ready, push the point of a knife into centre of one – if it comes out clean, the custards are cooked.

3 Whisk the egg yolks, caster sugar and orange liqueur, if using, in a mixing bowl until thoroughly blended. Whisk in the hot cream and strain the mixture into a large jug (pitcher). Divide the custard equally among the six ramekins.

4 Pour enough boiling water into the roasting pan to come about halfway up the sides of the ramekins. Cover the pan with foil and bake for about 30 minutes, until the custards are just set. Remove the ramekins from the pan and leave to cool. Return to the dry roasting pan and chill.

5 Preheat the grill (broiler). Sprinkle the brown sugar evenly over the surface of each custard and grill (broil) for 30–60 seconds, until the sugar melts and caramelizes. (Do not let the sugar burn or the custard curdle.) Place in the refrigerator to set the crust and chill completely before serving.

Energy 996kcal/4116kJ; Protein 6g; Carbohydrate 32g, of which sugars 32g; Fat 95g, of which saturates 57g; Cholesterol 430mg; Calcium 110mg; Fibre 0g; Sodium 47mg.

Chocolate Mandarin Trifle

Trifle is always a tempting treat, but when a rich chocolate and mascarpone custard is combined with amaretto and mandarin oranges, it becomes irresistible.

Serves 6–8

4 trifle sponges
14 amaretti
60ml/4 tbsp Amaretto di Saronno or
  sweet sherry
8 mandarin oranges

For the custard
200g/7oz plain (semisweet) chocolate,
  broken into squares
30ml/2 tbsp cornflour (cornstarch) or
  custard powder
30ml/2 tbsp caster (superfine) sugar
2 egg yolks
200ml/7fl oz/⅞ cup milk
250g/9oz/generous 1 cup
  mascarpone

For the topping
250g/9oz/generous 1 cup fromage
  frais or farmer's cheese
chocolate shapes
mandarin slices

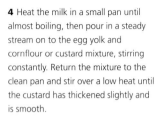

1 Break up the trifle sponges and place them in the base of a large glass serving dish. Crumble the amaretti over and then sprinkle with Amaretto or sweet sherry.

2 Squeeze the juice from two of the mandarins and sprinkle into the dish. Segment the rest of the mandarins and put in the dish.

3 Make the custard. Melt the chocolate in a heatproof bowl set over a pan of barely simmering water. In a separate bowl, mix the cornflour or custard powder, sugar and egg yolks to a smooth paste.

4 Heat the milk in a small pan until almost boiling, then pour in a steady stream on to the egg yolk and cornflour or custard mixture, stirring constantly. Return the mixture to the clean pan and stir over a low heat until the custard has thickened slightly and is smooth.

5 Stir in the mascarpone until melted, then add the melted chocolate, mixing it thoroughly. Spread evenly over the trifle base, leave to cool, then chill in the refrigerator until set.

6 To finish, spread the fromage frais over the custard, using a spatula, then decorate with chocolate shapes and the remaining mandarin slices just before serving.

COOK'S TIP
Always use the best chocolate which has a high percentage of cocoa solids, and take care not to overheat the chocolate when melting as it will lose its gloss and look "grainy".

Energy 569kcal/2394kJ; Protein 12.5g; Carbohydrate 80.3g, of which sugars 61.3g; Fat 23.1g, of which saturates 12.8g; Cholesterol 135mg; Calcium 162mg; Fibre 2.9g; Sodium 115mg.

Chocolate Hazelnut Galettes

If only all sandwiches looked and tasted as good as these chocolate rounds.

Serves 4

175g/6oz plain (semisweet) chocolate, broken into squares
45ml/3 tbsp single (light) cream
30ml/2 tbsp flaked (sliced) hazelnuts
115g/4oz white chocolate, broken into squares
175g/6oz/³⁄₄ cup fromage frais or farmer's cheese
15ml/1 tbsp dry sherry
60ml/4 tbsp finely chopped hazelnuts, toasted
physalis, dipped in white chocolate, to decorate

1 Melt the plain chocolate in a bowl over hot water, then remove from the heat and stir in the cream.

2 Draw 12 × 7.5cm/3in circles on sheets of non-stick baking parchment. Turn the paper over and spread the plain chocolate over each marked circle, covering in a thin, even layer. Sprinkle flaked hazelnuts over four of the circles, then leave to set.

3 Melt the white chocolate in a heatproof bowl set over a pan of barely simmering water, then stir in the fromage frais and dry sherry. Gently fold in the chopped, toasted hazelnuts. Leave to cool until the mixture holds its shape.

4 Remove the chocolate rounds carefully from the paper and sandwich them together in stacks of three, spooning the hazelnut cream between each layer and using the hazelnut-covered rounds on top. Chill in the refrigerator before serving.

5 To serve, place the galettes on individual plates and decorate with chocolate-dipped physalis.

COOK'S TIP
Strictly speaking, white chocolate is not really chocolate. It is made from cocoa butter, but contains no cocoa solids.

VARIATION
The chocolate could be spread over heart shapes instead, for a special Valentine's Day dessert.

Energy 597kcal/2489kJ; Protein 10.7g; Carbohydrate 48.1g, of which sugars 47.2g; Fat 41.1g, of which saturates 17.5g; Cholesterol 13mg; Calcium 182mg; Fibre 2.6g; Sodium 55mg.

Chocolate and Chestnut Pots

Prepared in advance, these are the perfect ending for a dinner party. Remove them from the refrigerator about 30 minutes before serving, to allow them to "ripen".

Serves 6

250g/9oz plain (semisweet) chocolate
60ml/4 tbsp Madeira
25g/1oz/2 tbsp butter, diced
2 eggs, separated
225g/8oz/scant 1 cup unsweetened
*   chestnut purée*
crème fraîche or whipped double
*   (heavy) cream, to decorate*

1 Make a few chocolate curls for decoration, then break the rest of the chocolate into squares and melt it with the Madeira in a pan over a gentle heat. Remove from the heat and add the butter, a few pieces at a time, stirring until melted and smooth.

COOK'S TIPS
• The quickest and easiest way to make chocolate curls is to use a vegetable peeler. Make sure the chocolate is at room temperature, then hold it firmly and shave off curls from one side. Transfer them using a cocktail stick (toothpick) to avoid damaging them.
• If Madeira is not available, use brandy or rum instead.
• These chocolate pots can be frozen successfully for up to 2 months.

2 Beat the egg yolks quickly into the chocolate mixture, then beat in the chestnut purée, mixing well until completely smooth.

3 Whisk the egg whites in a clean, grease-free bowl until stiff. Stir about 15ml/1 tbsp of the whites into the chestnut mixture to lighten it, then fold in the rest smoothly and evenly, using a metal spoon or rubber spatula.

4 Spoon the mixture into six small ramekins and chill in the refrigerator until set. Serve the pots topped with a generous spoonful of crème fraîche or whipped double cream and decorated with the plain chocolate curls.

Energy 348kcal/1455kJ; Protein 5g; Carbohydrate 41.4g, of which sugars 29.9g; Fat 18g, of which saturates 9.9g; Cholesterol 75mg; Calcium 42mg; Fibre 2.6g; Sodium 56mg.

Cold Lemon Soufflé with Almonds

Terrific to look at, yet easy to make, this dessert is mouthwatering, ideal for the end of any party meal.

Serves 6

vegetable oil, for greasing
grated rind and juice of 3 large lemons
5 large (US extra large) eggs, separated
115g/4oz/generous ½ cup caster
    (superfine) sugar
25ml/1½ tbsp powdered gelatine
450ml/¾ pint/scant 2 cups double
    (heavy) cream

For the almond topping
75g/3oz/¾ cup flaked (sliced) almonds
75g/3oz/¾ cup icing
    (confectioner's) sugar

1 To make the soufflé collar, cut a strip of baking parchment long enough to fit around a 900ml/1½ pint/3¾ cup soufflé dish and wide enough to extend 7.5cm/3in above the rim. Fit the strip around the dish, tape and then tie it around the top of the dish with string. Using a pastry brush, lightly coat the inside of the paper collar with oil.

2 Put the lemon rind and yolks in a bowl. Add 75g/3oz/6 tbsp of the caster sugar and whisk until the mixture is creamy.

COOK'S TIP
Heat the lemon juice and gelatine in a microwave, on full power, in 30-second bursts, stirring between each burst, until it is fully dissolved.

3 Place the lemon juice in a small heatproof bowl and sprinkle over the gelatine. Set aside for 5 minutes, then place the bowl in a pan of simmering water. Heat, stirring occasionally, until the gelatine has dissolved. Cool slightly, then stir the gelatine and lemon juice into the egg yolk mixture.

4 In a separate bowl, lightly whip the cream to soft peaks. Fold into the egg yolk mixture and set aside.

5 Whisk the whites to stiff peaks. Gradually whisk in the remaining caster sugar until stiff and glossy. Quickly and lightly fold the whites into the yolk mix. Pour into the prepared dish, smooth the surface and chill for 4–5 hours.

6 To make the almond topping, brush a baking tray lightly with oil. Preheat the grill (broiler). Sprinkle the flaked almonds over the baking tray and sift the icing sugar over. Grill (broil) until the nuts turn a rich golden colour and the sugar has caramelized.

7 Leave to cool, then remove the almond mixture from the tray with a palette knife or metal spatula and break it into pieces.

8 When the soufflé has set, carefully peel off the paper. If the paper does not come away easily, hold the blade of a knife against the set soufflé to help it keep its shape. Sprinkle the caramelized almonds over the top before serving.

VARIATIONS
• This soufflé is wonderfully refreshing when served semi-frozen. Place the undecorated, set soufflé in the freezer for about an hour. Just before serving, remove from the freezer and decorate with the caramelized almonds.
• You can also vary the flavour slightly by using the juice and rind of 5 limes.

Energy 628kcal/2611kJ; Protein 14g; Carbohydrate 36g, of which sugars 35g; Fat 49g, of which saturates 25g; Cholesterol 304mg; Calcium 109mg; Fibre 2g; Sodium 108mg.

Clementines in Cinnamon Caramel

The combination of sweet, yet sharp clementines and caramel sauce with a hint of spice is divine. Served with Greek yogurt or crème fraîche, this makes a delicious and refreshing dessert.

Serves 4–6

8–12 clementines
225g/8oz/generous 1 cup
  granulated (white) sugar
2 cinnamon sticks
30ml/2 tbsp orange-flavoured liqueur
25g/1oz/¼ cup shelled pistachio nuts

1 Pare the rind from two clementines using a vegetable peeler and cut it into fine strips. Set aside.

2 Peel all the clementines, removing all traces of the bitter, white pith, but keeping them intact. Put the fruits in a serving bowl.

3 Gently heat the sugar in a small, heavy pan until it melts and turns a rich golden brown. Immediately turn off the heat.

4 Cover your hand with a dishtowel to protect it and pour in 300ml/½ pint/ 1¼ cups warm water (the mixture will bubble and splutter). Gradually bring to the boil, stirring constantly until the caramel has dissolved. Add the shredded clementine peel and cinnamon sticks, then simmer gently for 5 minutes. Stir in the orange-flavoured liqueur.

5 Leave the syrup to cool for about 10 minutes, then pour it over the clementines. Cover the bowl with clear film (plastic wrap) and chill for several hours or overnight.

6 Blanch the pistachio nuts in boiling water. Drain, cool and remove the dark outer skins. Sprinkle over the clementines and serve immediately.

Energy 235kcal/998kJ; Protein 2g; Carbohydrate 53g, of which sugars 53g; Fat 2g, of which saturates 0g; Cholesterol 0mg; Calcium 50mg; Fibre 2g; Sodium 29mg.

Lime Sorbet

3 Freeze the mixture in an ice-cream maker, following the manufacturer's instructions.

4 If you do not have an ice-cream maker, pour the mixture into a metal or plastic freezer container and freeze for about 3 hours, until softly set.

5 Remove the mixture from the container and chop coarsely into 7.5cm/3in pieces. Place in a food processor and process until smooth. Return the mixture to the freezer container and freeze again until set. Repeat this freezing and chopping process two or three times, until a smooth consistency is obtained.

6 Serve in scoops decorated with slivers of lime rind.

This light, refreshing sorbet is a good dessert to serve after a substantial main course.

Serves 4

250g/9oz/1¼ cups sugar
grated rind of 1 lime
175ml/6fl oz/¾ cup freshly squeezed
* lime juice*
15–30ml/1–2 tbsp freshly squeezed
* lemon juice*
icing (confectioners') sugar,
* to taste*
slivers of lime rind, to decorate

1 In a small, heavy pan, dissolve the sugar in 600ml/1 pint/2½ cups water, without stirring, over medium heat. When the sugar has dissolved, bring to the boil and continue to boil for 5–6 minutes. Remove the pan from the heat and leave to cool.

2 Combine the cooled sugar syrup and lime rind and juice in a measuring jug (cup) or bowl. Stir well. Taste and adjust the flavour by adding lemon juice or some icing sugar, if necessary. Do not over-sweeten.

COOK'S TIP
If using an ice-cream maker for these sorbets (sherbets), check the manufacturer's instructions to find out the freezing capacity. If necessary, halve the recipe quantities.

Energy 251kcal/1067kJ; Protein 0g; Carbohydrate 66g, of which sugars 66g; Fat 0g, of which saturates 0g; Cholesterol 0mg; Calcium 11mg; Fibre 0g; Sodium 4mg.

Frozen Grand Marnier Soufflés

2 Heat the milk until almost boiling and pour it on to the yolks, whisking constantly. Return to the pan and stir over a gentle heat until the custard is thick enough to coat the back of the spoon. Remove the pan from the heat. Stir the soaked gelatine into the custard. Pour the custard into a bowl and leave to cool. Whisk occasionally, until on the point of setting.

3 Put the remaining sugar in a pan with 45ml/3 tbsp water and dissolve it over a low heat. Bring to the boil and boil rapidly until it reaches the soft ball stage or 119°C/238°F on a sugar thermometer. Remove from the heat. In a clean bowl, whisk the egg whites until stiff. Pour the hot syrup on to the whites, whisking constantly. Leave the meringue to cool.

4 Add the Grand Marnier to the cold custard. Whisk the cream until it holds soft peaks and fold into the cooled meringue, with the custard. Pour into the prepared glasses or dishes. Freeze overnight. Remove the paper collars and leave at room temperature for 15 minutes before serving.

Light and fluffy, yet almost ice cream, these delicious soufflés are perfect and wonderfully easy for a special dinner. Start preparations the day before as the desserts have to be frozen overnight.

Serves 8

200g/7oz/1 cup caster
(superfine) sugar
6 large (US extra large) eggs, separated
250ml/8fl oz/1 cup milk
15ml/1 tbsp powdered gelatine,
soaked in 45ml/3 tbsp cold water
60ml/4 tbsp grand marnier
450ml/¾ pint/scant 2 cups double
(heavy) cream

1 Wrap a double collar of baking parchment around eight dessert glasses or ramekins and tie with string. Whisk together 75g/3oz/scant ½ cup of the caster sugar with the egg yolks, until the yolks are pale. This will take about 5 minutes by hand or about 3 minutes with an electric hand mixer.

COOK'S TIPS

• The soft ball stage of a syrup is when a teaspoon of the mixture dropped into a glass of cold water sets into a ball.
• If you prefer, you can make just one dessert in a large soufflé dish, rather than eight individual ones, or serve in very small glasses for a buffet.

Energy 493kcal/2050kJ; Protein 9g; Carbohydrate 31g, of which sugars 31g; Fat 37g, of which saturates 21g; Cholesterol 277mg; Calcium 98mg; Fibre 0g; Sodium 101mg.

Iced Lime Cheesecake

This frozen dessert has a deliciously tangy, sweet flavour but needs no gelatine to set the filling, unlike most unbaked cheesecakes. It is not difficult to prepare and an added advantage is that it can be made several days beforehand.

Serves 10

175g/6oz almond biscuits (cookies)
65g/2½oz/5 tbsp unsalted butter
8 limes
115g/4oz/generous ½ cup caster (superfine) sugar
90ml/6 tbsp water
200g/7oz/scant 1 cup cottage cheese
250g/9oz/generous 1 cup mascarpone
300ml/½ pint/1¼ cups double (heavy) cream

1 Lightly grease the sides of a 20cm/8in springform cake tin (pan) and line with a strip of baking parchment. Break up the almond biscuits slightly, put them in a strong plastic bag and crush them with a rolling pin.

2 Melt the butter in a small pan and stir in the biscuit crumbs until evenly combined. Spoon the mixture into the tin and pack it down with the back of a spoon. Freeze the biscuit mixture while you make the filling.

3 Finely grate the rind and squeeze the juice from five of the limes. Heat the sugar and water in a small pan, stirring until the sugar dissolves. Bring to the boil and boil for 2 minutes without stirring, then remove the syrup from the heat, stir in the lime juice and rind and leave to cool.

4 Press the cottage cheese through a sieve into a bowl. Beat in the mascarpone, then the lime syrup. By hand, lightly whip the cream and then fold into the cheese mixture. Pour into a shallow container and freeze until thick. If you are using an ice cream maker, add the lightly-whipped cream and churn in an ice cream maker until thick.

5 Meanwhile, cut a slice off either end of each of the remaining limes, stand them on a board and slice off the skins. Cut them into very thin slices.

6 Arrange the lime slices around the sides of the tin, pressing them against the paper.

7 Pour the cheese mixture over the biscuit base in the tin and level the surface. Cover and freeze the cheesecake overnight.

8 About 1 hour before you are going to serve the cheesecake, carefully transfer it to a serving plate and put it in the refrigerator to soften slightly.

Energy 445kcal/1850kJ; Protein 5g; Carbohydrate 29g, of which sugars 21g; Fat 35g, of which saturates 22g; Cholesterol 83mg; Calcium 92mg; Fibre 0g; Sodium 251mg.

White Chocolate Parfait

This dessert is everything you could
wish for in one mouthwatering slice.

Serves 10

225g/8oz white chocolate, chopped
600ml/1 pint/2½ cups whipping cream
120ml/4fl oz/½ cup milk
10 egg yolks
15ml/1 tbsp caster (superfine) sugar
25g/1oz/scant ½ cup desiccated (dry
  unsweetened shredded) coconut
120ml/4fl oz/½ cup canned sweetened
  coconut milk
150g/5oz/1¼ cups macadamia nuts

For the chocolate icing (frosting)
225g/8oz plain (semisweet) chocolate
75g/3oz/6 tbsp butter
20ml/generous 1 tbsp golden (light
  corn) syrup
175ml/6fl oz/¾ cup whipping cream
curls of fresh coconut, to decorate

1 Line the base and sides of a 1.4 litre/
2⅓ pint/6 cup terrine mould
(25 × 10cm/10 × 4in) with clear film
(plastic wrap).

2 Place the chopped white chocolate
and 50ml/2fl oz/¼ cup of the cream in
the top of a double boiler or in a
heatproof bowl set over a pan of
barely simmering water. Stir until
melted and smooth. Set aside.

3 Put 250ml/8fl oz/1 cup of the cream
and the milk in a pan and bring to
boiling point.

4 Meanwhile, whisk the egg yolks and
caster sugar together in a large bowl,
until thick and pale.

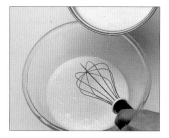

5 Add the hot cream mixture to the
egg yolks, beating constantly. Pour
back into the pan and cook over a low
heat for 2–3 minutes, until thickened.
Stir constantly and do not allow the
mixture to boil. Remove the pan from
the heat.

6 Add the melted chocolate,
desiccated coconut and coconut milk,
then stir well and leave to cool.

7 Whip the remaining cream until
thick, then fold into the chocolate and
coconut mixture.

8 Put 475ml/16fl oz/2 cups of the
parfait mixture in the prepared mould
and spread evenly. Cover and freeze
for about 2 hours, until just firm.
Cover the remaining mixture and chill.

9 Sprinkle the macadamia nuts evenly
over the frozen parfait. Pour in the
remaining parfait mixture. Cover the
terrine and freeze for 6–8 hours or
overnight, until the parfait is firm.

10 To make the icing, melt the
chocolate with the butter and syrup in
the top of a double boiler or in a
heatproof bowl set over a pan of
barely simmering water, stirring the
mixture occasionally.

11 Heat the cream in a pan, until just
simmering, then stir into the chocolate
mixture. Remove the pan from the
heat and leave to cool until lukewarm.

12 To turn out the parfait, wrap the
terrine in a hot towel and set it upside
down on a plate. Lift off the terrine
mould, then peel off the clear film.
Place the parfait on a rack over a
baking sheet and pour the chocolate
icing evenly over the top. Working
quickly, smooth the icing down the
sides with a palette knife or spatula.
Leave to set slightly, then freeze for a
further 3–4 hours.

13 Cut into slices using a knife dipped
in hot water. Serve, decorated with
curls of fresh coconut.

COOK'S TIP
When melting chocolate over a pan of hot
water, do not let the base of the bowl
touch the surface of the water. Keep the
water at simmering point.

Energy 769kcal/3189kJ; Protein 11g; Carbohydrate 37g, of which sugars 34g; Fat 65g, of which saturates 36g; Cholesterol 302mg; Calcium 161mg; Fibre 1g; Sodium 127mg.

Iced Christmas Torte

Not everyone likes traditional Christmas pudding. This makes an exciting alternative, but do not feel that you have to limit it to the festive season. Packed with dried fruit and nuts, it is perfect for any special occasion.

Serves 8–10

75g/3oz/¾ cup dried cranberries
75g/3oz/scant ½ cup pitted prunes
50g/2oz/⅓ cup sultanas (golden raisins)
175ml/6fl oz/¾ cup port
2 pieces preserved stem ginger,
*   finely chopped*
25g/1oz/2 tbsp unsalted butter
45ml/3 tbsp light muscovado
*   (brown) sugar*
90g/3½oz/scant 2 cups fresh
*   white breadcrumbs*
600ml/1 pint/2½ cups double
*   (heavy) cream*
30ml/2 tbsp icing (confectioners') sugar
5ml/1 tsp mixed (pumpkin pie) spice
75g/3oz/¾ cup brazil nuts,
*   finely chopped*
sugared bay leaves (see Cook's Tip)
*   and fresh cherries, to decorate*

1 Put the cranberries, prunes and sultanas in a food processor and process briefly. Tip them into a bowl and add the port and ginger. Leave to absorb the port for 2 hours.

2 Melt the butter in a frying pan. Add the sugar and heat gently until it has dissolved. Tip in the breadcrumbs, stir, then cook over a low heat for about 5 minutes, or until lightly coloured and turning crisp. Leave to cool.

COOK'S TIP
To make the sugared bay leaves wash and dry the leaves, then paint both sides with beaten egg white. Sprinkle with caster (superfine) sugar. Leave to dry on baking parchment for 2–3 hours.

3 Tip the breadcrumbs into a food processor or blender and process to finer crumbs. Sprinkle one-third into an 18cm/7in loose-based springform cake tin (pan) and spread them out to cover the base of the tin evenly. Freeze until firm.

4 Whip the cream with the icing sugar and mixed spice until it is thick but not yet standing in peaks. Fold in the brazil nuts with the fruit mixture and any port that has not been absorbed.

5 Spread a third of the mixture over the breadcrumb base in the tin, taking care not to dislodge the crumbs. Sprinkle with another layer of the breadcrumbs. Repeat the layering, finishing with a layer of the cream mixture. Freeze the torte overnight.

6 Chill the torte for about 1 hour before serving, decorated with sugared bay leaves and fresh cherries.

Energy 504kcal/2098kJ; Protein 6.3g; Carbohydrate 38.4g, of which sugars 21g; Fat 36.4g, of which saturates 17.8g; Cholesterol 61mg; Calcium 92mg; Fibre 2.3g; Sodium 209mg.

Blackforest Gâteau

Morello cherries and kirsch lend their distinctive flavours to this ever-popular gâteau.

Serves 8–10

6 eggs
200g/7oz/1 cup caster (superfine) sugar
5ml/1 tsp vanilla essence (extract)
50g/2oz/½ cup plain (all-purpose) flour
50g/2oz/½ cup (unsweetened)
  cocoa powder
115g/4oz/½ cup unsalted
  butter, melted

For the filling and topping
60ml/4 tbsp kirsch
600ml/1 pint/2½ cups double
  (heavy) cream
30ml/2 tbsp icing (confectioners') sugar
2.5ml/½ tsp vanilla essence (extract)
675g/1½ lb jar pitted morello cherries,
  well drained

To decorate
icing (confectioner's) sugar, for dusting
grated chocolate
chocolate curls
fresh or drained canned morello cherries

1 Preheat the oven to 180°C/350°F/ Gas 4. Grease three 19cm/7½ in sandwich cake tins (layer pans). Line the bases with baking parchment. Combine the eggs, sugar and vanilla essence in a bowl and beat with a hand-held electric mixer until pale and thick.

2 Sift the flour and cocoa powder over the mixture and fold in lightly and evenly with a metal spoon. Gently stir in the melted butter.

COOK'S TIP
To make chocolate curls, spread melted chocolate over a marble slab to a depth of about 5mm/¼ in. Leave to set. Draw a knife across the chocolate at a 45° angle, using a seesaw action to make long curls.

3 Divide the mixture among the prepared cake tins, smoothing them level. Bake for 15–18 minutes, or until the cakes have risen and are springy to the touch. Leave them to cool in the tins for about 5 minutes, then turn out on to wire racks and leave to cool completely. Remove the lining paper from each cake layer.

4 Prick each layer all over with a skewer or fork, then sprinkle with kirsch. Using a hand-held electric mixer, whip the cream until it starts to thicken, then beat in the icing sugar and vanilla until the mixture begins to hold its shape.

5 To assemble, spread one cake layer with a thick layer of flavoured cream and top with about half the cherries.

6 Spread a second cake layer with cream, top with the remaining cherries, then place it on top of the first layer. Top with the final cake layer.

7 Spread the remaining cream all over the cake. Dust a serving plate with icing sugar, and position the cake carefully in the centre. Press grated chocolate over the sides and decorate the top of the cake with the chocolate curls and fresh or drained cherries.

Energy 570kcal/2371kJ; Protein 2.9g; Carbohydrate 44g, of which sugars 39.6g; Fat 42.8g, of which saturates 26.7g; Cholesterol 107mg; Calcium 67mg; Fibre 1.2g; Sodium 137mg.

Marbled Swiss Roll

Simply sensational – that's the only
way to describe this superb cake.

Serves 6–8

90g/3½oz/scant 1 cup plain
(all-purpose) flour
15ml/1 tbsp (unsweetened)
cocoa powder
25g/1oz plain (semisweet)
chocolate, grated
25g/1oz white chocolate, grated
3 eggs
115g/4oz/generous ½ cup caster
(superfine) sugar

For the filling
75g/3oz/6 tbsp unsalted butter
175g/6oz/1½ cups icing
(confectioners') sugar
15ml/1 tbsp (unsweetened)
cocoa powder
2.5ml/½ tsp vanilla essence (extract)
45ml/3 tbsp chopped walnuts
plain and white chocolate curls, to
decorate (optional)

1 Sift half the flour with the cocoa
powder into bowl. Stir in the grated
plain chocolate. Sift the remaining
flour into another bowl; stir in the
grated white chocolate.

2 Preheat the oven to 200°C/400°F/
Gas 6. Grease and line a 30 x 20cm/
12 x 8in Swiss roll tin (jelly roll pan).
Whisk the eggs and sugar in a
heatproof bowl then set over a pan
of hot water until thickened.

3 Remove the bowl from the heat and
tip half the mixture into a separate
bowl. Fold the white chocolate mixture
into one portion, then fold the plain
chocolate mixture into the other. Stir
15ml/1 tbsp boiling water into each
half to soften the mixtures.

4 Place alternate spoonfuls of the two
mixtures in the prepared tin and swirl
lightly together to create a marbled
effect. Bake for about 12–15 minutes,
or until firm. Turn out on to a sheet of
non-stick baking parchment.

5 Trim the edges to neaten and cover
with a damp, clean dishtowel and
leave to cool.

6 To make the buttercream filling, beat
the butter, icing sugar, cocoa powder
and vanilla essence together in a bowl
until smooth, then mix in the walnuts.

7 Uncover the sponge cake, lift off
the baking parchment and spread the
surface with the buttercream. Roll up
carefully from a long side and place on
a serving plate. Decorate with plain
and white chocolate curls, if you like.

Energy 361kcal/1518kJ; Protein 5.6g; Carbohydrate 51.1g, of which sugars 42g; Fat 16.4g, of which saturates 7.4g; Cholesterol 92mg; Calcium 67mg; Fibre 1.1g; Sodium 125mg.

Chocolate Layer Cake

The cake layers can be made
ahead, wrapped and frozen.

Serves 10–12

unsweetened cocoa, for dusting
225g/8oz can cooked whole beetroot
(beet), drained and juice reserved
115g/4oz/½ cup unsalted
butter, softened
500g/1¼lb/2½ cups light brown sugar,
firmly packed
3 eggs
15ml/1 tbsp vanilla essence (extract)
75g/3oz cooking (unsweetened)
chocolate, melted
275g/10oz/2¼ cups plain
(all-purpose) flour
10ml/2 tsp baking powder
2.5ml/½ tsp salt
120ml/4fl oz/½ cup buttermilk
chocolate curls (optional)

For the chocolate ganache frosting
475ml/16fl oz/2 cups whipping cream
500g/1¼lb dark (bittersweet) or plain
(semisweet) chocolate, chopped
15ml/1 tbsp vanilla essence (extract)

1 Preheat the oven to 180°C/350°F/
Gas 4. Grease two 23cm/9in cake tins
(pans) and dust the bases and sides
with cocoa powder. Grate the beetroot
and add to the beetroot juice. With an
electric mixer, beat the butter, brown
sugar, eggs and vanilla essence for
3–5 minutes, until pale and fluffy.
Reduce the speed of the mixer and
beat in the chocolate.

2 Sift the flour, baking powder and
salt into another bowl. With the
mixer on low speed, alternately beat
the flour mixture in quarters and the
buttermilk in thirds into the egg
mixture. Add the beetroot and juice
and beat for 1 minute. Divide
between the cake tins and bake for
30–35 minutes, or until a cake tester
inserted in the centre comes out clean.
Cool for 10 minutes in the tins, then
turn out and cool completely.

3 To make the ganache frosting, heat
the cream in a heavy pan over a
medium heat until it just begins to
boil, stirring occasionally to prevent it
from scorching.

4 Remove the pan from the heat and
add the chocolate, stirring constantly
until it is until melted and smooth. Stir
in the vanilla. Strain into a bowl and
chill in the refrigerator, stirring every
10 minutes, for about 1 hour, until the
frosting is spreadable.

5 Assemble the cake. Place one layer
on a serving plate and spread with
one-third of the chocolate ganache
frosting. Turn the cake layer bottom
side up and spread the remaining
ganache over the top and side of the
cake. If using, top with the chocolate
curls. Leave the ganache to set for
20–30 minutes, then chill in the
refrigerator before serving.

Energy 9521kcal/39888kJ; Protein 94.2g; Carb 1196.3g, of which sugars 972.4g; Fat 518.1g, of which sat 312.1g; Cholesterol 1472mg; Calcium 1419mg; Fibre 27.5g; Sodium 1382mg.

Raspberry and White Chocolate Cheesecake

Raspberries and white chocolate are an irresistible combination, especially when teamed with rich mascarpone on a crunchy ginger and pecan nut base.

Serves 8

50g/2oz/4 tbsp unsalted butter
225g/8oz/2⅓ cups ginger nut biscuits, (gingersnaps) crushed
50g/2oz/½ cup chopped pecan nuts or walnuts

For the filling
275g/10oz/1¼ cups mascarpone
175g/6oz/¾ cup fromage frais or farmer's cheese
2 eggs, beaten
45ml/3 tbsp caster (superfine) sugar
250g/9oz white chocolate
225g/8oz/1⅓ cups raspberries

For the topping
115g/4oz/½ cup mascarpone
75g/3oz/⅓ cup fromage frais or farmer's cheese
white chocolate curls and raspberries, to decorate

1 Preheat the oven to 150°C/300°F/ Gas 2. Melt the butter in a pan over a low heat, then stir in the crushed biscuits (cookies) and nuts. Press the mixture evenly into the base of a 23cm/9in springform cake tin (pan).

2 To make the filling, beat together the mascarpone and fromage frais in a bowl, then beat in the eggs and caster sugar until evenly mixed.

3 Break up the white chocolate and melt it gently in a heatproof bowl set over a pan of barely simmering water.

4 Stir the melted chocolate into the cheese mixture and gently fold in the raspberries.

5 Tip the filling into the prepared tin and spread it evenly with a palette knife or spatula, then bake for about 1 hour, or until just set. Switch off the oven, but do not remove the cheesecake. Leave it until cold and completely set.

6 Release the tin and lift the cheesecake on to a plate. Make the topping by mixing the mascarpone and fromage frais in a bowl and spread over the cheesecake. Decorate with chocolate curls and raspberries.

Energy 666kcal/2776kJ; Protein 11g; Carbohydrate 52g, of which sugars 40g; Fat 48g, of which saturates 28g; Cholesterol 121mg; Calcium 225mg; Fibre 3g; Sodium 406mg.

Chocolate and Cherry Polenta Cake

This delicious dessert has an unusual nutty texture.

Serves 8

50g/2oz/⅓ cup quick-cook polenta
200g/7oz plain (semisweet) chocolate
5 eggs, separated
175g/6oz/¾ cup caster
    (superfine) sugar
115g/4oz/1 cup ground almonds
60ml/4 tbsp plain (all-purpose) flour
finely grated rind of 1 orange
115g/4oz/½ cup glacé (candied)
    cherries, halved
icing (confectioners') sugar, for dusting

1 Place the polenta in a heatproof bowl and pour over just enough boiling water to cover, about 120ml/ 4fl oz/½ cup. Stir well, then cover the bowl and leave to stand for about 30 minutes, until the polenta has absorbed all the excess moisture.

2 Preheat the oven to 190°C/375°F/ Gas 5. Grease a deep 22cm/8½in round cake tin (pan) and line the base with non-stick baking parchment. Break the chocolate into squares and melt it in a heatproof bowl set over a pan of barely simmering water.

3 Whisk the egg yolks with the sugar in a bowl until thick and pale. Beat in the melted chocolate, then fold in the polenta, ground almonds, flour and orange rind.

COOK'S TIP
Citrus fruits are often "waxed" to preserve their appearance. For grating, use unwaxed fruit or thoroughly wash the orange in hot water first.

4 Whisk the egg whites in a clean, grease-free bowl until stiff. Stir 15ml/ 1 tbsp of the whites into the chocolate mixture, then fold in the remainder. Finally, fold in the cherries.

5 Scrape the mixture into the prepared tin and bake for 45–55 minutes, or until well risen and firm to the touch. Cool on a wire rack. Dust with icing sugar to serve.

Energy 420kcal/1764kJ; Protein 9.6g; Carbohydrate 56.4g, of which sugars 45.5g; Fat 18.8g, of which saturates 5.8g; Cholesterol 120mg; Calcium 89mg; Fibre 2.2g; Sodium 53mg.

Blueberry-hazelnut Cheesecake

The base for this cheesecake is made with ground hazelnuts – a tasty and unusual alternative to a biscuit base.

Serves 6–8

350g/12oz blueberries
15ml/1 tbsp clear honey
75g/3oz/6 tbsp sugar
juice of 1 lemon
175g/6oz/¾ cup cream cheese, at room temperature
1 egg
5ml/1 tsp hazelnut liqueur (optional)
120ml/4fl oz/½ cup whipping cream

For the base

175g/6oz/1⅔ cups ground hazelnuts
75g/3oz/⅔ cup plain (all-purpose) flour
pinch of salt
50g/2oz/4 tbsp butter, softened
65g/2½oz/⅓ cup light brown sugar, firmly packed
1 egg yolk

1 For the base, put the hazelnuts in a large bowl. Sift in the flour and salt, and stir to mix. Set aside.

2 Beat the butter with the brown sugar until light and fluffy. Beat in the egg yolk. Gradually fold in the nut mixture, in three batches, until thoroughly combined.

3 Press the dough into a greased 23cm/9in pie tin (pan), spreading it evenly against the sides. Form a rim around the top edge that is slightly thicker than the sides. Cover with clear film (plastic wrap) and chill for at least 30 minutes.

4 Preheat the oven to 180°C/350°F/ Gas 4. Meanwhile, for the topping, combine the blueberries, honey, 15ml/ 1 tbsp of the sugar and 5ml/1 tsp lemon juice in a heavy pan. Cook the mixture over a low heat, stirring occasionally, for 5–7 minutes, until the berries have given off some liquid but still retain their shape. Remove the pan from the heat and set aside to cool.

5 Place the pastry base (pie shell) in the oven and bake for 15 minutes. Remove from the oven and set aside to cool completely while you are making the filling.

6 Beat together the cream cheese and remaining sugar until light and fluffy. Add the egg, 15ml/1 tbsp lemon juice, the liqueur, if using, and the cream and beat until smooth and thoroughly blended.

7 Pour the cheese mixture into the pastry shell and spread evenly with a palette knife or spatula. Bake for 20–25 minutes, until just set.

8 Let the cheesecake cool completely on a wire rack, then cover with clear film (plastic wrap) and chill in the refrigerator for at least 1 hour.

9 Spread the blueberry mixture evenly over the top of the cheesecake. Serve at cool room temperature.

COOK'S TIP

The cheesecake can be prepared 1 day in advance, but do not add the fruit topping until just before serving.

Energy 443kcal/1838kJ; Protein 8g; Carbohydrate 25g, of which sugars 18g; Fat 35g, of which saturates 14g; Cholesterol 107mg; Calcium 85mg; Fibre 3g; Sodium 131mg.

Fresh Berry Pavlova

Pavlova is the simplest of desserts, but it can also be the most stunning. Fill with a mix of berry fruits if you like – raspberries and blueberries make a marvellous combination.

Serves 6–8

4 egg whites, at room temperature
225g/8oz/1 cup caster (superfine) sugar
5ml/1 tsp cornflour (cornstarch)
5ml/1 tsp cider vinegar
2.5ml/½ tsp pure vanilla
   essence (extract)
300ml/½ pint/1¼ cups double
   (heavy) cream
150ml/¼ pint/⅔ cup crème fraîche
175g/6oz/1 cup raspberries
175g/6oz/1½ cups blueberries
fresh mint sprigs, to decorate
icing (confectioners') sugar,
   for dusting

1 Preheat the oven to 140°C/275°F/ Gas 1. Line a baking sheet with baking parchment. Whisk the egg whites in a grease-free bowl to stiff peaks. Whisk in the sugar to make a stiff, glossy meringue. Sift the cornflour over and fold it in with the vinegar and vanilla.

2 Spoon the meringue mixture on to the paper-lined sheet. Spread into a round, swirling the top, and bake for 1¼ hours, or until the meringue is crisp and lightly golden. Switch off the oven, keeping the door closed, and leave the meringue to cool for 1–2 hours.

3 Carefully peel the paper from the meringue and transfer it to a serving plate. Whip the cream until it forms soft peaks, fold in the crème fraîche, then spoon the mixture into the centre of the meringue case. Top with the raspberries and blueberries and decorate with the mint sprigs. Sift icing sugar over the top and serve.

Energy 394kcal/1639kJ; Protein 3g; Carbohydrate 35g, of which sugars 32g; Fat 028g, of which saturates 18g; Cholesterol 73mg; Calcium 40mg; Fibre 05g; Sodium 47mg.

Fresh Cherry and Hazelnut Strudel

Serve this wonderful old-world treat as a warm dessert with crème fraîche or custard, or leave it to cool and offer it as a scrumptious cake as part of a buffet-style brunch.

Serves 6–8

75g/3oz/6 tbsp butter
90ml/6 tbsp light brown sugar
3 egg yolks
grated rind of 1 lemon
1.5ml/¼ tsp grated nutmeg
250g/9oz/generous 1 cup
  ricotta cheese
8 large sheets filo pastry
75g/3oz ratafias, crushed
450g/1lb/2½ cups cherries, pitted
30ml/2 tbsp chopped hazelnuts
icing (confectioners') sugar, for dusting

1 Preheat the oven to 190°C/375°F/ Gas 5. Soften 15g/½oz/1 tbsp of the butter in a bowl and beat in the sugar and egg yolks until light and fluffy. Beat in the lemon rind, nutmeg and ricotta.

2 Melt the remaining butter in a small pan. Working quickly, place a sheet of filo on a clean dishtowel and brush it generously with melted butter. Place a second sheet on top and repeat the process. Continue until all the filo has been layered and buttered, reserving some of the melted butter.

3 Sprinkle the crushed ratafias over the top, leaving a 5cm/2in border around the outside. Spoon the ricotta mixture over the ratafias, spread it lightly to cover, then sprinkle over the cherries.

4 Fold in the filo pastry border and use the dishtowel to help roll up the strudel, Swiss-roll (jelly-roll) style, beginning from one of the long sides of the pastry. Grease a baking sheet with the remaining melted butter.

5 Place the strudel on the baking sheet and sprinkle the hazelnuts over the surface. Bake for 35–40 minutes, or until the strudel is golden and crisp. Dust with icing sugar and serve immediately if serving hot.

Energy 317kcal/1326kJ; Protein 6.5g; Carbohydrate 34.2g, of which sugars 22.9g; Fat 18.1g, of which saturates 9.1g; Cholesterol 109mg; Calcium 54mg; Fibre 1.2g; Sodium 93mg.

Chocolate Chestnut Roulade

This is a dream dinner party finale to have chocoholics swooning. The combination of intense flavours produces a very rich dessert, so serve it well chilled and in thin slices. It slices better when it is cold.

Serves 10–12

vegetable oil, for greasing
175g/6oz dark (bittersweet)
    chocolate, chopped
30ml/2 tbsp (unsweetened) cocoa
    powder, sifted, plus extra for dusting
50ml/2fl oz/¼ cup freshly brewed
    strong coffee or espresso
6 eggs, separated
75g/3oz/6 tbsp caster (superfine) sugar
pinch of cream of tartar
5ml/1 tsp vanilla essence (extract)
glacé (candied) chestnuts,
    to decorate (optional)

For the chestnut cream filling
475ml/16fl oz/2 cups double
    (heavy) cream
30ml/2 tbsp rum or
    coffee-flavoured liqueur
350g/12oz can sweetened
    chestnut purée
115g/4oz dark (bittersweet)
    chocolate, grated
thick cream, to serve

1 Preheat the oven to 180°C/350°F/ Gas 4. Oil the base and sides of a 38 × 25cm/15 × 10in Swiss roll tin (jelly roll pan). Line with baking parchment, allowing a 2.5cm/1in overhang.

2 Melt the chocolate in the top of a double boiler, over a low heat, stirring frequently. Set aside. Dissolve the cocoa in the coffee. Stir to make a smooth paste, and set aside.

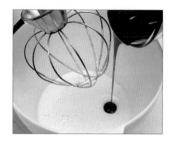

3 In an electric mixer or in a bowl using a whisk, beat the egg yolks with half the sugar for about 3–5 minutes, or until pale and thick. Gradually beat in the melted chocolate and cocoa-coffee paste until just blended.

4 In another bowl, beat the egg whites and cream of tartar until stiff peaks form. Sprinkle the remaining sugar over in two batches incorporating each thoroughly, and continue to beat until the whites are stiff and glossy. Then beat in the vanilla essence.

5 Stir a spoonful of the whisked whites into the chocolate mixture to lighten it, then fold in the remainder.

6 Spoon the mixture into the tin and level the top. Bake for 20–25 minutes, or until the cake is firm, set and risen, and springs back when lightly pressed with the fingertips.

7 Meanwhile, dust a clean dishtowel with the extra cocoa powder. As soon as the cake is cooked, carefully turn it out on to the towel and gently peel off the baking parchment from the base. Starting at a narrow end, roll the cake and towel together Swiss-roll fashion. Leave to cool completely.

8 To make the filling, whip the cream and rum or liqueur until soft peaks form. Beat a spoonful of cream into the chestnut purée to lighten it, then fold in the remaining cream and most of the grated chocolate. Reserve a quarter of the chestnut cream mixture.

9 To assemble the roulade, unroll the cake and spread with the filling, to within 2.5cm/1in of the edges. Gently roll it up, using the towel for support.

10 Place the roulade on a plate. Spoon the reserved chestnut cream into an icing (pastry) bag and pipe rosettes along the top of the roulade. Dust with more cocoa and decorate with glacé chestnuts and grated chocolate.

Energy 469kcal/1961kJ; Protein 6.2g; Carbohydrate 53.5g, of which sugars 44.9g; Fat 27.1g, of which saturates 15.2g; Cholesterol 163mg; Calcium 68mg; Fibre 1.7g; Sodium 57mg.

Tarte au **Citron**

You can find this classic lemon tart in
bistros all over France.

Serves 8–10

350g/12oz unsweetened or sweet
   shortcrust pastry
grated rind of 2 or 3 lemons
150ml/¼ pint/⅔ cup freshly squeezed
   lemon juice
90g/3½oz/½ cup caster
   (superfine) sugar
60ml/4 tbsp crème fraîche
4 eggs, plus 3 egg yolks
icing (confectioners') sugar, for dusting

1 Preheat the oven to 190°C/375°F/
Gas 5. Roll out the pastry thinly and
use to line a 23cm/9in flan tin (tart
pan). Prick the base of the pastry all
over with a fork.

2 Line the pastry case (pie shell) with
foil or baking parchment and fill
with baking beans. Bake for about
15 minutes, until the edges are set
and dry. Remove the foil and beans
and continue baking for a further
5–7 minutes, until golden.

3 Place the lemon rind, juice and sugar
in a bowl. Beat until combined and
then gradually add the crème fraîche
and beat until well blended.

4 Beat in the four eggs, one at a time,
then beat in the remaining egg yolks
and pour the filling into the pastry
case. Bake for 15–20 minutes, until the
filling is set. If the pastry begins to
brown too much, cover the edges with
foil. Leave to cool. Dust with a little
icing sugar before serving.

Energy 271kcal/1134kJ; Protein 6g; Carbohydrate 26g, of which sugars 10g; Fat 16g, of which saturates 6g; Cholesterol 165mg; Calcium 57mg; Fibre 1g; Sodium 179mg.

Pear and **Almond Cream Tart**

This tart is equally successful made with other kinds of fruit, and some variation can be seen in almost every good French pâtisserie.

Serves 6

350g/12oz unsweetened or sweet
*   shortcrust pastry*
3 firm pears
lemon juice
15ml/1 tbsp peach brandy or water
60ml/4 tbsp peach preserve, strained

For the almond cream filling
115g/4oz/¾ cup blanched
*   whole almonds*
50g/2oz/¼ cup caster
*   (superfine) sugar*
65g/2½oz/5 tbsp butter
1 egg, plus 1 egg white
few drops almond essence (extract)

1 Roll out the pastry thinly and use to line a 23cm/9in flan tin (tart pan). Chill the pastry case (pie shell) while you make the filling. Put the almonds and sugar in a food processor and pulse until finely ground; they should not be pasty. Add the butter and process until creamy, then add the egg, egg white and almond essence and mix well.

2 Place a baking sheet in the oven and preheat to 190°C/375°F/Gas 5. Peel the pears, halve them, remove the cores and brush with lemon juice to prevent them from discolouring.

3 Put the pear halves, cut-side down, on a board and slice thinly crossways, keeping the slices together.

4 Pour the almond cream filling into the pastry case. Slide a palette knife or spatula under one pear half and press the top with your fingers to fan out the slices. Transfer to the tart, placing the fruit on the filling like the spokes of a wheel. If you like, remove a few slices from each half before arranging and use them to fill in any gaps in the centre.

5 Place the tart on the baking sheet and bake for about 50–55 minutes, until the filling is set and golden brown. Place the tart on a rack and leave to cool.

6 Meanwhile, heat the brandy or water and the preserve in a small pan over a low heat, then brush over the top of the hot tart to glaze. Serve the tart warm, at room temperature.

Energy 576kcal/2407kJ; Protein 9g; Carbohydrate 54g, of which sugars 27g; Fat 37g, of which saturates 12g; Cholesterol 70mg; Calcium 114mg; Fibre 5g; Sodium 335mg.

Chocolate Amaretti Peaches

This delicious dessert can also be made with fresh nectarines.

Serves 4

115g/4oz amaretti, crushed
50g/2oz plain (semisweet)
*   chocolate, chopped*
grated rind of ½ orange
15ml/1 tbsp clear honey
1.5ml/¼ tsp ground cinnamon
1 egg white, lightly beaten
4 firm ripe peaches
150ml/¼ pint/⅔ cup white wine
15ml/1 tbsp caster (superfine) sugar
whipped cream, to serve

1 Preheat the oven to 190°C/375°F/ Gas 5. Mix together the crushed amaretti, chopped chocolate, grated orange rind, honey and cinnamon in a bowl until well combined. Add the beaten egg white and mix to bind the mixture together.

2 Halve and stone (pit) the peaches and fill the resulting cavities with the chocolate and amaretti mixture, mounding it up slightly.

3 Arrange the stuffed peaches in a lightly buttered, shallow ovenproof dish that will just hold the peaches comfortably in a single layer. Pour the wine into a measuring jug (cup) and stir in the sugar.

4 Pour the wine mixture around the peaches. Bake for 30–40 minutes, until the peaches are tender. Serve them immediately with a little of the cooking juices spooned over and the whipped cream.

Energy 166kcal/705kJ; Protein 3g; Carbohydrate 26g, of which sugars 26g; Fat 4g, of which saturates 2g; Cholesterol 1mg; Calcium 19mg; Fibre 3g; Sodium 20mg.

Pears in **Chocolate Fudge Blankets**

Warm poached pears coated in a rich chocolate fudge sauce – who could resist?

Serves 6

6 ripe eating pears
30ml/2 tbsp lemon juice
75g/3oz/scant ½ cup caster
 (superfine) sugar
1 cinnamon stick

For the sauce
200ml/7fl oz/⅞ cup double
 (heavy) cream
150g/5oz/scant 1 cup brown sugar
25g/1oz/2 tbsp unsalted butter
60ml/4 tbsp golden (light corn) syrup
120ml/4fl oz/½ cup milk
200g/7oz plain (semisweet) chocolate

1 Peel the pears thinly, leaving the stalks on. Scoop out the cores from the base. Brush the cut surfaces with lemon juice to prevent them from turning brown.

2 Place the sugar and 300ml/½ pint/ 1¼ cups of water in a large, heavy pan. Heat gently, stirring constantly, until the sugar dissolves. Add the pears and cinnamon stick with any remaining lemon juice, and, if necessary, a little more water, so that the pears are almost covered.

3 Bring to the boil, then lower the heat, cover the pan and simmer the pears gently for 15–20 minutes.

4 Meanwhile, make the sauce. Place the cream, sugar, butter, golden syrup and milk in a heavy pan. Heat gently, stirring constantly, until the sugar has completely dissolved and the butter and syrup have melted, then bring to the boil. Boil, stirring constantly, for about 5 minutes, or until the sauce is thick and smooth.

5 Remove the pan from the heat. Break up the chocolate and stir in a few squares at a time.

6 Using a slotted spoon, transfer the poached pears to a dish and keep hot. Boil the syrup rapidly to reduce to about 45–60ml/3–4 tbsp. Remove and discard the cinnamon stick and then gently stir the syrup into the chocolate fudge sauce.

7 Serve the pears in individual bowls or on dessert plates, with the hot chocolate fudge sauce spooned over.

Energy 613kcal/2570kJ; Protein 3.6g; Carbohydrate 84.8g, of which sugars 84.5g; Fat 31.2g, of which saturates 19.1g; Cholesterol 58mg; Calcium 90mg; Fibre 4.1g; Sodium 77mg.

Summer Berries in Warm Sabayon Glaze

This luxurious combination of summer berries under a light and fluffy alcoholic sauce is lightly grilled to form a deliciously crisp, caramelized topping.

Serves 8

900g/2lb/8 cups mixed summer berries,
   or soft fruit
8 egg yolks
115g/4oz/generous ½ cup vanilla sugar
   or caster (superfine) sugar
250ml/8fl oz/1 cup liqueur, such as
   Cointreau, Kirsch or Grand Marnier,
   or white dessert wine, plus extra
   for drizzling (optional)
a little icing (confectioners') sugar,
   sifted, and mint leaves, to
   decorate (optional)

1 Divide the fruit among eight individual heatproof glass dishes or ramekins. Preheat the grill (broiler).

2 Whisk the egg yolks in a large heatproof bowl with the sugar and liqueur or wine. Place the bowl over a pan of hot simmering water and whisk constantly until the yolks have become thick, fluffy and pale.

3 Pour equal quantities of the sauce into each dish. Place under the grill for 1–2 minutes, or until just turning brown. Sprinkle the fruit with icing sugar and decorate with mint leaves just before serving, if you like.

VARIATION
To omit the alcohol, use a juice substitute, such as grape, mango or apricot.

Energy 266kcal/951kJ; Protein 4g; Carbohydrate 31g, of which sugars 31g; Fat 6g, of which saturates 2g; Cholesterol 202mg; Calcium 56mg; Fibre 6g; Sodium 14mg.

Hot Chocolate Zabaglione

A deliciously chocolate-flavoured variation of a classic Italian dessert, this is a perfect way to end a celebratory meal.

Serves 6

6 egg yolks
150g/5oz/³/₄ cup caster
*   (superfine) sugar*
45ml/3 tbsp (unsweetened)
*   cocoa powder*
200ml/7fl oz/⁷/₈ cup Marsala
(unsweetened) cocoa powder or icing
*   (confectioners') sugar, for dusting*
almond biscuits (cookies), such as
*   amaretti, to serve*

1 Half fill a medium pan with water and bring to the simmering point.

2 Place the egg yolks and sugar in a heatproof bowl and whisk well until the mixture is pale and all the sugar has dissolved.

3 Add the cocoa powder and Marsala, then place the bowl over the simmering water. Whisk until the consistency of the mixture is smooth, thick and foamy.

4 Pour quickly into tall heatproof glasses, dust lightly with cocoa powder or icing sugar and serve immediately with almond biscuits.

COOK'S TIP

Marsala is a fortified wine from Sicily. It may be dry or sweet and flavoured versions, including chocolate and coffee, are also produced.

Energy 235kcal/989kJ; Protein 4.5g; Carbohydrate 31g, of which sugars 30.1g; Fat 7.1g, of which saturates 2.5g; Cholesterol 202mg; Calcium 48mg; Fibre 0.9g; Sodium 83mg.

Amaretto Soufflé

A mouthwatering and luxurious soufflé with rather more than a hint of Amaretto liqueur.

Serves 6

130g/3½oz/½ cup caster (superfine) sugar
6 amaretti, coarsely crushed
90ml/4 tbsp Amaretto liqueur
4 eggs, separated, plus 1 egg white
30ml/2 tbsp plain (all-purpose) flour
250ml/8fl oz/1 cup milk
pinch of cream of tartar (if needed)
icing (confectioners') sugar, for dusting

1 Butter a 1.5 litre/2½ pint/ 6¼ cup soufflé dish and sprinkle it with a little of the caster sugar.

2 Preheat the oven to 200°C/400°F/ Gas 6. Put the amaretti in a bowl. Sprinkle them with 30ml/2 tbsp of the Amaretto liqueur and set aside.

3 Using a wooden spoon, carefully mix together the egg yolks, 30ml/ 2 tbsp of the remaining caster sugar and all of flour in another bowl.

4 Heat the milk to just below boiling point in a heavy pan. Gradually add the hot milk to the egg mixture, stirring constantly.

5 Pour the mixture back into the pan. Set over a low heat and simmer gently for 3–4 minutes, or until thickened, stirring occasionally.

6 Stir in the remaining Amaretto liqueur, then remove the pan from the heat and leave to cool slightly.

7 In a clean, grease-free bowl, whisk all the egg whites until they will hold soft peaks. (If not using a copper bowl, add the cream of tartar as soon as the whites are frothy.) Add the remaining caster sugar and continue whisking until stiff.

8 Add about one-quarter of the whites to the liqueur mixture and stir in with a rubber spatula to lighten. Add the remaining egg whites and fold in gently.

9 Spoon half of the mixture into the prepared soufflé dish. Cover with a layer of the moistened amaretti, then spoon the remaining soufflé mixture on top to cover.

10 Bake for 20 minutes, or until the soufflé is well risen, just set and lightly browned. Sprinkle with a little sifted icing sugar to decorate and serve the soufflé immediately.

Energy 230kcal/969kJ; Protein 7g; Carbohydrate 33g, of which sugars 30g; Fat 6g, of which saturates 2g; Cholesterol 160mg; Calcium 83mg; Fibre 0g; Sodium 86mg.

Hot Mocha Rum Soufflés

Serve these superb soufflés as soon as they are cooked.

Serves 6

25g/1oz/2 tbsp butter, melted
65g/2½oz/generous ½ cup
  (unsweetened) cocoa powder
75g/3oz/generous ⅓ cup caster
  (superfine) sugar
60ml/4 tbsp strong black coffee
30ml/2 tbsp dark rum
6 egg whites
icing (confectioners') sugar, for dusting

1 Preheat the oven with a baking sheet inside to 190°C/375°F/ Gas 5. Grease six 250ml/8fl oz/1 cup soufflé dishes with the melted butter.

2 Mix 15ml/1 tbsp of the cocoa powder with 15ml/1 tbsp of the caster sugar in a bowl. Tip the mixture into each of the dishes in turn, rotating them so that they are evenly coated. Tip out any excess.

3 Mix the remaining cocoa with the coffee and rum.

4 Whisk the egg whites in a scrupulously clean, grease-free bowl until they form firm peaks. Gradually add the remaining caster sugar, whisking constantly. Stir a generous spoonful of the egg whites into the cocoa mixture to lighten it, then gently fold in the remaining whites.

5 Spoon the mixture into the prepared dishes, smoothing the tops. Place on the hot baking sheet, and bake for 12–15 minutes, or until well risen. Serve the soufflés immediately, lightly dusted with icing sugar.

COOK'S TIPS

• When serving the soufflés at the end of a dinner party, prepare them just before the meal is served. Pop in the oven as soon as the main course is finished and serve freshly baked.

• When whisking egg whites, use a glass, earthenware or stainless steel bowl or, best of all, a copper one. As a result of a chemical reaction with the copper, the foam is more stable. However, do not leave the egg whites in a copper bowl for more than about 15 minutes or they will turn grey. A plastic bowl is not suitable as it is difficult to be sure that it is completely grease-free.

Energy 137kcal/574kJ; Protein 5g; Carbohydrate 14g, of which sugars 13g; Fat 6g, of which saturates 4g; Cholesterol 9mg; Calcium 18mg; Fibre 0g; Sodium 190mg.

Chocolate Crêpes with Plums and Port

This dish can be made in advance and always looks impressive.

Serves 6

50g/2oz plain (semisweet) chocolate
200ml/7fl oz/⅞ cup milk
120ml/4fl oz/½ cup single (light) cream
30ml/2 tbsp (unsweetened)
  cocoa powder
115g/4oz/1 cup plain
  (all-purpose) flour
2 eggs

For the filling

500g/1¼lb red or golden plums
50g/2oz/¼ cup caster (superfine) sugar
30ml/2 tbsp port
vegetable oil, for frying
175g/6oz/¾ cup crème fraîche

For the sauce

150g/5oz plain (semisweet) chocolate
175ml/6fl oz/¾ cup double (heavy)
  cream
30ml/2 tbsp port

1 Break the chocolate into squares and place in a pan with the milk. Heat gently until the chocolate has melted. Pour into a blender or food processor and add the cream, cocoa powder, flour and eggs. Process until smooth, then tip into a jug (pitcher) and chill for 30 minutes.

2 Meanwhile, make the filling. Halve and stone (pit) the plums. Place them in a pan and add the sugar and 30ml/2 tbsp of water. Bring to the boil, then lower the heat, cover and simmer gently for about 10 minutes, or until the plums are tender.

3 Stir in the port and simmer for a further 30 seconds. Remove the pan from the heat and keep warm.

4 Have ready a sheet of non-stick baking parchment. Heat a crêpe pan, grease it lightly with a little oil, then pour in just enough chocolate batter to cover the base of the pan, swirling to coat it evenly.

5 Cook until the crêpe has set, then flip it over to cook the other side. Slide the crêpe out on to the sheet of parchment, then cook 9–11 more crêpes in the same way.

6 To make the sauce, break the chocolate into squares and place in pan with the cream. Heat gently, stirring until smooth. Add the port and heat gently, stirring, for 1 minute.

7 Divide the plum filling between the crêpes, add a spoonful of crème fraîche to each and roll them up carefully. Serve immediately in shallow plates, with the chocolate sauce spooned over the top.

Energy 867kcal/3604kJ; Protein 10.6g; Carbohydrate 57.4g, of which sugars 41.7g; Fat 67g, of which saturates 36.7g; Cholesterol 184mg; Calcium 175mg; Fibre 3.4g; Sodium 115mg.

Chocolate Chip and Banana Pudding

Hot and steamy, this superb light pudding tastes extra special served with chocolate sauce.

Serves 4

200g/7oz/1¾ cups self-raising
   (self-rising) flour
75g/3oz/6 tbsp unsalted butter
2 ripe bananas
75g/3oz/⅓ cup caster (superfine) sugar
60ml/4 tbsp milk
1 egg, beaten
60ml/4 tbsp plain (semisweet)
   chocolate chips
glossy chocolate sauce and whipped
   cream, to serve

1 Prepare a steamer or half fill a pan with water and bring it to the boil. Grease a 1 litre/1¾ pint/4 cup heatproof bowl. Sift the flour into a bowl and rub in the butter with your fingertips until the mixture resembles breadcrumbs.

2 Mash the bananas in a bowl. Stir them into the flour mixture, with the caster sugar.

3 Whisk the milk with the egg in a jug (pitcher) or small bowl, then beat into the pudding mixture. Stir in the chocolate chips and mix well until thoroughly combined.

4 Spoon the mixture into the heatproof bowl, cover closely with greaseproof (waxed) paper and a double thickness of foil, and steam for 2 hours, topping up the water as required.

5 Run a knife around the top of the pudding to loosen it, then turn it out on to a warm serving dish. Serve hot, with the chocolate sauce and a spoonful of whipped cream.

COOK'S TIP

To make glossy chocolate sauce: Place 130g/4½oz/scant ¾ cup caster (superfine) sugar in a pan with 120ml/4fl oz/½ cup water, and heat until the sugar has dissolved. Stir in 175g/6oz plain (semisweet) chocolate, broken into squares, until melted. Then add 25g/1oz/2 tbsp butter and melt in the same way. Do not let the sauce boil. Add 30ml/2 tbsp brandy or the grated rind of an orange. Serve warm.

Energy 528kcal/2220kJ; Protein 8.1g; Carbohydrate 79.3g, of which sugars 40.9g; Fat 22g, of which saturates 13g; Cholesterol 89mg; Calcium 222mg; Fibre 2.5g; Sodium 320mg.

Hot Chocolate Cake

This is wonderful served as a
dessert with a chocolate sauce.

Makes 10–12 slices

200g/7oz/1¾ cups self-raising
  (self-rising) wholemeal (whole-
  wheat) flour
25g/1oz/¼ cup (unsweetened)
  cocoa powder
pinch of salt
175g/6oz/¾ cup soft margarine
175g/6oz/¾ cup soft light brown sugar
few drops vanilla essence (extract)
4 eggs
75g/3oz white chocolate
chocolate leaves and curls, to decorate

For the white chocolate sauce
75g/3oz white chocolate
150ml/¼ pint/⅔ cup single
  (light) cream
30–45ml/2–3 tbsp milk

1 Preheat the oven to 160°C/325°F/
Gas 3. Sift the flour, cocoa powder
and salt into a bowl, adding in any
bran remaining in the sieve.

2 In a separate bowl, cream the
margarine, sugar and vanilla essence
together with a wooden spoon until
light and fluffy, then gently beat in one
of the eggs.

3 Gradually stir in the remaining eggs,
one at a time, alternately folding in
some of the flour, until the mixture is
blended in.

4 Coarsely chop the white chocolate,
then stir it into the mixture. Spoon into
a 675–900g/1½–2lb loaf tin (pan) or
an 18cm/7in greased cake tin. Bake for
30–40 minutes, or until just firm to the
touch and beginning to shrink away
from the sides of the tin.

5 Meanwhile, prepare the sauce.
Break the white chocolate into squares
and place in a pan with the cream.
Heat very gently until the chocolate
has melted. Add the milk and stir until
the sauce is cool.

6 Slice the cake and serve in a pool of
sauce, decorated with chocolate leaves
and curls.

Energy 343kcal/1432kJ; Protein 5.4g; Carbohydrate 35.7g, of which sugars 23.1g; Fat 20.8g, of which saturates 7.1g; Cholesterol 71mg; Calcium 124mg; Fibre 0.8g; Sodium 221mg.

Chocolate Almond Meringue Pie

This dream dessert combines three very popular flavours.

Serves 6

175g/6oz/1½ cups plain
  (all-purpose) flour
50g/2oz/⅓ cup ground rice
150g/5oz/⅔ cup unsalted butter
finely grated rind of 1 orange
1 egg yolk
flaked (sliced) almonds and melted
  chocolate, to decorate

For the filling
150g/5oz plain (semisweet) chocolate
50g/2oz/4 tbsp unsalted (sweet)
  butter, softened
75g/3oz/⅓ cup caster
  (superfine) sugar
10ml/2 tsp cornflour (cornstarch)
4 egg yolks
75g/3oz/¾ cup ground almonds

For the meringue
3 egg whites
150g/5oz/¾ cup caster
  (superfine) sugar

1 Sift the flour and ground rice into a bowl. Add the butter and rub in with your fingertips until the mixture resembles breadcrumbs. Stir in the orange rind. Add the egg yolk, mix well and bring the dough together. Roll out on a lightly floured surface and use to line a 23cm/9in round flan tin (pie pan). Chill in the refrigerator for 30 minutes.

2 Preheat the oven to 190°C/375°F/Gas 5. Prick the pastry base all over with a fork, cover with greaseproof (waxed) paper weighed down with baking beans and bake blind for 10 minutes. Remove the pastry case (pie shell).

3 To make the filling, break the chocolate into squares and melt in a heatproof bowl set over a pan of barely simmering water. Cream the butter with the sugar in a bowl, then beat in the cornflour and egg yolks. Fold in the almonds, then the chocolate. Spread in the pastry case. Bake for a further 10 minutes.

4 To make the meringue, whisk the egg whites until stiff, then gradually add half the sugar. Fold in the remaining sugar.

5 Spoon the meringue over the chocolate filling to cover it completely, lifting it up with the back of the spoon to form peaks. Reduce the oven temperature to 180°C/350°F/Gas 4 and bake the pie for 15–20 minutes, or until the topping is pale gold. Serve warm, sprinkled with almonds and drizzled with melted chocolate.

Energy 800kcal/3363kJ; Protein 12g; Carbohydrate 86g, of which sugars 56g; Fat 48g, of which saturates 24g; Cholesterol 246mg; Calcium 115mg; Fibre 3g; Sodium 48mg.

Christmas Pudding

This recipe makes enough to fill one 1.2 litre/2 pint/5 cup bowl or two 600ml/1 pint/2½ cup bowls. It can be made up to a month before Christmas and stored in a cool, dry place. Steam the pudding for 2 hours before serving.

Serves 8

115g/4oz/½ cup butter
225g/8oz/1 heaping cup soft dark
brown sugar
50g/2oz/½ cup self-raising
(self-rising) flour
5ml/1tsp ground mixed (apple
pie) spice
1.5ml/¼ tsp grated nutmeg
2.5ml/½ tsp ground cinnamon
2 eggs
115g/4oz/2 cups fresh white
breadcrumbs
175g/6oz/generous 1 cup sultanas
(golden raisins)
175g/6oz/generous 1 cup raisins
115g/4oz/½ cup currants
25g/1oz/3 tbsp mixed (candied) peel,
chopped finely
25g/1oz/¼ cup chopped almonds
1 small cooking apple, peeled, cored
and coarsely grated
finely grated rind or 1 orange or lemon
juice of 1 orange or lemon, made up
to 150ml/¼ pint/⅔ cup with brandy

2 Beat the butter and sugar together until creamy and combined. Beat in the flour, spices and eggs. Stir in the remaining ingredients thoroughly. The mixture should have a soft dropping (pourable) consistency.

3 Turn the mixture into the prepared bowl(s) and level the surface with the back of a spoon.

4 Cover with another disc of buttered greaseproof paper.

1 Cut a disc of greaseproof (waxed) paper to fit the base of the heatproof bowl(s) and grease the disc and bowl(s) well with butter.

5 Make a pleat across the centre of a large piece of greaseproof paper and cover the bowl(s) with it, tying it in place with string under the rim. Cut off the excess paper. Pleat a piece of foil in the same way and cover the bowl(s) with it, tucking it around the bowl neatly, under the greaseproof frill. Tie another piece of string around and across the top, as a handle.

6 Place the bowl(s) in a steamer over a pan of simmering water and steam for 6 hours. Alternatively, put the bowl(s) into a large pan and pour around enough boiling water to come halfway up the bowl(s) and cover the pan with a tight-fitting lid. Check the water is simmering and top it up with boiling water as it evaporates. When the pudding(s) have cooked, leave to cool completely. Then remove the foil and greaseproof paper. Wipe the bowl(s) clean and replace the greaseproof paper and foil with clean pieces, ready for reheating.

TO SERVE

Steam for 2 hours. Remove and discard the paper and foil, run a knife around the bowl(s) and turn the pudding out on to a warm plate. Leave it to stand for about 5 minutes before removing the pudding bowl(s) (the steam will rise to the top of the bowl and help to loosen the pudding). Decorate with a sprig of holly. Serve with brandy or rum butter, whipped cream or freshly made custard.

Energy 448kcal/1902kJ; Protein 2.4g; Carbohydrate 99.8g, of which sugars 92.5g; Fat 7.1g, of which saturates 3.6g; Cholesterol 20mg; Calcium 67mg; Fibre 0.9g; Sodium 123mg.

Index